Scots Plays
of the
Seventies

To Donna & Roy

Love,

Billy.

27-12-01

Scots Plays
of the
Seventies

edited by

Bill Findlay

SCOTTISH CULTURAL PRESS

This edition published 2001 by
SCOTTISH CULTURAL PRESS
Unit 13d, Newbattle Abbey Business Annexe,
Newbattle Road, Dalkeith EH22 3LJ
Tel: 0131 660 6366 ◆ Fax: 0131 660 6414
email: info@scottishbooks.com
web: www.scottishbooks.com

British Library Cataloguing in Publication Data
A catalogue entry for this book is available from the British Library

ISBN: 1 84017 028 X

The Publisher acknowledges subsidy from the Scottish Arts Council
towards the publication of this volume

THE SCOTTISH **ARTS** COUNCIL

Internal design by Carol Rodger

Printed and bound by Bell & Bain Ltd, Glasgow

The Editor

Bill Findlay is a lecturer in the Department of Drama, Queen Margaret University College, Edinburgh, and assistant editor of *IJoST: International Journal of Scottish Theatre*, which was launched by the Department in June 2000. He is editor of *A History of Scottish Theatre* (Polygon, 1998) and *Frae Ither Tongues: Essays on Modern Translations into Scots* (Multilingual Matters, forthcoming).

He has translated into Scots, with his Canadian collaborator Martin Bowman, Jeanne-Mance Delisle's *The Reel of the Hanged Man* (Stellar Quines Theatre Company), and seven plays by Michel Tremblay: *The Guid Sisters*, *The Real Wurld*, *Hosanna* (all Tron Theatre); *The House Among the Stars* (Traverse Theatre and Perth Theatre); *Forever Yours, Marie-Lou* (LadderMan); *Albertine in Five Times* (Clyde Unity Theatre); and *Solemn Mass for a Full Moon in Summer* (Traverse Theatre and The Barbican Centre).

His other work includes Scots translations and versions of Gerhart Hauptmann's *The Weavers* (Dundee Rep Theatre), Pavel Kohout's *Fire in the Basement* (Communicado Theatre Company), Teresa Lubkiewicz's *Werewolves* (Theatre Archipelago), and Raymond Cousse's *Bairns' Bothers* (Mull Theatre).

Contents

Introduction

As editor of *A History of Scottish Theatre* (1998) I said in the preface that two impediments to advancing wider appreciation of Scotland's tradition in drama were lack of a history of Scottish theatre from the Middle Ages to the present day (now supplied by that book) and 'anthologies of playtexts of historical or canonical importance'.[1] This collection of seventies' plays is intended as a contribution to beginning to remedy the latter deficiency. Recent years have seen publication of a number of anthologies of contemporary plays from the 1980s and 1990s,[2] which is a very welcome trend, as is the growing list of published plays by individual contemporary writers; but it is indicative of a problem that has long bedevilled Scottish drama – the non-availability of published plays – that only one anthology is in print for any period before 1980.

A consideration in the choice of plays here anthologised is that all six were published in the 1970s (see the select bibliography for details), yet, notwithstanding their importance in the development of modern Scottish drama, they have long been out of print; in most cases because they were published by small presses which subsequently folded. Indeed, as early as 1987, one of the playwrights included here, Tom McGrath, was expressing regret that 'the Seventies surge' seemed never to have happened, for 'only a few of the plays had been published and they were out of print'.[3] His comment confirms the important contribution that publication can make to ensuring continuing awareness of past developments and to maintaining the visibility of plays (and, come to that, playwrights) – even those from the recent past – both for readers and for potential producers/directors. It is significant that the Scottish Society of Playwrights recognised this at its inception in 1973 and declared as one of its first objectives the recovery, preservation, and dissemination-through-publication of playtexts. Sadly, it is a reflection of what has been a recurring start-stop problem that the SSP's admirable efforts in publishing playtexts foundered within a decade.[4]

The only previous collection of plays from the 1970s, *A Decade's Drama: Six Scottish Plays* (1980), has also long been out of print. The six plays included in that anthology were Stanley Eveling's *Mister*, Hector MacMillan's *The Rising*, C. P. Taylor's *Walter*, Stewart Conn's *Play Donkey*, Robert David MacDonald's *Chinchilla*, and John Byrne's *Threads*. These plays were chosen by the unnamed editor because, along with the work of seven other playwrights, they were broadcast on BBC Radio Scotland as part of a series 'celebrating a decade of drama in Scotland' that was organised by Stewart Conn as head of radio drama there. In a foreword to the volume, the late Allen Wright, drama critic of *The Scotsman*, wrote:

If anyone should imagine that contemporary drama in Scotland is poised somewhere between the kailyard and the kitchen sink, these six examples of vigorous and imaginative play-writing will come as a revelation. The territory over which they range is immense – extending from the opulently decadent salons in which Diaghilev languished, to the more rugged realms of John Byrne's recollections of a party in Paisley.

C.P. Taylor's *Walter*, wrestling with his racial and religious heritage, is miles away from the militant weavers of MacMillan's *Rising*, and Stanley Eveling's philosophical sea-dog is a very different creature from the blunt mercenary soldier in Conn's *Play Donkey*. The variety of subjects, and the diversity of literary style lend interest to this collection, which makes no claim to be fully representative of Scottish drama in the seventies but which does succeed in proclaiming its vitality.[5]

As Allen Wright indicates, the profusion and variety of work produced in the seventies poses a problem for an anthologiser. Given the inevitable limitations on length, in common with *A Decade's Drama* this present volume 'makes no claim to be fully representative of Scottish drama in the seventies'. Nor, I should add, does it claim or seek to be a 'best of' collection, either in relation to the seventies generally or the individual writers represented. In this last regard, most of the six writers produced other plays then that compete in importance for inclusion here, such as Bill Bryden's *Benny Lynch* (1975), Hector MacMillan's *The Sash* (1974), Stewart Conn's *Play Donkey* (1977), Donald Campbell's *The Widows of Clyth* (1979), and Tom McGrath's *Animal* (1979). (Details of other plays by these writers are included in the biographical notes prefacing each of the plays anthologised, and the select bibliography lists all their published plays.)

Key plays by other seventies' writers that have been omitted are John McGrath's *The Cheviot, The Stag and The Black, Black Oil* (1973), Robert David MacDonald's *Chinchilla* (1977), and John Byrne's *The Slab Boys* (1978), but the omission was driven by knowledge that these plays remain available in print (as do other seventies' plays by those three authors).[6] Omitted, too, are important plays by Tom Gallacher, Stanley Eveling, and C. P. Taylor, all of whom made formative contributions to sixties' and seventies' Scottish drama. Their work in the sixties, along with that by other playwrights, helped to lay the foundations for the fuller flourishing of native drama that occurred in the seventies. However, as Randall Stevenson has suggested, there is a difference in emphasis between their work and that of many seventies' playwrights, such as those represented in this volume, in that the latter 'investigated Scotland's history, speech and state of mind more directly than had Eveling, Gallacher, or even C. P. Taylor in the 1960s'.[7] A statement by Tom Gallacher himself clarifies the distinction, for while he was an enthusiastic supporter of the new developments in the 1970s, such as formation of the Scottish Society of Playwrights, he wrote of his own work in the sixties: 'I wasn't writing Scottish plays. I wrote plays mostly in English, with a European outlook.'[8] It would be good to have a separate collection of plays devoted to Gallacher, Eveling and Taylor, reflecting the different texture to their work and recognising their prominent roles as figures straddling *both* the sixties and the seventies.

There is an apparent gender bias in my selection in that all six playwrights are men. However, this is a reflection of the reality that very few women playwrights were active in the 1970s and none wrote or had staged a play in that decade that had the critical or box office success of those plays that can now be considered seventies' landmarks. Ena Lamont Stewart, A. J. Stewart, and Joan Ure were prominent in the founding of the Scottish Society of Playwrights in 1973, and the SSP, supportively, went on to publish Ena Lamont Stewart's *Men Should Weep*, Joan Ure's *Five Short Plays*, and A. J. Stewart's *The Man from Thermopylae*.[9] However, A. J. Stewart's best work was by then behind her (*The Man from Thermopylae* had first been staged to international acclaim in 1959); and Ure's mainly short plays, from the 1960s and 70s, did not achieve significant breakthrough. Ena Lamont Stewart had enjoyed popular success in the 1940s with her plays *Starched Aprons* (1945) and *Men Should Weep* (1947), but thereafter, though she had continued writing, had experienced what she described as 'The Wilderness Years'.[10] She later claimed as the source of this neglect: 'Men select the plays that are put on. They are more likely to put on a play by a man than a woman. Male chauvinism is rife in Scottish theatre.'[11] In the mid-1970s she revised *Men Should Weep* in preparation for publication by the SSP, but that revised text, which has subsequently become recognised as a modern classic, was not staged till 1982, so it falls outwith the decade anthologised. (The 1980s, it should be said, saw a radical shift, with a wave of new women playwrights coming to the fore – one of whom, Marcella Evaristi, had early work such as *Dorothy and the Bitch* and *Scotia's Darlings* staged at the Traverse in the late seventies.)

To compound the apparent gender bias in my selection, the six plays centre on male worlds. This is in part a reflection of the above reality but also of the fact that it is the characteristic focus of most seventies' plays. That said, a number of plays by men did foreground women, such as John McGrath's *Little Red Hen* (1975) and *Out of Our Heads* (1976), Tom McGrath's *Sisters* (1978), and Donald Campbell's *The Widows of Clyth* (1979). Since he is represented in this volume, it should be mentioned, too, that Stewart Conn's *I Didn't Always Live Here*, staged at the Citizens' Theatre in 1967, deals with the lives of two elderly Glaswegian women.

There comes a time when out of respect for itself a country must collect its resources, and look at its assets and shortcomings with an eye that is both sharp and warm: see what is there, and what is not there, what could be there. Perilously, without any political underpinning yet, Scotland is now consciously at that stage. [12]

This percipient diagnosis early in the 1970s, by the poet and critic Edwin Morgan, of a mood of national stock-taking, and of Scotland having arrived at a critical juncture, was to be reflected in seventies' drama, just as it was in developments in Scottish society generally. For the 1970s was a pivotal decade in modern Scottish history, witnessing a resurgence of Scottish identity that impacted on culture and politics. The roots of this nationalist sentiment lay in the sixties and beyond but it took on a new urgency in the seventies, as evidenced by the 1973 Kilbrandon Report of the Royal Commission on the Constitution, which came down in favour of a new dispensation for Scotland, and the eventual granting of a Devolution Referendum in 1979. Although a majority of voters in that referendum supported the devolution option, the notorious 40 per cent rule stymied the popular will. As the 1980s showed, this disappointment, coupled with the deep unpopularity of Thatcherism in Scotland, only served to advance disenchantment with the constitutional status quo, leading in time to the resounding vote in the 1997 referendum for the setting up of a Scottish Parliament with greatly enhanced powers over what was offered in 1979. With hindsight, one can see that the 1970s represent a crucial staging-post on that journey to the reconvening in 1999 of the first Scottish Parliament since 1707 – albeit a subordinate rather than, as then, an autonomous one.

A factor in the new mood of national assertiveness in the 1970s was the discovery of North Sea oil in Scottish waters. This discovery affected many areas of Scottish life, including theatre, as the playwright Tom Gallacher testified:

> ... the burgeoning riches of oil off the Scottish coast accomplished a sea change in the Arts as well. The public, and those whose job it is to reflect public opinion, became aware that Scottishness was an asset, not a liability. The pride of self-sufficiency showed at the box office to a degree which astonished the theatre managements. [13]

The first commercial oil-field, the Forties, was discovered in 1970, encouraging a Klondyke-like rush to locate more 'black gold', and provoking the Scottish National Party to launch an effective populist campaign under the slogan 'It's Scotland's Oil'. The issue of ownership implicit in that slogan reflected a larger unease about the majority involvement of foreign multi-nationals and the siphoning of benefits away from Scotland (e.g. in 1973 almost 90 per cent of oil-related equipment had to be imported[14]). One of the most popular plays of the period – now regarded as a classic of political theatre – John McGrath's *The Cheviot, The Stag and The Black, Black Oil* (1973), brilliantly caught the popular mood of unease about the oil industry's impact on Scotland, as confirmed by the play's huge popular success when 7:84 (Scotland) Theatre Company barnstormed around the country with it, from village halls to city theatres.

A related cause for concern was the decline of Scotland's traditional heavy industries such as engineering, mining, iron and steel, and shipbuilding. This was crystallised in the threatened closure of John Brown's shipyard (Upper Clyde Shipbuilders) in 1971, which provoked a work-in led by communist shop stewards Jimmy Airlie and Jimmy Reid. The scale and dignified discipline of the workers' protest hit the international headlines and brought forth a huge groundswell of support from all over Scotland. However, the outcome was that John Brown's was taken over by Marathon Engineering Company of Texas for oil-rig building – a portent of North Sea oil and its importance to the Scottish economy. The UCS work-in not only highlighted yet again the 'branch economy' nature of Scotland's industrial infrastructure, but offered further proof of how Scots' sense of national identity in modern times had, and has, a strong basis in working-class experience and left-inclining political sympathies – as seen in a significant number of seventies' plays.

The UCS work-in inspired two important theatre events. *The Great Northern Welly Boot Show* (1972) was directly based on the events at UCS and proved a popular hit in Glasgow and Edinburgh. Combining drama and music with political satire, it foreshadowed *The Cheviot, The Stag and The Black, Black Oil* (and shared some of the same performers). Among those involved with the show who achieved later significance as seventies' playwrights, and in other ways, were Billy Connolly, Tom McGrath, and John Byrne. The other influence that the UCS sit-in had was on Bill Bryden's *Willie Rough* (1972). Though set in the Greenock shipyards in 1914–16, Bryden's play had, for audiences, obvious parallels with more recent radical events on 'Red Clydeside'. Willie Rough is a shop steward involved in a bitter industrial and political conflict in which he leads a strike that paralyses the shipyards. Looking back at the early seventies from the perspective of 1982, the playwright Donald Campbell acknowledged the contemporary relevance of *Willie Rough* but saw the play as embodying the larger mood of the period, too:

> Apart from its excellence as a piece of drama, there is no doubt that *Willie Rough* is a more adequate reflection of the spirit of the times in which it was written and first performed. By 1972, the rediscovery of Scottish identity which had been gathering momentum throughout the sixties was about to move into a completely new phase. The most dramatic manifestation of this ... was the return of no fewer than eleven Scottish National Party Members of Parliament to Westminster in the two General Elections of 1974. This political development, however, was not the cause of this new Scottish awareness, but had come about, rather, as a result of it. In all manner of areas, from merchant banking to scientific research, new and distinctively Scottish institutions were being set up and distinguished exiles were coming home to commit their talents to Scottish society in a spirit that

transcended politics. In the arts ... the re-emergence of the Scottish identity was particularly noticeable.[15]

It is perhaps significant that four of the dramatists in this collection were also 'exiles' who, along with some other writers, chose to return to Scotland in the late sixties and early seventies. Hector MacMillan, for example, had been living abroad for ten years, latterly in Switzerland. Of his decision to return home in 1967 he wrote: 'Scotland was on the threshold of an exciting historical development and the things I wanted to write about were connected both with its history and with the processes of change. I wanted to be present. To be involved.'[16] That sense of excitement about homecoming, of the country being on the threshold of something momentous, is also communicated in an essay by Bill Bryden about his return in 1971:

> When the train from King's Cross climbed slowly over Beattock Summit a great roar erupted from the bar, 'Scot-laaand, Scot-laaand'. It reminded me of my childhood, coming back from Wembley, celebrating one of my country's rare victories over England. The year of Jim Baxter's goal. We had been defeated many times since then but I didn't think of that, neither did the men in the bar. There were no border guards in kilts to check our passports but, there was no doubt about it, we were entering a whole different country. I knew. I was going home.[17]

Like Hector MacMillan, Bryden, too, wanted to contribute. He returned from the Royal Court in London, at the invitation of Clive Perry and Richard Eyre, to be associate director at the Royal Lyceum Theatre in Edinburgh, motivated by the belief that 'a truly Scottish theatre could exist, expressing Scotland for the people of Scotland'.[18] His goal – shared by a number of Scottish companies since early in the twentieth century – was to establish a Scottish National Theatre on the model of the Abbey Theatre Company in Dublin, and thereby 'to show Scotland to Scotland – her past and her present – to prepare for her future, which seems blessed by economic development if the oil under her waters is really there'.[19]

Bryden gathered together an ensemble company of prominent Scottish actors and developed a policy of commissioning new Scottish work. That policy's importance in the resurgence of indigenous drama, as well as the importance of the Lyceum's contribution generally in the first half of the decade, is reflected in this anthology in the inclusion of three plays premiered at the Lyceum and directed by Bryden: his own *Willie Rough* (1972), Stewart Conn's *The Burning* (1973), and Roddy McMillan's *The Bevellers* (1974). That Roddy McMillan was in the company of actors assembled by Bryden, and that Stewart Conn became the theatre's Literary Manager from 1973 to 1975, gives an added sense of the creative energy centred on the Lyceum. Unfortunately, that focus of energy, which Bryden wanted to apply to development of the Lyceum into Scotland's national company, was relatively short-lived, notwithstanding the legacy of achievement. The possibility of the Lyceum being accorded Scottish National Theatre status, and moving to a new multi-purpose complex nearby on Castle Terrace, had been under discussion since 1970 but was eventually ruled out in 1975. Soon after, the Lyceum's artistic director, Clive Perry, left to head up Birmingham Rep, and Bill Bryden, ironically, was invited in 1974 to join the National Theatre in London.

Alasdair Cameron has rightly cautioned that a false impression can be given that 'Scottish drama went to sleep for twenty years in 1950, to be awakened by Bill Bryden's kiss at the Lyceum in 1970'.[20] As indicated earlier, playwrights in the 1960s were preparing the ground for the 1970s' flowering, and new Scottish work was seen in that decade at theatres such as the Lyceum, the Gateway, and the Traverse, all in Edinburgh, the Citizens' and the Close in Glasgow, and at Pitlochry Festival Theatre and elsewhere. New work was seen in earlier decades, too; indeed, there were manifesto-led initiatives to promote native drama, such as distinguished the work of Glasgow Unity Theatre in the 1940s and the Scottish National Players in the 1920s.[21] Characteristic features of seventies' drama were detectable in earlier periods as well, providing a line of continuity with developments in that decade. For example, it has been said that the early 1950s

possessed a group of writers whose work – despite its limitations – opened up several areas of interest successfully extended by later playwrights: exploitation of the vitality of Scottish speech; use of Scottish history as a source of subjects and themes; and development for the stage of some of the forceful, disturbing realities of Lowland urban life.[22]

Nonetheless, there is general agreement that the 1970s' resurgence, whilst it had precursors, marked a more definitive shift. Moreover, most commentators agree that the Bryden years at the Lyceum in the first half of the seventies, in their commitment to Scottish actors and writers, and in the receptiveness of audiences to new Scottish work, were seminal in their influence.[23] As early as 1983, Donald Campbell, from his perspective as both a playwright and a historian of Scottish theatre, concluded: 'The impact that Bill Bryden made on Scottish drama during his few short years at the Lyceum cannot be overemphasised ... Partly as a result [of his influence as a director and dramatist] ... the decade of the seventies witnessed the greatest upsurge of native dramatic writing that Scotland has ever known'.[24]

Fortunately, after Bryden's and Perry's departure from the Lyceum, the momentum was continued through the Traverse Theatre and the inspired directorship of Chris Parr. In Donald Smith's words, Parr 'caught the national mood' and 'turned the Traverse into the dynamo of new Scottish theatre between 1975 and 1980', generating something of the same excitement that had been attached to the Lyceum.[25] Representative of the Traverse's importance in that period are two plays in this volume that premiered there: *The Jesuit* by Donald Campbell (co-presented with The Heretics) and *The Hardman* by Tom McGrath with Jimmy Boyle. Representative, too, of the fact that complementary developments were happening elsewhere in Scottish theatre is Hector MacMillan's *The Rising*, which premiered at Dundee Rep (as did his other history play *The Royal Visit*). The sum effect of the disparate but sustained activity over the decade, embracing small and large building-based companies, and new touring companies such as John McGrath's 7:84, was that a steady stream of new work was produced in close proximity. As Alan Bold notes, this 'contributed to the impression that the Scottish theatre was alive as never before, with one fine play following another'.[26]

ॐ

In 1968, in an interview with Allen Wright of *The Scotsman*, Clive Perry, artistic director of the Royal Lyceum, expressed regret that Scottish writers concentrated over-much on historical subjects and tended to see the development of a national drama as primarily a means for preserving an anachronistic form of Scots language:

> I don't believe the public are willing to sit through a play whose vocabulary they don't understand. As regards the future of Scottish theatre, it may be that there is no such thing as a totally individual Scots language left. National drama with a tongue of its own is not for the future. Plays about contemporary Scotland will be in English with only a slight accent.[27]

Perry's greatest commercial success at the Lyceum, Jay Presson Allen's adaptation of *The Prime of Miss Jean Brodie*, staged in the same year as that observation, 1968, seemed to confirm that the future for Scottish drama, linguistically, lay 'in English with only a slight accent'. But, ironically, the Lyceum was soon to demonstrate triumphantly that the reverse was the case; and it did so because Clive Perry had not closed his mind to the possibility of a new drama arising of a different kind to that envisaged by his reading of the theatrical landscape in the late sixties – as evidenced by his subsequent invitation to Bill Bryden to join the company and his support for the policies that Bryden initiated. In fact, in the same year that he made this statement, he received Stewart Conn's *The Burning*, which he passed to Bryden to direct on his arrival in 1971.

Relevant to Perry's forecast in 1968 is the opinion expressed by Edwin Morgan in 1972:

> There is … a great deadlock to be broken in the theatre, where directors and managements seem to be hypnotised rigid by the polarity of Received Standard versus Costume Scots – neither of which any Scotsman actually speaks. Only rarely do Scottish theatre audiences hear that modest and unforced reflection of their own living speech-habits which English or American audiences take for granted.[28]

xvi

In an essay in the previous year, 'Registering the Reality of Scotland', Morgan regretted 'heavily entrenched positions regarding language in Scotland', preferring to see the 'untidiness' that is the reality acknowledged and given a voice in writing:

> I would rather see the mixed state that exists being explored and exploited, more truthfully and spontaneously and hence more seriously than at present, by writers, and by playwrights and novelists in particular. It may be that we have a blessing in disguise. But if we want to uncover it we shall have to use our ears more and our grammar-books less.[29]

In effect, though different in emphases, Morgan's and Perry's diagnoses overlap, in that both perceived a deadlock existing, in part because of Scottish theatre's tendency to promote work in Lallans, or 'Costume Scots'. Morgan's views proved prescient in that a distinguishing feature of 1970s' drama was to be exploration and exploitation of just that 'mixed state', comprising the distinctive particularities of spoken Scots.

This key development has influenced the choice of plays in this anthology. The chosen plays exemplify the range of dramatic language that arose, from varieties of urban vernacular – as found in *Willie Rough*, *The Bevellers*, *The Hardman*, and even *The Jesuit*, where Campbell uses register contrasts in his history play and has his soldier characters speak in a modern demotic Scots – through to a range of individualistic solutions to creating an accessible Scots medium for rendering historical subject matter. In this last regard, *The Burning*, *The Rising*, *The Jesuit*, and *Willie Rough* – a history play of sorts because of its pre-World War I setting – demonstrate in each case the playwright's forging of a Scots medium that is appropriate to the period and the nature of the work, yet remains accessible to a contemporary audience. Even when a non-naturalistic medium is employed, as in *The Burning* and *The Jesuit*, which are set in the sixteenth and seventeenth century, respectively, the stress is on intelligibility. Stewart Conn, for example, explained in his original note to *The Burning*, now prefaced to the play here: 'There is no attempt at a reconstruction of sixteenth-century speech. I have aimed at the idea rather than the reality; at a hardness of diction, yet suppleness of rhythm, capable of suggesting the period and coping with the play's contemporary concepts – while remaining clearly intelligible.' This spirit of experimentalism was shared by Donald Campbell, who in his own words, saw 'exploration of the complexities and potential of the idioms of Scottish speech' as 'one of the central concerns of my work.'[30]

A similar sense of 'making it new' can be seen in work of a contemporary urban cast such as *The Bevellers* and *The Hardman*. Roddy McMillan's unflinching view of the realities of workplace life is the more powerful because his urban vernacular is harshly realistic in a manner that would have been unthinkable when he similarly dealt with working-class life in Glasgow in his previous play, *All in Good Faith* (1954). A contributory factor here was doubtless the abolition in 1968 of the Lord Chamberlain's power to censor or even ban plays in Britain for reasons which included any 'profanity or impropriety of language'. But one also has a sense with *The Bevellers* of a dam bursting after McMillan's long lay-off from playwriting, such is the powerful replication of proletarian Glaswegian speech and the excoriating rush and invention of the invective, as seen in this passage of dialogue where Rouger has been interrupted in his spiteful seduction of a workmate's girlfriend and threatens to take out his frustration on the offending party, a first-day apprentice:

> Ya knee-crept, Jesus-crept, swatchin little fucker, ah'll cut the bliddy scrotum aff ye! Ah'll knacker an' gut ye, ah'll eviscerate ye! Ya hure-spun, bastrified, conscrapulated young prick, ah'll do twenty year fur mincin you. Ye hear me? Ah'll rip ye fae the gullet tae the groin, ah'll incinerate ye! Ah had her – right therr – ah had her, spread-eagled, waitin fur the knife – an' you blew it. You blew the chance o pittin wan in her, an' wan on Charlie. He's never had her, but ah wid have had her. Another minute, ah wid have scored where he's never scored, an' you shankered it, ya parish-eyed, perishin bastart. Well, whit she didnae get, you'll get. Come doon here, come doon ah'm tellin ye, ah'll pit a shot in your arse that'll feel like thunder.

The Hardman shares with *The Bevellers* an impulse to represent working-class Glaswegian speech faithfully, but Tom McGrath, influenced by the theories of Grotowski and others, also wanted to explore 'sculptural theatre', which entailed using language 'sculpturally' and giving it 'rhythmic and percussive aspects', complemented by having a percussionist on stage.[31]

The sum effect of the vitality and diversity of Scots language harnessed by playwrights in the seventies, and continued through to today, is that, as Randall Stevenson concludes in his overview in *Scottish Theatre Since the Seventies* (1996), 'it is probably Scots speech that is the most fundamental influence on the drama'. He adds: 'Variously developed in the work of Donald Campbell, Bill Bryden, Roddy McMillan, Stewart Conn and others in the 1970s, it is a resource which has greatly empowered the progress of Scottish theatre over the past quarter century'.[32]

❧

Related to the issue of language is that two other defining characteristics of seventies' Scottish drama are engagement with urban life – and with West-Central urban life in particular – and new approaches to historical subject matter. Both of these have, as indicated above, consequences for choice of medium; and both of them, as defining characteristics of drama in the decade, have, along with linguistic developments, influenced the choice of plays in this collection.

All three of these characteristics, it could be said, reflect the more general seventies' mood of raised identity alluded to earlier. A popular BBC Television series at the time was *Who Are the Scots?*; that question could be applied not just to the nation's history but to modern and contemporary Scotland, too, which for dramatists meant, to borrow Edwin Morgan's formulation, registering the realities of Scotland both past and present. Expressing the linguistic reality gave added potency to examining those other realities through theatre; as Lindsay Paterson has pointed out, 'When dramatists such as Hector MacMillan, Tom McGrath, and Donald Campbell started writing in a Scots that could be felt to be real ... the first thing [they] did was to harness the sheer energy of working-class Scots into a vigorous theatricality in which issues of wide social significance could be debated incisively'.[33] Issues to be raised in this way through Scots-language drama included, for example: confrontation with unpalatable aspects of modern Scotland, such as Catholic-Protestant sectarianism, dealt with in Hector MacMillan's *The Sash* (1973), and to varying degrees in *Willie Rough*, *The Burning*, *The Jesuit*, and *The Hardman*; the bleakness and inescapable drudgery of working life in a dirty and dangerous basement workshop found in *The Bevellers*; the brutal punishment rather than rehabilitation of a convicted killer, incarcerated, literally, in a cage and driven through officially-sanctioned violence to smearing himself in excrement in protest, as in *The Hardman*.

Tom McGrath worked with a real-life convicted murderer from the Glasgow ganglands, Jimmy Boyle, in creating *The Hardman*, but said that he saw the fictional lead character in the play, Johnnie Byrne, as

> a true dramatic character, not just a re-presentation of a real-life model. This makes for a crucial difference between *The Hardman* and both Jimmy's book, *A Sense of Freedom*, and the film of the book. ... I tried to make *The Hardman* its own reality about which the audience were free to make their own conclusions.[34]

McGrath had earlier written: 'He [Jimmy Boyle] is a man with a question mark over his head. I had to dramatise that question mark.'[35] The controversy that surrounded *The Hardman* demonstrated that asking such questions, not just about an individual's culpability but about society's, could prove uncomfortable (literally so, as shown when the show was heckled in Glasgow). An influential conference held in Edinburgh in 1973, organised by the magazine *Scottish International*, brought 450 people together from all over Scotland to discuss Scotland's future. (*The Cheviot, The Stag and the Black, Black Oil* had its first, triumphant, performance at this event). The conference title was a question: *What Kind of Scotland?* The posing of that and related questions was a feature of Scottish society in the seventies, and affected drama, too. The question mark that Tom McGrath placed over Johnnie Byrne could be seen to be placed over their lead characters by other dramatists as well. Is the eponymous Willie Rough a naïve would-be radical or a clear-sighted visionary? Is the martyr priest John Ogilvie in *The Jesuit* admirably principled or arrogantly fanatical? Is Rouger, the sadistic persecutor and attempted sodomiser of the callow, first-day apprentice, Norrie Beaton, in *The Bevellers*, the product of nature or of familial and social nurture? Such questions implicitly invited audiences to engage with the wider implications for Scottish society, and to ponder: What kind of Scotland?

Related to this was that dramatists dealing with historical subject matter were both interrogating history and posing contemporary questions to audiences. In Alasdair Cameron's words: 'Whereas previously dramatists had contented themselves with depicting historical events or characters, or using a historical setting to explore the possibilities of Scots as a dramatic language, in the 1970s, exploring history was at last used as a means of exploring the present.'[36] The seventies saw the beginning of a renaissance in historiography in Scotland, which cast fresh, and sometimes first light on diverse aspects of the country's past. This was echoed in the theatre, where historical drama was in its own way revisionist in choice and treatment of subject matter, and written with an eye on lessons for the present. As was noted earlier, Bill Bryden was inspired 'to show Scotland to Scotland – her past and her present – to prepare her for the future'.[37] Hector MacMillan similarly said that 'the things I wanted to write about were connected both with its [Scotland's] history and with the processes of change'.[38] MacMillan expanded on this in an essay in 1970, when commenting on 'the complaint that Scots writers seem far too keen on historical drama':

> In this complaint there is ... substance, though the reasons behind the harking-back seem to escape most of the complainers. Important Scots history has been omitted and falsified throughout our education over the past 200 years or so, and the fondness for historical themes is almost certainly largely a conscious or subconscious attempt to redress the balance. If such attempts result in mere 'costume' drama then rejection can be defensible. If, however, the attempt results in a 'historical' play that fills a genuine gap in our knowledge and understanding, then it should be recognised as such and presented to the public in Scotland. Some writers will offer contemporary plays now, but others will continue to concentrate on re-establishing a true connection to our past, and this process is an essential step on the way to establishing a Scots tradition in the Theatre.[39]

There are links here in Stewart Conn's motivation with *The Burning*, which he said, in his prefatory note to the published play, 'did not spring from any predisposition on my part towards Scots historical drama; but from what struck me as the theatrical potential of the theme, and its relevance today'. *The Burning* was also in part a reaction against an earlier play dealing with the same period, Robert MacLellan's *Jamie the Saxt* (1937). Conn regarded it as the kind of 'costume drama', compounded by being written in a 'costume Scots', to which Hector MacMillan refers above: 'I think that too much of the language is sentimental cliché. It reduces the struggle between James VI and his cousin, the Earl of Bothwell, to a level of mawkish comedy which precludes any serious analysis of the politics and the threat of danger of the time.'[40] The mainspring for

Donald Campbell's *The Jesuit* was a reaction against the conventional, too. In an interview he said that he wrote the play

> really in a fit of anger because in the *Edinburgh Evening News* someone had suggested that since the quartercentenary of the Reformation was coming up, there ought to be a competition of plays about John Knox. I thought that's exactly the opposite of what we need! So I went and looked for someone who was the opposite of John Knox and I found Ogilvie.[41]

It should be emphasised that in all of the above cases these were individual rather than shared, programmatic approaches to dramatising history – just as was the case with writers dealing with contemporary urban material – but they are nonetheless indicative of a larger mood of revisionism in choice and treatment of subject matter. For, as Donald Smith has observed, 'the 1970s began a cultural shift in which Scottishness reshaped and reasserted itself against both external forces *and its own stereotypes*' [my emphasis].[42]

MacMillan in *The Rising* and Bryden in *Willie Rough* were giving voice to inherited *oral* histories of radical working-class struggle that had previously gone unrecorded in published history. In his original note to the play, republished here, MacMillan wrote:

> *The Rising* is based on events that happened in Scotland in the year 1820; far enough away from us now to be regarded as long-past history, yet so close that it is still just possible for someone alive today to have learnt of them from an eye-witness. It is a story that has been kept alive from generation to generation by a relatively small number of committed Scots. I had the good fortune to learn it … as a child by the fireside. I had the additional good fortune to learn the story from the best possible source – from my father, Robert Galbraith MacMillan – one of the most committed of those committed Scots.

In an echo of this, Bill Bryden wrote that in *Willie Rough* 'the leading character was based on the memory of my grandfather',[43] whose name was Willie Rough (Bryden's full name is William Campbell Rough Bryden). As noted earlier, *Willie Rough* was history with obvious analogies that audiences could draw with contemporary events on Clydeside. *The Rising*, too, carried a contemporary resonance, as MacMillan confirmed in his prefatory note:

> It was never my intention to produce any kind of conventional stage play. I set out to recreate on stage the essence of a part of our history. I have tried to do so in a manner that will appeal on as many different levels as possible to the people whose forebears created that history in the first place and who are still deprived full knowledge of it.

It is relevant to note that John McGrath's *The Cheviot, The Stag and the Black, Black Oil* similarly had its genesis in the author's exposure to *oral* recollections of the Highland Clearances,[44] and overtly drew parallels between historical and contemporary experience.

In common with Bryden and MacMillan, Donald Campbell's work is informed by what he terms 'a proletarian consciousness'.[45] In the religious conflict depicted in *The Jesuit*, the soldiers, whom Alan Bond significantly describes as 'remarkably contemporary figures'[46], are representative of how ordinary people are exploited to fight for the causes of their social superiors. One of them articulates his perception of this to his comrades:

> Ach, whit gars me grue the maist is the fact that aa this argy-bargy is aboot sweet fuck-all! *(Holds the naked sword up before him.)* The haun that hauds this sword has killed mair men nor I hae years o my life – and whit for? Whit some bluidy jyner said or didnae say in Palestine hundreds o years syne! Christ, it gies me the boke tae think o it! ... It's aye the same – the meenisters and the priests and the high-heid anes'll dae the argyin and the stirrin up – but when it comes tae the killin and the deein ... it'll no be the meenisters that'll dae the fechtin or the killin or deein – it'll be you and me and Sandy and young laddies like Wullie! (II.4)

Stewart Conn's *The Burning* similarly shows how innocent citizens are trapped by struggles for religious or political power, in this case between King James VI and the Earl of Bothwell. Towards the end of the play, Bothwell says to the King: 'We are the upper and nether millstones, you and I. One way or another, it is those trappt in the middle, must pay the price' (II.6). As Randall Stevenson has noted, 'this vision of the common people oppressed by an unjust history' is a constant running through all of the above history plays.[47]

As a young playwright looking with frustration at the theatre scene in Scotland in 1961, an impassioned Stewart Conn wrote:

> I feel that what is wanted in Scotland is a break with parochial values, a drama of the people for the people and by the people, a return if necessary to pre-positional statements with which an audience can identify itself and from which it will benefit. Let our plays be 'theatre', alive, organic first – and literary afterwards. Illuminative and cathartic as against superficially satisfying, our drama must become part of the life of the community, and the Scottish Theatre part of a revitalised national consciousness.[48]

Conn's wish was to be achieved in the 1970s, when a vital new drama emerged that both reflected and contributed to 'a revitalised national consciousness' and was written as 'a drama of the people for the people'. For, as we have seen, in language, choice and treatment of subject matter, and general sympathies, a characteristic trait of seventies' Scottish drama is that it is markedly national and democratic in nature. That democratic, or popular, impulse is also evident in the variety of forms, style and techniques adopted by dramatists with the objective of lending their work accessibility, immediacy, and directness of effect. Added to this, there is a general emphasis on clarity, with the plays tending to share a simplicity of structure and staging, and often featuring short, episodic scenes, reflecting variously the influence of Brecht and of popular culture such as television and film. A noticeable feature, too, is that the plays call for a strongly collaborative style of ensemble acting, and demand from actors a confidence in speaking Scots speech with natural ease. Also, music and song are often an enlivening presence: *The Rising* features a folk group placed above the action to provide a running soundtrack and songs which advance and comment on events; *The Burning* is regularly punctuated by songs in a folk idiom; *The Hardman* opens with an ironic refrain from *The Song of the Clyde* and has a percussionist on stage throughout supplying an instrumental commentary.[49] A further dimension to the playwright-audience relationship in the work of the period was highlighted by Tom McGrath. In an interview, he said that, in common with contemporaneous Scottish drama, but in contrast with English drama of the same period, *The Hardman*

> just *is* of its own reality. This makes Scottish drama very different from what David Edgar and his kind are doing: it's a drama that's being expressed from *inside* something, whereas they are much more analytical in their mode of expression.

He added that he saw his kind of theatre 'to be more in a folk tradition than an intellectual one'.[50] That notion of 1970s' drama being written *from inside* a 'folk', or people's, culture – irrespective of whether 'folk' or 'people' is defined in national or class terms, or an elision of the two – can be seen as a further factor in the close rapport that playwrights enjoyed with their audiences in that decade.

Allen Wright commented in 1977 that 'a few years ago, theatre directors used to argue that Scottish plays did not attract audiences but that generalisation was demolished by the success' of plays by Bill Bryden, Hector MacMillan, and others.[51] This sea change was achieved partly through the dramaturgical means just discussed and partly through a synergy, or reciprocation, between playwrights and audiences, both of whom were influenced by the new national mood. It was a mood in which, to paraphrase Hector MacMillan, 'a new and enquiring audience was hungry for Scottish work',[52] and the playwrights provided the dramatic nourishment. Of the engagement with the particularities of common Scottish experience and the receptivity of audiences to it, Bill Bryden wrote, in relation to the enthusiastic reception given to the premiere of *Willie Rough* at the Royal Lyceum:

> The first performance was concrete proof that a talented ensemble of Scottish actors in a Scottish play was a unique experience. Watching this performance was not like watching English actors or German of French. It was neither better nor worse. It was different. ... There was no company in the world could do this particular play better than we could and *we were being supported by the people* [my emphasis].[53]

That italicised statement can stand as a resonant declaration of why the 1970s were such special years for the Scottish people and for the advancement of Scottish drama; a specialness illustrated by the six plays in this selection.

Bill Findlay

Notes

1. Bill Findlay, ed., *A History of Scottish Theatre* (Edinburgh: Polygon, 1998), p.ix.
2. Alasdair Cameron, ed., *Scot-Free: New Scottish Plays* (London: Nick Hern Books, 1990); Ian Brown and Mark Fisher, eds., *Made in Scotland: An Anthology of New Scottish Plays* (London: Methuen, 1995); Philip Howard, ed., *Scotland Plays: New Scottish Drama* (London: Nick Hern Books, 1998).
3. Tom McGrath, 'Blowing the Changes', in *Chapman*, 49 (Summer 1987), p.60.
4. See Audrey Bain's article on the history of the Scottish Society of Playwrights, 'Striking It Rich?', in *Theatre Scotland*, 3:11 (Autumn 1994), pp.16–24.
5. *A Decade's Drama: Six Scottish Plays* [no editor named] (Todmorden: Woodhouse Books, 1980).
6. John McGrath, *The Cheviot, The Stag and the Black, Black Oil* (London: Methuen, 1981; with subsequent reprints). In print, too, is: John McGrath, *Six-Pack: Plays for Scotland* (Edinburgh: Polygon, 1996); among the six plays are *The Cheviot* and two others from the seventies, *Out of Our Heads* (1976) and *Joe's Drum* (1979). Robert David MacDonald, *Three Plays: Webster, Summit Conference, Chinchilla* (London: Oberon Books, 1991). John Byrne, *The Slab Boys Trilogy* (London: Penguin, 1987; with subsequent reprints). Another seventies' play by John Byrne, *Writer's Cramp* (1977), is included in the anthology *Scot-Free* (see note 2 above).
7. Randall Stevenson, 'Scottish Theatre 1950–1980', in *The History of Scottish Literature: Vol. 4, Twentieth Century*, ed. Cairns Craig (Aberdeen: Aberdeen University Press, 1987), p.356.
8. Tom Gallacher, 'To Succeed at Home', in *Chapman*, 43–44 (Spring 1986), p.88.
9. For discussion of the work of Ena Lamont Stewart and Joan Ure, see: Jan McDonald, 'Scottish Women Dramatists Since 1945', in *A History of Scottish*

Women's Writing, ed. Douglas Gifford and Dorothy McMillan (Edinburgh: Edinburgh University Press, 1997), pp.494–513; and Audrey Bain, 'Loose Canons: Identifying a Women's Tradition in Playwriting', in *Scottish Theatre Since the Seventies*, ed. Randall Stevenson and Gavin Wallace (Edinburgh: Edinburgh University Press, 1996), pp.138–45. Ena Lamont Stewart's *Men Should Weep* features in Adrienne Scullion's 'Feminine Pleasures and Masculine Indignities: Gender and Community in Scottish Drama', in *Gendering the Nation*, ed. Christopher Whyte (Edinburgh: Edinburgh University Press, 1995), pp.169–204. (This essay also includes analysis of Roddy McMillan's *The Bevellers*.)

10. Quoted in Bain, p.18. In those otherwise barren years, Stewart's *The Heir to Ardmally* was staged at Pitlochry Festival Theatre in 1958.

11. Quoted in Elizabeth MacLennan, *The Moon Belongs to Everyone: Making Theatre with 7:84* (London: Methuen, 1990), p.112.

12. Edwin Morgan, *Essays* (Cheadle: Carcanet New Press, 1974), p.164. The essay originally appeared in *The Times Literary Supplement* of 28 July 1972.

13. Gallacher, p.89.

14. Christopher Harvie, *No Gods and Precious Few Heroes: Scotland 1914–1980* (London: Edward Arnold, 1981), p.159.

15. Donald Campbell, *A Brighter Sunshine: A Hundred Years of the Edinburgh Royal Lyceum Theatre* (Edinburgh: Polygon, 1983), p.208.

16. From statement by him on the back cover of: Hector MacMillan, *The Sash* (Glasgow: Molendinar Press, 1974).

17. Bill Bryden, 'Bricks on our Shoulders', in *Theatre 74*, ed. Sheridan Morley (London: Hutchinson, 1974), p.12.

18. *Ibid.*, p.127.

19. *Ibid.*, p.130.

20. Alasdair Cameron, *Study Guide to Twentieth-Century Scottish Drama* (Glasgow: University of Glasgow, Department of Scottish Literature, 1990), p.90.

21. See Chapters 4 and 5 of *A History of Scottish Theatre*.

22. Stevenson, p.349.

23. Some criticism was, however, raised that 'the Lyceum is attempting too much too quickly', with the programme becoming 'unbalanced in its favouring of the new and untried', leaving audiences 'a little disgruntled': see Kenneth Roy, 'What's gone wrong at the Lyceum?', in *Scottish Theatre*, 40, pp.12–13. Also, a prominent playwright expressed scepticism about how real a change the Lyceum had effected in 1970–75: see Hector MacMillan, 'The Future of Political Theatre in Scotland', in *New Edinburgh Review*, 30 (August 1975), pp. 32–3.

24. Campbell, p.207.

25. Donald Smith, '1950 to 1995', in *A History of Scottish Theatre*, p.275 and p.274.

26. Alan Bold, *Modern Scottish Literature* (London: Longman, 1983), pp.313–14.

27. Quoted in Campbell, p.203.

28. Morgan, p.163.

29. Morgan, p.156. The essay, 'Registering the Reality of Scotland', was first published in *Planet*, 4 (February–March, 1971).

30. Donald Campbell, 'A Focus of Discontent', in *New Edinburgh Review*, 45 (Spring 1979), p.5.
31. Gavin Selerie, ed., *The Riverside Interviews 6: Tom McGrath* (London: Binnacle Press, 1983), p.188.
32. Randall Stevenson, 'Introduction', in *Scottish Theatre Since the Seventies*, ed. Randall Stevenson and Gavin Wallace (Edinburgh: Edinburgh University Press, 1996), p.4 and p.5.
33. Lindsay Paterson, 'Language and Identity on the Stage', in *Scottish Theatre Since the Seventies*, p.75 and p.76.
34. *The Riverside Interviews*, p.188.
35. Quoted in *ibid.*, p.36, from an article by Tom McGrath in *Time Out*, 25 November 1977.
36. Cameron, p.99.
37. Bryden, p.130.
38. As note 16 above.
39. Hector MacMillan, 'Scots Theatre – or Theatre in Scotland', in *Catalyst*, 3:3 (Summer 1970), p.15.
40. Interview with Stewart Conn in: Ian Brown, 'Cultural Centrality and Dominance: The Creative Writer's View – Conversations between Scottish Poet/Playwrights and Ian Brown', in *Interface*, 3 (Summer 1984), p.56.
41. From an interview with John Clifford, 'Till all the words run dry', in *Theatre Scotland*, 4:13 (Spring 1995), p.23.
42. Smith, p.270.
43. Bryden, p.128.
44. See John McGrath's 'The Year of the Cheviot', prefaced to the Methuen edition of *The Cheviot, The Stag and the Black, Black Oil*, p.vi.
45. Interview with John Clifford (see note 41 above), p.28.
46. Bold, p.316.
47. Stevenson, 'Scottish Theatre 1950–1980', p.357.
48. Stewart Conn, 'Theatre in Scotland 1961', in *New Saltire*, 1 (Summer 1961), p.62. Conn wrote plays in the 1960s that were staged but considers them 'apprentice work' (quoted in Stevenson, 'Scottish Theatre 1950–1980', p.357).
49. The seventies' work that best exemplifies all these features, and in its politics more explicitly reveals the democratic impulse behind them, is *The Cheviot, The Stag and The Black, Black Oil*.
50. *The Riverside Interviews*, p.193 and p.194.
51. Allen Wright, 'Writers and the Theatre', in *Scottish Writing and Writers*, ed. Norman Wilson (Edinburgh: The Ramsay Head Press, 1977), p.49.
52. The paraphrasing is Audrey Bain's: see Bain, p.19.
53. Bryden, pp.127–8 and p.129.

Willie Rough

by

Bill Bryden

First performed at the Royal Lyceum Theatre, Edinburgh,
on 10 February 1972, directed by Bill Bryden

Bill Bryden is hereby identified as author of this work in accordance with
Section 77 of the Copyright, Designs and Patents Act 1988

Bill Bryden

Bill Bryden was born in Greenock in 1942 and educated at Greenock High School. He started his career in television in 1963 as a researcher and scriptwriter with Scottish Television. He left in 1965 to take up a Director Traineeship at the Belgrade Theatre, Coventry, followed by an Assistant Directorship at the Royal Court Theatre in London. From 1971 to 1974 he was Associate Director of the Royal Lyceum Theatre, Edinburgh, where with Clive Perry he developed a repertoire of new plays by Scottish dramatists and drew together a company of Scottish actors (including Roddy McMillan) as the nucleus of a projected but unrealised Scottish National Theatre. His productions there included Roddy McMillan's *The Bevellers,* Stewart Conn's *The Burning* (both of which he commissioned), and his own plays *Willie Rough* and *Benny Lynch.* He directed Sir David Lindsay's *Ane Satyre of the Thrie Estaitis* for the 1973 Edinburgh International Festival.

Frustrated by funding difficulties in transforming the Lyceum company into a Scottish National Theatre, he accepted an offer to join the National Theatre in London in 1974. He was appointed an Associate Director in 1975, with subsequent responsibility for the Cottesloe Theatre. Among his many outstanding productions there was *The Mystery Plays,* which won him the Evening Standard, Olivier, and Variety Club Awards for Best Director. He also directed the premiere of David Mamet's *Glengarry, Glen Ross.*

For the National Theatre he wrote *Old Movies* (1977), and for the Scottish Theatre Company, *Civilians* (1981), set in Greenock during the Second World War. He wrote the screenplay for a Hollywood feature film, *The Long Riders* (1980), and wrote and directed *Ill Fares the Land* (1982), a Channel 4 film about the evacuation of St Kilda.

From 1985 to 1993 he was Head of Drama at BBC Scotland Television, for whom he wrote and directed *The Holy City* (1985), and devised and executively produced John Byrne's award-winning series *Tutti Frutti.*

He was one of the ten directors of the opera film *Aria* (1985). Productions he has directed at the Royal Opera House, Covent Garden, include *Parsifal* (1989) and *The Cunning Little Vixen* (1990). He wrote the libretto for Robin Orr's opera *Hermiston,* staged by Scottish Opera in 1975.

To mark Glasgow's year as Cultural Capital of Europe in 1990 he was commissioned to write and direct *The Ship,* a large-scale promenade production performed in a vast shipbuilding-shed in Govan. For the same space he wrote and directed *The Big Picnic* (1994), subsequently televised on BBC2. In the 1990s he directed a number of plays in London's West End and elsewhere.

In 1990 he received the Gulliver Award for the Performing Arts in Scotland, and in 1993 was made a CBE. He holds honorary Doctorates from the University of Stirling, Queen Margaret University College, and the Guildhall School of Music and Drama.

I CARRY A BRICK on my shoulder in order that people may know
what my house was like.

Bert Brecht

GREENOCK

This grey town
That pipes the morning up before the lark
With shrieking steam, and from a hundred stalks
Lacquers the sooty sky; where hammers clang
On iron hulls, and cranes in harbours creak,
Rattle and swing, whole cargoes on their necks;
Where men sweat gold that others hoard or spend,
And lurk like vermin in their narrow streets:
This old grey town
Is world enough for me.

John Davidson

Characters

MR PENROSE, *clerk*

GEORDIE MacLEOD

SAM THOMSON

WILLIE ROUGH

HUGHIE

PAT GATENS

EDDIE, *publican*

JAKE ADAMS, *foreman*

APPRENTICE

KATE, *Willie's wife*

BERNADETTE, *Pat's wife*

SANNY, *policeman*

PETER, *policeman*

CHARLIE McGRATH

NURSE

WORKERS

The action is set in Greenock, Scotland, between February 1914 and June 1916.

Act One

1. Shipyard Employment Office: February 1914

The shipyard horn blasts loud and long. Three men are sitting on a simple wooden bench opposite a cluttered wooden desk with an empty chair behind it. WILLIE *is reading a newspaper. Beside him* SAM *is rolling a cigarette. Next to* SAM *sits* GEORDIE. SAM *lights his cigarette, and, while they wait,* GEORDIE *begins whistling impatiently.* MR PENROSE, *the clerk, comes in, ignoring their reaction to his arrival. He sits down on the empty chair, and rearranges his papers.*

MR PENROSE   Who's first? (GEORDIE *stops whistling, gets up quickly, and goes over to the desk.*) Name?
GEORDIE   I've tae see Jake Adams.
MR PENROSE   I asked you your name.
GEORDIE   My name? George R. MacLeod, an' I've tae see Jake Adams.
MR PENROSE   *(giving up trying to fill in the form)*   You'll find him down the yard. Ask somebody where the tanker is.
GEORDIE   What's it cried, like?
MR PENROSE   Pardon?
GEORDIE   What's its name, pal?
MR PENROSE   It hasn't got one yet. You'll have to build it first.
GEORDIE   I'll find 'im okay. Thanks, pal.

GEORDIE *goes out.*

MR PENROSE   Next? (SAM *rises and goes to the desk, still smoking his roll-up.*) Name?
SAM   Same as him.
MR PENROSE   I suppose you're George R. ...
SAM   Not at all. Jake.
MR PENROSE   And what's Jake short for?
SAM   I'm no Jake. I'm Sam. I'm lookin for Jake, but. Jake Adams. I've come tae the right place, I hope.
MR PENROSE   Yes.
SAM   Jake Adams is the foreman, right?
MR PENROSE   He's one of our foremen, yes.
SAM   Well, I want tae see 'im. He's startin me this mornin. I'm Sam Thomson.
MR PENROSE   You'll find him down the yard. Ask somebody where the tanker is.
SAM   Thanks for nothin', Jimmy. (SAM *goes to the door. He opens it, then turns to face* MR PENROSE *again.*) Hey?
MR PENROSE   Yes.
SAM   Is it as hard tae get out o here as it is tae get in?

5

MR PENROSE   I beg your pardon?

SAM   Just a wee joke. Cheer up.

SAM *goes out.*

MR PENROSE *(not pleased)*   Next! (WILLIE *folds up his newspaper, rises, walks over to the desk, and takes off his cap.)* I suppose you're looking for Jake Adams as well?

WILLIE   Who's Jake Adams?

MR PENROSE   Name?

WILLIE   Rough. R, O, U, G, H.

MR PENROSE   I can spell.

WILLIE   Sorry. I wis just tryin tae help.

MR PENROSE *(delighted that at last he can fill in a form)*   Rough by name and rough by nature, eh?

WILLIE   Aye.

MR PENROSE   First name?

WILLIE   William.

MR PENROSE   Any others?

WILLIE   The wife an' two weans.

MR PENROSE   Names, I mean. Any middle names?

WILLIE   No... just thae two... Willie Rough.

MR PENROSE   Date of birth?

WILLIE   The eighteenth o January 1883.

MR PENROSE   That makes ye...?

WILLIE   Thirty-wan.

MR PENROSE   How long have you been idle?

WILLIE   The last job stopped the week o Christmas.

MR PENROSE   Tough luck.

WILLIE   We still had Christmas.

MR PENROSE   It's getting so that it doesn't mean a thing, Christmas.

WILLIE   I can see you've nae weans.

MR PENROSE *(less familiar)*   Do you have your lines?

WILLIE   Aye. *(Taking some papers out of his pocket, he hands them to the* CLERK. *The* CLERK *reads them.)* ... My time's been out a good while nou... I'm a good tradesman. I've got references.

MR PENROSE   Organised, I see.

WILLIE   Oh, ye *must,* Mr... eh?

MR PENROSE   Penrose. Religion?

WILLIE   Prod'sant.

MR PENROSE   Do you go?

WILLIE   Aye. I'll need tae find a good kirk doun here.

MR PENROSE   You're not a Greenock man, then?

WILLIE   Na. I walked frae Johnstone this mornin.

MR PENROSE   That's fifteen miles.

WILLIE   Felt like fifty in the dark.

MR PENROSE   Oh.

WILLIE   I left early in case there was any chance o a start.

MR PENROSE   Well... I don't see how I can help you, Mr Rough.

WILLIE   What dae ye mean?

MR PENROSE   We've nothing at present.

WILLIE   I thought I'd get a start.

MR PENROSE   There's no work.

WILLIE   What dae ye mean, nae work? Them other two men got a start. Nae fillin in any forms. Nae nothing! I'm no stupit. What's the password, Mr Penrose?

MR PENROSE   I don't know what you're talking about. Look, if you call in at the end of the week there just might be something. I'll see what I can do.

WILLIE   I left the house at half-four this mornin. I walked tae Greenock tae get a job, and I'm no goin hame 'ithout wan!

MR PENROSE   Hot-headedness will get you nowhere, Rough. It's nothing to do with me.

WILLIE   Who's it tae dae wi, then?

MR PENROSE   I'm not the management. I'm a clerk. Shouting at me won't affect the issue one way or another.

WILLIE   I think I've been wastin my time talkin tae you. Who's the heid man?

MR PENROSE   I'm sorry.

WILLIE   You're no. You don't even know me. What does an application form tell ye about a man? You're no the least bit sorry.

MR PENROSE   If I could help you, I would.

WILLIE   Let us see the top man, then.

MR PENROSE   Mr Cosgrave isn't interested in the problems of employing one riveter, and you know it.

WILLIE   Aye, he should be, but.

MR PENROSE   That's as may be.

WILLIE   I'm a good man, Mr Penrose.

MR PENROSE   Look, I'll tell you what.

WILLIE   What?

MR PENROSE   Find one of the foremen. Preferably one that's a Protestant. Talk to him. He might be able to start you.

WILLIE   How can he start me when you cannae?

MR PENROSE   Because.

WILLIE   Because what?

MR PENROSE   Because that's the way things are. Every yard on the Clyde does things that way, and we're no exception.

WILLIE   What a state o affairs!

MR PENROSE   That's the way it is.

WILLIE   Well, what dae I dae first? Join the Masons, or something?

MR PENROSE   I don't think it need come to that. You'll find one of the foreman in the James Watt Bar across the road at dinner-time. Name of Jake Adams. He's never out of there.

WILLIE   Right y'are. I've never got a start in a pub afore. *(He moves towards the door.)*

MR PENROSE   Have you got any money?

WILLIE   How?

MR PENROSE   You might have to buy him a refreshment.

WILLIE   I've got four an' a tanner.

MR PENROSE   You're fine, then.

WILLIE   Aye. *(He goes to the door, but turns back just before leaving.)* I must thank ye very much.

MR PENROSE   You haven't got a start yet.

WILLIE   I will, but. I've got tae.

WILLIE *goes out.* MR PENROSE *pulls the application form into a bundle and throws it into the waste-paper basket.*

2. The James Watt Bar: February 1914 (same day)

The Public Bar is so small that when a few workers come in it will seem crowded. The bar is on one side. At the other side there are two round tables, and a long bench against the wall provides seating for both. The entrance to the Family Department is beside the bar, and a door at the back opens on to the street.

EDDIE, *the publican, behind the bar, is studying the racing form. Two other men are seated on the long bench behind one of the round tables, talking.* PAT *is in his late thirties;* HUGHIE, *a small, wiry man, must be nearly sixty, but it's difficult to tell exactly how old he is. They are arguing chiefly to pass the time; and, though they tend to shout, their dispute is neither violent nor serious.*

PAT   He is!

HUGHIE   He isnae! Ye don't know.

PAT   I know aa-right. He's my wean, in't 'e?

HUGHIE   Aye, but he's only six months auld. Ye cannae tell yit.

PAT   I can tell.

HUGHIE   Hou can ye tell 'at a wean's gonna be clever at that age?

PAT   He's got a big heid. That's a sign o intelligence.

HUGHIE   It's no!

PAT   I'm tellin ye it is!

HUGHIE   An' I'm tellin you it's no! Listen tae me. There's a wumman lives doun ablow me. She's got a boy wi a big heid, and he's daft!

PAT   Aye, but that's different. Och, ye cannae argyie wi you, Hughie!

An APPRENTICE *comes in. He's about fourteen years old.*

EDDIE   Hey, get out!
APPRENTICE   Keep yer hair on, wigs are dear.
EDDIE   You're too young tae be in here. What dae ye want?
APPRENTICE   I'm over wi the gaffer's line.
EDDIE   Who's your gaffer?
APPRENTICE   Jake Adams.
EDDIE   That's all right, then, son.

The APPRENTICE *crosses to the bar, and gives* EDDIE *a piece of paper.*

APPRENTICE   He says there should be somethin' back frae yesterday.
EDDIE   Oh. Just let me check up. *(He looks at his list of bets.)* Aye, he has, right
    enough. *(Sadly.)* He had a winner at Hamilton, and a place as well, but
    Ballykameen wis naewhere. They're still out lookin for it wi a bale o hay. That's
    (counting) eh… five tae wan at a tanner's hauf a croun, and he's a tanner back's,
    three shillins, an' wan an' three for the place. Four an' three, son. Is that what Jake
    said it would be?
APPRENTICE   He didnae tell me.
EDDIE   That's what it is, well. Nou, what's he on the day? *(He looks at the slip of
    paper.)* Confident, I see. Two bob each way on the favourite in the first race at
    Ayr, an' a shillin tae win on Chansin Damour. Five bob. By Jeese, he's breakin
    out the-day. Look son, gie us ninepence, and he's on. *(The* APPRENTICE *gives him
    the money.)* Right ye are, son. Ye can have a drink, if ye want.
APPRENTICE   Never touch it. My faither's a Rekkabite.

The APPRENTICE *goes out.*

EDDIE   Hey, Hughie!
HUGHIE   What's that, Eddie?
EDDIE   Will ye go a wee message for us?
HUGHIE   Is there a drink in it?
EDDIE   I'll gie ye a hauf.
HUGHIE   I never say 'No' to a wee refreshment, Edward… There's no too much
    walkin in it, is there?
EDDIE   Just run over an' get me the *Outlook.*
HUGHIE   I don't know whether I'll be runnin.
EDDIE   Ach, ye know what I mean. Just get us the paper. I want tae see the latest
    price o that horse Jake Adams is on. It's no even in the bettin in this wan.

HUGHIE, *whose left leg has been amputated just above the knee, picks up a heavy
wooden crutch from under the table, gets up, and hobbles over to the bar to get
the money from* EDDIE, *then crosses quickly to the door which opens on to the street.*

9

HUGHIE   I'd pour out that hauf, Eddie. It's great how the prospect o a wee goldie fairly gies a man acceleration.

HUGHIE *goes out into the street.*

EDDIE   *(pouring out* HUGHIE'S *drink)*   How about you, Pat?
PAT   Na, I'm fine, Eddie. I'll need tae get back tae the job. I'm supposed tae be out for a message.

WILLIE *comes in and crosses to the bar.*

EDDIE   Yes?
WILLIE   A hauf gill o Bell's.

WILLIE *gives him money.* EDDIE *gives* WILLIE *his change, then returns to the racing page.* PAT *looks at* WILLIE; WILLIE *waits, drinking his whisky.*

EDDIE   …Chansin Damour… it's funny, it's no in the bettin.
PAT   I know what you want, Eddie.
EDDIE   What's that?
PAT   You want everybody's horse tae go on the bing. By the law o averages somebody's got tae win sometime.
EDDIE   What dae you know about Chansin Damour, Pat Gatens?
WILLIE   It's by Pride and Prejudice out o French Dressin. It was a close fourth at Bogside a while back. It woulda won if I hadnae been on it. It's due a win. There's an apprentice on it the day.

HUGHIE *comes back into the Public Bar with the newspaper.*

PAT   You're too late, Hughie.
HUGHIE   How?
PAT   We know aa about Jake Adams' horse nou. This fella tellt us.
HUGHIE   Dae I still get my drink?
EDDIE   Aye.
HUGHIE   That's aa-right, then. *(He lifts* WILLIE'S *glass and drinks his whisky.)*
EDDIE   Hey, Hughie. That's his.
HUGHIE   Hell of a sorry.

HUGHIE *lifts his own glass and drinks that down, then dances over to join* PAT.

EDDIE   You're a bettin man, I see… eh…
WILLIE   Willie. Willie Rough. No, I wouldnae say that. I'm just interested in horses an' dugs. I only bet when I'm at the meetin. Sometimes I can pick a winner in the flesh. I've nae luck wi the papers.

EDDIE   Is 'at a fact?

PAT   He's no wan o the mugs, Eddie.

EDDIE   *(to* WILLIE*)*   Ye local, like?

WILLIE   Na, I'm frae Johnstone. Came doun this mornin tae try tae get a start ower by.

SAM *and* GEORDIE *come in from the street.*

EDDIE   What'll it be, boys?

SAM   Two pints.

WILLIE *looks at* SAM *and* GEORDIE, *then moves over to the empty table and sits down.* PAT *slides along the bench to be beside him, and* HUGHIE *follows suit.*

PAT   I couldnae help owerhearin your, eh, conversation, like… Tryin tae get started, are ye?

WILLIE   Aye. It's like gettin out o prison.

HUGHIE   It's harder 'ithout your faculties, believe me.

PAT   Shut it, Hughie!

HUGHIE   It's aa-right for some folk.

PAT   *(to* WILLIE*)*   You want tae speak tae wan o the gaffers. That's the system.

WILLIE   I know.

PAT   You've come tae the right place.

WILLIE   Will ye point 'im out tae us when he comes in?

PAT   Aye, sure.

WILLIE   You workin?

PAT   I'm at the hole-borin. Pat Gatens.

WILLIE   Willie Rough.

PAT   This is Hughie.

WILLIE   Hello.

HUGHIE   Pleased tae meet ye.

They shake hands. Several workers come into the pub. Most of them order a whisky and a bottle of beer; and when they have been served, they begin chatting in groups round the bar. They are dirty, and have obviously been working. All of them wear caps (which they call 'bunnets'). The small bar soon begins to look crowded.

WILLIE   Thae two ower there. They got a stairt this mornin. Aa I got was a lecture frae the time-keeper.

PAT   Penrose?

WILLIE   Aye.

PAT   Holy Willie. He's a Wee Free or something. He disnae drink or onything!

HUGHIE   Some folk's no wise.

They drink. JAKE *comes in. He is about forty-five years old. He wears a suit and matching bunnet. He looks cleaner than the rest. He is not tall but powerfully built.*

GEORDIE   Can I buy ye a drink?

JAKE   That's very good o ye, Geordie. I'll have a hauf gill o Bell's.

EDDIE   Right ye are! *(He pours out the drinks.)*

HUGHIE *(confidentially)*   That's your man there, Willie… the gaffer.

PAT   Shut it, Hughie. He might be frae Johnstone, but he's no stupit.

HUGHIE   Sorry I spoke.

JAKE *(to* EDDIE)   My boy was tellin me ye're no too pleased about my win yesterday.

EDDIE   Naebody likes tae lose.

JAKE   Come on, Eddie, the bookie never loses, and you know it. Got a tip frae the course the day – Chansin Dammer.

EDDIE   Outside chance.

JAKE *(laughing)*   It'll walk hame. I've a good mind tae get the whole yard on it just tae spite ye, Eddie.

EDDIE   Hey! Steady on, Jake! Ye want tae bankrupt us aathegither?

JAKE   Aye, likely. Take mair than wan cert tae dae that.

EDDIE   Remember, we've a maximum pey-out here, Jake.

JAKE   I'm sure the lads would take payment in kind frae the likes o you, Eddie. They've a gey long time tae wait tae next New Year, an' thay'll be some that's no daein much drinkin, or first-fittin either, this time.

EDDIE   How no?

JAKE   King and Country, Eddie.

EDDIE   Aye, ye might be right.

JAKE   I'm bloody sure I'm right. They'll be runnin doun tae the Toun Hall tae enlist like the RCs queuein up for their wee bit o soot on Ash Wednesday. Just you wait.

Leaving the bar, JAKE *goes towards the entrance to the Family Department, passing* WILLIE'S *table.*

PAT   Hello-rerr, Jake. Got that wee message for ye.

JAKE   Ye werenae long gettin back.

PAT   This is Willie Rough – Jake Adams.

JAKE   Fine day.

PAT   He's eh… wonderin, like, if there's any chance o a start, Jake.

JAKE   Impossible at the moment, son. I started a couple o new men this mornin.

PAT   He's wan o yours, Jake.

JAKE   I see. I cannae promise. I'm goin in there.

JAKE *goes out into the Family Department.*

HUGHIE *(to* WILLIE*)*   There ye are, then.

WILLIE   What?

HUGHIE   G'in and see 'im.

WILLIE   I'm no deif, Hughie, he said it was impossible.

HUGHIE   That'll be right, I don't think!

WILLIE   Okay. What dae I dae nou?

PAT *produces a packet of Gold Flake cigarettes and offers one to* WILLIE.

PAT   Fag?

WILLIE   Ta.

HUGHIE *(seizing one before* WILLIE *can)*   You're a gentleman, Patrick.

PAT   When are you gonna buy some?

HUGHIE   The next hallecaplump Tuesday 'at faas on a Wednesday.

PAT   I havenae got a light, Willie. Go an' ask Jake Adams for a match.

WILLIE   Haud on. I've got a box in my pocket.

PAT   Just dae what I tell ye.

WILLIE *gets up and goes into the Family Department.* PAT *gives* HUGHIE *a light and then lights his own cigarette.*

HUGHIE   It's a bit slow on the uptak. Just doun frae the hills, ye ask me.

PAT   It's aa-right for us. We know the gemm. But how onybody's expectit tae know how ye go about it beats me.

HUGHIE   It's hardly worth 'is while onywey. The likes o him'll be itchin under 'is khaki afore ye can say 'Jock Robinson'.

WILLIE *comes back into the Public Bar.*

HUGHIE   Well?

WILLIE   Well what?

PAT   What happened?

WILLIE   Nothin'. I asked him for a light. He gies me a box o matches an' says, 'Keep the box. There's only wan in it.'

HUGHIE *and* PAT *exchange looks. They have a secret.*

HUGHIE   Light your fag, then.

WILLIE *(opening the matchbox)*   Christ! Ther' money in here. Hauf-a-croun.

HUGHIE   Pat, what did I tell ye afore? He's daft, an' he *hasnae* got a big heid. Look, Willie, ye don't expect Jake Adams tae gie somebody a light like any other body, dae ye?

PAT   Have ye got a hauf-croun?

WILLIE   Aye.

PAT   Well, pit it in the box wi the other wan, an' gae ben there, an' gie 'im the box back. Tell him there were three in it, and ye used wan.

HUGHIE   That's safe enough. Walls have ears, Willie.

WILLIE   Bribery and corruption.

PAT   Well, ye want the job, dan't ye?

WILLIE   Aye.

PAT   That's aa-right, well.

WILLIE   It's *no* right.

PAT   Listen tae me, pal. I don't know you. I only met ye five minutes ago. Ye tellt me ye wantit a job, right?

WILLIE   Right.

PAT   Well, will ye shut that fuckin box an' tak it ben there an' get wan? You're no the only wan idle, ye know. Maist folk think it's worth a few bob tae get a start these days.

HUGHIE   Pat knows, Willie…

WILLIE   Gie's a light.

PAT *lights* WILLIE'S *cigarette.* WILLIE *rises and goes out into the Family Department.*

PAT   …Want a drink, Hughie?

HUGHIE   You know me, Patrick. Refuse naething but blows.

PAT   You get them up then.

PAT *gives* HUGHIE *money.* HUGHIE *gets up and goes over to the bar.*

HUGHIE   Three Bell's, Eddie.

EDDIE   Three Bell's. Aa-right for beer?

HUGHIE   Aye.

WILLIE *comes back into the bar and sits down again beside* PAT.

WILLIE   What happens nou?

PAT   Ye wait, Hughie's gettin 'em up.

HUGHIE   *(to* SAM, *who stands at the bar reading a newspaper)*   Is that the wan o'clock *Telegraph?*

SAM   What dae ye think it is? Scotch mist?

HUGHIE   Can I hae a wee scan at it?

SAM   Buy your ain.

HUGHIE   Keep the heid. Civility costs naething.

SAM   Away ye go. I'm studyin form here.

HUGHIE   Ye can keep that page. Gie's the rest.

SAM   Oh, is that aa? Here ye are. *(He hands over most of the newspaper.)* I thought ye wantit the runners.

HUGHIE   Na, I just want tae see if they've set a date for it yet.

SAM   For what?

HUGHIE   The war, what dae ye think?

SAM   You're no thinkin o volunteerin, are ye, Hughie?

HUGHIE   I've had mine. You wait. It's no a Sunday School Picnic tae fuckin Largs.

EDDIE   *(handing over drinks)*   That'll be wan an' nine.

HUGHIE   It's on the counter.

HUGHIE *takes the drinks over to the table, making two trips.*

PAT   Look, I'm tellin ye. It's no money doun the drain. Ye'll be aa-right.

WILLIE   I'd better be. I'm skint...

PAT *and* WILLIE *begin drinking, while* HUGHIE *is fetching the rest of their drinks.*

PAT   Ye mairrit, like?

WILLIE   Aye. I've got two weans. A boy and a wee lassie.

PAT   I've got five.

HUGHIE *(bringing the last of the drinks)*   He's tryin tae win the Pope's medal.

PAT   Shut yer face, you! What's in the paper?

HUGHIE   The usual.

PAT   Dae ye think ye'll be joinin up, Willie?

WILLIE   Na.

PAT   How no?

WILLIE   It's no my war when it does come. Nor yours, neither.

HUGHIE   Aye, but ye've got tae go but. I mean, I didnae start the last wan, but I had tae go. An' look what happened tae me. I left wan leg in a midden bin in fuckin Africa, bi-fuck!

WILLIE   But naething cam out o't at aa, did it? Can ye no see? What's five weans gonna dae 'ithout their faither? Ye see... it's aa arranged frae start tae finish. It's been worked out, like. The time-tables o trains that'll tak the boys back an' furrit frae the Front have aa been organised. Ye wouldnae believe it. The war's got tae come nou, because folk want it. An' it's no only the politicians, either.

PAT   Naebody wants war.

HUGHIE   Naebody wise, onywey.

WILLIE   You're wrang there. Just tak a look at thae men ower at the counter there.

PAT   What about them?

WILLIE   They'll volunteer tae a man when the times comes. Some o them are learnin tae march at nights up our way aaready.

PAT   Aye. I go mysel'... the odd time.

WILLIE   Sorry I spoke, then.

HUGHIE   Hey, you... Willie, for Christ's sake, ye're no a German spy, àre ye?

PAT   Och, Hughie, wheesht! *(To* WILLIE.) So what dae ye suggest we dae... supposin... just supposin the war braks out? Take a fortnight's holidays an' take the weans tae Rothesay for a dip?

WILLIE   Stay where ye are. Here in Greenock, where ye belang. Sure, we've got tae try our hardest tae prevent this imperialist war: *(rhetorically)* but if it starts, as start, God help us, it surely will, it's our duty to oppose it. Out of the crisis of the war we must find the means to bring an end tae capitalism.

HUGHIE   A Red Flagger, for fuck's sake!

PAT   Hey! Keep the heid, Willie. Ye sound like wan o they manifestos, or somethin' lik that. Drink up. It might never happen.

HUGHIE   What cam intae ye at aa?

WILLIE   *(smiling)*   Nothin' cam intae me. Ye ever hear o John McLean's meetins up in Paisley?

HUGHIE   John McLean... for fuck's sake...

WILLIE   He's a great man. I really believe that. His meetins are the only thing I've got tae look forward tae 'cept gaun hame tae the wife an' the weans at night. An' just look at me nou. I'm sore ashamed o mysel, sae I am! Willie Rough sittin here waitin tae see if he's bought 'imsel' a job.

PAT   Look, your politics is naething tae dae wi me. I'm no clever enough tae hav politics. I just vote Labour lik everybody else. But listen tae me. Ye're no exactly whisperin, an' if ye say much mair, ye'll be out o that yaird afore ye're in it!

HUGHIE   Aye. Come see, come saa, Willie.

PAT   You've got a wife an' weans tae feed. Remember that.

WILLIE   Aye. Sae I'll sit quiet. I'll drink my drink an' say nothing! I'll say nothing, no because I'm feart, but because I don't know what I want tae say. I'll wait.

HUGHIE   I'll say wan thing, Willie. Ye've kinna put the tin lid on the conversation. We're lik three folk at a funeral waitin tae see if the widow wumman's teetotal. I mean...

JAKE comes out of the Family Department, and HUGHIE stops talking. JAKE walks past their table towards the street door, stops, and turns to WILLIE, who goes on looking straight ahead.

JAKE   Hey, Rough! (WILLIE *turns to face him.*) Ye start in the mornin.

JAKE goes out.

WILLIE   Thanks, eh... Mr Adams.

PAT and HUGHIE are delighted: WILLIE now owes them a drink.

PAT   What did I tell ye?

HUGHIE   Pat knows. Pat's the wee boy.

WILLIE   I should buy the baith o ye a hauf, but I've just got my bus fare hame for the night an' the morra left.

HUGHIE   Nae dout we'll all congregate at this very spot for a few refreshments at a later date, Willie. I'm free when ye get your pay next Saturday.

WILLIE *(to* PAT) Dae ye work a week's lyin time?

PAT Aye.

WILLIE A week on Saturday, then. *(He rises.)* I must thank ye very much, Pat. I suppose I'd better get up hame an' tell the wife.

PAT Aye, ye'll need tae find a house doun here.

WILLIE I'll go and see some factor the-morra.

PAT Willie?

WILLIE Aye?

PAT Hope ye don't mind, like, but I've got a wee bit o advice. Keep aa that John McLean propaganda tae yoursel', for Christ's sake. At least, wait till ye've taen your jaicket aff an' worked a few hours.

WILLIE *(getting ready to go)* I know what ye mean.

PAT I go tae the drillin an' that, but I don't think I'm gonna go tae the Front either.

HUGHIE Ye've baith naething tae worry about. Even if they get tae the stage of sendin the Press Gang out, you'll baith be on work of national importance.

WILLIE I don't know what's worse.

HUGHIE Better a live coward nor a deid hera.

PAT Aye.

HUGHIE Well, cheerybye, Willie.

WILLIE Cheerio.

WILLIE *goes out.*

HUGHIE …Fairly gies ye 'is life story, dan't he?

PAT Nice enough fella.

HUGHIE Aye… the-nou. But you wait. Just you watch that yin. He'll be mair confident wi a pound or two in 'is pocket. He'll be haunin out leaflets and pamphlets an' God kens what aa else. Wait tae ye see.

PAT Well, it'll be a chynge frae the *War Cry.*

HUGHIE He'll just hav tae watch he disnae get 'is jotters… or worse… he'll get his heid bashed in and find himsel' six fit doun below South Street.

PAT Aye… mebbie you're right, Hughie…

EDDIE Hughie!

HUGHIE What?

EDDIE Will ye go a wee message for us?

HUGHIE It'll cost ye a pint.

EDDIE I'd be better goin mysel'.

HUGHIE Please yoursel'.

EDDIE Half a pint.

HUGHIE I'll hav tae talk tae the Message Boys' Union about this. A pint's the rate for the job. Ye'll hae a strike on your hauns.

EDDIE Don't joke about the likes o that, Hughie, for Christ's sake. A strike's no funny.

HUGHIE   Aye. It isnae, is it? They'd be nae mair doubles, trebles, an' roll-ups then, Eddie, and naebody would be able tae afford the price o a pint, either. Ye'd hav tae gie't awa.

EDDIE   I'd raither sit here an' drink it mysel'.

HUGHIE   That's the sort o thing you would dae!

EDDIE   Would you come in an' help me finish up the stock, Hughie?

HUGHIE   Gie me plenty o warnin so's I can get intae trainin.

EDDIE   Aye. That'll be right. Look, Hughie, go over tae Timpson's and pick up my shoe repairs. It's their half-day.

HUGHIE   Gie's the money. *(He goes over to the bar.)*

EDDIE   Haud on.

EDDIE *takes out his purse. He looks inside it carefully to find the money, then takes it out, coin by coin.* HUGHIE *is leaning against the bar. Suddenly he swipes the air with his crutch as if it were a club.*

EDDIE   What ye daein?

HUGHIE   *GOT IT!*

EDDIE   Got what?

HUGHIE   Just a wee moth, Eddie.

3. The Shipyard: May 1914

The horn blows. PAT, SAM, *and* GEORDIE *march in step down the yard. The* APPRENTICE *follows, watching them with admiration.*

GEORDIE   Squa-a-a-d... halt!

Raggedly, they halt.

PAT   It's wan-two, *HALT,* wan-two. Ye don't just stop. What dae they learn ye up at the drillin?

WILLIE *comes in and stands looking at them.*

SAM   It's aa-right for you. You were at the back.

GEORDIE   Aye. We couldnae see you.

APPRENTICE   He's as bad.

PAT   Shut up, you!

WILLIE   Pat?

PAT   Aye.

WILLIE   What ye daein?

PAT   Marchin.

WILLIE   Thought ye'd chucked aa that.

PAT   Keepin my haun in. Just in case.

WILLIE   Ye're aa aff your heids.

GEORDIE   Who dae ye think you are?

WILLIE   I know I'm as well haudin my breath wi the likes o you, Geordie. When's 'is union meetin?

SAM   Quarter an hour.

WILLIE   They couldnae run a minauge, so they couldnae.

APPRENTICE   I've got a baa. Gie's yer jaicket for a goal, Willie.

WILLIE *gives the* APPRENTICE *his jacket. The* APPRENTICE *makes a goal with his own jacket and* WILLIE'S.

GEORDIE   Aa-right. Two-a-side.

APPRENTICE   I'll go goalie.

SAM   You're no playin.

APPRENTICE   It's my baa!

SAM   In ye go, then.

PAT   Me an' Willie against the rest.

SAM   Fair enough.

GEORDIE   Right! To me, son.

The APPRENTICE *throws the ball to* GEORDIE. *The game begins. The tackling is quite tough.*

APPRENTICE   Come on, the Rangers!

The game gets rough. Eventually PAT *scores a goal.*

PAT   Goal!

GEORDIE   That's no fair. Ye held my jaicket.

APPRENTICE   'Na, he didnae!

GEORDIE   He did, Sam! Nae kiddin.

SAM   Thae Fenians is aa the same.

PAT   Mind your mouth, son.

SAM   What'll you dae about it?

PAT   I'll dae plenty.

GEORDIE   You, an' what army?

PAT   Two against wan, is it?

GEORDIE   Na. A square go, anytime ye like. Haud my jaicket, Willie.

WILLIE   Ye no feart ye'll catch the cauld?

PAT   Haud 'is jaicket, Willie. I'll mangalate 'im!

WILLIE   Ye'd be better mangalatin your piece. What happens when the gaffer comes
   roun? Bagged on the spot, the baith o ye.
PAT   I suppose ye're right, Willie.
GEORDIE   Ye crappin it?
PAT   If ye're serious… Roun the back aifter the meetin.
WILLIE   Ye're like a couple o weans on the school play-grun.
GEORDIE   You stay out o this. We'll settle it.
WILLIE   Settle what?
GEORDIE   Eh?
WILLIE   What are ye fightin about? If Jake Adams wisnae about, I'd tak on the baith
   o ye mysel'.
APPRENTICE   Let's see ye, Willie.
WILLIE   *(kicking him in the backside)*   You get tae fuck an' boil my can. Get me ten
   Capstan full strenth, tae. I gied ye the cash.

The APPRENTICE *goes.* WILLIE *picks up his jacket.* GEORDIE *passes the ball to* SAM.
Slowly the game begins again. PAT *sits down exhausted.* JAKE *walks down the
yard.*

JAKE   Hav ye got nothin' better tae dae wi your time than kickin a baa about?
WILLIE   Waitin for the Union meetin tae start, Jake.
JAKE   That'll dae yez a lot o good, I don't think!
WILLIE   Twopence an hour rise. Forty-five bob a week frae nou on.
JAKE   An' what did the band play?

JAKE goes out. GEORDIE *and* SAM *continue to kick the ball to each other, once they
are sure that* JAKE *is gone.*

WILLIE   Pat?
PAT   What?

WILLIE *goes over to* PAT, *who is stretched on the ground.*

WILLIE   I know Jake's no in the Union.
PAT   You stupit?
WILLIE   I wish tae hell he wis.
PAT   What good would it dae the likes o him?
WILLIE   Time we got tae the meetin. I can see some o the boys goin doun nou.
SAM   Aye. We'd better shift.

GEORDIE *and* SAM *go out carrying the ball. The* APPRENTICE *comes in carrying*
WILLIE'S *can of tea.*

APPRENTICE   Hey! Where dae youz think ye're goin wi my baa? *(He gives* WILLIE *his tea.)* Come back wi my baa, ye thievin bastarts!

The APPRENTICE *runs off after* SAM *and* GEORDIE. WILLIE *sips his tea.* PAT *gets up.*

PAT   Takin your tea in wi ye, then?

WILLIE   Keeps me awake when the shop steward's forgot 'is glesses an' cannae read the treasurer's report.

PAT   Aye. He's a bit auld for it. Know what?

WILLIE   What?

PAT   I'm gonna propose you.

WILLIE   What for?

PAT   Election o office-bearers the-day. 'S about time we had a chynge. Don't look sae pleased about it. Ye might no get it, an' if ye dae, it'll be 'cause naebody else wants it.

WILLIE   Ye're hell of a good tae me, Pat. I don't deserve it.

PAT   It's nae bother at aa.

WILLIE   Are ye for mairchin intae the meetin, like?

PAT   Can ye no take a joke? You're that serious about everythin'.

WILLIE   They cannae wait for the war tae break out.

PAT   Neither can you.

They go off to the meeting.

4. A Street: July 1914

KATE, WILLIE'S *wife, is waiting for him. At her feet are two bags full of shopping.*
WILLIE *comes along the street, in a hurry.*

KATE   You're a fine yin. That's three tram cars we've missed. It's bad enough when ye're workin, but ye've knocked aff for the Fair, an' you're still late.

WILLIE   I wis daein my correspondence.

KATE   I don't want tae go tae Rothesay the-morra. Ye've pit me aff the notion.

WILLIE   Ye'd think I liked bein Shop Steward, tae hear you.

KATE   It's a chynge from McLean, anyhow. At least ye can dae it in your ain toun.

WILLIE   *(picking up the shopping-bags)*   The weans aa-right?

KATE   A lot you care. They'll be wonderin what their faither looks like.

WILLIE   I'll tak them for a douk the-morra. I like a wee paddle mysel'.

KATE   What about me? Hav I tae sit up the lum as usual?

WILLIE   I'm takin ye out the-night. We're goin tae Pat Gatens's club.

KATE   I don't like goin out wi other folk.

WILLIE   Bernadette's nice.

KATE   I know, but I mairrit you. Sometimes I wish I wis back hame, in Campbeltown.

WILLIE   Campbeltown wis too quiet when ye were in it.

KATE   Aye. But there's nae meetins there. Ye don't hav tae read pamphlets doun there. People tell ye aa ye need tae know.

WILLIE   Three fishin-boats an' a distillery.

KATE   At least your man comes hame the odd night.

WILLIE   You'll no be sayin that when we get the twopence-an-hour rise.

KATE   I'll believe that when ye lea me forty-five shillins on the table wan Friday night. You're awful askin us out wi the Gatenses. People'll think we're turnin our coats. Is it that club up the Port?

WILLIE   Aye.

KATE   Ye'll be at the Chapel next.

WILLIE   What's the maitter wi you? I've got my holiday pay in my pocket. Dae ye blame me for wantin tae gie you a night out? I don't know. When ye're in, ye want out, an' when ye're out ye want tae gae hame again.

KATE   Mebbie ye shoulda mairrit somebody else.

WILLIE   What's got intae you?

KATE   Ye know I'm no very good at talkin tae folk.

WILLIE   Ye're as good as onybody. We're as good as onybody.

KATE   Just don't you get above your station, Willie Rough.

WILLIE   Would ye stop criticisin me aa the time! I left the yard happy. I'm on holiday. I've got my pay in my pocket. I'm takin the wife an' the weans doun the watter the-morra. I wis as happy as Larry till I met you.

KATE   Have you ever tried tae get throu the shops on Fair Friday?

WILLIE   So that's it.

KATE   What a crush! I havenae got hauf the things I need.

WILLIE   Come on up hame, an' I'll gie ye a wee hauf afore we go out.

KATE   I didnae mean it, Willie. I'm just exhausted. I could dae wi goin tae my bed.

They hear a tram car approaching. They lift the bags and look at the approaching vehicle.

WILLIE   We'll come hame early.

KATE   Ye know what happens then?

WILLIE   Ye werenae complainin last night.

KATE   Oh, you!

The noise of the tram car comes nearer and nearer.

5. The James Watt Bar: September 1914

Patriotic posters are now displayed in the Public Bar – 'YOUR KING & COUNTRY NEED YOU!' and 'WOMEN OF BRITAIN SAY "GO!"' The bar is crowded. Many of the men are either drunk or well on the way to it. EDDIE *is behind the bar, as usual. Across it from him is* JAKE. *Round one of the tables* HUGHIE *has gathered his troops. All of them are singing. Amongst them are* SAM *and* GEORDIE, *who have volunteered and are already wearing khaki uniforms.* HUGHIE *and his mob are wearing spectacles of many different shapes and sizes, swapping them with each other, and trying them on.* WILLIE *and* PAT *are sitting together at the other table trying to ignore* HUGHIE'S *gang.* WILLIE *himself has had too much to drink; he's in an aggressive mood.*

HUGHIE and his cronies sing at the top of their voices, each in their own key, of course.

HUGHIE *(with all his gang, singing)*
    Oh, Greenock's no a bonnie toun, you'll hear some folk complain
    For when they go tae Greenock there is nothing else but rain;
    Da da da da da da da da da da da da da DEEEE!
    For I'm proud that I'm a branch of the *GREEN-OAK TREE!*

    Here's tae the Green Oak that stands doun by the Square
    Here's tae its tounsfolk a-slumbering there:
    Here's tae its tounsfolk wherever they may be –
    For I'm proud that I'm a branch of the *GREEN-OAK TREE!*

A triumphant cheer goes up from the singers as they reach the end of their song.

SAM   Best of order there! Best of order!

GEORDIE   Aye. Best of order for Shughie!

HUGHIE   Boys. We know what we're here for the-night, an' it's no joke. As an auld sodger that done his bit in the last wan, I'd just like tae say that I'm proud tae be in the company of these brave young fellas that are about tae do their bit in the defence o the Realm – Geordie MacLeod an' Sammy Thomson *(cheers)* ...An' I'd just like tae add that the first blow in the battle against the Hun has been struck. It was struck the-night. An' we struck it, so we did! *(Prolonged cheers.)*

EDDIE   You'll no be sayin that when the Polis come.

HUGHIE   There might be a few German sympathisers in this toun, Eddie MacCausland, but not in the Force. Patriots! Patriots to a man! Now lads, while we're talkin serious, who's buyin the beer?

GEORDIE   My turn, lads.

HUGHIE   Same all round, Geordie. Same all round.

GEORDIE *goes over to the bar.* EDDIE *begins pouring out the large order of drinks.*

JAKE *(to* GEORDIE)   Where the fuck did ye get thae glasses?

GEORDIE   The spoils of war, Jake.

JAKE   Ye're no at the Front yet, Geordie, tell us where ye got them?

GEORDIE   How? Dae ye want a pair?

JAKE   There's nae use talkin tae you. You're paralytic.

GEORDIE   Here, take a pair. *(He gives* JAKE *some spectacles.)* Take two!

JAKE *(handing them back)*   I'm havin nothing tae dae wi it.

GEORDIE   Aye. Ye were kinda conspicuous by your absence. Hauf the toun was
there, but I never seen you.

JAKE   What's that supposed tae mean?

GEORDIE   If the cap fits.

JAKE   Ony mair o that, Geordie MacLeod, an' ye'll have two big keekers that ye'll
no be able tae see out o wi ten pair o specs.

GEORDIE   Keep the heid, Jake. It's a free country.

JAKE   Mebbie – but no for long when we're dependin on the likes o you tae defend
it!

GEORDIE   I take exception tae that remark!

JAKE   Ye can take fuckin Syrup o Figs, if ye like.

EDDIE   Easy, lads. Here ye are, Geordie, away over there, an' lea Jake alane.

GEORDIE   If I wisnae drunk...

EDDIE   If ye werenae drunk, ye'd be flat on your back at Jake's feet, an' you know
it. Nou, here's your drink. Take them over.

GEORDIE *pays for the drinks and carries them over to* HUGHIE *and the others.*
HUGHIE *moves over to the bar.*

HUGHIE   Wis Geordie giein ye a wee bit o trouble, Eddie? It's the blood-lust, I
think. He cannae wait tae go.

EDDIE   What side are you on, Hughie?

HUGHIE   How dae ye mean?

EDDIE   Well, afore the war broke out, ye were never done stickin up for Willie
Rough over there.

HUGHIE   Well the-night it suits me tae be patriotic. The-morn, we'll see.

EDDIE   Look, tak aa yer cronies ben there tae the ither bar, will ye? I'm no wantin
ony trouble if the Polis come.

HUGHIE   Anything tae oblige, Eddie.

HUGHIE *goes over and begins to herd his cronies through the door into the Family
Department.*

HUGHIE   Come on, boys, we're tae muve.

SAM   How?

HUGHIE   Eddie says it, that's how. Come on, Sam.

SAM   I'm nice and comfortable sittin here.

EDDIE   Next door, or outside!

SAM *rises, staggers to the door, and walks through.* HUGHIE *steadies him on his way, and is just about to go through himself.*

PAT   Hughie!
HUGHIE   What?
PAT   Come 'ere, Willie an' me want tae talk tae ye.

HUGHIE *comes up to* WILLIE *and* PAT.

PAT   *(to* HUGHIE)   You want tae look at yoursel'.
HUGHIE   If you were me, would you want tae look at yoursel'?
WILLIE   Ye're steamboats.
HUGHIE   Ye're no lookin sae sober yoursel', Willie.
WILLIE   That may be. But I'm ashamed, that's how I'm drunk. You're just drunk.
HUGHIE   I never need a reason tae be drunk, Willie.
PAT   Hughie, where did aa they glasses come frae? The haill pub's weirin them.
HUGHIE   We done Lizars.
JAKE   Ye what?
HUGHIE   Lizars. Ye ken the opticians in West Blackhall Street?
WILLIE   Aye.
HUGHIE   Well a big crowd o the lads, like… Aye, a rare crowd, an wee boys, tae… we broke the windae an' climbed in an' wrecked the place. The only pairs o glesses 'at arenae broke are the wans ye see in here the-night.
PAT   But, what did ye dae it for?
HUGHIE   They're fuckin Germans! I mean… we just cannae tolerate German sympathisers in this toun. Case you don't know, there's a war on, Pat. We've got tae fight the enemy within.
WILLIE   So that's it. Christ, ye've nae sense, the haill lot o' ye. Wan minute they're signin on for the Army, an' the next they're paradin about Cathcart Square lik a shower o bloody clowns, an' nou ye're breakin shop windaes. Hav ye nae sense? Has the war demented the haill toun?
HUGHIE   I didnae start it, Willie.
WILLIE   Who did?
HUGHIE   I don't know.
WILLIE   Na. Naebody ever knows who starts the like o this. They're aa in at the finish, tho.
HUGHIE   I didnae think ye'd be sae het up about it, Willie.
WILLIE   Well, I am. Pat and me. We've been at meetins aa week. We're tryin tae get a rise in two months. Dae you know what twopence an hour means tae this toun? We're tryin tae pruve that we're no representin a bunch o loonies, an just when ye're gettin somewhere, they're out throwin bricks through windaes. This on tap o everything else.

HUGHIE   What else?

PAT   McLean was arrested at a rally in Glesga. The School Board hav bagged him nou.

HUGHIE   That's hard lines.

WILLIE   What dae *you* care?

HUGHIE   I care aa-right. I see that you care, an' I care about you, so I *care.* I can see that ye're no sae sober, either.

WILLIE   But Lizars isnae a German shop, even, is it?

PAT   Not at all. He's frae Stirling or somewhere.

HUGHIE   What dae ye mean, frae Stirling? Lizar. Lie Zar – frae Stirling, my arse! He's frae fuckin Berlin!

PAT   Ye mighta checked up afore ye done 'is shop.

HUGHIE   It's no a Greenock name, is it? Even I know that. Lie-Zar. Sounds foreign enough. He's a fuckin Gerry aa-right.

WIILIE   Ach away an' join your gang! It's a pity ye cannae drink specs, in't it?

HUGHIE   It is that, Willie.

PAT   What about the Polis?

HUGHIE   What about them?

PAT   Dae they no know about ye wreckin the shop?

HUGHIE   If ye ask me, I think they knew an' just let us enjoy wirsel's.

WILLIE   Oh, Pat, are we the only two sane men in this madhouse?

HUGHIE   Mebbie you're the loonies, boys. Hav ye thought about that?

HUGHIE *goes next door to join his friends. Cheers, within, followed intermittently by snatches of shouting and singing.*

PAT   I'd better get ye hame, Willie.

WILLIE   Wan for the road, Pat.

PAT   Are ye sure ye want wan?

WILLIE   A wee Bell's, Pat.

PAT   Right. *(He gets up and goes to the bar to get the drinks.)*

JAKE   *(to no one in particular)*   So they done the opticians?

PAT   Two John Bell's, Eddie. Jake, what'll ye hav?

JAKE   Na, I'm fine.

EDDIE   I see Willie's well on. It's no usual for him.

PAT   I think he thinks he's been let doun.

EDDIE   How dae ye mean?

PAT   Well, he's that serious about everythin', ye know.

EDDIE   Aye, I know.

JAKE *moves over towards* WILLIE'S *table.*

PAT   An' wi the negotiations about the rise goin on, an' aa the rest o't, he wants the men tae keep the slate clean, like.

JAKE *(at* WILLIE'S *table)*   Hello, Willie.

WILLIE   Sit doun, Jake. Dae ye think there's three o us?

JAKE   What?

WILLIE   'At's no stupit?

PAT *(to* EDDIE)   An' McLean's in the jyle.

EDDIE   Aye. I've often heard Willie go on about 'im. 'War against the warmongers', an' aa that. If ye ask me, jyle's the best place for 'im.

PAT *(refusing to be involved in a conversation with* EDDIE)   Naebody's asking you, Eddie. *(He puts down money for the drinks.)*

PAT *returns to* WILLIE'S *table with their drinks.*

JAKE   How's the weans, Pat?

PAT   No bad, Jake. No bad. But... the wee lassie's no daein sae good.

JAKE   You've a couple o weans, dan't ye, Willie?

WILLIE   Aye. A boy an' lassie.

JAKE   That's nice.

WILLIE   I havenae seen much o them lately.

JAKE   Aye, ye've been kept busy.

WILLIE   You any weans, Jake?

JAKE   No. We had wan but it was still-born, the wife cannae hav any mair.

WILLIE   Oh... *(They drink.)* I always meant tae thank ye, Jake.

JAKE   Thank me for what?

WILLIE   You know what for. I bought a job off ye like everybody else.

JAKE   Ye mean the graftin?

WILLIE   Aye. What made ye stop?

JAKE   Ye cannae depend on a couple o bob in a match-box aa your days.

WILLIE   That's no aa I wis gettin at, Jake. I wis talkin about your attitude. Even although ye're a gaffer, ye're solid behind a hunner-percent union shop.

JAKE   So'd anybody be that's wise.

PAT   What brought ye roun?

JAKE   I can read as well, ye know.

PAT   Aye, I suppose ye can.

They drink. GEORDIE *comes in from the Family Department, and passes* WILLIE'S *table on his way to the bar to place his order.*

GEORDIE *(to* EDDIE)   Same again, Eddie.

EDDIE   Have ye no had enough?

GEORDIE   First time I've heard o a publican no wantin tae sell a man a drink.

EDDIE   Nou I didnae say that, did I?

EDDIE *pours out the drinks.* GEORDIE *waits.* WILLIE *rises, then moves over towards* GEORDIE.

WILLIE   Geordie MacLeod. I never thought ye could be sae stupit. Ye're stupit!

PAT   Willie, you're drunk.

WILLIE   Just look at yersel'. Tommy fuckin Atkins, Defender of the Realm!

GEORDIE   Just watch what yer sayin, Willie. I'll mangalate you.

WILLIE   Ye know what? I think that's what I want ye to dae. I want tae see stars, an'
    I wouldnae care if I never saw anither khaki jacket.

GEORDIE   Well, ye're goin the right wey about it.

EDDIE   Easy, boys. No fightin. Outside, if ye want tae hav a set-to!

GEORDIE   Don't worry yoursel', Eddie! He couldnae punch a hole in a wet paper.

WILLIE *is nearer to* GEORDIE *now, but less aggressive.*

WILLIE   Tell me wan thing, Geordie.

GEORDIE   What?

WILLIE   When I brought McLean doun here, an' he tellt ye the truth about this war,
    I looked at ye, an' your mouth was wide open. Ye were spellbound, bi-Christ,
    listenin tae that man. Ye believed 'im. I know ye believed 'im. An' then Willie
    Gallacher cam doun frae the Albion. Ye were there that night as well. He tellt ye,
    an' McLean tellt ye, an' at wan meetin after another I've tellt ye mysel', an' here
    ye are like a whippet strainin at the leash. Over the top! Tell me where we went
    wrong, Geordie, 'cause I've got tae know. Honest, I've got tae know!

GEORDIE   Mebbie I got fed up wi your Red Flags an' songs an' aa that shite. You
    can stay here an' sing the 'Internationale', an' the 'Red Flag', tae, but when ye're
    daein it, remember that me an folk like me are fightin for ye. Ye cannae be serious
    tae think that I'd miss the chance o goin tae the front. Ye'll change your mind, but
    by that time it'll be all over..

WILLIE   Would ye believe me, Geordie, if I tellt ye I hope it will?

GEORDIE   Just answer me this, Willie Rough.

WILLIE   What?

GEORDIE   Supposin somebody attacks me wi a big stick on the way hame the-night.

WILLIE   What?

GEORDIE   Just supposin that happened. Would I be justified in usin a big stick tae
    defend mysel'?

WILLIE   Aye.

GEORDIE   Well, then?

WILLIE   Well, what?

GEORDIE   That's the war, in't it, an' the British Army's the big stick against the
    Germans?

WILLIE   I don't know who you've been talkin tae the-day, but that's kinna fancy for
    the like o you.

GEORDIE   I asked ye the question, an' you answered it.

WILLIE   Look, Geordie. If somebody attacks ye on the road hame the-night I've nae
    objection tae you usin a big stick – two, if ye can handle the baith o them. An' if
    Bethmann Hollweg uses a big stick tae attack Sir Edward Grey, I cannae complain

if Sir Edward Grey uses a big stick back tae Bethmann Hollweg, but there's wan thing I'm fuckin sure o, an' that is that I'm no gonna be the big stick, an' I've done aa I can tae stop the workin class bein used as the big stick. You're in the wrong fight, Geordie. Sure I want ye tae win. If ye want bands playin, we'll hav bands playin, but the victory shouldnae be for the Imperialist Allies. It should be *your* victory. I'm talkin about Geordie MacLeod, the hauder-on, no Private MacLeod, G.!

GEORDIE   I'm no kiddin ye, Willie. Any mair o that talk, an' they'll be lockin ye up for treason.

WILLIE   You'll be in beside me for breakin an' enterin if ye don't tak these stupit glesses aff!

GEORDIE   Can I tak my drinks, Eddie? Next door they'll be thinkin it's a dry area.

EDDIE   Here ye are.

GEORDIE *takes the drinks through to the Family Department.* WILLIE *sits down beside* JAKE *and* PAT.

JAKE   What wis aa that about?

PAT   I'm gonna get you hame.

WILLIE   I've just thought o something.

PAT   What?

WILLIE   I might never see Geordie MacLeod again.

JAKE   Christ, you're cheery!

Two policemen, SANNY *and* PETER, *come in. They walk to the bar.* HUGHIE *steps out of the Family Department, still wearing his stolen spectacles: but, seeing the policemen, he pops back into the Family Department very, very quickly.*

HUGHIE *(off)*   Act normal.

VOICES *(off)*   It's the Polis… Shut up… They'll no know we're here if ye haud your wheest…

SANNY *(a Highlander, to* EDDIE)   Where's Hughie?

EDDIE   What's he done?

PETER   He was seen at Lizars the-night. Hauf the toun done the shop.

EDDIE   Hughie's no hauf the toun.

PETER   Mebbie no, but his wan leg wis recognised.

EDDIE   Aye. It would be, wouldn'it?

SANNY   Is 'e been in or no?

EDDIE   'E'll no get time or anything, will 'e?

SANNY   Not at all. We'll let 'im out in the mornin.

PETER   It'll soon blow over. We're just goin throu the motions.

EDDIE   I wisnae sure whether Lizars were Germans or no.

SANNY   Well, they're no frae Port Glasgow. I'll teli ye that for nothing.

PETER   They must be Germans.

JAKE   How dae ye make that out?

SANNY   Well, they wouldnae hav done the shop if they werenae, would they?

EDDIE   Good thinkin, Sanny. They're next door. Quiet as ye can, boys.

SANNY *and* PETER *both go to the door of the Family Department.* SANNY *opens the door.*

SANNY   Come on Hughie. Nou dinnae gie us ony bother, lads.

HUGHIE *comes back into the Public Bar, followed by all the others.*

HUGHIE   What's the trouble, eh, constable?

SANNY   Where did ye get thae specs?

HUGHIE   Timothy White's.

SANNY   Aye, that'll be right.

HUGHIE   I sweir tae God.

SANNY   Dae ye ey wear the two pair?

HUGHIE   Aye. The odd time. If I'm readin an' lookin a long distance ower the tap o the paper at the same time.

PETER   Ye're never stuck, are ye, Hughie?

HUGHIE   Where's the hauncuffs?

SANNY   We've ran out o hauncuffs. Hauf the toun's in the jyle.

HUGHIE   That's fine, then. We'll no be stuck for company. Can we hav a cairry-out, Eddie, tae drink in the jyle?

PETER   Na, ye cannae! Come on, youz!

SANNY *and* PETER *lead the criminals out. At the door* PETER *turns.*

PETER   Eddie…

EDDIE   What?

PETER   You should be shut.

EDDIE   Aye. I'm just going for the gates for the windaes nou. Somebody might get the idea that the MacCauslands are frae Munich!

PETER   Right. Goodnight, well.

EDDIE   'Night, Sanny.

PETER *goes out.*

EDDIE *(to the three still at the table)*   Did ye no hear 'im? Time up, boys.

PAT *(to* WILLIE*)*   Come on. I've got tae get you hame.

WILLIE   I'll be okay.

JAKE   Come on Pat. I'll get ye up the road.

PAT   I'm waitin for Willie.

WILLIE *(aggressively)*   I'm okay, I tellt ye!

PAT   Aa-right. Don't bite my heid aff.

EDDIE   It's okay, Pat. I'll get 'im up the road.

PAT   Fine. Thanks, Eddie. See ye in the mornin, Willie.

JAKE   On time, or ye're quartered.

PAT *and* JAKE *go out into the street.*

EDDIE   I'll just pit the gates on, an' we'll be on our way.

EDDIE *goes out behind the counter to get the gate for the window.* WILLIE *rises, staggering slightly. One of the posters decorating the bar catches his eye. He goes nearer to it, stares at it.*

WILLIE   *(reciting)*   Your King and Country need ye,
Ye hardy sons of toil:
But will your King and Country need ye,
When they're sharin out the spoil?

6. Pat's House: October 1914

PAT *and* BERNADETTE, *his wife, are kneeling together near a child's coffin which has been placed on the kitchen table.*

PAT   Our Father, Who art in Heaven, hallowed be Thy name. Thy Kingdom come. Thy will be done, on earth as it is in Heaven.

BOTH   Give us this day our daily bread, and forgive us our trespasses, as we forgive them that trespass against us. Lead us not into temptation, but deliver us from evil... Amen.

PAT   Hail Mary, full of grace, the Lord is with thee. Blessed art thou among women, and blessèd is the fruit of thy womb, Jesus.

BOTH   Holy Mary, Mother of God, pray for us sinners, now and at the hour of our death... Amen. *(They go on until they have said the Hail Mary ten times.)*

BOTH   Glory be to the Father (WILLIE *comes in, dressed in his working clothes, but wearing a black tie, and stands quietly, cap in hand, until their prayer is over),* and to the Son, and to the Holy Ghost, as it was in the beginning, is now, and ever shall be... Amen.

WILLIE *raises his head and waits.* PAT *rises. They look at* BERNADETTE...

PAT   Bernadette...

BERNADETTE   Thanks for comin, Willie.

WILLIE   Your mother wants tae see ye in the room.

BERNADETTE   I don't want tae go ben there just yet, I'll just start greetin again.

PAT   It's time ye went, hen. The men are here for her.

WILLIE   Aye. Ye'd be best tae go.

BERNADETTE   I wish I could go tae the graveside.

PAT   No. It would only upset ye aa the mair. I'll see the wee yin up the road.

WILLIE   Pat's right, Mrs Gatens. *(She goes out.* PAT'S *hand is on the coffin.)* Greet, if ye want tae, Pat. There's naebody but me tae hear ye.

PAT   Greetin's for weemin an' weans.

WILLIE *turns to go.*

PAT   Don't go, Willie. As sure as God they'll never get me out o' here if you go. I'll staun here thinkin o what she might hae grown tae. I never really thought o her as a wean. It's a fact. We had Anthony first, then Patrick an' Michael. Aa boys. I woulda done onything for thae boys, but Bernadette she wanted a wee lassie. When Teresa came it wis like a blessin, Willie. She wis a wee smasher. She's only two year auld, but I kept thinkin o her up. Ye know what I mean? Filled out an' 'at. Quite the young lady, ye know, breakin everybody's heart frae Kilmacolm tae Gourock. I kept wonderin if I'd be able tae talk tae her then. I wisnae carin if folk said I spoiled her. I woulda gien her the skin aff my back, Willie, so I would. Every faither's got a favourite. I'm sure ye have yoursel'… When she was a wean, she had a wee convulsion or two just after Bernadette brought her back frae the Maternity. It was that bad we couldnae sleep for worry a couple o nights. I thought then she might no live, it was that bad. But we did what Nurse Lonie said, an' she came on fine. But what can ye dae about the scarlet fever, Willie? We're no even gien the chance. I'd chynge places wi her if I could, Willie. Honest. We're a good family. We go tae eight o'clock Mass every Sunday. An' it's no just 'cause it's my duty tae go an' tae mak the weans go. I *believe* in going. Ye see some folk… they're in an out o the jyle. We've met them oursel's, Willie. We see them marchin about the toun in khaki uniforms as if that made them intae saints. We're no saints, either, Willie, but you an' me, we've tried our best tae be decent folk. I've never sided wi a Catholic against you, Willie, an' you've never waved an Orange banner in my face, either. We're no Hibs or Masons, are we?

WILLIE   No.

PAT   Ye believe in God an' ye tell your weans tae believe in something as well an' then that scarlet fever comes… *(He almost breaks down.)* Can He no pick on somebody else? We'll remember this year aa-right, Willie.

WILLIE   There's a lot o families lost somebody.

PAT   Aye. Ye know I forgot aa about everythin'. The only thing I believed in was our Teresa, an' she was away. Ye cannae think o onybody else sufferin as much as you dae. Just think if I'd stayed at the drillin an' joined up. I wouldnae be here. Can ye imagine gettin a note in a week or a fortnight mebbie tellin ye ye havenae got a wee lassie ony mair?

WILLIE   Aye. Geordie MacLeod's wife got a note yesterday forenoon.
PAT   Aye. Ye tellt us: 'Missing, believed killed in action'.
WILLIE   Aye.
PAT   I never had much time for him. Ach, he wisnae a bad fella, Geordie. I cannae see ony end tae't.
WILLIE   They think they'll be hame for the New Year.
PAT   What year, but?…
WILLIE   Are ye ready nou, Pat?
PAT   Aye. Ready as I'll ever be.

PAT *lifts the coffin and carries it out.*

7. The hills above Greenock: December 1914

WILLIE, JAKE, *and* PAT *are walking together.* WILLIE *is carrying a small leather case.* JAKE *has a* WHIPPET *on a leash. They stop and look down from the hillside to the town and the river beyond.*

WILLIE   Look at it! Spellbindin. Ye'd never think Greenock could look sae fine.
JAKE   Aye. It's aa-right frae up here. It's no sae fine when ye're stuck in the rain in the middle o't.
PAT   What the hell are yez talkin about? I'm freezin. Who ever heard o goin a walk up the hill in December?
JAKE   Willie wanted tae see me. Ye cannae keep a whippet shut up in a kennel.
WILLIE   We'll no be a minute, Pat. I've got tae explain tae Jake what's goin on.
PAT   I can go hame, then.
WILLIE   Och, haud your tongue an' sit doun, Pat.
PAT   Sit doun! I'll get a chill in my arse if I sit doun.

WILLIE *sits down.* JAKE *and* PAT *crouch near him. The* WHIPPET *strains at the leash.* JAKE *strokes its long nose.*

JAKE   What's on your mind, Willie?
WILLIE   It's the negotiatin committee, Jake. I know your collar an' tie's kept ye out o the Union, but your attitude's always been sympathetic.
JAKE   No always.
WILLIE   Ye know what I mean. I thought ye might be able tae help us.
JAKE   Willie, I'm in a funny position. It's none o my business. Neither the Union nor your negotiatin committee. Christ, if any o the high heïd-yins saw me even talkin tae you two, I'd get the fuckin bag!
WILLIE   I havenae slept for a week, Jake. That's honest. It's got tae be twopence an

hour or nothin'. I know that. But I'm feart I'm gonna let the men doun.

PAT   Ther' mair nor you on that committee. Govan, Clydebank. Every yaird an' factory on the Clyde's represented...

JAKE   Pat's right, Willie. Ye cannae blame yoursel' for the whole shootin-match.

WILLIE   Sure I can. The rest are like corn on the wind.

JAKE   Well, if they're aa sae glaikit, it should be nae bother tae get a haud o them by the scruff o the neck an' tell them tae sit on their arses till the employers up their offer tae twopence an hour. Ye don't need me tae tell ye that. I'm away tae run my dug. *(He rises and moves away with the dog.)* ...

WILLIE   I hoped you could gie me some information.

JAKE   How dae ye mean?

WILLIE   We went tae this meetin up in Glesga. Sit doun, Jake. (JAKE *crouches beside* PAT.) We tellt the employers. Twopence an hour. Basic rate increase o twopence an hour. That's from thirty-six tae forty-five bob for the fifty-four-hour week. Clear. Right?

JAKE   Aye. Then *they* tellt ye they were skint.

WILLIE   That's right. They pleaded poverty an offered us a hapenny.

JAKE   I hope ye told them where tae pit it.

WILLIE   They knew we would. They didnae come up the Clyde in a banana-boat. They came tae the meetin tae go as far as three farthins, so they offered us that. We said, 'Ye're not on,' an' they chucked it.

JAKE   An' that's where ye are? Three farthins an hour increase. It's nothin' tae dae wi me, but ye musta spent mair than that on train-fares.

PAT   It's better than nothin'.

WILLIE   What would ye say tae a penny an hour, Pat?

PAT   A penny would make a difference. I can see the men settlin for that.

WILLIE   There ye are! Oh, the big bugs know all about you. They can read ye lik a book, Pat. That's what they want. Can ye no see? Even at the committee meetin the other day... a committee member, bi-Christ... chief o the 'Brassies'... 'A penny, an' we'll settle' ...he kept sayin it over an' over... 'A penny, an' we'll settle' ...I thought he might end up singin it... playin right intae their haunds... as bad as you, Pat... tryin tae force the Engineers tae settle for hauf.

JAKE   Haud on. Haud on, Willie. What have the Engineers got tae dae wi this?

WILLIE   I'll start frae the beginnin.

JAKE   I wish ye would.

WILLIE   Two separate negotiatin committees, right? The A.S.E., representin the Engineers. An' the Allied Trades, that's us. Both aifter the same thing. Twopence an hour. Right?

JAKE   With ye.

WILLIE   We, the Allied Trades, go in. They offer a hapenny. We tell them tae stuff it. Three farthins. Still stuff it. Then, in a roundabout way at the negotiations, they let us know that they'll go tae a penny, unofficially, like, knowin the bulk o our members'll lap it up an' settle.

JAKE   But what's your point?

WILLIE   They're usin us, Jake. They're usin us tae get the Engineers tae settle. The smaller unions, like us, are bein used to betray their fellow workers. If somethin's no done fast, they'll offer the penny, official, our committee will accept it, and the Engineers'll have tae settle, tae. That's what I wanted tae see ye about, Jake.

JAKE   What dae ye want? Time aff?

WILLIE   No. You know folk, Jake. Find me an Engineer that's on the A.S.E. negotiatin committee. Let me talk tae'm, an' mebbie between us we can organise a united front tae tell the employers tae stick the penny up their arse before they've got the cheek tae offer it tae us.

JAKE   Ye'll get me hung, Willie. Christ, I wish they'd conscript ye, an' get ye tae hell away frae here.

WILLIE   They might, ye never know.

JAKE   I'm bloody sure they win't. They don't want a bloody mutiny on their hauns. *(They laugh.)* ...I think I know a bloke. Works in Browns. Mebbie no. Might be Fairfields. Up the river.

PAT   Well, if 'at's the meetin over, I'm goin doun hame. I'm freezin. *(He moves away.* WILLIE *stands beside* JAKE.*)* ...

WILLIE   What's this bloke frae Glesga like?

JAKE   You should get on well. He done time for throwin shite at some Councillor up there a coupla years back.

PAT   Oh, Christ, they'll baith hav bombs in their pockets at the next meetin.

JAKE   But what if Charlie agrees wi ye? His name's Charlie McGrath. He's only wan.

WILLIE   As long as he's the right wan. Thae meetins are beyond description. Wan o the managin directors giein ye a wee talk about patriotism, an' how we should grist tae the mill, an' shouther tae the wheel, an' roll wir sleeves up, an' set a stout heart tae a stey brae, an' tripe lik that. It's aa lies. He wis near greetin when he described 'the plight of our glorious brothers in foreign fields'. The tears wis formin in his eyes. He made this speech... well, it wis mair liker a hymn... real tears... I couldnae believe it. The auld hypocrite. I tellt him tae join up. He chynged his tune aifter that. Sat like a dummy for the rest o the day.

JAKE   So it looks like ye'll be a wee while gettin the twopence, Willie?

WILLIE   It's a rotten prospect, Jake, but I think it'll take nothing short of strike action.

JAKE   Ever been out on strike, son?

WILLIE   No.

JAKE   Well, don't be in a hurry tae see what it's like. It would be aa-right tae start wi. I suppose. It's a kind o bravery for civilians. Aa thae folk 'at havenae gone tae the Front... there's some 'at think we're mebbie a wee bit feart... so ye down tools an' show what ye're made o, a wee bit. Me an' the ither hats'll go tae work... we'll drink tea an' dae nothin'... no 'at that'll be much o a chynge for us... but we'll look about us an' see it... the deserted shipyaird... lik a graveyaird full o bogie-men, an' the big cranns lookin doun on us lik vultures. An' the boats'll no chynge that wee bit week-bi-week, like they dae when ye're workin...

just stay the same… waitin for ye tae come back tae finish them aff. An' aa you… you'll be staunin on street corners… the money ye've pit by'll soon be done, so you'll no be in the pub. Ye'll be nae better 'an the man 'at cannae get a job, or disnae want a job, or had wan an' got the bag! You must look after the boys, Willie. Don't pit this toun intae that situation.

WILLIE   It would be mair than just this toun. It would be right up that river doun there.

JAKE   Christ!

WILLIE   Oh, I meant tae tell ye. Comin back frae the meetin I passed Greenlaw Goods Station. Know what I saw?

PAT   Na. What?

WILLIE   Two big guns ready tae be cairted aff tae the Front. Huge bloody things they were.

PAT   What's wrang wi that?

WILLIE   They've been sittin there for six weeks. The bosses are no gonna muve them till the Government pays higher transportation fees.

JAKE   'S 'at a fact?

WILLIE   Them an' their 'boys in the trenches'! Ye know what else? They're sendin war materials tae neutral countries at ridiculous profits knowin full well that the stuff's eventually being sold to the Germans tae blaw the boys tae fuck *out* o the trenches!

JAKE   I wouldnae trust any o them as far as I could shite, so I wouldnae.

PAT   They're bastarts, so they are. Hey, I'm cauld.

JAKE   Aye. It's time we were muvin. I cam up here tae run the dug, no tae listen tae propaganda aa night. (PAT *strokes the* WHIPPET.) …Don't pet him, Pat. He'll never win a race if ye dae that.

PAT   Oh, I see. Dae ye chase hares, like?

JAKE   Aye.

PAT   Ever catch anythin'?

JAKE   Aye. Fuckin pneumonia. (He *walks the* WHIPPET *a few steps away from them. He talks to the dog, whistles, then shouts as he slips it from the leash. The* WHIPPET *runs off.* WILLIE *and* PAT *have moved over, fascinated by* JAKE'S *handling of the* WHIPPET.) …Go, Teemo! (*He whistles.*) …

PAT   Seems fast enough tae me.

JAKE   I swear to Christ – some day I'll take that dug out for a walk and run away frae it! (*They are still watching the dog's journey.*)

WILLIE   Thanks, Jake.

JAKE   Aye. I'll pit ye in touch wi Charlie McGrath. All right?

WILLIE   Sooner the better.

JAKE   He's your man, aa-right… Oh, that bloody idiot dug. He's lost, bi-Christ! It's aa-right. Your daddy's comin… (*He goes off after his dog.* WILLIE *goes down to look at the view once again.*)

WILLIE   Would ye look at that view?

PAT   I've seen it afore. Come on. My teeth are chitterin.

WILLIE   It musta been great here afore the cranns came, and all this mechanisation. Can you imagine haein a wee farm up here? Away from everybody. Every time ye ploughed your field, an' that, ye could come over here for a wee rest an' just look doun at the river frae the Tail o the Bank tae the Holy Loch. Great times. Mebbie. Mebbie no. Even smells different up here. And it's quiet.

PAT   You're a romancer, Willie. Come on tae fuck!

They both go.

8. The James Watt Bar: February 1915

HUGHIE *and* EDDIE *have the place all to themselves. It's before lunchtime.*

HUGHIE   Dae ye ken hou mony that is?

EDDIE   Aye. Ye tellt us. It's twenty thousan.

HUGHIE   Sure it is. But, I mean, can ye *see* twenty thousan?

EDDIE   How dae ye mean?

HUGHIE   Well, ye dinnae get what it's like frae the report wance the War Office is throu wi't. Ye dinnae get the smell, for wan thing.

EDDIE   There's nae point upsettin folk ony mair than ye need, is there?

HUGHIE   Mebbie no. Gie's a Bell's, Eddie. On the slate.

EDDIE   I'm gonna get a clock in here. I'll tak the hauns aff an' I'll write on a bit o paper across its face: *'NO TICK'*.

HUGHIE   But, in the meantime, Eddie, …

EDDIE   Ye said ye'd pey me at the New Year.

HUGHIE   I didnae say what wan, but. Come on, Eddie. Are ye?

EDDIE *pours out the drink,* HUGHIE *comes over to the bar to get it.*

HUGHIE   Here's continuin prosperity tae ye, Eddie, in 1915. Aa-ra best!

EDDIE   Ye're a bit late.

HUGHIE   Flies in, din't it? It's Feb'ry aaready. *(He drinks.)* …

EDDIE   Did ye hear about wee Danny Blair frae East Crawford Street? Nice lad.

HUGHIE   Aye. I mean, ye cannae help likin a bloke wi a po-stumous decoration.

EDDIE   V.C.

HUGHIE   Aff 'is heid.

EDDIE   How?

HUGHIE   The two men he went out tae save's aa-right. Wee Danny's deid, bi-fuck. Valour! Out o-ra question. Look at me. I've only got wan leg, an' I wis a coward. We had a hera in our squad an aa. He's deid, tae.

EDDIE   There are some things worth deein for, Hughie.

HUGHIE   What? You tell me.

EDDIE   Your country right or wrong.

HUGHIE   You're aff your heid, as well!

EDDIE   You werenae sayin that the night before they went away. I remember it well. Ye were staunin there talkin like wan o thae posters on the waa.

HUGHIE   I say mair nor my prayers, Eddie. Ye don't honestly think I believe any o it? I don't mean I'm a pro-German or anything, ye know? I mean, I'm on the right side, but I know. I've seen them. If ye gied hauf o them a gun in peace-time, they'd be locked up in the loony-bin for runnin amok, bi-Christ.

EDDIE   Where is everybody?

HUGHIE   Yaird gates. Big Union meetin.

EDDIE   Again?

HUGHIE   Aye. The Engineers have lowered themsel's tae talk tae the Allied Trades. Motion o solidarity. Twopence an hour or nothing.

EDDIE   They'll settle for a penny. Bet ye anything.

HUGHIE   Of course they will. Willie Rough's dementit. He cannae win.

EDDIE   Nae chance.

HUGHIE   They'll be after him soon. Mark my words, Edward.

EDDIE   Who will?

HUGHIE   The Press Gang. Listen tae me. Twenty thousan men deid or missin. Have ye got that?

EDDIE   Eh?

HUGHIE   Morton's playin the Rangers at Cappielow, right? Capacity crowd. Ye cannae breathe for Rangers supporters. Nou, imagine every single wan o' thae men at that game. Twenty thousan. Imagine the whole fuckin lot o them blown right out o Sinclair Street intae the Clyde. Weans orphaned. Wives weidowed. Can ye imagine the size o the funeral? But there's nae big funeral. Wee Danny's mammy'll get the medal. The'll be naething left o him. Bits. Even if 'is watch escaped unhurt, as it were, somebody's snaffled 'at!

EDDIE   Screw the bobbin, Hughie. Ye cannae take a man's glory away.

HUGHIE   Neither ye can, considering he only got it throu the post this mornin an' him deid.

EDDIE   They thought they'd be hame for the New Year.

HUGHIE   Propaganda. Pure an' simple. I'll gie ye the answer in one dreaded word. Conscription.

EDDIE   It's no as bad as that, is it?

HUGHIE   Dae ye think anither twenty thousan are itchin tae volunteer? Not at all. This time, it's you, you, an' you.

EDDIE   Mebbie ye're right. To tell ye the truth, Hughie, I havenae lost wan regular since yon night ye done Lizars.

HUGHIE   In this toun there's folk that's stupit, but there's mair folk that's no sae stupit. Am I right or am I wrong?

EDDIE   Ye're right.

HUGHIE   Ye want a message?

EDDIE   No. Ye want a drink?

HUGHIE   Aye. I've got money comin tae me.

EDDIE   How do you live, Hughie?

HUGHIE   I go messages for you.

EDDIE   Money, I'm talkin about.

HUGHIE   Anybody in by?

EDDIE   No.

HUGHIE   Ye'll no tell onybody?

EDDIE   What dae ye take me for, a clype?

HUGHIE   It's the *Telly*. Wan o the reporters is giein me a wee back-hander.

EDDIE   What for?

HUGHIE   I gie 'im the odd tip about the situation ower by.

EDDIE   Does Willie know?

HUGHIE   What dae you think?

EDDIE   I think he disnae.

HUGHIE   You'd be right. Listen tae me…

CHARLIE *comes in. He's about thirty, dressed in quite a smart suit and a cap. He has just come down from Glasgow.*

CHARLIE   Excuse me. Have ye seen Willie Rough?

HUGHIE   Yaird gates. Big meetin.

CHARLIE   He tellt me he'd be here.

HUGHIE   He'll no be long. I'm Hughie. This is Eddie.

CHARLIE   Charlie McGrath. I'm a frien o Willie's frae Glesga.

EDDIE *(serving)*   Yes?

CHARLIE   Have ye got lemonade?

EDDIE   Aye.

HUGHIE   He's got whisky an' aa.

CHARLIE   I don't drink.

HUGHIE   How? Was ye an alcoholic or something?

EDDIE   Lea' the fella alane, Hughie. *(He pours out some lemonade for* CHARLIE.*)*

HUGHIE   There's nae accountin for taste.

CHARLIE *(to* HUGHIE*)*   You have another, Hughie?

HUGHIE   That's very kind o ye, Charlie. I'll hav a gless an' a pint.

EDDIE *pours out another drink.*

CHARLIE   I don't know whether tae go over tae the yard or no.

HUGHIE   You look a bit agitaitit.

CHARLIE   I've got news for Willie. They've downed tools at Weirs o Cathcart. By the end o this week every man on the Clyde'll be out on strike.

EDDIE   Well, don't look sae cheery about it.

HUGHIE   If it's no a war, it's a strike. Is there naething cheery happenin at aa?

39

EDDIE   Disnae seem like it.

HUGHIE   There's nae point Weirs comin out about the rise. Negotiations havenae broken doun or onything, hav they?

CHARLIE   It's not the rise this time. Shortage of labour.

HUGHIE   Well?

CHARLIE   They've brought engineers over frae America.

HUGHIE   What's wrang wi that? They're no darkies or onything, are they?

CHARLIE   No, they're not, if ye must know. Anyway, they brought in thae Yanks. Skilled men all right, but what dae they do?

HUGHIE   What?

CHARLIE   Return tickets. Ten shillins a week more than our own men, an' a guaranteed ten-poun bonus at the end o six months. They've really done it this time. They're skilled men, but they don't know wan end o a discharge-pump frae the other. Willie Rough an' me. We knew they'd make their mistake. We waited. Here it is. Weirs o Cathcart – the bosses themsel's are gonna be instrumental in gettin twopence an hour frae Glesga tae the Tail o the Bank!

EDDIE   When, but?

HUGHIE   Aye. That's pit your gas in a peep!

CHARLIE   Not at all. Don't you believe it. I've lived for this morning. Can ye no see? War or nae war, this'll show that the unions'll survive. The working man's been the goods an chattels of the employer class for far too long. We're in nae state tae think or feel or even live as human beings. A day like this is to exploit our hatred and kindle it intae rebellion. The day we tell them we're united. The-morra, we frighten them tae death. They can stick the Defence o the Realm Act. From now on they'll have to reckon wi us as a fighting organ of the working classes!

HUGHIE   The Band o Hope, bi-Christ!

WILLIE *comes in with* PAT *and two other workers.*

CHARLIE   Willie.

WILLIE   I thought it was you.

CHARLIE   Have ye heard about Weirs?

WILLIE   Aye. I heard.

CHARLIE   Well... are ye out? Are ye on strike?

WILLIE   Aye.

WILLIE *and* PAT *move over to their table.* CHARLIE *follows.*

CHARLIE   We knew wan o they Toffs would dae somethin' daft, didn't we? A Bell's, Willie?

WILLIE   Aye, thanks.

CHARLIE   Pat, you do the needful.

CHARLIE *gives* PAT *some money.* PAT *goes over to the bar.*

PAT   Glass o lemonade an two Bell's, Eddie.

HUGHIE   Eh. Three Bell's. Fairly lashin out, that yin. Mair like a christenin nor a strike.

PAT   Wait tae I tell Bernadette.

HUGHIE   Nae alternative, tho.

PAT   Still, wait tae I tell Bernadette.

CHARLIE   It's good news, Willie.

WILLIE   Listen tae me, Charlie McGrath. I've just pit eight hunner men on the street, an' afore the day's out there'll be thousans, an' I don't think that's very good news, so I don't!

CHARLIE   But it's the mistake. The clowns have done it. They know where to stick their penny an hour. It's twopence or nothin'.

WILLIE   I wish I wis like you, Charlie. I dae sometimes. Honest. Ye're like that crann over there. Just like steel. Ye don't get that wee tightness in your stomach as if ye were gaunna spew your ring up. Aa mornin, when you've been thinkin about organisation, I've been thinkin about next week or the week aifter, when the excitement wears a bit thin, an' they're dyin tae get back across that street tae make the price o a hauf or a loaf or three eggs. Ye cannae live on the win'.

CHARLIE   I thought ye'd be glad, that's aa.

WILLIE   Glad? Ye've nae feelings at all, have ye?

HUGHIE *lifts his crutch and moves to the door.*

EDDIE   Ye goin tae *your* work nou, Hughie?

HUGHIE   You shut it. Cheerio, lads. Ye'll be back on Monday wi the increase aa sewn up.

PAT   I hope tae Christ we are!

HUGHIE *goes out.* JAKE *comes in and goes to the bar.*

EDDIE   Hello, Jake. Ye'll be gey lonely over the road this aifternoon.

JAKE   Mebbie I'll be able tae teach that dug o mine how tae win a race.

EDDIE   Aye. Ye cannae be a gaffer if ye havenae got a squad.

PAT   I don't know what I'll dae. Bernadette'll soon want me out o the road. There's aye the picketin, I suppose.

JAKE *sees* CHARLIE.

JAKE   Charlie. Long time.

CHARLIE   Dae ye want a drink, Jake?

JAKE   Dae ye no think we better buy wir ain?

Act Two

9. A Street: February 1915

KATE *and* BERNADETTE *meet. Both are wearing scarves round their heads. Each carries a shopping-bag, but neither has made many purchases.* KATE *is visibly pregnant.*

KATE   Hello.

BERNADETTE   Hello, Katie. It's that close.

KATE   We're due rain, I'm thinkin.

BERNADETTE   Aye. When are ye due?

KATE   April.

BERNADETTE   Oh. No be long now.

KATE   The men'll be back by then, surely.

BERNADETTE   Och, sure it's terrible. Pat comes hame an' says 'We're out. Solid!' Pleased wi 'imsel', like, and I says, 'Who's gonna feed us?' an' he says, 'There's mair important things than your belly,' an' I says, 'What? What's mair important,' an' he goes on about infiltration an' agitation an' God knows what aa else, an' I says, 'Agitation'll no feed ye, nor four weans, neither,' an' he says, 'Be quiet,' an' I says, 'Na,' an' wan thing led tae anither, an' I got a skyelp on the face.

KATE   Oh.

BERNADETTE   We made it up again, tho. Your Willie must be worse. I mean, he's in charge, so 'e is, an' you expectin an' everything. How are you managin?

KATE   We manage.

BERNADETTE   Ye just hav tae.

KATE   Aye. That's about it. Willie says he'd live on tatty-peelins tae get 'is rights.

BERNADETTE   Pat's just as determined. An' there's nae sign o' it endin?

KATE   Willie never talks tae me about it.

BERNADETTE   I thought he would. I mean… he must hav a lot on's mind.

KATE   Aye, but he's deep, my Willie. He keeps maist o't tae 'imsel'.

BERNADETTE   I wouldnae let Pat keep any secrets frae me.

KATE   I don't bother. The Union's the men's business. If they got the rise, it would be worth it.

BERNADETTE   Is your rent up?

KATE   Aye. I got a letter frae the factor this mornin.

BERNADETTE   So's ours. I went tae see wan o the Labour men on the Council. He tellt me no tae pay it.

KATE   Did 'e?

BERNADETTE   Aye. It seems there's a big protest goin on. It wis startit by a wumman up in Glesga. I've got a poster. Wait tae ye see. *(She takes the poster from her bag.)* …Haud that end.

KATE *takes one end of the poster, and they spread it out between them. It reads* '*DO NOT PAY INCREASED RENT*'.

BERNADETTE   Do... not... pay... increased... rent... There ye are.

KATE   Do ye think it's aa-right?

BERNADETTE   Aa-right or no, I'm no giein them ony mair. Two shillins! Where dae they think we get it, Katie? The men might as well be idle. The strike amounts tae the same thing. Nothin' a week!

KATE   We cannae afford it. If the men get the rise, mebbie. It'll be different then.

BERNADETTE   It's never ony different. Ye'll get a shillin a week extra on the mantelpiece on a Friday, an' by the weekend breid's gone up twopence, sugar's up a penny, an' there's anither penny on a pot o jam an' cookin-fat. Afore ye can draw breath, the car-fare's up a hapenny. Then you're in the toun an' back, in an' back, that's a penny a day, an' ye're right back where ye started. Skint. An' you know what happens next?

KATE   The rent?

BERNADETTE   Na. The men's out again. Lockout. Strike. Arbitration. Negotiations. Meetins, meetins, an' mair meetins. They're no wise.

KATE   Ye don't think they like bein on strike, dae ye?

BERNADETTE   I wouldnae pit it past them. My Patrick got 'is photo in the *Telegraph* the other day, an' in ablow't 'is name... He says, 'Look, Bernadette! – Patrick Gatens!' He's still got it in his wallet. He cut it out an' kept it.

KATE   I wis gonna keep some o the things they said about Willie in a wee book, but he wouldnae let us.

BERNADETTE   How no?

KATE   He says the papers is, what d'ye cry it? ...biased against the men.

BERNADETTE   Oh, I cannae mind what they said about Pat. I just saw 'is name, like.

KATE   *(suddenly looking ahead)*   Oh. Is 'at the time? I've got tae go an' see Nurse Lonie.

BERNADETTE   She's 'at nice, isn't she?

KATE   Aye.

BERNADETTE   She's been in Greenock for years, ye know. I'm sure she'll be the midwife when our weans' weans is born.

KATE   So it's aa-right about the rent, ye think?

BERNADETTE   I'm no payin it. I cannae.

KATE   I just hope they don't get the polis on tae us.

BERNADETTE   The men would wreck the factor's offices if that happened.

KATE   Aye. It disnae take much tae set them aff these days. I'll have tae go.

BERNADETTE   Oh. I hope I havenae kept ye back.

KATE   No.

BERNADETTE   I meant tae tell ye. Five fish. I bought five haddock. Know how much they wantit?

KATE   No.

BERNADETTE   Wan an' thruppence. Wan an' thruppence! Would ye credit it?

Thruppence for wan fish. An' they're wee things. Tiddlers.

KATE   It's after four o'clock.

BERNADETTE   Oh, I'm terrible, so I am! What are we staunin here for? I'll walk ye doun. I forgot tae get a wee biscuit in.

They begin to go.

BERNADETTE   Aa we need's MacFarlane Langs tae pit a penny on digestives.

KATE   Is Pat on the picket?

BERNADETTE   Aye. I'd like tae see 'im tryin tae stop me if I wantit tae go in tae work.

KATE   They've got tae dae it.

BERNADETTE   You're as bad as the men.

KATE   Where can I get wan o thae banners about the rents?

BERNADETTE   They're aa over the toun.

KATE   Like the Coronation.

They both go off.

10. The Temperance Institute: February 1915

PAT *and* CHARLIE *are sitting behind a long table.* WILLIE *stands between them addressing a Union meeting. He holds some papers in his hand.*

WILLIE   It's been a hard week. I've felt it. You've aa felt it. For wance the pubs are kinna empty, so the publicans have felt it. But, brothers, there's a few shipyards an' a torpeda factory no far from this hall, an' they're empty an' aa, so the bosses have felt it! *(Cheers.)* I want to record some things on the minutes. First of all, as just wan o' the organisers in this toun I want to say that I'm proud o every wan o yez. Your solidarity's a credit tae ye, an' I ask ye tae carry on till this great strike is over and *won! (Cheers.)* I don't want to stand up here aa mornin, but I've got to acquaint ye wi a few facts. I've always tried tae tell ye the truth. An' the truth about the Unions during this strike stinks tae high heaven. Not with us. Not with the rank an' file, but the support given tae the Government by the national Trade Union leaders, including the Allied Trades… and the A.S.E.… our ain high-ups, boys! Their support o the Government is an act of the grossest treachery to the working man! I've been told personally by a member of the National Executive that he was willing to agree with that wee Welsh… gentleman… Davie Lloyd George, to call off this strike an' to 'suspend' trade-union rights till the war's done. I'll tell ye exactly what he said. He said, 'It's aa-right for you blokes, but we've been called up by the Government. We could feel a threat behind what they told us.' I says, 'What threat?' 'The threat of imprisonment,' says he. 'Who for?' says I. 'For us,' he said. Best place for traitors, I thought. But the tragic fact remains that the people at the top o' the tree... men who should be strong behind us... are, at the moment, daein it on their trewsers! They'll attempt to break us. But they'll never break us! *(Cheers.)* We're ready for them, aye, an' we'll be ready for Davie Lloyd George, tae, should he want to take us on! *(Cheers.)* Brothers, at this moment the very life of trade unionism is at stake. But remember, the committee behind this strike must always be known as the Labour-Withholding Committee. The very word 'strike' will send them panicking to the Defence of the Realm Act, or the Munitions Act, or some other instrument against the working people of this country, and as sure as there's a God in heaven they'll hae us aa breakin' up stanes in Barlinnie. There's people in high places that hate and despise us, brothers. That means we're strong! Before we get back on the picket, I must make two things clear. This is not an unofficial strike. Not at all. This is a spontaneous strike – a swift and necessary action because of the introduction of privileged employees at Weirs. But up to a point we've ourselves to blame. Six months ago, in the same shop, Weirs o Cathcart, Chinese were employed. These Chinee workers were paid *less* for the same job, and no action was taken. When I learned this, my first words, in all confidence, were, it wouldnae have happened in a Greenock shop! *(Cheers.)* Brothers, we're in for more hard times in the week to come. I'm sorry tae say that nane o us are gonna get any richer. An' we're no gonna get fat, either. But we will be a credit to our muvement, an' a credit tae oursel's... One final an' very important item on the agenda. It pruves we're no skint on Clydeside yet. The strike bulletin has made a profit of seven an' a tanner! *(Cheers.)*

11. The James Watt Bar: February 1915

The strike is still on, and so there are very few men in the Public Bar. EDDIE *stands behind the bar reading the evening paper.* HUGHIE *is sitting beside* SAM *at one of the tables.* SAM *is home on leave from the front. He is wearing uniform. His right arm has been amputated, and the sleeve of his tunic is pinned across his chest.*

SAM   Aa packed in there like herrin in a box, so we were. Some ospital. I don't think the doctors knew what wis wrang wi ony o us.
HUGHIE   That's no the worst o't, believe you me.
SAM   What are ye talkin about?
EDDIE   Lea Sam alane, Hughie. He must have a lot on's mind.
HUGHIE   Never mind Eddie, Sam. This is the first drap o drink he's sellt aa week.
EDDIE   I'll pit you outside.
SAM   I wish I had steyed at hame. Honest.

HUGHIE   Not at all. Dinnae start sayin the likes o that, Sam. What would we have done 'ithout ye?

SAM   What about aa them bastarts across the road? Ye don't get blown tae bits runnin a strike.

HUGHIE   I understaun how ye feel.

SAM   Dae ye? You think, 'cause you were in that wee hauf-arsed rammy out there in Africa, you know what it's aa about, but ye don't. You havenae got the faintest idea what it's like in France. 'Over the top', bi-Christ! Five hunner men goin over the top at wan go, an' mebbie twenty-five gettin back alive, an' no aa in the wan bit, either. What dae ye think these boys think o thae bastarts across the road lyin in their ain beds every night… out on bloody strike, bi-Christ? Dae ye think ye understaun that?

HUGHIE   Sure I dae, Sammy boy, sure I dae, but just you wait tae folk start tryin tae help ye. 'Can I get ye this, Sam, can I get ye that? Would ye like tae go for a wee walk? Dae ye fancy a game o puttin? Oh, sorry, I forgot. It wis your airm, wisnae't?' Treat ye worse nor a wean, so they dae.

SAM   Aye. It's lik that in the house.

JAKE *comes from the street and walks over to the bar.*

HUGHIE   How a' ye, Jake?

JAKE   No bad, Hughie, no bad. Sam. What are ye for, boys?

HUGHIE   Mine's a wee pint.

SAM   No, thanks.

JAKE *orders a half and a half-pint for himself and a pint for* HUGHIE.

SAM   You win all round, don't ye, Jake?

JAKE   What ye sayin?

SAM   Well, you didnae go tae France, an' the haill toun seems tae be on strike, bar you!

JAKE   *(paying for drinks)*   Aye. I'm past it, son.

HUGHIE   Ye've got your whole life in front o ye, Sam.

SAM   What life? … What sort o life dae yez think I've got, eh? Twenty-wan. Twenty-wan year auld. Time just out, an' then this happens. A wan-airmed hauder-on! Where dae ye think I'll get a job?

JAKE   Ye'll get a start, Sam.

SAM   Much'll it cost us?

HUGHIE   Now, now, Sam.

SAM   How much, Jake?

JAKE   I might change my mind in a minute.

SAM   Aye, it's up tae you, Jake, in't it? I coulda won a fuckin battle, but when I come hame, it's still up tae you whether I can earn a copper or no.

JAKE   I understand why ye're bitter, son. Just forget it.

SAM   Forget it?

JAKE   Come on. Have a drink.

SAM   Would ye no rather buy a flag? It'll only cost ye a hapenny. I'll rattle my tin can, if ye like.

JAKE   I came in here for a drink, no an argument.

HUGHIE   Aye, cheer up, lads. It might never happen. Sam'll hae a glass o Bell's.

JAKE   Gie 'im what he wants, Eddie.

EDDIE *pours out a drink.*

HUGHIE   Seen Willie the-night, Jake?

JAKE   No. He's speakin up the Temperance Institute.

EDDIE *gives* JAKE *his drink.*

JAKE   There's your whisky.

SAM *rises and moves over to the bar to collect his drink.*

SAM   *(to* JAKE*)*   Sorry I lost the place, Jake.

JAKE   That's aa-right. Come an' see me when it's settled.

SAM   When's 'at gonna be?

JAKE   Hard tae say. Willie's got them solid, an' that Charlie McGrath's never done agitatin. While yet.

HUGHIE   Thought Charlie wis a pal o yours, Jake.

JAKE   I know 'im. I cannae help that. He's no close or anything. Thank Christ. Too quick off the mark, if ye ask me.

SAM   Who is 'e?

JAKE   Frae Glesga. Engineer. Doun helpin Willie tae organise the strike.

SAM   Christ, they're better organised when they're out on the street than when they're at the tools.

HUGHIE   Aye. Nothing's simple ony mair. I thought bein on strike meant they sat in the house.

EDDIE   It looks like it the-night.

WILLIE *and* CHARLIE *come in from the street.*

HUGHIE   *(sotto voce)*   It's the secret service.

SAM   Ye look pleased wi yoursel', Willie.

WILLIE   Hello, Sam. This is Charlie McGrath.

CHARLIE   Hello.

SAM   *(to* CHARLIE*)*   Are you the commandin officer?

JAKE   You want somethin', Charlie? (CHARLIE *sits down at one of the tables.*)

CHARLIE   No for me, Jake.

JAKE   I forgot. *(He goes over to the table where* CHARLIE *is sitting.* WILLIE *orders a drink.)*

WILLIE   A pint, Eddie.

JAKE   How's it goin?

WILLIE   Good meetin the-night. (WILLIE *and* JAKE *sit down beside* CHARLIE, JAKE *in the middle.* WILLIE *is looking at his notes.)*

JAKE   Sam's no feelin too good.

WILLIE   Oh.

JAKE   Understandable.

WILLIE   Sorry, Jake, I wisnae listenin. What were ye sayin?

JAKE   You've got mair important things on your mind.

CHARLIE *(to* WILLIE)   I'll try tae get aa that copy for the Strike Bulletin before the weekend. Went well the-night, I thought.

WILLIE   Champion.

CHARLIE *(taking bundles of paper out of his case)*   We'd better stack these voting forms.

They begin stacking the forms. JAKE *rises and goes over to the bar to join* SAM *and* HUGHIE.

SAM *(to* HUGHIE)   I wisnae expectin a pipe band an' a hera's reception or anything, but, Christ, ye'd think folk might be pleased tae see ye. Willie Rough looked right throu us, so he did.

JAKE   A bit touchy, aren't ye?

SAM   Would ye look at them? Like a coupla stick-men for a squad o hures…

JAKE   I don' know what tae dae wi mysel' the night.

SAM   Are they no talkin tae you, either? I don't know what's worse… bein wan-airmed like me, big men lik them, or sittin in the middle lik you.

JAKE   Aa-right, Sam, that's enough o your patter for wan night.

SAM   They don't need you ony mair, Jake. Look at them. They've got what they want. You're a back number.

JAKE   I don't know what the fuck I'm doin here!

JAKE leaves the pub. WILLIE *and* CHARLIE *go on piling up the ballot papers. They do not see* JAKE *go.*

12. The hills above Greenock: February 1915

WILLIE *stands staring straight ahead at the view below him.* CHARLIE *is sitting on the ground near him. He is scribbling on a jotter. He licks his pencil, then scribbles some more…*

WILLIE   It's great up here, so it is.

CHARLIE   Eh?

WILLIE   Aa this speakin's murderin me. My voice's goin. What ye writin?

CHARLIE   An article.

WILLIE   For a paper?

CHARLIE   There's nae paper would print what I want tae write, an' you know it.

WILLIE   Well, what is it?

CHARLIE   I'm gonna start wan.

WILLIE   A paper?

CHARLIE   Aye.

WILLIE   On your strike pay, like?

CHARLIE   Don't be funny. Ye've got tae think what comes after. What's the next demand? What's the next step? We cannae trust tired auld union men. We've got tae see a way ahead oursel's.

WILLIE   Aye, it's a rare gift tae be able tae see what's ahead o us. McLean's got it. He's a great man. I've never met anybody like him, an' you havenae, either, if ye were tae be honest about it.

CHARLIE   He's a dreamer. He's a wonderful dreamer, but he's still a dreamer. Sure, he tellt everybody what the war wis about, an' he did gie this river a bit o pride that it was badly in need o, but surely you can see 'at that's no enough.

WILLIE   Try as ye might, Charlie, ye'll no make me think any the less of him. If I hadnae heard him, how dae ye think I'd hav the gumption tae run this strike? I'm tellin thae men what tae dae. That's a hell of a responsibility.

CHARLIE   Sure it is. But what's next? If Weirs send the Yanks packin, dae we go back, or dae we wait till Christmas for the twopence an hour?

WILLIE   We go back before we break our strength.

CHARLIE   Then what?

WILLIE   You go back tae your patriots across the negotiatin table, an' I go back tae mine.

CHARLIE   That's gonna dae us a lot o good.

WILLIE   The Weirs situation is a different issue frae the tuppence an hour. When we've got some of our strength back, we'll go for that.

CHARLIE   You're wrong: we must use our solidarity *now* for the overthrow o the whole system.

WILLIE   What ye gonna dae? Dae ye want tae string up Mr Cosgrave an' the whole jingbang o them in Cathcart Square an' sell tickets?

CHARLIE   Mr Cosgrave! Can ye no see further than your ain midden, Willie?

WILLIE   I've got enough on my mind giein thae men the spunk tae stay out. If every shop wis as solid as mine we'd be laughin.

CHARLIE   What's that supposed tae mean?

WILLIE   Where's your shop? Glesga. That's where you should be. What ye daein here?

CHARLIE   You asked me down a while back. Remember?

WILLIE   Thanks for comin. Ye can skidaddle aff hame again as far as I'm concerned. Away hame an' write a book about it. This is the first half-hour's peace I've had in the last fortnight, an' I've come up here tae enjoy it. I want tae be up here lookin doun there. That's my wey o gettin free o't for a wee while. I can see my house, an' the school my laddie goes tae. There's the yard an' my church, an' the Municipal Buildings. Somehow I've always got mair go in me when I've been up here.

CHARLIE   You should get doun on yer hauns an knees an' offer a prayer for our salvation.

WILLIE   There's some things ye don't joke about. Whit are ye, anyway?

CHARLIE   Ye mean am I a Catholic, Prod'sant, Wee Free, or Anabaptist, I suppose. I'm nothing. Nothing tae dae wi any o that nonsense, anyhow. How can ye staun there talkin about 'my church'? Ye seen the light, or something? Ye tryin tae convert me?

WILLIE   I'm no tryin tae convert anybody. A man has tae staun for somethin'. My religion's nothin' tae dae wi anybody else. I'm no explainin it. It's wan o the things that's mine.

CHARLIE   But ye tellt me the strike was condemned out o the pulpit in the Mid Kirk. Some o them think we're gettin a hand-out frae Berlin.

WILLIE   They're just feart. My minister wouldnae dare. We'd walk solid out o there an' aa, if he did.

CHARLIE   Dae ye walk under ladders? (WILLIE *reacts, but says nothing.*) ...Ye know when tae stop, dan't ye? That's hauf the trouble wi you.

WILLIE   There's somethin' tae you, Charlie. Sometimes I wish ye were at the bottom o the Clyde wi a hunnerweight o scrap roun your neck, but you've got a way wi ye, and I swear tae God I covet it sometimes.

CHARLIE   Ye're better away doun tae the kirk, then, ye've time for a psalm an' a lesson before the shop meetin.

WILLIE   Right. Right. Hauf time. We're like a couple o weans. Ye've got me as bad as yoursel'.

CHARLIE   I wish ye were. (*He returns to his jotter, rereads what he has written, then licks his pencil, and scribbles some more.*) ...

WILLIE   I wish the gorse wis out. (*He lies flat looking at the sky. Silence... Then sitting up.*) Ye mean a whole paper?

CHARLIE   Aye. What dae ye think?

WILLIE   Well... I thought it wis like the Strike Bulletin.

CHARLIE   Na. A real radical paper that prints exactly what's happenin aa over the world, an' what should be happenin. No quarter. What about you writin somethin'? Ye write maist o the Bulletin.

WILLIE   That's different. That's my job.

CHARLIE   If I ever get it goin, I'll pay ye tae change your mind.

WILLIE   If I write anything for a socialist paper, I'll write it 'cause it needs written, I'll no be after any cash in hand!

CHARLIE   So ye will write something?

WILLIE   I might an' I might no.

CHARLIE   Nae hurry…

WILLIE   What dae ye think?

CHARLIE   What?

WILLIE   The wife's out on a rent parade the-day.

CHARLIE   Is 'at a fact? They're aa over Glesga.

WILLIE   No wonder the sheriff's officers are feart, faced wi a pack o wild weemin armed wi brushes, clathes-poles, an' God knows what else. I wouldnae like tae face them. There'll be hunners o prosecutions, I tellt Katie.

CHARLIE   Mebbie I should be askin her tae write a wee bit for my paper.

WILLIE   I'll write it. I'll dae the article for ye. Satisfied?

CHARLIE   Satisfied.

WILLIE   Hey! That's twenty-five past three on the Mid Kirk clock. Ye comin?

PAT   *(off)*   Willie!

WILLIE   I tellt ye ye should be at hame.

PAT   *(nearer)*   Willie!

WILLIE   *(to* CHARLIE*)*   Who's 'at?

CHARLIE   Dae they want you?

PAT   *(nearer still)*   Willie! Willie (PAT *arrives, breathless, holding his shoulder in pain. His head is bleeding.* HUGHIE *follows close behind him.* PAT *collapses exhausted.* WILLIE *and* CHARLIE *go over to him, followed by* HUGHIE.) …Willie, ye've got tae get doun by. They cam aff the three o'clock train… strike-breakers… I don't know who's payin 'em. There's broken heids everywhere.

HUGHIE   Right throu the picket they went.

CHARLIE   Where are they?

HUGHIE   In the yard. Where dae ye think? (CHARLIE *runs off very quickly.)* No, Charlie. It's no you that's wantit. Charlie!

WILLIE   Nou, caa canny. Canny, boys. Are the polis there?

HUGHIE   No many.

PAT   It wis sudden, like. I've never seen any o them afore.

HUGHIE   Hard men. The bastarts. Listen tae me, Willie Rough, you get doun that yard at wance, afore Charlie starts an ever bigger rammy an' pits the baa on the sclates aathegither.

WILLIE   He'll no dae anythin' till I get there.

HUGHIE   I'm lame, but you're fuckin blind!

WILLIE   Can ye get up, Pat? *(He lifts* PAT *to his feet.)*

PAT   I had tae come an' get ye, Willie. I didnae ken what tae dae. I wis feart tae dae the wrang thing.

HUGHIE   Come on! Are you waitin tae it gets dark?

WILLIE   I'm comin. I've just got tae think what I'm gonna dae.

HUGHIE   Think on the road doun. Are ye fit, Pat?

PAT   Don't worry about me.

WILLIE   Gie'm a haun, Hughie.

HUGHIE   Who's gonna gie *me* a haun?

PAT   I'm aa-right, I tellt yez!

PAT *goes off.*

WILLIE   Nou, you bloody well stay out o it, Hughie.
HUGHIE   Aye. We'll see. We'll see. We'll see.

WILLIE *runs off.* HUGHIE *follows.*

13. A ward in Greenock Royal Infirmary: February 1915

HUGHIE *is lying on a simple, iron hospital bed. His eyes are shut.* WILLIE *comes in quietly and moves over to him.* HUGHIE *opens his eyes.*

HUGHIE   What?
WILLIE   Hello, Hughie.
HUGHIE   Is 'at you, Willie? Aye. I'm glad it's you.
WILLIE   Is the pain bad?
HUGHIE   I don't know. It's that dope. I cannae feel a thing, so there's nae wey o tellin how bad I am. The doctor musta decided I wouldnae be able tae thole it. If he's right, I'm finished.
WILLIE   Don't talk daft, Hughie. You'll be on your feet in nae time.
HUGHIE   *(smiling)*   Hav I got any feet?
WILLIE   Och, Hughie!
HUGHIE   Figure o speech. Dinnae be saft, Willie. I've got used tae only haein the wan. What's the difference? Sure, I hope ye're right. I don't care if I hav tae wheel mysel' about on a wee bogie like a damaged wean as lang as I get out o here. Skatarry's no in it.
WILLIE   But it wisnae your fight, Hughie. I tellt ye to stay out o it.
HUGHIE   I wis tryin tae help ye, Willie. When I saw our boys gettin stuck intae thae dirty bastards, I just had tae try an blooter wan or two wi the auld crutch. I couldnae help mysel'. I'm leanin against this waa layin about me, when this big red-heidit fella starts runnin for the gates. He had somethin' in his haun, ye see? I shouted: 'Where the fuck did that come frae?' It looked lik a gun, but I thought it was a wee toy. It didnae look lik a real wan. I didnae think it was gonna blow ma fuckin leg aff.
WILLIE   I don't know what tae say, Hughie. I swear tae God, I wish I wis lyin there in your place.
HUGHIE   What did the band play?
WILLIE   Ye're the only man who rushed in the gates wi us that had nothin' tae gain.
HUGHIE   Are ye daft aathegither? Everybody in this toun shoulda been behind ye. We aa shoulda rushed past the polis tae get our hauns on thae bastarts. If you an' the men had no been so resolute. If ye hadda been in two minds about goin back,

they wouldnae had tae send anybody doun frae wherever it was they cam frae. You an' folk like ye are costin some o the big bugs a fortune, so yez are. They dinnae like that too much. They'll hav tae invite ye back e'nou. Wait tae ye see. Ye havenae got a wee dram about ye?

WILLIE   Eddie gied me a gill o Lang's for ye. The Bell's is aa done.

HUGHIE   Oh, Lang's is just champion. Gie's it.

WILLIE *looks round to see if there are any doctors or nurses about, then quickly hands the bottle to* HUGHIE. HUGHIE *opens it and takes a long slug.*

HUGHIE   I can really taste it. Down. Down. Down she goes. That's hell of a good o ye, Willie. To the last drop.

WILLIE   Keep some o it.

HUGHIE   Just a wee tait mair.

WILLIE   You're a hell of a man.

HUGHIE *(finishing the whisky)*   The last drop. I used tae hav a set o whisky glesses, ken? Afore the wife deed. They were engraved. Ye saw a man on the gallows bein hung, like. Below 'im it said 'The last drop'... on the bottom o the gless, like... Dae ye no see it?

WILLIE   I'll come back in the mornin.

HUGHIE   I might no be here. Onywey, we drove them out. I suppose that means we wun?

WILLIE   The doctor said I should only stay a wee while.

HUGHIE   Willie, would ye tak a wee bit o advice, if I gied it ye?

WILLIE   What's 'at?

HUGHIE   Gie's your haun. Listen. Try tae keep the company o our ain lads. Pat an' Jake an' 'at. Stay awa frae Charlie McGrath. He's... Ye know what I think o him. Just dae what I tell ye. How's Pat?

WILLIE   It's just a sprain.

HUGHIE   That's good. *(Groaning in pain.)* Mebbie this auld heart couldnae staun them takkin the leg aff, or mebbie I'm just no as young as I wis, but that pain's gey bad, dope or nae dope. It's funny. Ye ken, in Africa I kent I'd come hame. This is a different thing aathegither. Willie, I think ye'd better get the priest.

WILLIE   I never knew ye were a Catholic, Hughie.

HUGHIE   Waddins an' funerals.

WILLIE   I'll get wan.

HUGHIE   I'll pit in a good word for ye up the stair. Here! Mebbie it's doun by I'm goin.

WILLIE   I'll come back wi the priest.

HUGHIE   I wish ye didnae have tae. (WILLIE *moves a step away.*) Try an' get, eh... what d'ye cry him? Flynn. Aye. Canon Flynn, an' hope tae Christ he remembers me.

WILLIE   Eh... Hughie... what's your ither name, again?

HUGHIE *(smiling)*   Naebody knows it. Frizell. Stupit name, in't it? Hughie Frizell.

WILLIE   Anythin' ye want?

HUGHIE   I don't think the priest would appruve o my last request.

WILLIE   Eh?

HUGHIE   It's that lang since I've had my hole, so it is. I wouldnae mind a wee bit o stuff.

WILLIE   *(laughs)* …The pain bad?

HUGHIE   It's muvin about inside me. I doubt the haill engine's giein it up as a bad job.

WILLIE   I'll no be long.

WILLIE *goes out.*

HUGHIE   Nurse? … (HUGHIE *is in pain. The* NURSE *seems a long time coming. Eventually she comes in, a plain, scrubbed girl with dark hair.)* Nurse, could ye oblige me wi a cigarette?

NURSE   You know you're not supposed to be smoking.

HUGHIE   But ye'll gie me wan, win't ye? *(She gives him a cigarette, then lights it for him. He takes a long draw.)* …Ye got *(weakly)* a heavy date the-night?

NURSE   No.

HUGHIE   *(growing weaker and weaker)*   Ye a local lassie?

NURSE   Kilmarnock.

HUGHIE   I like it doun there.

NURSE   It's nice enough, I suppose.

HUGHIE   *(weaker)*   Ye've got a nice face.

NURSE   *(serious, but humouring him)*   You're terrible!

HUGHIE   *(now very faintly)*   Honest… *(The* NURSE *takes the cigarette from his mouth. He closes his eyes. She leaves, carrying the cigarette awkwardly to save the ash from falling on the polished floor.* HUGHIE *reopens his eyes. He stares in front of him.)*

14. The Shipyard: April 1915

There are a few tin drums and a couple of wooden boxes to sit on. The APPRENTICE *comes in carrying some metal tea-cans with handles. He is just going off to make the tea. The horn blows loud and long for lunch-time.* PAT *comes in, carrying his own tea-can.*

PAT   Hey, you!

APPRENTICE   What?

PAT   Will ye boil my can?

APPRENTICE   Much ye gie us?

PAT   I'll gie ye a kick up the arse if ye don't.
APPRENTICE   Where's your ain can-boy?
PAT   Yeeprez.
APPRENTICE   Oh. My gaffer says I'll hav tae go if conscription comes in. Will I?
PAT   What age are ye, son?
APPRENTICE   Fifteen past. I'm nearly sixteen, so I am.
PAT   Christ!
APPRENTICE   Here's Jake comin. It's time I wisnae here.

The APPRENTICE runs off taking PAT'S can. PAT sits down on one of the boxes. JAKE comes in. The others are in their working-clothes, and all wear caps. They are dirty, and speak louder than before.

JAKE   Patrick.
PAT   Hello-rerr, Jake.

JAKE sits down on a drum. PAT begins to unwrap his 'piece', which consists of thick sandwiches wrapped in newspaper.

JAKE   Did ye see that boy?
PAT   Aye. He's away tae boil the cans.
JAKE   Dead slow an' stop, that yin.

WILLIE comes in. He sits down on a drum and takes out his 'piece'.

WILLIE   Workin hard, Pat?
PAT   Aye, kept goin. What about you?
WILLIE   Rush job.
JAKE   Aye. Cosgrave's been at me about it. It was supposed tae be finished in the month o Feb'ry, but the strike put the kybosh on that. He'll be lucky tae deliver by the Fair, so 'e will, an' that's three months away.

The APPRENTICE comes on carrying the steaming cans of tea. He gives one to each of the men.

JAKE   Did ye hav tae plant it first?
APPRENTICE   I've only got wan pair o hauns.
JAKE   Changed days since I wis a boy.
APPRENTICE   Wis 'at in the good old days?
JAKE   Nane o your lip. Scram!
APPRENTICE   Can I no hav my piece wi youz?
JAKE   No, ye cannae. We're talkin. Get tae fuck.

The APPRENTICE goes. Each man has a little tin of sugar in the breast-pocket of his dungarees, and a medicine-bottle full of milk in his jacket-pocket. They stir their tea with pencils.

PAT What ye got the-day, Willie?
WILLIE Cheese.
PAT Gie ye a corn' mutton for a cheese wan.
WILLIE Right y'are.

They exchange sandwiches. The men eat their lunch and drink the tea from their cans, blowing on it first. PAT *is still reading the paper.*

PAT Listen tae this. *(Reading paper.)* Churchill… 'We will sacrifice our last shilling and our last man.' Our last man! Hey, I don't like the way he's talkin about me.
WILLIE He's no talkin about you, Pat. He's talkin about himsel'.
JAKE Nae flies on him. He's got a good job.
PAT He's dead jammy, so 'e is. *(They go on eating and drinking.)*
JAKE Oh, Willie, I meant tae tell ye.
WILLIE What's 'at, Jake?
JAKE The wife got a wee present for your new wean.
WILLIE Oh, ye shouldnae hav bothered, Jake.
JAKE It's just a wee mindin.
WILLIE That's hell of a good o ye.
JAKE A wee rattle.
PAT Three nou?
WILLIE Aye.
JAKE Are you two havin a race, or something?
WILLIE I don't know what tae call her. Katie thought it was gonna be a wee boy.
JAKE We've been talkin about adoptin wan.
WILLIE Ye should, Jake.
PAT Hey, listen tae this, lads. It's about us. Christ almighty! Wait tae ye hear this.
WILLIE Out wi't, then.
PAT 'If one asks what event disillusioned the Liberal Government – the answer is the Clyde dispute, and nothing else.'
JAKE Mebbie it was worth it, then.
WILLIE I wis never sae sure o anythin' in my life.
PAT What exactly is this Clyde Workers Committee?
WILLIE I'm stayin away frae that.
PAT But they asked ye on tae it, din't they?
WILLIE Aye, sure. But ye'd never be at your ain fire-side. Too much. It's aa-right for the likes o Charlie. He's no mairried or anything. He can shoot 'is mouth aff three nights on a Sunday, an' naebody'll complain.
PAT I'd sooner hav you tae represent us than the likes o him.
WILLIE Charlie McGrath's tryin as hard as anybody else I know tae get better

conditions o work on this river. Him an' the whole Workers Committee'll no
staun any shite frae anybody. Aye, an' that's includin Lloyd George himsel', so it
is.

JAKE   I think ye'd quite like tae be on it, aa the same, Willie.

WILLIE   What if I would?

JAKE   They need somebody a wee bit level-headit.

WILLIE   Oh, I keep in touch wi them, like, tae keep our branch informed. I'm writin
a wee article for their magazine.

PAT *takes the magazine from his pocket.*

PAT   Is it in this wan?

WILLIE   No. It'll be in the next wan.

JAKE *looks over* PAT'S *shoulder.*

JAKE   *The Worker,* 'Organ of the Clyde Workers Committee'. It looks quite
interestin. Gie's the wire when your name's in it.

PAT   Keep that, if ye like, Jake. I've read everythin' I wantit tae read in it.

JAKE   I cannae be seen wi the likes o this!

WILLIE   What's wrang wi't?

JAKE   Are you forgettin I'm a foreman? Can ye imagine me at a meetin up the
stairs, an' that faain out o ma pocket, an' Cosgrave pickin it up an' readin about
what's gonna happen tae the likes o him when the Revolution comes? I'd be out o
here faster than my dug gets aff 'is mark. *(They all laugh.)* By Jeeze, that's no
very fast, maist o the time.

WILLIE   It's no like you tae be feart, Jake.

JAKE   I'm keepin my nose clean.

WILLIE   Ye chynge wi the win', Jake.

JAKE   What about you? You're savin a lot on train fares these days.

WILLIE   I tellt ye. This branch an' this yaird an' this toun's aa that concerns me at
present. 'S 'at no enough for wan man?

PAT   Dis this new Rent Act mean 'at our rents'll no go up at aa, even if the war goes
on anither year?

WILLIE   Ten years! Till the end o the war, an' six months beyond, rents are
restricted. It's in black an' white.

PAT   Bi-Christ, thae weemin did what the men couldnae dae. We're still waitin on
that rise.

WILLIE   Formality nou, Pat. Keep the workers happy. That's the new plan.

JAKE   What's the catch?

WILLIE   Conscription. They'll be losin men aa over the place. Potential tradesmen,
anyway.

PAT   Aye. That boy there. He's only fifteen, bi-Christ. He'll hav tae go, tae. Ye're
aa-right if your time's out. We're aa-right.

JAKE   Who's gonna boil the can?

WILLIE   Dilution. Weemin'll be platin an' caulkin an' hole-borin an'...

JAKE   An' a few things mair, if I know some o the dirty buggers in here. *(They laugh.)*

JAKE   Can you imagine this yaird wi nae swearin?

PAT   Is this dilution serious, Willie?

WILLIE   Mebbie no here, but the torpeda factory'll definitely get its quota.

PAT   How much are they gonna pey them?

JAKE   How? Ye thinkin o gettin the wife out heatin rivets?

PAT   No, just curious. What's the rate, Willie?

WILLIE   Washers. They'll pay them in washers. Plenty there for the Clyde Workers Committee tae get their teeth intae. By Jeese, I'm glad I turned doun that big Committee job.

JAKE   Are ye sure o that, Willie?

WILLIE   Aye. When ye get on that train tae Glesga it's aa politics.

PAT   I'm glad ye're daein a wee bit for the *Worker,* tho. We're quite a famous shop because o you.

WILLIE   I don't know if they'll pit the article in or no. I wrote it in the heat o the moment, like.

PAT   When?

WILLIE   When I cam hame frae Hughie's funeral.

JAKE   It's taken ye a hell of a long time tae get it in.

WILLIE   I wis gonna send it, then I wisnae, ye know? It's in my pocket. If Charlie comes doun, I'll gie'm it. If he disnae, I willnae.

JAKE   Ye feart they'll tell ye it's rotten?

WILLIE   Mebbie that's it.

JAKE   *(rising)*   I'll away an' see that job lined aff.

PAT   Stick in, Jake. Ye'll be up the stair yet.

JAKE   I'm savin up for a bowler hat.

JAKE *goes off.*

WILLIE   *(taking a last sip of tea)*   I meant tae tell ye, Pat.

PAT   What?

WILLIE   Somebody threw a brick at us last night.

PAT   When?

WILLIE   On the road hame. It just missed us.

PAT   Mebbie it wis a wee boy playin.

WILLIE   No. It wisnae.

PAT   How dae ye know?

WILLIE   It was too near the bloody mark.

15. Princes Pier, Greenock: May 1915

CHARLIE *sits on a bollard reading* WILLIE'S *article.* WILLIE *stands looking out to sea. Foghorns alternate with an occasional snatch of military music – a brass band one time, pipes and drums another…*

WILLIE   Would ye credit it? 'More men… More men.'

CHARLIE   This is good, Willie.

WILLIE   Ye can read it when ye get hame. Just look at them boats. Filled tae the brim, so they are. A lot o them's just boys.

CHARLIE   We cannae win that fight nou, Willie. Worry about what's goin on at hame. Dilution.

WILLIE   What dae I care about a few weemin goin tae make torpedas when the Clyde's full of troopships in front o me?

CHARLIE   There's folk that want the war tae carry on a bit longer.

WILLIE   Aye. They'll be retirin on their winnins when it's done.

CHARLIE   No only them, but. There's friens o mine that think we could take advantage o the war.

WILLIE   Ye're way ower my heid again, Charlie.

CHARLIE   What are ye talkin about? It's aa in your ain article here. 'Should the workers arm?' I thought it wis a bit strong for the likes o you.

WILLIE   I wrote that a long time ago.

CHARLIE   Did ye mean it?

WILLIE   Aye, sure I meant it… *(Realising he's caught.)* You're a fly man, Charlie. Don't try to make me intae some kind o a revolutionist. I'm no John McLean. Aye, an' I'm glad I'm no. Ye cannae dae much for your shop breakin up stanes in Peterheid. But I'll tell ye wan thing. If you an your cronies are gonna pit the Red Flag on top o the City Chambers in George's Square, that'll be because it wis in your ain heids tae dae it. Don't pit the blame on some scribbles o mine.

CHARLIE   Ye're a changed man, Willie. What's the maitter?

WILLIE   Nothin'.

CHARLIE   It's done a lot o damage tae be nothing.

WILLIE   Folk hav been gey suspicious o me since the strike.

CHARLIE   But ye knew that would happen.

WILLIE   Aye, but knowin's wan thing, an' havin it happen tae ye's anither. Somebody chucked a hauf-brick at us. If I'd got in the road, I'd be deid. An' last Sunday, last Sunday in the pulpit o my ain church, fire an' brimstone aa about us! I could tell the Minister wis talkin about me. There wisnae wan that said 'Cheerio' tae either Katie nor mysel' aifter the service, so there wisnae. That's the faithful for ye.

CHARLIE   You don't have to stay here, ye know. Ye could muve up tae Glesga. Take your place on the committee.

WILLIE   I've muved enough. I like Greenock. I'm stayin. It's too big. The whole thing's got too big for a man tae understaun. Too much has happened since I cam tae this toun. Look at thae boats. Rule Britannia! Us an' folk afore us built some o thae boats, an' look what they're carryin nou. An' it's no only the wans that'll no come back that worry me, it's the woundit an' aa. What the fuck are we gonna dae wi' them? Folk don't need that many baskets. An' you, Charlie, wi your revolt. That's war an' aa. I want the quiet back again. That's aa I want. The quiet.

CHARLIE Ye're no the man ye were, Willie. I sometimes wish we really were 'in league wi the dreaded Hun'.

WILLIE Ye aff your heid?

CHARLIE They'd gie us guns like a shot, so they would.

WILLIE Guns! Dae you know what ye're talkin about?

CHARLIE We know aa-right.

WILLIE Is 'at aa ye dae on that Committee? Ye havenae forgotten about the rise, I hope.

CHARLIE That'll be throu in nae time at all. We're busy just nou settin up a welcomin party when the wee man comes tae see us.

WILLIE He's braver'n he looks, comin up here.

CHARLIE He's refused tae talk tae the Committee. Don't you worry yoursel'. He'll see us.

WILLIE Lloyd George. I wouldnae mind five minutes wi him.

CHARLIE Ye've missed your chance, Willie. *(The pipes and drums which have been coming and going now sound much nearer. Tune:* Happy we've been aathegither.) ...

WILLIE Would ye listen tae that!

CHARLIE I'll miss my train. Nou, dae ye want me tae take this for the paper or no?

WILLIE I gied ye't, didn't I?

CHARLIE Ye want it printed?

WILLIE I want it printed. (CHARLIE *puts the article away in his pocket. The pipes sound louder and louder.)* ...The bands don't get any quieter, an' the songs are still hell of a cheery. It's aa lies. Frae Lloyd George right doun tae some big fat polis playin the pipes!

CHARLIE They make a hell of a noise at the best o times. *(On the other side, very near, a brass band strikes up* See the Conquering Hero Comes, *very loudly.)* Jesus Christ!

WILLIE Surrounded!

They both go off.

16. The hills above Greenock: December 1915

WILLIE *and* KATE, *both wearing overcoats, walk past the stump of a dead tree.*
WILLIE *is pushing the pram. He brings it to a halt and looks down at the town.*

KATE   We'll catch our death up here.

WILLIE   It's great, the snow.

KATE   Ye're as bad as William wi's sledge.

WILLIE   It's as well I got Pat tae make 'im that. He'll no be gettin much else this Christmas.

KATE   But they'll no jyle ye, Willie. Surely. They canna. How am I supposed tae feed three weans wi my man in the jyle?

WILLIE   I don't know what's gonna happen.

KATE   Are ye feart, Willie?

WILLIE   Aye.

KATE   They might let ye aff.

WILLIE   No chance. How dae ye think they're havin the trial in Edinburgh?

KATE   But it wis only words, Willie. A wee article in a paper. Very few read it. Oh, Willie I wish ye'd never written it!

WILLIE   What's done's done.

KATE   I've never been tae Edinburgh.

WILLIE   You're no comin.

KATE   I want tae be wi ye, Willie.

WILLIE   As sure as God's in heaven, I'll get a year, or at the very least six months, an' I don't want tae see your face when they haul me out o that court.

KATE   I'll bring the weans tae see ye.

WILLIE   No. Tell them I'm away tae England tae work.

KATE   We've never tellt them lies, Willie, an' I'm no about tae start, so I'm no. They'll find out anyway.

WILLIE   How?

KATE   Folk'll tell their weans, an' their weans'll soon tell William in the school playgrund. There's no many secrets in this toun.

WILLIE   No. Ye're right. Oh, I'm stupit! I wis in two minds whether tae gie it tae Charlie or no.

KATE   I wish ye'd never clapped een on him, so I dae.

WILLIE   It's past, Katie. At least, it soon will be. The day aifter the-morra they'll at last hav me in some kind o uniform. I wonder if they've really got wee arrows on the jaicket.

KATE   What are we gonna dae, Willie?

WILLIE   There's nae point greetin about somethin' we don't know. I might be lucky an' only get the six months, but wi that Zeppelin raid over Edinburgh last night the jury'll be sharpenin the knife, I'm thinkin. Six months isnae long. It's mair'n six months since wee Sarah was born.

KATE   I knew somethin wis gonna happen, Willie. I knew it. Just as we were beginnin tae get over the strike, an' people starin at us a wee bit less, this has tae happen. We were just back tae normal. We were gettin on our feet, so we were. We mighta saved a shillin or two nou that the rent's no chynged. We need a bigger house, Willie, wi three weans.

WILLIE   Dae ye think I want tae go tae the jyle? What's gonna happen tae the Union when I'm in Peterheid? Christ only knows.

KATE   If ye'd worry a bit mair about yoursel' insteid o other folk, we might no be in this mess nou. What possessed ye tae write that stuff? If Charlie McGrath wants tae run the country, he can staun as an MP lik onybody else. The people would soon show who they wantit, an' it might no be him.

WILLIE   It wis my ain doin. I wisnae thinkin about anybody else. I wisnae even thinkin about you.

KATE   I don't understand ye Willie. What did ye dae it *for?*

WILLIE   I wis angry.

KATE   Ye'll hav time tae regret it nou, aa-right.

WILLIE   But I don't regret it…

KATE   It's freezin, Willie. Come on doun. The best way tae look at a white Christmas is through the room windae, when the fire's on.

WILLIE   I'm comin, Katie. When I get out, I think we'll pack up an' get away frae this place aathegither.

KATE   Australia or someplace lik that?

WILLIE   Canada, America mebbie.

KATE   But we don't know anybody, Willie.

WILLIE   We didnae know anybody here when we came. We're still strangers tae maist folk.

KATE   I don't think ye want tae, Willie. Ye're thinkin ye might hav tae, in't ye?

WILLIE   I'll no be short o time tae make my mind up, will I?

KATE   Come on doun intae the warm. I don't want her tae get a chill.

WILLIE   Right. It's nae life for you, Kate. Where hav ye been? Naewhere.

KATE   I'm no complainin.

WILLIE   That's true, Kate. Ye've never done much o that. *(He begins to walk away.* KATE *turns the pram towards home.)* …Well, we'll no be up here for a while. (KATE *walks over to him. She takes his arm. Together they walk off down the hill with the pram.)*

17. Edinburgh: a cell: December 1915

WILLIE *and* CHARLIE *sit waiting to be taken to prison.* CHARLIE *has some books beside him on the bench.*

CHARLIE   You in the huff? … Do I detect a wee wave o huffiness?

WILLIE   You might have said *somethin'.*

CHARLIE   No point.

WILLIE   Six months in prison's worth complainin about, is it no?

CHARLIE   Sure, it wis a fine wee speech ye made, Willie, but naebody wis listenin tae ye. This is Edinburgh…

WILLIE   Ye let me down, Charlie. *(He takes a fag from his packet of Gold Flake, lights it, and inhales deeply.)* ...I'll miss the New Year.

CHARLIE   Aye, an' I'll miss it next year as well. Still... what's the odds? Cannae be bothered wi't anyway.

WILLIE   I cannae fathom you, Charlie... Ye don't smoke, don't drink... nae wife... nae weans.

CHARLIE   No problems.

WILLIE   Apart frae eighteen months in the clink.

CHARLIE   What d'ye expect me tae dae about that, Willie? Burst out greetin? No point. I've been inside before, but I'm no gonna waste my energy fightin wi the warders this time.

WILLIE   Didnae take ye for a hard man, Charlie.

CHARLIE   Oh, not at all, reformed character. It's ages ago. Now I'm quite prepared to sit an' read Marx, Engels, an' *Moby Dick* over an' over again until they open the gates. It's not all tottie-howkin and breaking stones, you know.

WILLIE   It's a bloody holiday for you, in't it?

CHARLIE   You've got to face facts, Willie. What else can ye dae? Mebbie ye think ye can jump ower the waa, or something? Well, I've got news for ye – they're kinna high, an' ther' a hell of a lot o big teuchtar warders tryin tae keep ye in, for that's what they've been tellt tae dae. If ye think about the outside aa the time, ye'll go mad. It happens tae some. You've got tae use the heid. There's ways of makin a wee stretch like yours count. Look at the history of the Revolution. Many a reputation was made behind bars.

WILLIE   I'll say this for ye, Charlie: ye're the first man I ever met 'at *wanted* tae be in the jyle.

CHARLIE   There's worse places.

WILLIE   But we didnae commit a crime, Charlie. For the first time in my life I wrote doun something I believed in. Sure, I wis willin tae go tae jyle for my convictions, because I kent that wis the law. But the law's wrang. A man should be free tae criticise. If there's nae criticism, there'll be nae chynge, an' the same fools'll be runnin the country election aifter election, and the voice o the workin people will never be heard! That's what that sentence this mornin wis about, an' that's why I wis ashamed o your silence.

CHARLIE   But I'm tellin ye how tae win. If you stick wi me, 'Willie Rough' could amount tae something. You're no exactly a household word, are ye? You wait. In eighteen months' time, when I come out o the gates, folk'll know all about it. The newspapers'll even be there waitin for me.

WILLIE   Big man.

CHARLIE   Sure. See you. You cannae see further than your ain nose. When you were knockin your pan out doun there in Greenock, I wis gettin mysel' known, makin contacts, gettin some kinna future aa sewn up for mysel'. Engineerin! It's a mug's game. You think I'm daft?

WILLIE   Ye're a lot o things, Charlie, but ye're no daft.

CHARLIE   These friens o mine, Willie. They've got influence. They decide what goes... in the Unions... in the Party... they're in charge o our bit o the world, son, an' I've made damn well sure they'll look after me all right. As for you... you don't know the difference between Winston Churchill an' Tommy Hinshelwood.

WILLIE   Who's Tommy Hinshelwood?

CHARLIE   Big fella wis in my class at school. Havenae heard o'm since. A nobody, Willie. A number. A private o the line, or a stupid ship-builder who's content tae turn 'is ticket aa 'is life. I've made damn sure that's no how I'm gonna end up. The other day... Thursday, it wis... I wis walkin by the tenement I wis born in. The windaes wis aa smashed tae bits. Broken glass everywhere. Condemned. An' you know what? I wis ashamed tae tell the person 'at wis wi me 'at that wis the house I wis reared in. That attic, up that close, in that condemned tenement, wi'ts windaes aa broken. An' that disnae mean I'm ashamed o what I cam up frae, or o onything my faither or mither did by me. It just means 'at I want a hell of a lot mair out o life than ony o them got. I've found out how it's done, so I'm daein it. That's all.

WILLIE   Weill, ye'll no be daein it for a year an' a hauf, onywey. *(Smiling.)* We're safe till then.

CHARLIE   It's no funny, Willie. We're no aa as saft as you, thank Christ! When you get out, ye'll be back tae the yaird hopin everything's quietened doun a wee bit. Then it's back tae the bulk-heid bangin your hammer frae six o'clock till midnight, if they'll pay ye the overtime. I'm no goin back tae the tools for anybody.

WILLIE   Rivetin's my trade, Charlie. I'm good at it. I'll ey get a start at it. You cannae be up tae much as an engineer when ye're chuckin it.

CHARLIE   Ye're no gonna gie's a wee lecture on the glorious tradition of British craftsmanship, are ye? Ye've got tae go after the main-chance. There's nae future in bangin in rivets. A man like you could do very well workin wi the Union. Organisin... gettin better conditions for the boys, and the best part is that while ye're daein it, ye'll have a hell of a lot better conditions for yourself! Collar an' tie. Travellin expenses. No sweat. Nothing like it.

WILLIE   I'm happy enough in Greenock.

CHARLIE   Tae hell wi Greenock! I'm fed up hearin about Greenock. Come up tae the City. Get workin at headquarters. It would take ye about a week tae replace that balloon ye've got for a Secretary in the Allied Trades.

WILLIE   I've got a job, Charlie. I'm no aifter onybody else's.

CHARLIE   Know something, Willie?

WILLIE   What?

CHARLIE   You're a mug! *(He picks up a book.)* ...

WILLIE   They'll be comin for us soon. Six months'll no be lang goin in.

CHARLIE   Ye cannae wait tae get back hame, can ye? Just wan thing, Willie... take a note o the day I'm due out.

WILLIE   How? What are ye gonna dae?

CHARLIE   Treat mysel' tae a new suit.

18. The shipyard: June 1916

PAT *sits on a drum, sipping his can of tea and reading his paper.* WILLIE *comes in, dressed in a suit. He stops.* PAT *turns round.*

PAT   Willie Rough... hey! *(He gets up, walks over, and shakes* WILLIE'S *hand.)* ...Christ! How are ye, pal?

WILLIE   Fine, Pat.

PAT   When did ye get out?

WILLIE   Yesterday mornin.

PAT   In for a start, like?

WILLIE   Aye. Where's Jake?

PAT   He's doun the yaird. I'll get 'im.

WILLIE   There's nae hurry.

PAT   Christ, it's great tae see ye, Willie. I've missed ye, so I hav.

WILLIE   How's Bernadette?

PAT   She's fine. You?

WILLIE   I'm no bad.

PAT   How wis it?

WILLIE   Well, I'm in nae hurry tae go back, if that's what ye mean.

PAT   Na. I'm sure an' ye're no.

WILLIE   Busy?

PAT   Kept goin. There's a launch the-morra.

WILLIE   Aye. I passed the boat. Is 'at where Jake's workin?

PAT   Aye. I'll get 'im. Look, Willie, come doun the-morra. It's no every day Cosgrave's haunin out the free drink.

WILLIE   No. Aye, I'll take a race doun.

PAT   I cannae tell ye how good it is tae see ye back. Things've been quiet 'ithout ye.

WILLIE   It's a long time.

PAT   I want tae know aa about it. Just curious, like. But it's time I wisnae here. I've had my break. They'll bag me if I don't get back tae the job. I'll run over an' get Jake for ye. Ther' a wee drap tea there. *(Giving* WILLIE *his can.)*

WILLIE   Thanks, Pat. *(Drinking.)* I forgot what yaird tea tastes like.

PAT   Aye. Parish Priest's tea, the wife caas it.

WILLIE   It's good.

PAT   I'll away an' get ye Jake. Be seein ye.

WILLIE   Aye. Thanks, Pat.

PAT *goes off.* WILLIE *sits down on a box. He drinks his tea. After some time* JAKE *comes on.*

JAKE   Hello, Willie.

WILLIE   Jake!

JAKE   Long time, eh? How was it?

WILLIE   It wisnae exactly a wee holiday.

JAKE   Six months.

WILLIE   A hunner an' eighty-nine days.

JAKE   I bet ye're sorry ye spoke.

WILLIE   I am nut.

JAKE   Oh… I had my dug out at a meetin last night.

WILLIE   Did ye? How did ye do?

JAKE   Outclassed.

WILLIE   Hard lines.

JAKE   Honest tae Christ, ye work your drawers aff trainin thae dugs, so ye dae. But ye can only take them so far.

WILLIE   I wis wonnerin about a start, like.

JAKE   Aye. I wis thinkin that. Look… eh. It's hard the-nou… eh, Willie, ye know. I mean, I tried my hardest tae haud on tae your job, like, but ye know how it is. It's nothin' tae dae wi me, ye understaun. It's upstairs. Ye know what they're like. I got tellt by Cosgrave 'imsel' personally, like. If I wis the manager, it'd be different. It would be up tae me then, but I've got my boss, tae. You know how it is, Willie…

WILLIE   Barred, is it?

JAKE   I wouldnae go as far as tae say that.

WILLIE   What would ye say, Jake?

JAKE   It's no my fault!

WILLIE   Is it no? Whose fault is it, then? If that's no victimisation, what is? I've had men threaten strike action for less.

JAKE   Aye. That's what you would dae! But it's changed days nou, so it is. It's a different yaird aathegither frae the way you left it. There's nae mair o your cairry-on. Nae mair strikes. Nae mair weeks 'ithout a pay-packet. Nae mair debts docked aff the first pay. Aa that's over an' done. Paid on a Saturday, an' there's a wee bit o piecework, an' the rise is throu an' aa. There's nae need for any mair trouble.

WILLIE   An' how dae ye think ye got the rise? Tell me that, Jake.

JAKE   Don't start, Willie, for Jesus' sake. Ye're only out o the jail five minutes. I'm sorry. I mean that. But there's nothin' I can dae about it. Another yaird that disnae know ye might start ye. It's no the end o the world.

WILLIE   It's the end o somethin' tho, Jake, in't it? It's the end of staunin up tae Cosgrave an' everybody like 'im. An' when strong men, like you who were on our side, chynge your tune, it's the end o any chance o winnin. Oh, I wis feart o't, Jake. Somethin' tellt me it would happen, but nou that it's happenin tae me, I cannae believe it. I changed you. I did. I know I did. I changed you, Jake Adams. Who changed ye back? Is it too much tae trust a man? Is that too much? Dae ye believe in anythin' at aa, Jake? Tell me that.

JAKE   I don't know what ye expect frae me. You trusted people far too much. That's the trouble wi you.

WILLIE   I'm sure o wan thing. I trusted you, Jake. Honest tae Christ, I trusted you. I musta been aff my nut.

JAKE   It was different then, Willie. I wisnae actually involved in it, but I wis caught up in it. It wis like a fever up an' doun this river. McLean wis speakin wan night, Gallacher the next. You were tellin us what it meant. An' you were right *then,* Willie. But the war's a bit mair serious nou. Folk are dyin. They're no comin back. An' they're no folk we've never heard o. It's the man in the next close an' the boy next door that went tae the Sunday School. It's Greenock folk. Relatives an' friens, bi-Christ. We just stopped fightin the bosses an' got on wi the job. The likes o me find out ye cannae win. Ye can only make the best o what ye've got. An' aa that other stuff. Where did it get you? You an' your pamphlets an' your speeches. Six months in Peterheid, an' if ye cannae get a start, ye'll be at the Front wi a gun in yer haun.

WILLIE   I bet ye'd like tae see me marchin doun Princes Pier aa in khaki wi the band playin.

JAKE   I wouldnae mind. Folk as good as you hav had tae go. It's no near done yet. I'd go mysel' if I wis young enough.

WILLIE   The whole machine's been at ye, hasn't it, Jake? My wee bit o sense hasnae been aroun for a wee while.

JAKE   You think a hell of a lot o' yoursel', don't ye?

WILLIE   Mebbie I dae. Mair than I think o the likes o you, Jake. That's a fact.

JAKE   Ye're sayin things ye'll be sorry for. There was a time when I thought the sun shone out o ye. It's true, that, an' ye winnae believe me, but I'm sorry I cannae start ye.

WILLIE   In some roun-about wey, I suppose ye arc. Oh, God help ye, Jake, an' God help the country. When the likes o you stops botherin, the country's finished. Ye'll be forgettin tae go out an' vote next, an' that'll be the end. Ye deserve what's comin.

JAKE   Mebbie ye'll get a start in Lithgows or up there in Siberia.

WILLIE   If they've got you feart, Jake, the foremen up there must be really crappin it.

JAKE   Aye. Well… there's plenty o work in Glesga.

WILLIE   I've only been in Greenock a coupla years, Jake, but don't try throwin me out o my ain toun.

JAKE   What's sae great about Greenock?

WILLIE   There's bugger-aa great about it, but it's where I live, till I decide tae muve.

JAKE   Look, Willie, I'm tryin tae help ye.

WILLIE   Oh, stop it, for Christ's sake! Would ye stop tryin tae be nice? I cannae forgive ye. How can I? Ye've let me down. I wis sure about you, an' by Christ I wis wrong. I wish ye would go, Jake. If ye don't, I might hit ye. An' if I did, I might no stop. Ye know why? 'Cause you knew I trusted ye. Ye must have. You knew ye had that trust, an' knowin that ye broke it, like ye break a stick every night tae kinnle the fire. As easy as that. Away ye go, Jake. If ye see me comin toward ye, on West Blackhall Street, cross over. Don't say Hello as if nothin's happened. Forget ye were ever a brother o mine. (PAT *comes back along the yard towards* JAKE *and* WILLIE. *He stops near them.*)

JAKE   Cheerybye, Willie. There's a lot o folk in this yaird sorry ye ever walked in thae gates, an' I'm no wan o them, but I'll be as glad as them tae see the back o ye. I don't suppose I can shake your hand, so, as you say, I'll just go. *(To* PAT.*)* Ye've got wan minute tae get back on the job, Gatens!

JAKE *goes off.*

PAT   What's the maitter wi him?

WILLIE   The bastart'll no start me.

PAT   How no?

WILLIE   Orders. For wan man I've got a lot o folk hell of a feart.

PAT   Ye'll get a start somewhere.

WILLIE   Where?

PAT   They don't know ye everywhere, Willie.

WILLIE   But I want tae be known. I'm ashamed o nothin' I've done.

PAT   But ye've got to pay the rent an' 'at. How's Kate been managin?

WILLIE   She's been out washin stair-heids. How dae ye think I feel about that? Aa I want's a day's work, an' that's honest.

PAT   There's other jobs forbye rivetin.

WILLIE   Aye. The Army.

PAT   Don't be daft. There's the farmin. They need farmers the-nou. Get out o the grime. I wish I could go tae the country.

WILLIE   I like the grime. I've got tae stay, Pat. I've got tae show folk what it's like tae live by somethin' ye believe in. Mebbie I can change them by showin them that. Mebbie I cannae. But I've got tae haud my heid up, so that they can stick up for themselves an' no be feart tae demand what's theirs by rights. They can call me any name they like. They can brand me wi any slogan, any party, an' I'll answer tae them aa. They can jyle me again if they want tae, an' if they throw anither brick at my heid, it had better kill me! 'Cause I'm here, an' I'm gonna haunt Jake Adams an' every worker in this river an' Cosgrave an' aa. I'll haunt them till they see sense or tae my time's spent. I'll turn everything upside doun an' backside foremost or die tryin. There's worse tae come.

PAT   But ye havenae got a start yet, Willie.

WILLIE   But I will, Pat. I've got tae.

The horn blasts long and loud. PAT *slowly walks away.* WILLIE *is on his own.*

The Rising

by

Hector MacMillan

First performed at Dundee Repertory Theatre on
1 May 1973, directed by Stephen MacDonald

Hector MacMillan

Hector MacMillan was born in Glasgow in 1929. After leaving school at fourteen he did his National Service in the army. Among other jobs, he served in the Merchant Navy for four years, then worked as an electronics engineer, mostly in research, until becoming a freelance dramatist in 1967. Before then he had worked abroad for ten years, the last four in Switzerland. He has written of his decision to return home in 1967: 'Scotland was on the threshold of an exciting historical development and the things I wanted to write about were connected both with its history and with the process of change. I wanted to be present. To be involved.' He was a founder-member in 1973 of the Scottish Society of Playwrights and is a past Chairman.

His first play, *To Stand Alone,* was broadcast by Scottish Television in 1966. Other drama for Scottish Television and BBC Television includes *Solidarity* (1972), *Annals of the Parish* (1979), *Out in the Open* (1982), and *The Personal Touch* (1983). A television version of his play *The Sash* was broadcast by Radio Telefeis Eirean in the late 1970s. (BBC Scotland recorded the play for television, too, but it was never broadcast.) He has had plays, adaptations and translations broadcast by BBC Radio Scotland and Radio Clyde, and has written a substantial body of scripts for educational television and radio.

His work for theatre began in 1971 with *The Resurrection of Matthew Clydesdale* for Glasgow University Arts Theatre Group. His plays since include *The Rising* (1973), *The Sash* (1973), *Royal Visit* (1974), *The Gay Gorbals* (1976), *Oh What a Lovely Peace!* (1977), *Clann A Cheo* (1980), *Eine Kleine Nachtmutze* (1981), *Capital Offence* (1981), *The Funeral* (1988), *Tigh na Triubhais* (1989), *Bridging the Gap* (1990), *A Greater Tomorrow* (1997). He translated into Scots *The Hypochondriak* (1987), *Noblesse Obleedge* (1989), both by Molière, and *Figaro the Barber* (1991) by Beaumarchais. *The Hypochondriak* has been translated from Scots into Finnish and has proved a popular and critical success in Finland.

Author's Original Note

The Rising is based on events that happened in Scotland in the year 1820; far enough away from us now to be regarded as long-past history, yet so close that it is still just possible for someone alive today to have learnt of them from an eye-witness. It is a story that has been kept alive from generation to generation by a relatively small number of committed Scots. I had the good fortune to learn it in the way that so many of the best things in life are learnt, as a child by the fireside. I had the additional good fortune to learn the story from the best possible source – from my father, Robert Galbraith MacMillan – one of the most committed of those committed Scots.

The principal events depicted are based as accurately as possible on verifiable fact; dramatic licence and interpretative reconstructions have been kept to the absolute minimum. The facts alone make the dramatic and historical points more than adequately. It was never my intention to produce any kind of conventional stage play. I set out to recreate on stage the essence of a part of our history. I have tried to do so in a manner that will appeal on as many different levels as possible to the people whose forebears created that history in the first place and who are still deprived full knowledge of it.

The following characters are historically-based:

JAMES & MARY WILSON
JANET & DAVIE WALTERS
ROBERT HAMILTON
MATTHEW RONY
MARGARET McKEIGH
JAMES SHIELDS
MacGREGOR (Tolbooth jailer)
Lt. Col. ALEXANDER BOSWELL (of Auchinleck)
Rev. JAMES LAPSLIE (of Campsie Parish)
LORD SIDMOUTH
GEORGE IV

The following are historically-based composites:

JOHN & MEG FALLOW
DUNCAN MacINTYRE
CHARLOTTE

The character of PLACEMAN is in a category of its own. He too is a composite, but based on many people. SAMUEL HUNTER (editor of the *Glasgow Herald*), KIRKMAN FINLAY, M.P. (Lord Provost of Glasgow), and LORD PRESIDENT HOPE (of the Scottish Court of Sessions) are part of it; but as much as anything he is representative of an attitude shared by many of that class of Scot at that time. Sadly, it is an attitude that still lingers on; and sadder still, it lingers nowhere more tenaciously than among the ageing Executive of the Scottish Council of the British Labour Party.

Hector MacMillan, 1973

Characters

JOHN FALLOW	Small town businessman.
MEG FALLOW	His daughter.
JAMES WILSON	A weaver. A Strathaven man.
MARY WILSON	His wife.
JANET WALTERS	His daughter.
DAVIE WALTERS	His son-in-law. A weaver.
MATT RONY	Irishman. A mill worker.
RAB HAMILTON	A weaver.
DUNCAN MacINTYRE	Highlandman. A blacksmith.
CHARLOTTE	Old widow-buddy.
MARGARET McKEIGH	Young woman.
JAMES SHIELDS	Glasgow weaver.
JAILER	Highlandman.
Lt. Col. ALEX. BOSWELL	Yeomanry commander.
PLACEMAN	Scottish Establishment figure.
Rev. JAMES LAPSLIE	Minister.
GEORGE IV	The reigning Monarch.
LORD SIDMOUTH	Home Secretary.

ORATORS & MAGISTRATES
WOMAN ON THE ROAD TO CATHKIN BRAES
OTHER WEAVERS

FOLK MUSICIANS/SINGERS

Set

No formal set is called for. The movement between scenes should be fluid. A rostrum above the main action should be available for the MUSICIANS and SINGERS, another for PLACEMAN.

Other rostra of varied height and shape are the only permanent furnishings on stage.

Act One

Prologue

The thin high notes of an instrument playing 'The Rising'. Weathered writing on a wall: 'Agent Provocateur – Richmond!', '1817', 'Richmond is Lord Sidmouth's Spy'. A slow build in the intensity of the music as THE SINGERS *appear sitting close to the audience. Before they start singing a new warning has been added to the old, the dribs of wet limewash still trickling down: 'Sidmouth has many Spies!', '1820'.*

SINGERS   The weavers o Scotland aspired tae win freedom.
  They socht naethin less than the True Rights o Man;
  They joined in a union, its aim was Reform,
  A vote for each man and each woman their plan.

Music continues in the background as the radical orators occupy centre-stage one by one.

WALTERS   Citizens o Glesca! They tell us we live under the finest Constitution in the world; but apart f'the Magistrates and Cooncil, whae are self-electit, whit ither buddy has the richt tae vote on the operation o that Constitution? Not yin o the hale hundert an twinty thoosan souls in this city has ony mair say in choosin the Member o Parliament than they hae in choosin the Emperor o Morocco, the Dey of Algiers, or the bloody Grand Turk himsel!

Spokesmen for established government appear one by one above and behind the radicals. Each is aware of the others' presence and argument, but all address the larger audience before them.

PLACEMAN   So long as property, upon which our whole system is founded, shall continue to return the Government... I shall not despair.
HAMILTON   Fellow toonsmen! Ye ken as weel as me that yon wars against Napoleon hae pit a debt o one thoosand million pounds oan this deludit country. One thoosan million, that we hae tae accoont for in sweat, famine, fever, an stervation!
FALLOW   There are high and low, rich and poor, in this world. We should be contented and happy in the situation in which we are placed.
JANET WALTERS   The weemin are hertsick bringin bairns intae the warld, just tae see them happit under the sod for want o henest nourishment!
BOSWELL *(slightly arrogant)*   Are not millions of starving people the occasional necessary... *(searching for the right word)* slumps, in any manufacturing nation?
CHARLOTTE   Gin oor bairns dee o stervation, they leeve diseased an deformed in their foul cotton mills!
LAPSLIE *(in sepulchral tones he reserves for his biggest lies)*   There must be rich

and poor, there *must* be fortunate and unfortunate, for blessed purposes. For if there were no poor, there could be no... sweet, and holy charity.

RONY   They preach that the wars against Napolean were necessary. They were necessary so that they could all re-establish 'the Right Divine of Kings to Govern Wrong!'

JANET   Oh you're aw bold lads when the drums beat an a braw rid coat's clappit oan yir back. Weel it's time ye kent yir real enemy! It's time ye did some fechtin here for a cheynge!

MARGARET McKEIGH   Nae mair wull the weemin be jist machines tae produce their bluidy cannon-fodder!

ORATOR *(on a rostrum)*   Men and weemin o Scotland, I ask you now tae record publicly, and withoot fear, an overwhelmin vote in favour of oor just demands for Reform!

MACINTYRE   End the imperialistic wars!

MARGARET   Universal adult suffrage!

HAMILTON   Equality o rights!

WALTERS   Repeal o the cripplin Union wi England!

ALL RADICALS   Live free... or die!

THE MUSICIANS, *very much to the fore, resume the first verse of 'The Rising'.*

SINGERS   But naethin was heard o but Plots and Sedition,
High Treason, Rebellion, and Blasphemy Wild;
Because that the people had dared tae petition
In plain honest language, firm, manly, and mild.

Scene 1

Strathaven village square. The Strathaven folk gathered round a rostrum on which JOHN FALLOW, *considerably better dressed than the others, has taken his stand. A local employer, he tries hard to behave and speak 'correctly'. An invitation to take a glass of wine at 'The Big Hoose' would have him bubbling with excitement for a month before and a twelve month after.*

The others present include his daughter MEG, JAMES *and* MARY WILSON, JANET *and* DAVIE WALTERS, RAB HAMILTON, MATT RONY, DUNCAN MACINTYRE, *and* CHARLOTTE.

FALLOW   Fellow citizens of Avondale; I deem it my duty to warn you against the unlawful violence that has been preached at this meeting, *(checking* WALTERS' *attempt to interrupt)* and at others, throughout the length and breadth of the land.

WALTERS   Naebody here wants tae listen tae you, Fallow.

FALLOW   The right to speak; is that no part of what your... *(sneeringly)* Reform, is supposed to be about?

HAMILTON   *(quiet growl)*   We'll reform him gin he doesnae get aff that bluidy tub!

FALLOW   *(on his dignity)*   This is a public meeting, Hamilton. I have the same rights as the next man!

RONY   *(humorously)*   Another word and he'll get his *last* rites!

RONY, *an Irishman of about the same generation as* JAMES WILSON, *has become something of a favourite since he settled in Strathaven.*

MEG   *(shouting over the general amusement)*   There's no reason my father shouldn't speak at his leesure. The Fallows have lived in Strathaven as long as most of you here!

FALLOW   And longer than some, Maister Rony. Eh?

CHARLOTTE   *(pushing in before* RONY *can reply)*   Better keep your faimily oot o public meetins, Meg. Maist o's here ken mair aboot your ancestry than you seem t'dae yirsel!

CHARLOTTE *has a knowing, toothless cackle that triggers off the others.* MEG *is puzzled by the remark, but* FALLOW *avoids her questioning look. He is not popular; partly because of what he has that most of the others in the town lack.*

FALLOW   Now I'm not saying but wha... *(he tries again to get their attention)* I said I'm not saying but what there's a good many things wrong with the country at present; I agree with you about that. But violent talk is not the remedy, and it never can be!

HAMILTON   Then whit is your remedy?

FALLOW   *(refusing to be hurried)*   Ahh, weel; that's just the whole trouble with the half of you. You're all looking for simple answers. Easy solutions. You...

WALTERS   *(flaring)*   Oot wi your solution if you hae yin!

FALLOW   *(down his nose)*   Oh, now; I don't pretend to hae solutions to all this world's problems, *(jabbing his face at* WALTERS) like *some* I could name!

WALTERS, *the local rhymer and an intelligent, well-read man, turns away in disgust.*

WALTERS   B'Christ he's aboot as decisive as a pup wi its first hedgehog!

FALLOW   *(still fairly complacent)*   That notwithstanding, I believe I can put forward a proposal that would, in a very short time indeed, relieve the greater part of most of your alleged sufferings.

RONY   *(apparently serious)*   Mister Fallow, you're in a position to relieve all of our sufferings; here and now.

FALLOW   *(slightly surprised challenge)*   How, man?

RONY   *(relishing it)*   Shut your gob and get down!

Annoyed now, FALLOW *shouts above the jeering amusement.*

FALLOW   My proposal is that this meeting should petition His Majesty, King George the Fourth, for…

He is drowned out under a roar of scornful disapproval.

WALTERS   Nae mair petitions!
JANET   We're sick o writin them!
MACINTYRE   Never again!
CHARLOTTE   Petition yir erse, Fallow!
RONY   Not one more!
WALTERS   Get doon f'there!
HAMILTON   Jesus Christ, man! They treat oor petitions as bluidy jokes in Parliament!
FALLOW   *(struggling to continue)*   …should petition His Majesty for assistance, financial assistance, for…

The roar is even more derisive this time. HAMILTON, *a lithe, volatile man of about thirty, who like* MACINTYRE *has campaigned in the Napoleonic Wars, has had all he can take. He reaches for* FALLOW.

HAMILTON   Aw for Christ's sake man, get doon. Get doon!
RONY   *(grabbing for* FALLOW*)*   Pull the silly hoor outa that!

FALLOW *struggles to remain where he is.*

HAMILTON   Away wi'm!

JAMES WILSON, *the oldest of the weavers present, but a sturdy, vigorous man despite his sixty-odd years, shoulders his way none too gently into the struggle.*

WALTERS   Rab, Davie, Matt!
MEG   *(frightened)*   Leave my father alane the lot o ye!
WILSON   That's enough noo.
MEG   *(edging towards hysteria)*   Leave ma father alane!
WILSON   Duncan! *(Throws them off fairly roughly.)* That's enough noo. *(Grips* HAMILTON.*)* Rab! That's enough!
HAMILTON   He's wastin oor bluidy time!
WILSON   Even so. *(Checks the attempted reply.)* A fair hearing for aw.
MACINTYRE   Not for the likes of that, Jamie!
WILSON   *(right into his face)*   For every man or wummin that wants a say, Duncan.
WALTERS   But Jamie, he's…
WILSON   *(almost a shout)*   Let'm feenish!

WILSON *is a man who has earned and long enjoyed the respect of most of the Strathaven folk. The protest rapidly subsides.*

WILSON   Let him feenish whit he has tae say.

HAMILTON *(grudged relaxation)*   He'd better be bluidy quick aboot it, then.

WILSON *(getting off the rostrum)*   Ye may cairry oan noo, Maister Fallow.

FALLOW *(making the best of a bad job)*   I never intended to dae otherwise, Maister Wilson. *(Squares himself up again.)* This has just been a prime example of what I was warning you all against. The intemperate behaviour of far too many of your... so-called Radicals.

CHARLOTTE   Whit are ye so-called then, Fallow?

RONY   He's a so-called bloody man. *(Calls up to* FALLOW.*)* Away home an make your ould wummin's dinner!

FALLOW *(ignoring their amusement)*   My proposal is that the people of Strathaven should ask His Majesty for financial assistance, for those wishing to emigrate. To Canada, for instance. Or...

MACINTYRE   And big fat Geordie would chust hand over the money?

FALLOW   It would be a perfectly lawful way to proceed.

WALTERS   Goad man; your King Geordie's rookit!

HAMILTON   Yir King's loast mair money on weemin an gamblin as would transport every man, wummin an child in Scotland tae the ither end o the yirth an back!

WALTERS   It's because o him we're aw taxed tae ruination!

FALLOW   It would be a loan, not a gift! Them that accept would be bound to repay. In instalments.

JANET   It's Reform we're eftir, no forced emigration!

RONY *(to those around him)*   I've done all the emigratin I'll do in one lifetime! *(Calls to* FALLOW *angrily.)* Now will you come away down to hell outa that!

HAMILTON   Ay, you've had your say!

MACINTYRE   Come on. Down!

WALTERS   Ay, doon!

FALLOW *(hands out to stop them)*   All right! *(Making it clear he gives up.)* All right. I've said what I had to say. You'll no be warned. Just let me make it quite clear before I go that I publicly dissociate myself from all your proceedings here.

HAMILTON   Aw that's guid.

WALTERS   Ay, suits us fine.

FALLOW *(getting off the rostrum)*   Moderation is the yin constructive guidin principal in all thae things. Come on, Meg.

WILSON   It maun aye be the will o the majority that decides thae maitters, Maister Fallow.

FALLOW   If their bellies were stretched just a wee thing tighter the half of them wouldn't say cheep about Governments.

WILSON   For maist folk in Scotland aw the belly kens is the feel of the backbane!

FALLOW   For all that, you'll maybe find you've fewer on your side than you think, Maister Wilson. Guid day t'ye.

Some of the men bar his way as he tries to lead MEG *off.* THE MUSICIANS *begin to play 'Bruce's Address'. The men chant the words at him. It is horseplay, but for* MEG, *an attractive girl still in her teens, it is frightening.*

HAMILTON   'Wha – will be – a traitor knave?'
MACINTYRE   'Wha – can fill – a coward's grave?'
WALTERS   'Wha sae base as be a slave?'
ALL THREE   *(together)*   'Let him – turn – and flee!'
WILSON   *(recites against music, quietly serious)*
    'Wha for Scotland's King and Law,
    Freedom's sword will strongly draw,
    FREEMAN stand, or FREEMAN fa',
    Let him follow me!'
FALLOW   And that's another 'auld sang' that's long overdue for endin!
WILSON   The deepest memory's aye the last t'go.
FALLOW   It's Britain now, and thank God for it! Ye'd ken all about it if ye lived in some bits o the world!
MACINTYRE   *(bitterly)*   India, maybe. Where you'd have the land stolen from you and see your people butchered by armies of kilted men!
FALLOW   We're doin a damn sight more for the heathen as to'm, MacIntyre. And we're not needin the likes o you to come down here steerin-up honest workin bodies.
MEG   *(primly sarcastic)*   There's more nor one kind of heathen, y'know.
MACINTYRE   *(dismissively)*   Mallachd ort.
FALLOW   *(annoyed)*   Speak the king's English when you're speaking to my family, Duncan MacIntyre. Nane o your foreign curses here, m'lad!

RONY *makes a deep, mock-reverential bow to* FALLOW, *then reverses to present his backside.*

RONY   *(a smiling invitation)*   Poc mahone!
FALLOW   *(further annoyed by their laughter)*   Patriots an foreigners! Tryin tae set the clock back a hunder years! *(To* MEG *as he draws her away:)* There's just nae saying where it'll aw end up!
WILSON   In a better way o life for us?
FALLOW   *(stops)*   Singin a hymn like yon, it's a hingin you'll get!
WILSON   *(amused)*   It's a song that Burns wrote!
FALLOW   *(nastily)*   Like any other tradesman, he'd have his off days! *(Makes to leave again.)*
WILSON   *(calls)*   Oh Maister Fallow? *(When* FALLOW *stops and turns,* WILSON *begins to recite quietly.)*
    'Here's freedom to them that wad read,
    Here's freedom tae them that wad write,
    There's nane ever fear'd that the truth should be heard,
    But they wham the truth wad indite.'…

Whit kind o day did he write that oan?

FALLOW   He wasnae far short o bein grippit by the law himself!

HAMILTON *(reciting enthusiastically at* FALLOW*)*
'A fig for those by law protected!
Liberty's a glorious feast!'

WALTERS   'Courts for cowards were erectit,
Kirks were built t'please the priest!'

FALLOW *(moving back towards them)*   Ay, weel; you're nut the only yens ken your
Burns! Ah'll tell ye somethin else he said! *(Jabs it back at* WALTERS.*)*
'In Politics, if thou wouldst mix,
And *mean* thy fortunes be;
Bear this in mind, be deaf and blind,
Let *great* folk hear and see!'

JANET WALTERS *is a strong featured woman of about thirty. She has much of her
father's character in her, but with a sharper edge to her manner. She all but jabs
the fiercely brisk recitation up* FALLOW'S *nostrils.*

JANET   'If Ah'm designed yon lordin's slave
By nature's law designed
Why was an independent wish
E'er plantit in ma mind?'

FALLOW *(backing off rapidly)*   Oh, there's mair nor independent thoughts plantit in
your mind, Janet Walters. *(Nastily.)* Though you're maybe just your father's
daughter in that respect!

WILSON *(stung)*   Well at least ma lass *kens* her faither!

FALLOW *stiffens in shame and indignation.* MEG *is not sure what to make of it.
Some of the Strathaven folk find it funny, particularly* CHARLOTTE. *She puts her
index fingers to the side of her head like horns.*

CHARLOTTE *(to* WALTERS*)*   Cuckoo.

WALTERS *(making the sign back at her)*   Cuckoo!

Others join in the fun. Though no one addresses it directly to FALLOW, MARY
WILSON *is genuinely and deeply offended by this behaviour.*

MARY *(uncharacteristically sharp)*   Stop that, Davie Walters! Charlotte! Stop it!
The pair o ye should ken better!

The amusement subsides to continue more privately. MARY *turns to* FALLOW, *but
can find nothing to say. Trembling with rage and frustration* FALLOW *turns and
leaves without another word.* MEG, *close to tears, hesitates only a moment before
hurrying after him.*

MEG *(calls)* Father?

WILSON is *already regretting the words spoken in haste.*

MARY   That wasnae like ye, Jamie. *(He turns away from her.)* An it wasnae a
sensible thing tae dae at a time like this...
WILSON *(annoyed mainly with himself)* Wumman, Ah'm aware o that! *(Then
gestures an apology.)*
HAMILTON   Ah, whit odds. If the bitch doesnae ken she's the only yin that doesnae.
MARY *(rounding on him)* Village clishmaclavers!
CHARLOTTE   Aw, naw, but it's true, Mary.
MARY *(greatly displeased with her)* Oh, ye would hae the information!
CHARLOTTE   Oh, but dae Ah! For yin Hugmanay Jean Fallow got greetin-foo, an
she tellt me he hadnae pit a leg owre her since the nicht they got word they'd taen
the heid aff yon Marry-Antoinette!
MARY   That was mair nor twenty-five year ago!
CHARLOTTE   Ay, so? *(To the others.)* An whit age is Meg?

Her triumphantly knowing cackle gets the others going again. CHARLOTTE *is by
far the oldest of those present and, having tholed so much longer than the others,
she is not bound by the conventional limits. She is allowed to put her nose into
most domestic happenings in the village because usually her experience is
invaluable. So she knows everything that goes on – from accouchement to
fornication – and sometimes vice versa.*

HAMILTON *(on the rostrum)* Listen freens. Fallow yonder spoke tae ye o
moderation. The people o Avondale love moderation as weel as ony! But why talk
aboot it? Is there ony moderation in the way we're taxed? *(General agreement
there is not.)* Is there ony moderation in the patronage and pensions handit oot
b'the Government in London tae their ain kind? *(Louder negative from his
audience.) (The trump card.)* An was there ony moderation shown b'the
Government last year at Peterloo? When the cavalry rade their horses owre
innocent men, weemin, an children; hackin them doon wi their bluidy sabres?
(Roar of anger from his audience.) They tell us we owe allegiance tae the throne.
But the man whae occupies that throne has consistently spurned oor just pleas an
petitions. That bein the case, Ah say oor allegiance is noo forfeit! Men an weemin
o Avondale, Ah say... tae *Hell* wi gie'n oor allegiance tae such men!

A roar of approval for this, then freeze at its peak.
Silence.
The light goes as a spot picks out PLACEMAN, *on a rostrum to one side, looking
down on them... as he takes up a document the musicians play 'The Rising' as a
quiet background.*

PLACEMAN *(reading)* March the eighteenth, eighteen-twenty. To Lord Sidmouth, Secretary of State for the Home Department, London… M'Lord. On the assurances of reliable informants I am convinced that the radicals here are actively making final preparations for a general rising. I am advised that their plan is to set up a Scottish Assembly, or Parliament, in Edinburgh. The disaffected in England, *and* in Ireland, with whom they are in constant contact, are to set up similar assemblies… As already reported to you, the core of this movement is to be found among the weavers and cotton workers of the industrial towns and villages. They would appear to be imbued with the Republican ideals preached by that odious band of disaffected known as 'United Scotsmen' and 'United Irishmen'. Until now it has generally been believed that these criminals disappeared entirely after their abortive attempts to overthrow Government some twenty years ago. *(Significantly.)* Their aim, also, was the destruction of the unity of our Kingdom.

Scene 2

Strathaven. WILSON, HAMILTON *and* WALTERS.

WILSON   You lads'll hae tae learn tae guard your tongue better.

HAMILTON   Ehh, *(dismissing it)* there was a time for that!

WILSON *(pointedly)*   An Ah lived through it.

WALTERS   But Jamie, it's different noo. It's…

WILSON *(sharp)*   Oppressor and oppressed! Which never alters! (HAMILTON *doesn't want to hear the argument again.)* Rab, since Ah was a young man, aboot ages wi yoursel, Ah've worked wi every man o importance in the Reform movement in Scotland.

HAMILTON   What did aw their caution achieve?

WILSON *(sharp)*   Martyrdom?

WALTERS   Jamie, *(quietly insistent)* it is different this time. The folk are ready tae rise.

WILSON   They will be, given time.

HAMILTON   An given the truth!

WILSON   They'll get nae mair f'Gilbert McLeod!

HAMILTON *(unsettled)*   He micht yet get aff.

WILSON *(quiet, slightly scornful)*   The verdict oan Gilbert was decidit afore even they arrestit him. *(To* WALTERS.) An he published a lot o your writin in his paper. That'll no hae gone unnoticed.

WALTERS   Nane o't wis signed.

WILSON   The police raidit the shop.

HAMILTON   Gilbert wad hae burnt onythin that micht hae incriminatit Davie. He…

WILSON *(rounding on him)*   Had he time?

Neither of the younger men is sure.

WALTERS   He wis careful.

WILSON   Ay; *(nods)* an noo he's oan trial in the High Coort in Glesca for his life!
…Listen, Davie; Ah hae been a marked man maist o ma time. Ony son-in-law will
be a prime suspect for their… *(indicates the warnings behind them)* …Judas
Iscariots.

HAMILTON   *(a bit critical)*   A man be owre cautious.

WILSON   Cautious? B'christ, Rab, gin the time wis right Ah'd lead ye the high road
intae Glesca masel!

HAMILTON   Gin the folk are no ready noo they never will be!

WILSON   That's exactly whit they were sayin in Muir's time, but naebody rose tae
save him!

HAMILTON   *(grimly)*   They cam bluidy close tae it!

WILSON   Tam Muir was a freen o mine. He wis sentenced tae fourteen year in
Botany Bay an Ah could only staun there in the Coort an be ashamed o belangin
tae a people that could permit such injustice!

HAMILTON   This time they are ready!

WILSON   Ah saw Palmer, Maragarot, Gerald, Skirving; aw transportit alang wi
Muir, an *still* the people didnae rise! *(Over-riding the attempted reply.)* Ah saw
Watt executit in the same cause, Ah saw George Mealmaker o Dundee sentenced
tae fourteen year! Ah saw…

HAMILTON   There's nae question o your experience, Jamie; but this time the people
must rise! They've never been in such desperate straits afore!

WILSON   An never had a mair powerful and repressive regime haudin them there!

MARY'S *approach breaks the tension.*

MARY   Jamie? *(Indicates back where she has come from.)* Your brose is oan the
table, there. It's gettin cauld.

WILSON   Ay, Mary. Ah'll be in directly.

MARY   Wull ye tak some, Rab? Wull ye sit-in wi's?

HAMILTON   *(changes his mind about accepting)*   Naw, mistress; but thank ye.
(Turns away.)

MARY   *(trying to make it sound convincing)*   There's plenty.

HAMILTON   *(sour)*   B'christ, an for twenty year an mair there's been less even than
sufficient!

MARY *knows that to be true but would prefer the facts without the blasphemy.*

WALTERS   Ah'll get ye up the road.

MARY   Ay, ye dae that, Davie. For Ah'll no be accused o drawin ye awa frae your
ain wife's table.

WALTERS   *(affectionately)*   Oh, ye taught Janet weel, Mary. But mind ye, Ah believe your cookin still has that wee… *(He waggles a hand over the missing word.)*

MARY *pushes him towards* HAMILTON, *as pleased as ever with this piece of ritual family banter.*

MARY   Get oan wi ye. Dinna think tae turn ma heid the way ye dae wi them that's young an f…
WILSON *(cuts her off abruptly)*   Wheesht!

The others are startled.

WALTERS   Whit is't?

WILSON *gestures for silence. The sound of a sizeable cavalry troop approaching the village becomes more noticeable.*

HAMILTON *(to* WILSON)   Military!

He jumps up onto rostrum, followed by WILSON.

WALTERS   Is it the regulars?
HAMILTON *(turns back to him)*   It's the bloody Ayrshire Yeomanry!
WALTERS   Christ that's worse.
MARY *(frightened)*   Oh Jamie!
WILSON   It's aw richt, lass.
MARY   It's you they're eftir!
WILSON *(shakes head, a little amused)*   Ma reputations bad, but no that bad they'd sen a hunner cavalry t'grip me. *(The other Strathaven folk have begun to drift back to join the group watching the horsemen approach.) (Descending to her.)* They go wherever there's a meetin, noo. Just tryin tae intimidate folk wi their… Volunteer show.
WALTERS *(bitterly)*   Part-time sodgers; full-time fairmers, merchants, an manufacturers! Yon's the bastards we hae t'worry aboot!
MACINTYRE   Ay, they'll fight fiercer then any Regular to keep what they've gained.
HAMILTON   Stolen! For they own naethin that wasnae wrocht for by us!

Boos and jeers now from another small crowd offstage.

MAN'S VOICE *(offstage)*   Awa hame an mind yir ain affairs!
CHARLOTTE *(calls)*   Pair bluidy excuses for Scoatsmen!
MAN'S VOICE *(offstage)*   Traitors tae your ain kind!
WALTERS *(calls)*   Ah saw nane o ye at Waterloo!
HAMILTON *(calls)*   Naw, but they werenae missin at Peterloo!

The Strathaven folk begin to hiss – a protest sound that does not betray the protester.

JANET *(angry)*   Oh, wad ye look at the swagger o him that's leadin them!

RONY   Ay, him on the big grey. *(Calls.)* Hey sour-milk Jock? Away home an muck out your byre!

FALLOW *(greatly offended)*   That's Colonel Boswell you're aw shoutin at!

HAMILTON *(whips round on FALLOW)*   …Young Auchinleck?

FALLOW   Ay, Auchinleck!

That was all HAMILTON needed.

HAMILTON *(a roar)*   Lord Sidmouth's bloody butcher!

BOSWELL *(offstage)*   Squadron, halt!

The cavalry, close by now, clatter to an irregular stop. The jingle of the harness is heard, the snorting and neighing of animals. JANET reaches for HAMILTON and drags him off the rostrum. She and her husband put themselves in front of him. CHARLOTTE moves to help cover him too.

A CORPORAL appears behind them, to one side and remains on guard there, sabre drawn. A TROOPER takes up the position opposite. As the Strathaven folk react to this trap, BOSWELL approaches from a third direction.

In his early forties, he is a big, well set up man, with a naturally commanding presence. Like the other two soldiers he wears the Ayrshire Yeomanry uniform of Glengarry, blue tunic, white breeches and black riding boots.

BOSWELL *(menacingly)*   What man called out just now? *(Advancing slowly towards them.)* Come away, *(imperiously)* I'll have the truth from someone here! *(There is no reaction, only cold sullen stares. Suddenly, unexpectedly, he draws his sabre, letting the blade pass dangerously close to the nearest face.)* There's my blade, then. *(Those nearest fall back individually when he hacks at the air as if testing the feel of the weapon.)* Fetch out your best, Radical, steel. *(He establishes and holds a dominance before moving slowly on past them. In sarcastic Scots accent:)* Ye've grown gey quiet! *(Letting amusement show for a moment as he speaks to his guard.)* It seems the Strathaven men are better at words, than deeds. *(Without turning his head WILSON checks HAMILTON'S reaction. JANET puts a hand to him too.)* *(Stops, turns.)* I'm disappointed. *(Suddenly quite brutal.)* I promised my men they'd be riding up to their bridle reins in Radical blood! *(Turns and continues offstage.)*

HAMILTON, *barely able to contain his frustrated rage, shakes himself free of the restraining hands.*

HAMILTON   Ah've faced better men mony a time!

WILSON *(quietly)* Oan equal terms. No like this.

JOHN FALLOW *has gone offstage after* BOSWELL. MEG *has stopped to flirt with* THE TROOPER.

CHARLOTTE *(fairly quiet – for her)* Did somebody say yon was Boswell?
WILSON That's him, Charlotte.
CHARLOTTE The son o Doactor Johnson's Boswell?
WILSON The same.
CHARLOTTE *(amused)* Gin he's onythin like his faither he'll be ridin aw richt. *(Chuckles.)* But no up tae's bridle in blood. He'll be up tae's ballops here in somethin else awtegither! *(Toothless cackle.)*

The men are amused despite – or because of – the tense situation.

MARY *(genuinely shocked)* Charlotte!
JANET *(unable to hide her amusement)* Oh Charlotte ye'll get hung yin day.
MARY That's a terrible thing t'say!
CHARLOTTE Ahaw, *(rejecting the protest)* like faither like son!
WILSON *(more relaxed)* Ay, they're a queer mixture the Boswells.
HAMILTON *(still smouldering)* Ah'd like tae steer that mixture wi a pike!
BOSWELL *(offstage)* Come on, then! Where are all the Strathaven Radicals we've heard about?
WILSON Dinnae underestimate'm, Rab. *(To the others.)* But ye'd scarcely credit a blood-lustin Tory the like o that wad raise funds for a memorial tae Burns.
JANET *(surprised)* Did he, faither?
WILSON Ay, did he, Janet. No twa month past.
WALTERS Yin human heid can haud some gey queer thochts as neebors!
HAMILTON *(bitterly)* Some heids haud nae thochts at aw! Look at yon bitch, Fallow!

With her coy posturings MEG *has succeeded in drawing and holding* THE TROOPER'S *interest. He is a naive young man, dull offspring of an equally dull Kilmarnock merchant, but for the moment he is being made to feel quite the hero.*

JANET *(to her husband)* Maybe she doesnae ken her faither, but there's nae doot she's her mither's dochter.
MARY Oh, she's just an empty heidit lassie, Janet; fair teen oan wi the uniforms.
CHARLOTTE Christ, an she needna bother uniforms, Mary. Ah never yet saw gowd braid oan a man's coack!
MARY Charlotte!
WALTERS Hoo mony hae ye seen, Charlotte?
CHARLOTTE Oh, Ah've *(kicking a heel in towards herself)* dinged a few in, in ma day, Davie!

BOSWELL'S *reappearance puts a sudden end to their fun. He strides calmly and confidently through the group again, fixing on each man in turn a look that is part challenge, part intimidation with its suggestion of memorising for identification purposes. He stops near* JANET.

BOSWELL   We have already made some arrests, in Ayrshire... *(To* JANET:) You'd find you'd made a damned cold bed ... without your man. *(He exits roaring out the command:)* Headquarters squadrawwwwwwwwwn!

Four booming drumbeats spotlight THE MUSICIANS, *on their feet for a vigorous, use of the heroic jingo song 'The Plains of Waterloo'. Apart from a simple drum rhythm they sing unaccompanied.*

MALE SINGERS
   Here's a health to George, our royal King,
   And long may he govern!
   Likewise the Duke of Wellington,
   That noble son of Erin!
   Three years are added to our time.
   With pay and pensions too;
   For now we are recorded all –
   As 'The Men of Waterloo!'

Spotlight on JANET *as she sings 'The Men of Waterloo' to the same tune.*

JANET   *(angrily)*
   There's a fortune for their Iron Duke,
   An mony a gift o lan',
   Tho he had but yin life tae lose,
   Like ony ither man;
   The sodger left wi twae black stumps
   Maun crawl his hale life thro.

The shadowy figures of the other women are seen, shawled, and individually indistinguishable.

ALL WOMEN   For aw hae been forgetten, wha –
   Were 'Men o Waterloo'.
MALE SINGERS   On the eighteenth, in the morning
   Both armies did advance,
   On this side stood brave Albion's sons,
   On that the pride of France;
   The fate of Europe in his hands
   Each man his sabre drew,

And death or victory was the word –
On the Plains of Waterloo.
JANET   Fell mony a lad on Flanders field,
Was buried where he lay,
And there's nae pockets in a shroud
Will haud a hero's pay;
There's bounty for dependents
O aw the officer crew,
ALL WOMEN   But naethin for the widow's o – 'The Men o Waterloo'.

The drum beats fade into the distance. JANET *sings the last verse slowly, firmly – very bitterly.*

JANET   Oor orphan bairns, at six year auld
In factories maun slave,
Or sleep ablow the bridge's arch
Tae wait an early grave;
If pox and fever spare them yet,
They've mair time for tae rue,
ALL WOMEN   That ever they had faithers, wha –
Were 'Men o Waterloo'.

Spotlight on PLACEMAN *alone.*

PLACEMAN   *(reading from document)*   March the twenty-first, eighteen-twenty. To Lord Sidmouth, Secretary of State for the Home Department, London... M'Lord. I have been informed of your opinions on the matter of the disaffected of this place... It is with all the more regret, therefore, that I have to report an increase in unrest. Evil-minded persons have set fire to employers' premises; in places so far apart as Port Patrick in Wigtonshire, Paisley in Renfrewshire, Kirkcaldy in Fife... However, I am pleased to inform your Lordship that our endeavours to infiltrate Government agents in the Radical organisations have been completely successful. Some of our informants have succeeded in attaining positions of trust; even of importance.

Scene 3

LORD SIDMOUTH'S *office.* SIDMOUTH *leads the way in, followed by* BOSWELL *still in uniform but minus Glengarry and spurs.*

SIDMOUTH   Can you be quite certain, Colonel Boswell, that the rabble do not possess any significant number of cannons?

BOSWELL   As Lord Lieutenant of Ayrshire, I can say that in that county they possess none whatsoever.

SIDMOUTH *(turns)*   Elsewhere?

BOSWELL   There have been widespread searches in all the manufacturing areas. Armaments previously carried by merchant vessels have been rendered completely ineffective.

SIDMOUTH   Are you sure?

BOSWELL   Quite sure, m'Lord.

SIDMOUTH *(weighs up his visitor)*   …What about small arms? *(Moving on.)*

BOSWELL *(lightly)*   A few old fowling pieces. *(Amused.)* Oh, and some relics of the Jacobite troubles!

SIDMOUTH *is a tall, somewhat pompous man, and not at all easily amused. He turns.*

SIDMOUTH *(stiffly)*   Have you any reason to suppose they are no longer lethal?

BOSWELL   Well, no m'Lord; but…

SIDMOUTH   Confiscate them.

BOSWELL   Such a detailed search would take a great deal of time, m'Lord. We…

SIDMOUTH   Time, Colonel Boswell, is what we may not have! *(Resumes his icy manner.)* Doubtless you have read of the attempt last month to assassinate the entire Cabinet?

BOSWELL   News of the Cato Street affair was received in North Britain with considerable distress, and anger.

SIDMOUTH *(studying him closely)*   Indeed?

BOSWELL   May I say, personally, how relieved I am the plot was discovered in time.

SIDMOUTH   The plot, Colonel Boswell, was financed by and controlled from this room. (BOSWELL'S *reaction pleases* SIDMOUTH, *though that might not be very obvious to some people.)* Oh not instigated here… Simply *(gestures for the word)* …developed.

BOSWELL *(still puzzled)*   The Cabinet didn't intend to dine at Lord Harrowby's?

SIDMOUTH   We made arrangements to dine, individually, and quite safely; we then met afterwards at the Prime Minister's home to await the outcome of our efforts.

BOSWELL   …I had no idea.

SIDMOUTH   There has been some conjecture that the two bags, specially purchased by the conspirators to contain the severed heads of Lord Castlereagh and myself, might actually have been paid for by the Treasury. *(He permits himself the slight movement of the facial muscles that serves to indicate when he is amused.)* Lord Liverpool suggested this might come under the heading of… capital expenditure! *(He actually almost chuckles.)*

BOSWELL *(amused)*   Oh, capital indeed, m'Lord *(going to him)* capital indeed…

SIDMOUTH'S *abrupt ending of the amusement stops* BOSWELL *from clapping a comradely hand on the other man's shoulder. He lets it fall to smooth his own hair.*

SIDMOUTH *(dry and sharp again)* Parliament will not sanction anti-terrorist measures unless in a state of active alarm. Nothing alarms Parliament so much as an active terrorist. But! … The Home Office must be in control *(Moves away from him.)* We have that control here in the South. Ireland is under the care of Lord Castlereagh. … *(Turns.)* Which leaves only some doubt about your countrymen, Colonel Boswell.

BOSWELL *(Going to him. Earnest)* Indemnify me against the legal consequences, m'Lord, and I shall not be long in dispelling that doubt!

SIDMOUTH And will act as necessary?

BOSWELL Would have done so ere this were not for a handful of Whig lawyers, ever ready to leap to the defence of these miscreants!

SIDMOUTH A pity our Constitution allows the benefit of trial to even the most malevolent of wretches.

BOSWELL It would not be difficult to think of a more certain justice… and quicker!

SIDMOUTH The army have sometimes disappointed me.

BOSWELL I'll wager you will not be disappointed in the North British Yeomanry!

SIDMOUTH You seem certain.

BOSWELL They are volunteers, m'Lord. With a great deal at stake.

SIDMOUTH *(decides he has a right-thinking man here)* Colonel Boswell, the day may not be far off when I can offer you a suitable opportunity. Free from adverse… repercussions.

BOSWELL *(grimly)* Then for me, that day cannot arrive soon enough!

SIDMOUTH *(drawing him away)* I'm glad we are agreed. A little bloodletting is not always an unhealthy thing. *(Gestures the way out.)* Pour encourager les autres, *(hint of a smile)* to borrow a phrase.

They exit.

SINGERS 'Twas then that the weavers did rise and tak arms,
In manhood resolved tae live freely or die,
'Twas then that they drilled the sharp pikes in the gloamin,
'Twas then the betrayal by traitor and spy.

Scene 4

Strathaven smiddy. THE REVEREND JAMES LAPSLIE, *a big, black, menacing figure of a man, is standing just inside the door. With long flowing white hair. He has a build and manners more suited to a farmer than a minister. He advances slowly on*

WALTERS *and* MACINTYRE. MACINTYRE *has a blacksmith's hammer and tongs in his hands.* WALTERS *is holding a sickle.*

LAPSLIE   You'll be the smith, then?
MACINTYRE   I am.
LAPSLIE   Mmmm… Who would you be?
WALTERS   Just a tradesman, meenister.
LAPSLIE   With time on your hands?
WALTERS   *(of the sickle)*   It wastes time workin wi bad gear.
MACINTYRE   I'm putting a new edge on that heuk for him.
LAPSLIE   Are you throng with work, then?
MACINTYRE   As busy as can be expected in times like these.
LAPSLIE   Mmmm. *(He noses about the place.)* You wouldn't be busy making pikes?
MACINTYRE   I would not. And there's no use looking for any.
LAPSLIE   *(sharp)*   Watch your tongue, man… It's a trait of reformers to show little respect for the Kirk's representative! *(Resumes prowling.)* 'My son, fear then the Lord and the King: And meddle not, with them that are given to change: For them calamity shall rise suddenly, and who knoweth the ruin of them both?' *(Rapidly.)* Has anyone approached you to make pikes for the Radicals?
MACINTYRE   No.
LAPSLIE   Were you asked, what would be your response?
MACINTYRE   I would refuse.
LAPSLIE   And report it?
MACINTYRE   No.
LAPSLIE   Why not?
MACINTYRE   Because the man making such a request would be either a fool… *(quieter)* or a spy.
LAPSLIE   …What do they call you?
MACINTYRE   MacIntyre. Duncan MacIntyre.

LAPSLIE *silently transfers the question to* WALTERS.

WALTERS   Davie Walters.
LAPSLIE   Mhmm… *(Prowls again.)* Do you know one James Wilson in this town?
MACINTYRE   I, eh…
WALTERS   *(quickly)*   The smith's no long settled here. He doesnae ken awbody yet.
LAPSLIE   …In that case, I'll have your answer.
WALTERS   There's a great mony Wilsons in these parts … an no a few cried James.
LAPSLIE   *(not bothering to conceal his feelings)*   This one will be readily identified! A man in his sixties. A well known and unrepentant agitator most of his life! A Radical!
WALTERS   It's no awtegither uncommon noo.
LAPSLIE   There's only one of his calibre in this town! … *(Tries a persuasive approach.)* The authorities would look in a kindly way on any man helping to

preserve the peace of the Realm.

WALTERS   Oor ain meenister has already made that clear, frae the pulpit.

LAPSLIE   And? *(The two men remain motionless. Rapidly again:)* Are you aware, MacIntyre, that siding with Radicals is a sure passport to hell? Were you *tempted* to make pikes?

MACINTYRE   I was not.

LAPSLIE   Mind how you answer! *(Working up from a slow start.)* 'Simeon and Levi are brethren; instruments of cruelty are in their habitation!' Have you instruments of cruelty in your habitation, MacIntyre?

MACINTYRE   I have not.

LAPSLIE   Walters? (WALTERS *shakes his head.)* 'Oh, my soul! Come not into their secret; unto their assembly, mine honour be not thou united!' Were you tempted to join one of their unholy Reformers' unions?

WALTERS   Ah wis not.

LAPSLIE   Never do then! 'For in their danger they slew a man, and in their self-will they digged down a wall! *(In full flight.)* Cursed* be their anger, for it was fierce! And their wrath, for it was cruel! I will divide them in Jacob, and scatter them in Israel!' Genesis forty-nine, verses five to seven! *(He moves closer to them.)* *(Slyly.)* But it is also written in the good book that 'when thou doest *alms,* let not thy left hand know what thy right hand doeth... That thine *alms* may be in secret; and thy Father, which seeth in secret, himself shall *reward* thee, openly.'

He waits expectantly, his mouth half open. MACINTYRE *turns back to his bench.*

MACINTYRE   I have work to do.

LAPSLIE   Maybe you, then, would eh, ... *(glances at* MACINTYRE'S *back, then taps the side of his own nose)* show me my way through the town?

WALTERS *does not trust himself to speak. He brushes past* LAPSLIE *to join* MACINTYRE.

LAPSLIE *(jaw snaps shut)*   Just so! *(He moves back towards the entrance. Turns.)* But should heathen Radical principles tempt any man of this town to be careless of his immortal soul, let him not forget that a wretch convicted of Treason is first hanged... *(almost relishing it)* then beheaded... then his body is butchered, for public display in the four corners of the Kindom! *(Exits.)*

WALTERS *(slowly at first, trembling with rage)*
    'God knows, Ah'm no the thing Ah should be,
    Nor am Ah even the thing Ah could be,
    But twinty times Ah raither would be *(striking the hook into the bench)*
    An aetheist clean
    Than under gospel colours hid be
    Just for a screen!'

MACINTYRE *(quiet fury)*   We should have drowned the bastard! I should have held him there in the horse trough till the breath bubbles stopped and his sightless eyes looked up through the water at me out of hell!

The music for 'Pensioner Jamie' builds slowly up.

WALTERS   Ah, b'Christ, Duncan, *(relaxing)* maybe we did better tae gie'm naethin t'report. He's a dangerous man, the Reverend James Lapslie.

MACINTYRE   *(reciting against the music)*
My name's James Lapslie, I preach and I pray,
And for my 'informing' expect a good pay,
To the High Court of Session I went with my lies,
Self appointed, the foulest, of government spies.

THE SINGERS *take up the song in a lively manner.*

SINGERS   He spurred thro tae Embro his tale tae relate,
Tae swear perjured oaths, for tae seal a man's fate,
But the Lord o Justiciary couldn't use him in Law,
For even Corruption a limit must draw!

LAPSLIE, *a shadowy figure now, is seen standing in the distance. He is aware of what is being said, and* THE SINGERS *make it clear they refer to him.*

But England's King Geordie, and the traitor Dundas,
Made use o the witness that he did harass;
Tam Muir got transported tae Botany Bay,
(slow for last line)
And he got gold guineas for the part he did play!

Scene 5

Strathaven. WILSON *enters, followed by his wife,* HAMILTON, *and* JANET.

MARY   It's ye they're eftir, Jamie. From whit wis said, he kent fine whae he wantit afore he cam here!

WILSON   Ay, Lapslie kens me aw richt. Since awa back in Muir's time.

MACINTYRE   *(bitterly)*   It's a wonder he's been allowed to live as long.

MARY   *(quiet rebuke)*   That's no worthy o ye, Duncan.

HAMILTON   The man's livin proof that your Goad is deid!

WALTERS   *(stopping* MARY'S *reaction)*   Weel at the verra least, Mary, Lapslie proves that Goad's no oamnipotent. The Almichty wad need t'be hauf daft t'alloo yon t'represent'm!

MARY   That's enough o talk like that.

MACINTYRE   Oh, there's scarcely one o them that doesn't misuse the pulpit for his own private purpose.

HAMILTON   Ay! The biggest set o hypocritical bastards that ever...

MARY   *(shocked into yelling at him)*   An that's enough f'you, Rab Hamilton!

HAMILTON *turns away, shaking his head.*

WILSON   *(quietly)*   It's nae mair nor's true, lass. You...

MARY   *(covering her ears)*   Ah'll no listen!

WALTERS   Christ, that's how we're in this situation! Folk dinna want t'hear the truth!

JANET   *(quietly)*   Davie.

WALTERS   Damn it, you agree wi me!

JANET   But if ma mither doesnae want t'hear onythin against the Kirk, she's perfectly ent...

WALTERS   The Kirk!

MARY   Ay, the Kirk!

WALTERS   *(begins to recite, moving away from them)*   'Oh, ye pair, silly, Priest-ridden boddies, attend...'

MARY   Ah'll no bide t'hear blasphemy, mind!

WALTERS   'To ane that wad caution ye noo, *(to* MARY*)* as a friend! Against black coats, an grauvats sae white...'

JANET   Davie, that'll dae.

WALTERS   *(to the larger audience)*   'For greater imposters can scarcely exist, Than some whae are dubbed wi the title o – Priest!'

MARY   Ye're nae guidson o mine when ye speak like that, Davie Walters!

WALTERS   'For their plan is the pair human mind tae mislead, An barter their mystical jargon, for breid!'

MARY   Ah'll no bide t'hear sic blasphemy! *(Turns away.)*

WALTERS   *(quieter, returning towards the group)*   'Wi their black coats, an grauvats sae white.'

WILSON   *(Gestures he should not pursue the subject. Calls.)*   Mary?

MARY   *(stops)*   It's no richt tae talk against Goad's Holy Wark in sic a mainner! *(To* WALTERS:)* Aw meenisters dinna behave the same, ye ken!

WALTERS   'Oh ay, amang chaff, ye'll find pickles o wheat!'

MARY *exits, hands over ears.*

JANET   Stoap it noo! That's enough!

WILSON   *(moving after his wife)*   Mary. Come back here, lass.

JANET   Ye're ower ready t'force thae rhymes doon folk's thrapples. An ye've nae business upsetting your ain kith and kin!

WALTERS   It was written tae upset them!

HAMILTON   God knows, the maist o them's had their minds in religion's fetters lang enough.

JANET *(rounding on him)*   Well ma mither doesnae like it so that's an end o'it!

WILSON *returns to break the silence.*

WILSON *(worried)*   Ah'd be happier gin Ah kent the state o their plans in Glesca.

HAMILTON *(confident)*   Ah'll wager things are fair hummin aw-where!

JANET *(concerned)*   Faither, Ah think mither was richt aboot Lapslie.

WILSON   He learnt naethin aboot me, Janet, that he didnae ken awready.

JANET   He micht come back. Or somebody else!

WILSON   They'll hae spies aw-where, lass. We'll attract least attention in oor ain hame toon.

WALTERS   Ay, but for aw that, Jamie; maybe it wad be nae harm for ye t'get oot o Strathaven. Just for a while.

WILSON   Ah've lived in this village aw ma born days, son. *(Quietly firm.)* Gin it's tae be confrontation, it's on this soil ma feet wull be plantit.

A loud distinctive knock on the doors startles them.

WALTERS *(eager)*   Matt!

MACINTYRE, *nearest the door, hurries to answer.*

MACINTYRE   Come in, lad.

RONY *(as he is bustled to the fire)*   Well boys.

MACINTYRE *(to the others)*   Get him over to the heat, first.

Having walked the high moorland road into Glasgow and back, a total of thirty four miles in sleety March weather and inadequate clothing, RONY *is weary, droukit, and chitterin with cold.*

HAMILTON *(eagerly)*   What's the news, Matt?

RONY *(huddling himself for warmth)*   Ah God help us, and there's news all right! Glasgow's buzzin we near as many rumours as red-coats!

JANET   Sit in. *(Putting a blanket round his shoulders.)* Keep that roon ye.

RONY *(Nods to her. Speaks to the others.)*   Did you hear about McLeod?

WILSON   The trial's feenished?

RONY   ...Guilty. Five year in Botany Bay.

Reaction from everybody.

MACINTYRE *(to himself)*   For printing nothing but the truth.

95

WALTERS *(breathes it)*   Christ!

HAMILTON   For a man in McLeod's health, that's a daith sentence!

RONY   Ay it is. *(Bitterly.)* For there's a few alive in Van Diemen's Land at the end o three.

WILSON, *very thoughtful, drifts away from them.*

JANET *(offering a small bowl)*   Will ye tak a hot drink, Matt?

RONY   Ah, Janet, God bliss ye lass. I've scarce had a thing since yesterday. *(Sips eagerly, then the excitement of his news temporarily dispels hunger.)* Ah but listen, boys, sure we're just about there! God it's like the ould country in ninety-eight all over again!

WALTERS   Whit stage are they at, then?

HAMILTON   Are they ready?

RONY   Ready? They're out in the open, practisin their drill wi pikes!

WILSON *(sharp)*   Ye saw that for yirsel?

RONY   Last night! Even on the Glasgow Green!

WALTERS   Did the sodgers try tae stop them?

RONY   They didn't, Davie. And they didn't even look as if they wanted to.

WALTERS *(firmly)*   They're oan oor side!

MACINTYRE   I knew they would be!

HAMILTON   It was never in doot!

WILSON *(holding off their enthusiasm)*   Ah, steady noo. Steady... there could be ither reasons.

HAMILTON *(impatient)*   Whit reasons?

WILSON   Ah could think o several.

WALTERS   Jamie! The sodgers hae less love o the Government even nor us!

WILSON   The regulars! No the volunteers!

RONY   Oh, and there's plenty volunteers. Hunter of the *Glasgow Herald's* got over a thousand men in his Corps already.

WILSON *(not really surprised)*   As mony as that.

RONY   Ay, and half as many again in the Glasgow Armed Association.

WILSON *(very concerned)*   That's the danger! *(Moving away from them again.)* That's the enemy!

HAMILTON   Listen, lads; wi as little's a third o the regulars on oor side we'd rin that vermin intae the bluidy Clyde! We kin burst the Tolbooth open an free McLeod oorsels!

WILSON   Hoo mony pikes d'the Glesca Committee think we kin rely oan?

RONY   Some said Paisley could raise two, three, maybe four thousand.

WILSON *(sharp)*   Maybe?

RONY   Well the rumours are wild.

HAMILTON   Whit aboot Glesca itsel?

RONY   Och, God; three thousand, five thousand, ten thousand!

HAMILTON *(to WILSON)*   Ten thoosan pikes, Jamie!

WILSON   But nae firm figures! *(To* RONY:*)* Am Ah richt?

RONY   *(disappointed after all his efforts)*   …I did my best.

WILSON   Mmm. It doesnae sound t'me as if they're ready yet.

WALTERS   Glesca's only yin place! There's Ayr, Kilmarnock, Lanark, Falkirk! Just aboot every ither toon in the country!

WILSON   We need news, no rumours! That's whit wis wrang in ninety-eight, Matt. Wis it no?

RONY   *(forced to agree)*   Ay, was it. Rumours an… *(the ritual spit)* informers.

MACINTYRE   *(quietly)*   There's no rumour about the pikes, Jamie.

WALTERS   *(seizing at that)*   Duncan kens three workshops in Ruglen alane. The men workin aw nicht an turnin them oot b'the hunner!

HAMILTON   *(of* RONY*)*   An he saw the lads drillin them oot in the open!

WALTERS   *(an appeal)*   Jamie!

WILSON   *(comes to a decision)*   Matt, listen. Could ye go back intae Glesca?

RONY   *(dismayed)*   Now?

WILSON   In the mornin.

RONY   *(weary acceptance)*   I will, surely; but I hope someone can give me the len of another pair o boots.

JANET   Are yours feenished, Matt?

RONY   They feel as if they are, girl. *(Holds up foot.)* But you'll be able to see better than me.

The sole of the boot is nearly all gone, and dirt has caked the blood all over it.

JANET   Oh Matt, yir foot's in a terrible mess!

RONY   Sure I thought that on the road back but with seventeen mile still in front o me I was too frightened to look!

JANET   *(removing boot)*   Ye'll need t'wash aw that bluid an dirt oot.

WALTERS   *(after examining* RONY'S *foot)*   He kin traivel nae further oan that, Jamie.

WILSON   *(takes a brief look, then turns to* HAMILTON*)*   Rab?

HAMILTON   *(already on his way)*   Leave it t'me.

JANET   *(helping* RONY *up)*   Come oan, Matt.

WILSON   *(calls)*   Could ye mak it back the nicht?

HAMILTON   *(eager nod)*   Ay, were it twice as faur! *(Exits.)*

Supported by JANET *and* WALTERS, RONY *is led off for attention to his foot.*

RONY   *(in some pain)*   The thing is, boys… I've got a gentleman's fine soft feet… The only trouble is… *(sharp pain)* I didn't get his bloody horse an carriage as well!

PLACEMAN *speaks urgently against the music of 'The Rising'.*

PLACEMAN   To Lord Sidmouth. Secretary of State of the Home Department.

London. M'Lord. Thanks to the efforts of loyal informants we now have the name of every leading Radical in the West of Scotland. The mass of the disaffected are still not aware of our efforts. If we are allowed to act now we may be in a position to arrest the entire Glasgow committee!

Scene 6

Lord Sidmouth's office. SIDMOUTH *has entered, followed by* BOSWELL.

SIDMOUTH *(calls)*   Sir Placeman?

PLACEMAN, *slightly startled, hurries down to join them.*

PLACEMAN   M'Lord?

SIDMOUTH   You are not to make such arrests. Not on any account.

PLACEMAN   But some of the men on the Glasgow Committee are members of the Provisional Government for Scotland!

SIDMOUTH   Some of the members of the Provisional Government for Scotland... are Government men. (SIDMOUTH *enjoys* PLACEMAN'S *surprise.)* I will provide you with a list of those who are not to be arrested. Or if arrested, to be set free without charge; and of course, without publicity.

PLACEMAN   ...Of course.

SIDMOUTH *(beginning to pace the floor)*   Colonel Boswell is of the opinion that the Radicals in North Britain enjoy considerable popular support. Do you agree with that assessment?

PLACEMAN   It is not so much a question of support, m'Lord. The bulk of the working class is Radical.

SIDMOUTH *(turns)*   And that evil has been allowed to fester?

PLACEMAN   It was not always apparent on the surface.

SIDMOUTH *(icily)*   A cancerous condition seldom is. *(Resumes his pacing.)* When may we expect this... uprising, Colonel Boswell?

BOSWELL   Left to their own devices, I believe the disaffected would need at least another six months to be fully trained and ready.

PLACEMAN *(in answer to the silently transferred question)*   They certainly are not yet prepared; but any spark might serve to trigger them off now.

SIDMOUTH   We are now in a position to provide such a spark. Suppose we are also able to convince the North Britain rabble that the Day of Liberty had arrived. What then? Mm?

BOSWELL   Then for the first time I would have the opportunity to catch the vipers out of their lairs.

SIDMOUTH   Sir Placeman?

PLACEMAN *(troubled at this turn)*   If we are allowed to act now, m'Lord Sidmouth, we may avoid bloodshed all together.

SIDMOUTH   Exactly.

PLACEMAN *(shocked)*   …After the events of Peterloo, I should have thought the Government was seeking to avoid adverse criticism.

SIDMOUTH   We would not be criticised for putting down armed terrorists.

PLACEMAN   The use of agents-provocateurs?

BOSWELL   Do you deny the use of informers?

PLACEMAN   Gathering intelligence is one thing, Colonel Boswell. Deliberate provocation of violence is quite something else!

SIDMOUTH   The Home Office may not provoke violence, Sir, but it certainly has the right to control when it is to happen!

BOSWELL   We are dealing with men actively planning insurrection! Many of them experienced ex-soldiers! Should we allow *them* to choose the time and place?

SIDMOUTH   Is it not our bounden duty to seek the greatest possible advantage for the forces of Law and Order?

PLACEMAN *(greatly troubled)*   …I still believe we can arrest the leaders and put an end to the conspiracy now.

BOSWELL   And find these leaders replaced within a week?

SIDMOUTH   You said yourself they have widespread support.

PLACEMAN   With the greatest possible respect m'Lord; but perhaps the Government should have spent more time examining the causes of that support.

SIDMOUTH *(suddenly losing temper)*   Damn your causes, Placeman. Will you obey our instructions or not?

PLACEMAN   …It has always been my intention to serve Government to the utmost of my humble abilities.

SIDMOUTH *(quite in control again)*   Thank you.

PLACEMAN   Because of that, I feel I must ask if your Lordship is quite convinced that any violence, once started, can be adequately controlled.

SIDMOUTH   Oh yes. It shall be controlled. *(Moves closer to him.)* Between units of the regular army, and regiments of the various volunteer corps, I have amassed, north of Carlisle, a larger army than was used against Charles Edward Stuart in seventeen-forty-five. *(There is nothing* PLACEMAN *can now say.* SIDMOUTH'S *gesture indicates that they should retire.)* Please wait in the outer room.

The two men bow and exit. THE MUSICIANS *play a set of 'Variations' by Mozart.* SIDMOUTH *slowly pivots round to:*

Scene 7

The King's Chambers. They appear to be empty, but GEORGE *is heard, somewhere, crooning to the music in a rather pleasant baritone.*

SIDMOUTH *(calls)* Your Majesty…? *(He moves to be able to see away into the inner recesses.)* … *(Louder.)* Your Majesty? *(Moves closer to the rostra.)* … *(Impatiently loud.)* Your Majes…

GEORGE *(popping up unexpectedly close)* Oh really, Sidmouth!

SIDMOUTH *(startled)* I eh, do beg your Majesty's pardon.

GEORGE *(furious)* We left distinct instructions we were not to be disturbed!

SIDMOUTH I am sorry.

GEORGE Not on any account!

SIDMOUTH It is a matter of grave national importance.

GEORGE Then it certainly has nothing to do with us!

THE KING *prepares to resettle his vast bulk back out of sight, in the supine position in which it was disturbed.*

SIDMOUTH I am sorry, but I simply must speak with your Majesty!

GEORGE *(with very bad grace)* Ohhhh! *(Struggling to reach the perpendicular.)* Well, God's blood man; help us up! Up! Up! *(His twenty-odd stone enveloped in a gaudy tent of a dressing gown he stumbles on down past* SIDMOUTH.*)* What the devil can be so urgent we're expected to deal with damned business in the middle of the day?

SIDMOUTH *(pompous)* I regret to have to inform your Majesty that we seem to be threatened by a further outbreak of…

He breaks off to watch GEORGE *go towards the* MUSICIANS *frantically waving his arms for silence and puffing air past his lips.*

GEORGE How can anyone possibly enjoy Mozart in this man's company! *(Gestures briefly, apologetically, they should forget it.* THE MUSICIANS *accept their lot philosophically. To* SIDMOUTH:*)* In God's name, man; what are you trying to tell me?

SIDMOUTH *(deliberately lets him have it unsweetened)* The North British rabble is preparing for armed insurrection.

GEORGE *(his jowls quiver, but he bears up well)* …Hang the leaders. *(Turning back to his lair.)* It worked at Nottingham.

SIDMOUTH We must first find them guilty.

GEORGE *(stops, turns)* Why?

SIDMOUTH *(evenly)* Because if British justice is not to be discredited in the eyes of the world, even Radical agitators must be seen to benefit from it.

GEORGE *(sourly)* In the aftermath of the late revolution in France, your scruples bring us great comfort!

SIDMOUTH Your Majesty's person is safe from all harm in England… *(Checks any interruption.)* So long as the affairs of the government are in proper hands.

GEORGE   We have already suffered attempts on our life!

SIDMOUTH   There will be no revolution here.

GEORGE   Doubtless poor Louis Seize had the same assurances from his advisors!

SIDMOUTH   England is not France.

GEORGE   The rabble is the rabble!

SIDMOUTH   ...I believe your Majesty may have misunderstood. Whilst it is perfectly true that any Radical falling into our hands must be seen to enjoy the benefits of British Justice... and whilst the quality of that Justice must in no manner be diminished... nevertheless, and because it is necessary to safe-guard our Constitution, an appropriate number of guilty verdicts will be obtained.

GEORGE   With hangings to follow?

SIDMOUTH   Undoubtedly.

GEORGE   At least we can agree on some things. *(Gestures offstage.)* Will you take some sherry?

SIDMOUTH   I must decline for the moment. I trust your Majesty will excuse me. *(It is a matter of no concern to* GEORGE.*)* I think your Majesty should know that it is within our power to trigger off this insurrection... prematurely.

GEORGE   *(suddenly understands the whole business)*   You wish to put on record our Royal sanction for any measures that may prove necessary to deal with the eh... resulting confusion.

SIDMOUTH   *(trying to play the innocent)*   I am simply conveying the advice of your Majesty's ministers.

GEORGE   *(coldly)*   You would act in any case, Sidmouth... With or without our sanction.

SIDMOUTH   It is in your Majesty's own interests that we do so.

GEORGE   And in your interest to obtain our approval. In case your scheme misfires and a scapegoat be needed!

SIDMOUTH   *(moving away)*   ...The situation within which we find ourselves decrees that the future of England's Royal Family depends largely on the continuing power of England's aristocracy.

GEORGE   Aristocracy? Now? *(Venomously.)* Merchants! Our family was in existence a thousand years before such... arrivistes!

SIDMOUTH   *(first trace of emotion as he rounds on him)*   Louis Capet was the son of sixty kings. Yet less than thirty years ago the rabble stamped their feet in the blood...

GEORGE   *(moving away)*   Stop.

SIDMOUTH   *(louder)*   ...spewing from his headless corpse...

GEORGE   *(trying to shield himself)*   Stop!

SIDMOUTH   *(louder still, remorselessly)*   ...in the Place de la Revolution!

GEORGE   *(a shriek)*   Stop! *(Holding his head in his hands.)*

SIDMOUTH, *quite cold again, watches* THE KING *struggle to keep control of himself.*

SIDMOUTH *(dull)*   Your Majesty will be kept informed of all developments.

GEORGE exits *rapidly in search of protection for his threatened head. The remainder of the day will probably be spent with it burrowed out of sight between the twin bolsters of some extremely mammiferous object like Lady Connynghame.* SIDMOUTH *makes an ironically deferential bow, then turns to meet* BOSWELL *and* PLACEMAN *in:*

Scene 8

Lord Sidmouth's office.

SIDMOUTH   His Majesty has given complete approval for your plan, gentlemen. *(Even* BOSWELL *reacts slightly to this sudden transfer of responsibility.)* He has asked to be kept informed of all developments in North Britain.

SIDMOUTH'S *bland manner leaves* PLACEMAN *wondering if he only imagined an intentional barb.*

PLACEMAN   You may rest assured, m'Lord, that our despatches from Scotland will be both prompt and particular.
SIDMOUTH *(briskly)*   You will enjoy complete freedom, Colonel Boswell, to deal with events on the ground as the occasion demands.
BOSWELL *(accepting the implication)*   Thank you.
SIDMOUTH *(leading them slowly off)*   Let me know if you require supplies, finance, or additional arms.
BOSWELL   On the question of finance…
SIDMOUTH *(stops)*   Yes?
BOSWELL   I have already laid out above six hundred pounds of my own money; to equip, and uniform my Ayrshire Yeomanry.
SIDMOUTH   It will be refunded immediately, Colonel Boswell; and generously.
BOSWELL   Thank you. I have a large estate to…

SIDMOUTH *is already ignoring him and has put what looks like a friendly hand on* PLACEMAN'S *shoulder.*

SIDMOUTH   Your own prospects in office, Sir Placeman, will scarcely be harmed by a successful outcome to this whole distressing affair.
PLACEMAN *(stiff)*   I would in any case carry out my duties, m'Lord; to the utmost of my humble abilities.
SIDMOUTH *(bland again)*   Of course. *(Moves on past them.)* I expect your

informants will have told you of a man on the Glasgow Committee by the name of *(turns)* ...King?

PLACEMAN *(sternly)* I believe him to be one of their most dangerously active leaders.

SIDMOUTH *(amused)* Oh indeed he is. Very shortly that man will be issuing a grand Proclamation to your disaffected. *(Sharper.)* Make certain that while he is engaged in this the authorities do not obstruct him in any way whatsoever!

PLACEMAN *(incredulous)* ...Such a man is your agent?

SIDMOUTH It is always wise for Governments to take the precautions of infiltrating the, eh, *(with malicious emphasis)* in-fil-traitors.

SIDMOUTH *exits, leaving the two Scots to face the music that has been played as a soft background to the last few speeches: 'Such a Parcel of Rogues in a Nation.'*

SINGERS 'Fareweel tae aw oor ancient fame,
Fareweel oor ancient glory;
(Singing at the two men.)
Fareweel ev'n tae the Scottish name,
(BOSWELL *draws* PLACEMAN *away from these scurrilous louts.)*
Sae famed in martial story.
(THE SINGERS *now address the larger audience.)*
Noo Sark rins owre the Solway sands,
An Tweed rins tae the ocean,
Tae mark whaur England's Province stands
Such a parcel o rogues in a nation.'

THE SINGERS *hum along with the instrumental as* WILSON *recites against it.*

WILSON 'O would, ere Ah had seen the day
That treason thus could sell us,
Ma auld grey heid had lien in clay,
Wi Bruce an loyal Wallace!
But pith and power, till ma last hour
Ah'll mak this declaration;
We're bocht an sold for English gold
Such a parcel o rogues in a nation!'

Scene 9

Strathaven smiddy.

WALTERS Damn, it's as true the day as ever! Scotsmen lyin and buyin their way

103

intae London Parliament, for sake o whit they can get oot't!

MACINTYRE *(good humoured)* Well. *(Strikes a final blow on a pike-head. Holds it up.)* There's another sharp one to puncture their plans. Put a shaft to that, Jamie. *(Tosses it to* WILSON.*)* It'll knock a hole in any yeoman gullet!

WILSON *(who is fitting wooden shafts to the heads)* Keep yir voices doon.

WALTERS Hoo mony's that, noo?

MACINTYRE Eh…

WILSON Twa short o three dozen.

WALTERS *(delighted calls)* B'christ b'the mornin, Duncan, we'll be able to…

WILSON Keep your voices doon!… Guid kens wha micht be prowlin oot there!

MACINTYRE *(taking up another pike-head)* Ach, they hear nothing with the windows blocked-up, Jamie.

He raises the hammer to strike but freezes at the sound of a sudden, loud, distinctive knock. At a nod from WILSON, WALTERS *hurries to answer.*

WALTERS *(offstage)* Rab!

HAMILTON *(offstage)* It's oan, Davie! It's oan! *(He bursts in, wild with excitement.)* The Proclamation, lads! *(Pulls a bundle of posters from inside his shirt.)* The bluidy Proclamation!

WILSON It's stertit?

HAMILTON Ay, stertit, Jamie! Stertit! *(He drops the bundle as he opens one of the posters for them all to see. It is boldly headed: 'Address to the inhabitants of Great Britain and Ireland.')* Tak a look at that, lads! What d'ye think o't! Eh?

MACINTYRE Oh, *(a rising flood of release from frustration)* at last we can stand up like men against the whoreson bastards that oppress us, oppress our children, and would oppress our children's children. *(Snatches up a completed pike.)* Bring out your cavalry! *(Adopts crouched guard position.)* Here's the first Strathaven pikeman on the field!

WALTERS *(springing to the guard position at one side of* MACINTYRE*)* Here's the saicond!

HAMILTON *(jumping to the other side with a pike)* Mak it three!

The grouping suggests the traditional 'Hedgehog' of pikemen known as a Shiltrom. HAMILTON *breaks away from them again.*

HAMILTON *(excited)* Delegates hae been hurryin oot o Glesca aw day, Jamie. Each man wi as mony of thae as he can safely cairry. B'mornin they'll be postit in every toon and village in lowlan Scotland!

WILSON *(still studying the poster he has picked up)* Whae issued these, Rab?

HAMILTON *(jabs at the poster)* The committee for formin a Provisional Government!

WILSON Naw, naw, *(impatiently)* whit man actually issued them tae you?

HAMILTON Yin o the Glesca Committee.

WILSON   You're sure o'm?

HAMILTON   Christ, Jamie, Ah'm no glaikit! Ah've sat in wi the man at meetins for months!

WALTERS   What did Dan Jamieson say?

HAMILTON   Ah didnae see Dan. He hasnae been hame this week past.

WILSON   *(sharp)*   A week?

HAMILTON   There's mair nor him awa! Some arrestit, the rest in hidin tae plan this!

WILSON   *(still cautious)*   Eh, bide a wee, though. *(Of poster.)* This just says there's t'be a Risin. It doesnae say when!

HAMILTON   *(remembers)*   Ah! Here's the safe gaird. *(Fishes a bit of card from a pocket.)* Noo, that's yin hauf o a caird some o the committee rippit in twa afore ma verra een in Glesca. We accept nae instructions, o ony kind, unless the messenger can produce the matchin hauf o this. When such a man does arrive, we ken he's f'the Glesca committee, an we ken the words oot aw owre the West o Scotland tae... bundle an go!

RONY   *(burst in, greatly excited)*   Rab! Is it true, boy?

HAMILTON   *(exultant)*   Ay, true, Matt! True!

RONY   *(advancing slowly)*   The Risin?

HAMILTON   The Risin of the Moon!

RONY   *(arm out in invitation to dance)*   Tis, the...

The three younger men begin to birl with RONY *as in a reel.*

RONY, MACINTYRE, WALTERS, HAMILTON   *(together)*
   Risin of the Moon,
   Tis the Risin of the Moon, *(they stop dancing)*
   And hurrah me boys for FREEDOM! *(enthusiastic finale)*
   Tis the Risin of the Moon!

RONY   Ah, God, haven't we waited weary years for this day to dawn!

HAMILTON   An this time thae'll be nae mistakes, Matt! Nae mistakes!

RONY   Are the boys out in Glasgow?

HAMILTON   Tollcross t'Partick, Matt! Port Dundas t'Pollokshaws! North, South, East an West, the lads are drilling t'the drumbeat! The cotton spinners hae fired the mills an are marchin in their thoosans. In their thoosans!

The Bodhran beat for 'The Cotton Spinners' has built up insistently through these last speeches.

SINGERS   *(vigorously)*
   Saw ye the cotton spinners,
   Saw ye them gaein awa?
   Saw ye the cotton spinners,
   Merchin doon the Broomielaw!

Some o them had boots and stockins,
Some o them had nane ava,
Some o them had boots and stockings,
Merchin doon the Broomielaw!

*Continue brisk instrumental behind the Government men as they read their
proclamations in loud, urgent, official voices.*

PLACEMAN   Proclamation by the Lord Provost and Magistrates of the City of
Glasgow. April the third, eighteen-twenty. In consequence of the present
threatening appearances all shops are to be shut at the hour of six, this and every
following night, until tranquillity is restored. The inhabitants of the city are hereby
enjoined to retire to their homes as soon as possible thereafter.

THE FIRST MAGISTRATE *begins loudly before end of above.*

1st MAGISTRATE   Proclamation from the Sheriff of the County, and the Provost and
Magistrates of Paisley. While the present riotous condition continues, it is
expected that all well-disposed inhabitants will keep themselves within doors as
much as possible during the day, and have their entire household off the streets by
eight o'clock in the evening.

2nd MAGISTRATE   April the third, eighteen-twenty. Information has been received
which renders it necessary to adopt immediate precautions for preventing and
suppressing riot and disturbance in the town of Girvan, and for bringing to justice
the persons who may be concerned therein.

3rd MAGISTRATE   Kirkcaldy, April the third, eighteen-twenty. The Provost and
Magistrates of Kirkcaldy, hereby enjoin all well-disposed persons to be off the
streets of the town by eight o'clock every evening while the present riotous
conditions exist...

4th MAGISTRATE   The Provost and Magistrates of Stirling hereby order all shops in
the town to be shut by seven o'clock in the evening for the duration of the present
civil unrest...

5th MAGISTRATE   April the third, eighteen-twenty, Hamilton. The Provost and
Magistrates of the town hereby order all well-disposed inhabitants...

6th MAGISTRATE   In view of the present riotous conditions prevailing, the Lord
Provost and Magistrates of Ayr hereby order all...

7th MAGISTRATE   All strangers are hereby enjoined to withdraw from the town of
Dumbarton before seven o'clock at night.

8th MAGISTRATE   The Provost and Magistrates of Falkirk deem it proper to issue the
following orders...

The music swells up to drown out the last of these announcements.

SINGERS
Saw ye the cotton spinners,
Saw ye them gaen awa?
Saw ye the cotton spinners
Merchin doon the Broomielaw!
(occupying centre stage now)
Some o them had boots as stockins,
Some o them had nane ava,
Some o them had boots an stockins,
Merchin doon the Broomielaw!

THE SINGERS *repeat the song, fading into the distance as they move off after the others.*

Curtain.

Act Two

THE MUSICIANS *alone on stage at first, enjoying themselves with improvisations on 'The Cotton Spinners', instrumental only.* THE GOVERNMENT MEN *appear one after the other, to make their reports.*

PLACEMAN   Since the posting of the treasonable proclamation by persons styling themselves The Committee of Organisation for a Provisional Government, the labouring classes have struck work almost universally in the industrial West of Scotland.

1st MAGISTRATE   Where the strike of work is not complete, local Radical Committees enforce it.

2nd MAGISTRATE   Drilling by Radicals, in groups of up to one hundred, is now taking place during the hours of daylight.

3rd MAGISTRATE   Pikes are openly displayed for sale, at prices ranging from sevenpence to one shilling.

4th MAGISTRATE   Iron foundries have been broken into for materials and implements that may be fashioned into weapons.

PLACEMAN   Fortunately, the forces of rebellion do not appear, as yet, to have obtained access to firearms.

Scene 1

Strathaven village square. THE STRATHAVEN FOLK *gather round rostrum. A banner stretched between two posts, a skilled piece of local weaving and embroidery, bears the declaration: 'Scotland Free – or a Desert!'*

HAMILTON   *(haranguing crowd)*   Will we never know, nor appreciate, oor ain strength? Are oor hauns always t'be tied, oor backs bowed doon wi hunger and labour? *(Cries of 'No'.)* Are degradation an misery t'be the sole inheritance o oor children? Are oor bairns, and their bairns t' remain eternally the victims o a villainous aristocracy? *(Cries of 'No' and 'Nae longer', 'Never'.)* Then let cowards cry caution! Let the men o Strathaven trust t'their ain right hauns for their ain salvation! When the word comes f'Glesca, we should merch oot f'here as proud as oor forefaithers merched t'Bannockburn! For we also are fightin for a people's freedom, an for the freedom o oor native land! *(He jumps down from the rostrum to enthusiastic cheers.)* On ye go, Matt. Gie them it hot an strong, lad!

RONY   *(keen)*   Ay, by God an I will!

WILSON   *(checking* RONY'S *movement)*   If they gae intae this, Matt, they gae in kennin aw that's involved. Ah'll speak first.

Cheer greeting from crowd as WILSON *mounts the tub. Cries of 'Come on, Jamie!', 'Good old Jamie Wilson!', and 'Let's hear whit a real radical sounds like, Jamie!' He holds up his hands for silence.*

WILSON *(starts quietly)* Freens. Maist o ye here hae kent me this... twenty, thirty, forty, *(exchanging a smile with* CHARLOTTE*)* ay, mair nor fifty year, past. *(Sporadic acknowledgements.)* Ye will aw ken the political principles that hae guided me through the entire coorse o ma adult life... Some o ye will ken yoursel whit can cost tae abide by thae principles in times like these. *(Quiet assent from some.)*

MACINTYRE *(distant)* Ay, we do, Jamie.

RONY We do. We do.

WILSON We hae suffered the massacre o oor people, an the debasement o oor national character. We hae famine in the streets, and fever in oor hames. We hae been driven intae wars that were supposed t'guarantee future peace... an aw they hae done is sow the seeds o future wars... In the coorse o ma ain lifetime, Ah hae seen oor common lands stolen frae us, and folk herdit intae the manufactories, t'live an work under worse conditions than beasts o the field. We hae reached the state in the toons that smallpox is considered *The Poor Man's Friend...* for the wey it cuts doon the number o bairns' mooths, beggin at us for food we havenae got tae gie them. *(Very quietly.)* We have reached the point where such conditions will nae longer be tolerated. *(Murmur from crowd.) (Sharply.)* But! Let nae man, or woman, be under ony delusion. The confrontation, when it comes, will be between an ill-fed, ill-armed, ill-prepared army o the people... and the military might o an Empire. Let nane here think in terms o glory, or honours. It will be a fight for survival only. If we fail, there will be nae mercy shown us... That banner abune us bears oor forefaithers' slogans... *Scotland free – or a Desert. ... (Quieter with deep feeling.)* That is baith the issue facin us this day... and the terms oan which we maun fight. *(Murmur from crowd.) (Sharper.)* Citizens o Avondale! When the word comes frae Glesca for the people o Scotland t'rise, Ah'd raither five men merched oot o Strathaven wi that slogan burnin in their briests, *(indicating banner)* than ten times that number of men whae cannae face the fact that the road intae Glesca will lead only t'victory... or tae the scaffold at the fit o the Sautmerket!... Thank ye.

Low disturbed rumble from the crowd as he descends from rostrum.

HAMILTON *(annoyed)* Christ, that wasnae clever, Jamie. Ye've damped the hale thing doon!

WILSON It had t'be said.

FALLOW *and his daughter,* MEG, *begin to drift away.*

HAMILTON No at a time like this!

WILSON *(uncharacteristically sharp, and edgy)*   It has aye t'be said, Rab! An exactly at a time like this!

WALTERS   But Jamie, ye've pit some o the lads aff comin wi us!

The age difference between WILSON *and the other Radicals is now more apparent than ever.*

WILSON   Ah hae nae desire, son, t'dampen a lowe ah've spent maist o ma life keepin alive. But we're again oot there t'face an army! *(To the others.)* Gin yin man turns an rins when the fechtin starts he taks ten ithers awa alang wi'im!

MACINTYRE *(mild criticism)*   Some of us learnt our fightin in Europe, Jamie.

WALTERS   Maist o's!

HAMILTON   Nae Strathaven man'll rin!

WILSON   That thocht does ye nocht but credit, Rab. Maybe Ah've just lived owre lang t'think it still masel.

HAMILTON   But Jamie, if we…

WILSON *(rounds on him)*   If we fail this time, we set the hale cause back thirty, forty, fifty… maybe even a hunner years!

HAMILTON   We cannae fail!

WILSON   Gin folk cannae face the facts Ah just gied them there, then maybe they're no ready tae win freedom!

JANET *(calls, sharp)*   Faither!

They look to where she indicates. SHIELDS, *obviously a weaver like themselves, is standing some way back from them; hesitant, a little apprehensive-looking. The Strathaven folk are immediately suspicious.*

HAMILTON *(sharp)*   Whae would ye be?

SHIELDS   A weaver… Just a, weaver, like yoursels.

HAMILTON *(moving towards him)*   Ay?

MACINTYRE *(going with* HAMILTON*)*   A stranger, though.

SHIELDS   T'these parts, ay. *(Tentatively moving to meet the two.)*

HAMILTON   Tae whit part are ye no a stranger?

SHIELDS *(worried as the two men close in on either side, and a little behind him)*   Paisley.

WILSON   Ye're faur traivellt.

SHIELDS   Ah hae business in this airt.

WALTERS   In Strathaven itsel?

SHIELDS   Ah'm seekin yin, Wilson. Jamie Wilson.

HAMILTON   Oh?

SHIELDS   Is he here?

WALTERS   Why?

SHIELDS *(very unsure of himself)*   It's… business.

WILSON   What's your name?

SHIELDS   Shields.

It means nothing to any of them.

WILSON *(decides to tell him)*   Ma name is Wilson.
SHIELDS   Jamie Wilson?
WILSON   Whit's yir business?
SHIELDS   ... *(blurting it out)*   The committee in Glesca sent me. The Provisional Government!
HAMILTON *(roughly gripping his arm)*   Yir memory's short, man!

SHIELDS, *startled, does not comprehend.* RONY *moves in on him too now.*

WALTERS   Paisley, wis whaur ye said ye belanged!
SHIELDS   Ay, but Ah was sent b'the Glesca men.
MACINTYRE   Can you prove that?

SHIELDS *hesitates.*

WILSON *(quietly)*   Ye've cam here purporting tae represent some... provisional government. Ye're in a dangerous position, laddie.
SHIELDS   Are ye Jamie Wilson?
WILSON   ...Ay.

SHIELDS *decides to show them the half-card he carries.*

HAMILTON   Wha gied you that?
SHIELDS *(bolder because of the reaction produced by the card)*   Show me if you can match it first.
MACINTYRE *(a quiet but serious threat)*   Just answer the question.
SHIELDS *(hurriedly)*   It wis a man cried Lees.

Both HAMILTON *and* RONY *indicate to* WILSON *that they do not recognise the name.*

WILSON   Where did you see this Lees?
SHIELDS   In Glesca.
WALTERS   D'ye ken onybody else there?
SHIELDS   A Maister King. He's yin o the leaders. *(Of the piece of card he still holds.)* Ah wis tellt somebody here would hae the ither, matchin, hauf o this.

HAMILTON takes *the piece of card and passes it to* WILSON, *who takes the half-card from his own pocket and tries them together, watched closely by the others. It fits.*

WILSON *(offering his hand)*   Welcome, Shields. Ah'm the Jamie Wilson ye seek.

HAMILTON *(releasing* SHIELDS, *relaxing)*   Ah'm Rab Hamilton. *(Shakes his hand.)* What's the word for us?

SHIELDS *looks to see who else is near.*

WILSON   Ye can talk here, but keep it saft.

SHIELDS *(hurried)*   Can ye aw be ready b'dawn?

HAMILTON   Gin we're t'be ready, we'll be ready! Whit's the plan?

SHIELDS   Ye've t'be oan Cathkin Braes by first licht the morn. That's your meeting point wi the ithers!

WALTERS *(excited)*   Richt then lads! Get the pikes...

WILSON *(checks him)*   Haud on a wee...! Hoo mony ithers will there be oan Cathkin?

SHIELDS   Nae less nor five thoosan!

WILSON   Whae will lead that number?

SHIELDS   Kinloch o Kinloch's landit back f'France.

MACINTYRE *(pleased)*   The old rebel himself!

WALTERS   Ye couldnae get a better man, Jamie. You've said it often.

HAMILTON *(turns away)*   Come oan, then; we're wastin time!

WILSON   Rab!

HAMILTON *stops.* WILSON *draws him further away from the others.*

WILSON *(quietly)*   You made the arrangements in Glesca. Are ye fully convinced b'this man?

HAMILTON *(quietly)*   He couldnae ken whit he does if he wasnae genuine. And there's the card! How could he get that if it wasnae f'the Glesca committee?

WILSON   No yin single doot?

HAMILTON *(shakes head)*   Ah met this man King masel.

WILSON *(calls)*   Shields. Hae you been oan Cathkin?

SHIELDS   Naw. Maister King has. He says they're gaitherin awready an dependin on toons like Strathaven t'swell the numbers.

WILSON   We're t'march f'there oan Glesca?

SHIELDS *(nods)*   There's anither body o men on the Campsies. We're t'come in frae North and South at the yince.

RONY   That was always the plan, Jamie.

HAMILTON   It wis.

MACINTYRE *and* WALTERS *nod agreement.*

WILSON *(decides)*   Pass the word, Rab! We'll need t'be oan the road three oors afore dawn!

HAMILTON *(leaving)*   Ah'll attend tae it!

WILSON *(suddenly in command)* Duncan, get every available haun t'the Smiddy. There's shafts t'be pit oan pikes there yet!

MACINTYRE Ay! *(Leaves.)*

WILSON Matt, take Shields t'dry his claithes; then get yirsel ready for takin a message intae Glesca.

RONY Right! *(To* SHIELDS:) Come on, lad; we'll get them wet things off you! *(They leave.)*

WILSON Get the weemin folk, Davie. Set them t'makin cartridges!

WALTERS *(leaving)* Richt Jamie!

WILSON *(calls after them all)* Tell them Ah'll be doon masel, directly.

WALTERS *(calls back)* Fine!

As WILSON *turns away in the opposite direction he finds* MARY *there.*

MARY *(softly)* Jamie, ye'll no gang tae Cathkin... wull ye?

WILSON *(gently)* Ay, Mary. Ah'm for Cathkin.

MARY Fechtin's for young men.

WILSON It's for every man that can wield a blade this day.

MARY *(quietly frightened)* Jamie! *(Going to him.)*

He shelters her in his arms a moment, trying to see into the future above her head.

WILSON *(very soft)* Ah'll tak care, lass.

THE GOVERNMENT MEN *report to* PLACEMAN *loudly, officially.*

BOSWELL Government forces have mounted artillery on all bridges crossing the Clyde towards Glasgow!

LAPSLIE Regular troops are now standing to arms all over the city!

PLACEMAN And the Yeomanry?

BOSWELL Volunteer re-inforcements are proceeding with all haste to the main trouble spots in Glasgow and Paisley!

PLACEMAN The Radicals?

LAPSLIE Our information suggests that a clash between the Radical forces and Government troops is now unavoidable, and imminent!

PLACEMAN Thank you. *(Reads.)* April the third, eighteen-twenty. To Lord Sidmouth. The Home Department, London... M'Lord. There is a good deal of suspicion within Radical circles concerning the authenticity of the recent Proclamation. Fortunately, however, there is a great deal more of confusion. A major confrontation may not be possible in Glasgow itself but, God willing, we may still teach the rabble a lesson in the outlying country areas where their lines of communication are much less efficient.

Scene 2

Strathaven smiddy. MACINTYRE *is hammering metal at a bench.* CHARLOTTE *carries in a large cauldron and ladle.* MARY *and* JANET *are making cartridges.* WILSON *is putting shafts onto pike-heads.* HAMILTON *and* WALTERS *drag in a sack heavily laden with lead.*

WALTERS   Here ye are then, Charlotte! Anither load for yir broth pot!

MACINTYRE *(surprised)*   Mair lead?

HAMILTON   Ay, mair lead. *(Leaving it beside her.)* T'mak a richt fillin brew for the yeoman, eh?

She takes a strip of lead from the bag, holds it up.

CHARLOTTE   Goad help us, Ah thocht there was nane left in the toon! *(Drops it in the pot.)*

JANET *(suspicious)*   Whaur did ye get that lot?

WALTERS *(greatly pleased with himself)*   We rived it aff the kirk roof.

WILSON *(amused)*   Ah hope it doesnae rain next Sunday!

CHARLOTTE   Och, if it does, Jamie, the meenister'll just think it's somebody in the organ loft, pishin oan'm! *(Cackles delightedly.)*

MARY *(becomes upset)*   That's a form o blasphemy, Davie Walters! Pure blasphemy!

WALTERS   Whit is?

MARY   Daein a thing like that t'the kirk!

MACINTYRE *(kidding her)*   Ohh, Mary, isn't the lead off the kirk roof about the only useful thing we'll ever get out of religion!

MARY *(tosses down the bag of cartridges)*   Gettin yir richts is yin thing! But Ah dinna haud wi bringin the Kirk intae it!

WALTERS   Whit does the Kirk in Scotland ken aboot religion onyway?

JANET   Davie.

MARY   Gin I hear ony mair o that talk Ah'm for hame!

WILSON   Mary, lass, din…

WALTERS   They say that reform is sae heinous a sin,
That nane wha pursue it tae Heaven'll get in;
Wi their black coats, an gr…

JANET silences him with a very sharp dunt.

MARY *(very upset)*   Ye'd pit folk oan yir side against ye! *(Exits.)*

WILSON   Mary.

JANET   Mither!

JANET is quite displeased with her husband for the moment. Her father could be happier about him too. There is an uncomfortable tension in the air. They all decide to resume work without adding further to it.

CHARLOTTE   Whaur did ye get the poother t'fire aw thae baws Ah'm makin?

MACINTYRE   We've had a stock laid up this while back, Charlotte.

CHARLOTTE   *(nudges WALTERS)*   Did ye steal that an aw?

WALTERS   *(somewhat surly)*   The Strathaven committee contributed tuppence a man t'buy it.

CHARLOTTE   *(amused)*   Fower bawbees o gunpoother each?

WALTERS   *(edgy)*   Ay.

CHARLOTTE   Tae owerthrow the British government?

HAMILTON   *(annoyed)*   Gin ye find it aw that amusin, it's a wunner ye bother t'help!

CHARLOTTE   *(enjoying herself)*   Goad, son, an Ah wouldnae miss it! Ah havenae laughed sae muckle since John Fallow's horse drappit deid! *(Cackles.)* That's the first time it's done that, he said … Then he stappit hey in its mooth so's folk couldnae say it de'ed o stervation!

Her amusement is infectious. It takes the tension out of the atmosphere at once. Then a gunshot is heard fairly close.

CHARLOTTE   *(alarmed yelp)*   Oh my Christ!

JANET   *(tense)*   Faither?

They listen. Another single shot is heard, followed quickly by a third. WILSON *relaxes, smiles.*

WILSON   That's only fowlin pieces. Bein a bit o a gunsmith aw thae years has its uses. *(Winks.)* Eh?

JANET   Ye said naebody in the toon would get hurt!

WALTERS   Naw, *(lightly)* but some o the gentry micht need a wee bit persuadin afore they'll part wi an expensive musket or twa.

HAMILTON   The lads'll no aim t'hit, Janet. Unless they're aimed at first!

RONY bursts in, ready for his journey to Glasgow.

RONY   *(excited)*   God almighty, boys; did you hear our first Few-de-joy out there!

JANET   Wis that oor lot shootin?

RONY   Ahh, nobody hurt, Janet; nobody hurt. Just Gebbie the lawyer with two or three holes drilled straight through the middle of his… obstinacity! What's the message for Glasgow, Jamie?

WILSON   Tell them the Strathaven contingent will be on Cathkin Braes weel afore dawn, Matt.

RONY   Right.

WILSON   Every man will hae a pike, some swords, but we'll no hae mony guns unless we can pick mair up on the road in. If they've ony t'spare, we'd welcome them.

RONY   I'll tell them that. Anything else?

WILSON   No. Just mak as few steps on the road as you can, Matt. As it is you'll scarcely get t'Glesca afore we're at the rendezvous.

RONY   Right. *(Suddenly quiet, serious.)* God save you, old friend.

WILSON   *(taking the hand offered between his own)*   God save you too, Matt.

There is a brief moment of deep, silent understanding between the two older men.

RONY   *(heading for door)*   God willin, boys, I'll join you in the morning!
    (Exuberant again.)

JANET   *(calls)*   Look eftir yourself, Matt.

MACINTYRE   Be careful.

CHARLOTTE   Tak care!

HAMILTON   The Risin o the Moon, Matt!

RONY   *(offstage yell)*   The Risin o the Moon!

A door bangs shut. JANET *is first to break the silence.*

JANET   Ah hope he doesnae run intae their patrols.

WALTERS   Matt's an old hand at rebellions, Janet.

MACINTYRE   *(quietly, something fey in his attitude)*   By this time tomorrow, we'll all be old hands at rebellion.

There is an awkward silence. They all realise that MATT'S *departure has committed them irrevocably.*

WILSON   *(shaking the gloom off)*   Come oan, then! There's still work t'be done! *(To* SINGERS.)* Let's hae a song, lads!

CHARLOTTE   *(calls to them)*   Mak it Tammy Traddlefeet!

EVERYBODY   *(in time with hammer beats)*
    Whack! Row de dow dow,
    Fal lal de dal de diddle
    Whack! Row de dow dow,
    Fal-lal de diddle day!

SINGERS
    We weaver lads were merry blades
    When Osnaburg sell't weel,
    An when the price o ilka piece
    Wad pay a bowl o meal.
    The folk gat sale for beef an veal,
    For cash was rife wi evrrybodie;
    An ilka ale hoose had the smell

O roast pies, reekin toddie!
EVERYBODY
    Whack! Row de dow dow,
    Fal lal de dal de diddle,
    Whack! Row de dow dow,
    Fal-lal de diddle day!

THE MUSICIANS are left alone on stage.

SINGERS
    Gin times wad come like time that's gane,
    We'd soon be merry aw;
    We'd loup and prance, and jig and dance,
    Till we'd belike tae faw,
    O then ye'd see we'd happy be,
    An ilka wab we'd hae a drink oan,
    We'd laugh an sing 'Guid Save the King',
    An better songs we can think oan!

    Whack! Row de dow dow,
    Fal lal de dal de diddle,
    Whack! Row de dow dow,
    Fal-lal de diddle day!

They run straight on into the next song, 'the Weavers' March', as THE
STRATHAVEN MEN *are seen in the cold pre-dawn light, in the distance, setting out
on the road to Cathkin Braes with the women-folk gathered briefly to watch them
go. They march in time to the music.*

SINGERS
    Sae forwards lads, step heel and toe,
    In manhood bound, come weal come woe;
    There's nocht but freedom we wad know,
    Gin we follow the gallant weavers.

Scene 3

*The road to Cathkin Braes. The hour of false dawn on a cold, sleety, April morning,
at an altitude of about 1000 feet. There is still very little light. The wind soughs
through the gaunt limbs of leafless trees. Behind and above these the dark lowering
clouds drive hard over the heather moorlands. Led by* HAMILTON, THE STRATHAVEN

MEN *march into view. Armed with pikes, a sword, and one musket.* A YOUNG WOMAN *approaches from another direction. Straining to identify the marchers.*

WOMAN *(calls)*   Are you men comin frae Strathaven?
HAMILTON   Halt lads!

The marching stops, raggedly.

WOMAN *(anxiously)*   Is that the Strathaven contingent?

HAMILTON *and* MACINTYRE *approach warily, as if suspecting a trap, pikes held ready for immediate use.*

HAMILTON   Whae are ye t'be on the road at this oor?
WOMAN *(agitated)*   Are ye frae Strathaven?

WILSON *and* WALTERS *join the group.* WILSON *with a drawn sword in hand.*

WALTERS *(hard)*   Suppose we were, whit then?
WOMAN   Is Jamie Wilson in your party?
WILSON   Whae's askin? *(Recognising the voice* THE WOMAN *steps close to him and takes the hood of her cloak back from her face.* WILSON *steps closer and recognises her.)* Your father sent ye?
WOMAN   Ye've tae disband an scatter! The troops are aw-where!
HAMILTON   We're here tae meet their bluidy troops!
WOMAN   There's nae risin! Ye've been trapped!
HAMILTON *(angry)*   Whit the hell d'you mean nae risin?
MACINTYRE   There's five thoosand men waiting on us at Cathkin!
WOMAN   There's no even five men on Cathkin!
WALTERS   We had word f'Glesca!
WOMAN   Ah've just come f'there! The yeomanry's lyin in ambush at ilka cross-road! *(Moving away.)* Ye've tae disband and scatter intae the hills! *(Calls.)* Ye're walking intae a trap!
WILSON *(calls)*   Isabel?
WOMAN   Ah've ithers tae warn!
WILSON   Isabel, the rest o the Strathaven men's on the Kilbride high road. Can ye get t'them?
WOMAN   Ah'll dae that first. *(Exits.)*
HAMILTON *(yells)*   Tell them we're for gawn oan!
WOMAN *(in distance)*   Scatter an gae hame.

The singers snarl the song 'Radical Bodies, Gae Hame' to the weavers.

SINGERS
> The cavalry's comin, gae hame, gae hame.
> Wi riflemen runnin, gae hame, gae hame.
> The cavalry's comin, wi riflemen runnin,
> Sae Radical bodies, gae hame, gae hame!

HAMILTON *(murderously)* Whaur's that bastart Shields that brocht us the word? Has he run aw rea...

SHIELDS Ah'm here! *(Comes forward to join the others.)* Ah'm still here. *(Very worried.)*

MACINTYRE *(grimly)* What have you to say to us now, then?

SHIELDS Ah had orders f'the Glesca Committee only yesterday!

HAMILTON *(menacing)* Did ye...? Or did ye maybe think t'become a rich man b'sendin a few simple weavers t'their daith?

SHIELDS *(agitated)* Ah swear t'Christ Ah took the orders in guid faith! Ah cam t'Strathaven prepared t'march wi the rest o ye!

MACINTYRE But we haven't met the troops yet. Maybe you were thinking of slipping away before the fighting started.

WALTERS Ah've noticed he's been hingin back at the rear maist o the time!

SHIELDS Ah'm in this as deep as ony man here!

HAMILTON Ye'll be the first tae hing!

Rumble of agreement.

MACINTYRE We'll see to that!

WALTERS Ay, will we!

HAMILTON Maybe we should string the bastard up noo!

Increased agreement.

WILSON That'll dae!

HAMILTON *(grimly)* Jamie, every ithers son o us was seen by government men afore we left Strathaven.

WALTERS Fallow noted every move we made!

HAMILTON There's nae escape for us noo, but we can still hing the man responsible!

SHIELDS Ah'm nae spy nor informer! Ah swear it!

WILSON We've nae proof!

SHIELDS Ah swear t'Christ if it's betrayal, Ah'm betrayed alang wi you! Ah swear that! But Ah still think that lassie was wrang!

SHIELDS' *sincerity seems very genuine.*

HAMILTON *(relenting a very little)* Wad ye gang oan tae Cathkin wi us?

SHIELDS Ah will!

HAMILTON   Merchin aw the road in front o me?

SHIELDS   Yes!

WILSON *(resigned)*   Lads, it's aw up.

HAMILTON *(ignoring* WILSON)   Ye'll remember Ah've got a pike at yir back, Shields. The hale road. If ye even look like runnin, you'll be a deid man afore you've taen the saicond step!

SHIELDS   Ah'll go wi ye. Ah'm ready t'fight!

MACINTYRE   Put him between us, Davie. If he tries to leave, I've something to sink into the bastard too.

WILSON   Lads, tak ma word for it! Oor only hope noo is t'brek an scatter.

HAMILTON *(quietly grim)*   We've come this faur, Jamie. We'll see for oorsels whit's oan Cathkin Braes!

WILSON   A score o men cannae face an army!

HAMILTON   Maybe no. But we'll mak sure there's nae risin afore we turn for hame. *(Turns away. Keeping* SHIELDS *before him.)* Richt then lads! Marchin order, *(pushes* SHIELDS*)* forward!

WALTERS *(as the others exit)*   Whit are ye gaun t'dae, Jamie?… Ah promised Janet Ah'd never lea your side!

WILSON *(turning to face him, crushed)*   Ah'm gaun hame, Davie.

WALTERS *(torn)*   …Ah maun go wi the lads.

WILSON *can find no words. His slow gesture frees his son-in-law of any further obligation to remain.* WALTERS *is still reluctant, but finally hurries after his comrades.* WILSON *turns and slowly begins to make his way back alone to Strathaven.*

SINGERS
The cavalry's comin, gae hame, gae hame!
Wi riflemen runnin, gae hame, gae hame!
When cavalry's comin, an riflemen runnin,
A Radical's safest at hame, at hame!

WILSON has *stopped to look back in the direction taken by the younger men.*

WILSON *(to himself)*   Ah saw it. Christ Almighty, Ah saw it!

As he buries his head in his hands and exits, BOSWELL *appears above him.*

BOSWELL *(singing sarcastically at the receding figure)*
On Cathkin your camp was nae doot raither damp,
And when it began then tae rain, tae rain,
Tae keep yoursel warm frae the weet and the storm,
Ye were wise just tae step awa hame, awa hame!

He turns back from watching the route of the Strathaven Radicals. Becomes very official again as he reads his report.

To Lord Sidmouth, the Home Department, London. M'Lord. Although our agents were unable to provoke a major confrontation in Glasgow itself, we did succeed in drawing out several companies of armed rebels. A contingent from the town of Strathaven actually raised their standard on Cathkin Braes. They dispersed without engaging our forces, but at least one of their principal leaders has already been arrested. I am particularly pleased to report that a body of men from Glasgow, aided by others from Stirlingshire, were intercepted by cavalry whilst on their way to seize the arms and ammunition works at Carron. *(The introduction to 'Dark Bonnymuir'. Behind the next speech, a silhouetted impression of a Shiltrom of Pikemen is seen on either side of* PLACEMAN.*)* General Bradford reports that this Radical 'Army' opened fire on government forces when they were intercepted at a place known as Bonnymuir. General Bradford reports that the cavalry cut this body of men down, and secured nineteen of them as prisoners, in a skirmish that the well-disposed are now terming 'The Battle of Bonnymuir'.

JANET *(singing)*   They tell o hordes wha for gains, and for glory,
In faur distant conflicts their empires expand,
But gie me the lads ken their ain hameland story,
And will for its freedom arise and tak stand.

The other women, individually indistinguishable, take up the chorus.

ALL WOMEN   April the month, in the year aichteen-twenty
A cauld sleety dawnin, owre cloudit an dour,
Tho wearied wi marchin, wi mealpokes lang empty,
They plantit their pikes there, on Daurk Bonnymuir.
JANET   Nae bright scarlet doublets aw braided and frontit,
But twa-score a weaver lads for man's common-weal,
Wi pike and wi pitchfork the horsetroop confrontit,
Their lives tae their comrades resolved tae haud leal;
ALL WOMEN   Scotland, thy clans lang their freedom defendit,
Yet owre this proud prospect the weavers maun floo'er,
(Through the last two lines the women break away to either side to leave JANET *alone.)*
Tho betrayed and hackit doon, ere the conflict had endit
We ne'er shall forget the men o Daurk Bonnymuir.

Music fades out slowly through the remainder of BOSWELL'S *report.*

BOSWELL *(less complacent)*   I have also to report, m'Lord, that due to the jails in Paisley being overcrowded with Radical prisoners, it was necessary to transfer some of them to Greenock. The Port Glasgow Armed Association acted as escort.

The mob attacked these volunteers with stones and other missiles. Faced with such an attack from a mob of such overwhelming numbers, the volunteers had no alternative but to open fire.

Short, sharp burst of musketry fire. JANET, *spotlighted, reads from a document.*

JANET *(unemotionally)* Adam Clephans: age forty-eight: shot dead. John Boyce: age thirty-five: shot dead. Archibald Drummond: age twenty: shot dead.

BOSWELL Attempts have been made to load the character and conduct of the volunteers with reproach, obloquy and guilt. Such treatment is not to be tolerated against brave men who leave their businesses and their homes to defend their country against the worst of foes.

Burst of musketry fire.

JANET Mistress Catherine Turner: age sixty-five: leg amputated. Hugh Turner: age fifteen: leg amputated. Archibald MacKinnon: age seventeen: died of wounds.

BOSWELL A public declaration of Government support for the stand taken by the Port Glasgow force would serve to offset the present slander.

Burst of musketry fire.

JANET Peter Cameron: age fourteen: wounded. David McBride: age fourteen: wounded. Robert Spence: age eleven years: wounded.

BOSWELL *(huffed)* It is not to be tolerated, m'Lord, that these volunteers, when attacked by Radicals, or well-wishers of Radicals, should be made responsible for the consequences, or have their feelings lacerated while represented as shedding needlessly and heedlessly innocent blood!

Burst of musketry fire.

JANET James Kerr: age seventeen: shot dead. William Lindsay: age fifteen: shot dead. James McGilp: … *(looks up out over audience)* age eight: shot dead.

BOSWELL *(quite subdued)* In addition, and with deepest regrets m'Lord, I have to report that subsequent to the attack on the Port Glasgow volunteers, the rabble broke down the door of Greenock jail and assisted the Paisley Radicals to escape. *(Slowly recovering.)* However, we are making strenuous efforts to track down these criminals, as well as anyone suspected of assisting them. The military forces, assisted by local police, have begun a series of vigorous house-to-house searches in all suspect areas of North Britain.

Instrumental of 'The Rising' as a soft background to the latter part of their report.

SINGERS The laws were suspended, the prisons were glutted,

Indictments preferred, the Packed Juries enclosed,
The labourin poor, in their efforts outwitted,
Each thocht they expressed, by informers exposed.
At dawnin the hames o the rebels were raidit,
Braw men dragged awa at the point o the gun,
Fu mony a gallant lad focht till he drappit,
And some fled their hameland, and ne'er can return.

Scene 4

King's chamber. GEORGE *parading the room declaiming as if to a large audience.* SIDMOUTH *awaiting his reaction to the document.*

GEORGE *(from document)*   Deeply as we regrct that the machinations and designs of the disaffected should have led, in some of the country, to acts of open violence and insurrection, we cannot but cxpress our satisfaction at the promptitude with which these attempts have been suppressed. *(To* SIDMOUTH:*)* But we are not satisfied.

SIDMOUTH   The phrase is intended as an incentive.

GEORGE *(not convinced, but resumes his performance)*   The wisdom and firmness manifested by Parliament have greatly contributed to restore confidence throughout the Kingdom. We know that wc can rely on the continued support of Parliament in our determination to... *(He gives up impatiently, shaking his head.)*

SIDMOUTH   Something wrong?

GEORGE   Support of Parliament! It's not that we have any basic objection to mendacity, Sidmouth. We simply find our own fabrication more amusing. *(Thrusts the document back at him.)*

SIDMOUTH *(slightly annoyed)*   With a monarch at the head of our Constitution, the whole fabric of government in these islands would crumble. It is in the interests of all present members of Parliament to sustain Your Majesty's position.

GEORGE *(sarcastically)*   For in so doing they sustain their own?

SIDMOUTH   Living as we do, under the perpetual threat of democracy, we must all make sacrifices. *(Offers document back to* GEORGE.*)*

GEORGE *snatches it from him with a very bad grace. But the public performer takes over again.*

GEORGE   Deploring, as we all must, the distress which still unhappily prevails among the labouring classes, it is in the mcantime our common duty to protect the loyal, the peaceable, and the industrious. *(Conversationally.)* When would you have us present this to the public?

SIDMOUTH   It would probably have greatest impact if used as your Majesty's speech at the opening of the new session of Parliament.

GEORGE   Oh. *(A little brighter.)* Oh well it probably is good enough for that. *(Skims through the rest, picking out the key words only.)* Ahh… we trust that an awakened sense of the dangers… blah-blah-blah-blah… spirit of loyalty… hearts of the great body of the people… blah-blah… blessing of Divine Providence… blah… happiness, freedom, prosperity. Yes, it's the usual bloody rubbish, Sidmouth. *(Thrusts document back at him as he leaves.)* Now if there's nothing more of this annoying business to deal with we would much rather…

SIDMOUTH   *(loud)*   There is still the report on how the trials are proceeding in North Britain. I thought your Majesty would like to hear…

GEORGE   *(rounds on him)*   His Majesty wishes to hear nothing but verdicts, Sidmouth! D'you hear? Verdicts! Guilty verdicts! *(Exits.)*

SIDMOUTH, *managing to restrain himself, follows his monarch out.*

Scene 5

Court Room at Stirling. A gavel bangs loudly.

USHER   *(Offstage. Calls sharply.)*   Let the Bonnymuir prisoners be upstanding for the Lord President of the Court!

PLACEMAN, *unrecognisable at first in the white wig and red robes of office, takes up his normal reporting stance, but facing away from the audience.*

(offstage)   Andrew Hardie, John Baird, James Clelland, Thomas McCulloch, Benjamin Moir, Allan Murchie, James Wright, Thomas MacFarlane, Alexander Hart, Robert Gray, Thomas Pike, William Clarkson, David Thomson, Andrew White, Alexander Johnstone, Alexander Latimer, William Smith, John Barr, John Anderson, William Crawford, John MacMillan and Andrew Dawson.

The USHER'S *voice fades to an indistinct background after the first two or three of the above names are read out. Spotlight on* MARGARET MCKEIGH *as she reads her letter over.*

MARGARET   *(unemotionally)*   My dear and loving Margaret… I hope you will not take it as a dishonour that your unfortunate lover died for his distressed, wronged, suffering and insulted country… No, my dear Margaret I know you are possessed of nobler ideas than that.

PLACEMAN *turns to face the audience in court.*

PLACEMAN   You present a melancholy spectacle of two and twenty subjects of this country who have forfeited their lives to justice; a spectacle, I believe, unexampled in the history of this country.

Intercut PLACEMAN *and* MARGARET *after this.*

MARGARET   ...I shall die firm to the cause in which I embarked. Although we were outwitted and betrayed, yet I protest as a dying man it was done with good intentions on my part, and I may safely speak for the whole of those that were taken at Bonnymuir.

PLACEMAN   The crime of which you have been convicted is the crime of High Treason... Yet I am well aware that some of you may consider yourselves not as victims of justice, but as martyrs of liberty!

MARGARET   ...No person could have induced me to take up arms to rob or to plunder. I took them up for the restoration of those rights for which our forefathers bled, and which we have allowed shamefully to be wrested from us.

PLACEMAN   Repentance alone is not sufficient... Remember that you have to appear before a God who is not only possessed of infinite mercy, but also of inflexible justice!

MARGARET   ...Farewell... A long farewell to you and all worldly cares... I hope you will call frequently on my distressed and afflicted mother... At the expense of some tears I have destroyed your letters... Again, farewell, my dear Margaret... May God attend you, is the sincere prayer of your affectionate and constant lover while on earth... Andrew Hardie.

PLACEMAN   It only remains for me now to pronounce against one and all of you the last awful sentence of the law... In regard to you, Andrew Hardie... and John Baird... I can hold out no hope of mercy. You were selected for trial as leaders of that band of men who defied and challenged government forces at Bonnymuir. I am afraid that an example must be made of you... The sentence of the law is... that you, and each of you, be taken to the place whence you came, and that you be drawn on a hurdle to the place of execution, and there be hung by the neck until you are dead... And afterwards... your head be severed from your body...

A roar of disgust and disapproval off stage drowns out the last sentence.
PLACEMAN *remains calmly unmoved through it, then puts wig aside to report.*

PLACEMAN   To Lord Sidmouth. The Home Department, London... m'Lord. At the recent trials at Stirling, no fewer than twenty-two convictions on a charge of High Treason were recorded. It is our opinion that Government would be well served if all but two of these prisoners were to have their sentences commuted to transportation to a penal settlement for life. There is still considerable unrest among the population here, which might be stirred up needlessly. In any case, we can be quite certain of hanging the leaders in the persons of Baird, Hardie, and in particular James Wilson of Strathaven, who has long been a noted 'reformer' in that part of the world. Wilson's trial is nearing its conclusion at this moment at Glasgow, and will doubtless terminate in a manner quite in accordance with the sentiments you have expressed.

A gavel tapped loudly.

Scene 6

Court Room at Glasgow.

USHER *(Offstage. Calls.)*   Let the prisoner be upstanding for the Lord President of the Court!

WILSON enters very slowly. His hands and feet are manacled and chained. Almost four months in Glasgow's tolbooth have had a severe effect on him. He now looks his age – or more. PLACEMAN *dons his wig and turns to confront* WILSON.

PLACEMAN   James Wilson you have been indicted of High Treason. Upon this indictment you have been arraigned and pleaded Not Guilty. For your trial you have put yourself on God and your country… which country has found you guilty. What have you to say for yourself why the court should not give you judgement to die, according to law?

WILSON draws himself up, faces his accusers.

WILSON   M'Lords an gentlemen… Ah' will not attempt the mockery o a defence… Ye are about t'condemn me for attemptin tae overthrow the oppressors o ma country; but ye do not know, neither can ye appreciate, ma motives!

PLACEMAN   If you have anything to say in your own defence, Wilson, you should be well advised to say it now and briefly.

WILSON   All Ah wull say, is that Ah committ ma sacred cause, which is the cause o freedom, t'the vindication o posterity! *(Buzz in court. Gavel banged.)* Ye may condemn me tae immolation oan the scaffold, but ye cannae degrade me. If Ah hae appeared as a pioneer in the van o freedom's battles, if Ah hae attemptit tae free ma country frae political degradation, then ma conscience tells me that Ah hae done nae mair nor ma duty!

PLACEMAN *(controlled annoyance)*   The prisoner should take warning about using expressions that may well prove detrimental to any possible appeal.

WILSON *(dismissing him)*   Your brief authority wull soon cease! But the vindictive proceedings this day will be recordit in history!

Increased buzz of excitement in court. Gavel banged.

USHER *(offstage)* Silence in the court!

WILSON *(with passion now)* The principles for which Ah hae contendit are as immutable...

PLACEMAN Wilson!

WILSON ...as imperishable... as the eternal laws o nature!

PLACEMAN I cannot allow you to continue in this vein! You will not use this court as a platform for Radical ravings!

WILSON *(quieter)* Ma heid may faw on the scaffold, and be exposed as the heid o a traitor, but Ah appeal wi confidence tae posterity. When ma countrymen will hae exaltit their voices in bold proclamation o the rights and dignity o Humanity...

PLACEMAN Wilson!

WILSON ...an enforced their claim by the extermination o their oppressors...

PLACEMAN *(calls)* Master-at-arms!

Increased buzz of excitement in court.

WILSON *(over-riding everything)* ...then, and no till then, will some future historian dae ma memory justice!

PLACEMAN I warn you, Wilson, I have the powers...

WILSON *(his heart carrying him on)* Then will ma motives be understood... an appreciatit!

Hubbub breaks out. Gavel is banged vigorously.

USHER *(offstage)* Order! Order in court!

PLACEMAN I will have the court cleared if this disturbance continues!

Gavel banged.

USHER *(offstage)* Silence! Silence in court!

Gavel again. Noises fade.

PLACEMAN *(nettled)* I would ask the representatives of our newspapers present to use their discretion in reporting the prisoner's disgraceful outburst!

JANET *and* CHARLOTTE *are facing out over the audience.*

JANET *(bitterly)* The Glesca Herald reportit o ma faither's speech... 'He stammered out a few words in an incoherent manner'!

PLACEMAN *(quietly, firmly)*   James Wilson… You must be convinced of the impartiality and fairness with which the proceedings against you have been conducted.

CHARLOTTE   The prosecution was in the hands o an English lawyer, an conductit in accordance wi English Law.

JANET   Which breks the Treaty o Union!

PLACEMAN   By the exercise of your right to challenge, the jury by which you have been found guilty may be considered as chosen by yourself.

JANET   The juries were chosen frae a list o sworn anti-reformers; includin yeomanry officers.

PLACEMAN   The crime of which they have found you guilty, is the most dreadful that can afflict any nation.

JANET   Guilty, on the distortit testimony o folk like John Fallow.

The two women exit.

PLACEMAN   James Wilson, remember that the justice of God is as inflexible as his mercies are infinite. I trust you have not thrown off all allegiance to your heavenly sovereign, as it appears you have done to your earthly one… The ministers of religion, of every sect and persuasion, will be ready to assist you in preparing for the concern of your immortal soul… The sentence of the Law is that you be drawn on a hurdle to the place of execution, on the thirteenth day of August, eighteen-twenty, and after being hung by the neck till you are dead, that your head be severed from your body, and your body cut in quarters, to be at the disposal of the King!… And may the Lord have mercy upon your soul!

Instrumental of 'Parcel of Rogues' has come up behind the latter part of the sentence. WILSON *faces* PLACEMAN, *weary but unbowed.*

SINGER   What force or guile could not subdue,
Thro many warlike ages,
Is wrought now by a coward few,
For hireling traitor's wages,
The English steel we could disdain,
Secure in valour's station;
But English gold has been our bane
Such a parcel o rogues in a nation!

WILSON *exits slowly, head erect, the iron chains on his legs trailing the floor behind him.*

Scene 7

King's chamber.

GEORGE   We are not at all happy with the manner in which these trials were conducted, Sir Placeman!

PLACEMAN *throws off robe and wig. Bows.*

PLACEMAN   Your Majesty.

GEORGE   Not at all happy!

PLACEMAN *(hurrying down from rostrum)*   Your Majesty, we have three satisfactory verdicts.

GEORGE   You arrested several hundred of these rebels!

SIDMOUTH *(who has entered behind GEORGE)*   Of whom more than eighty were charged with High Treason?

PLACEMAN   Only fifty could be brought to trial, m'Lord.

GEORGE   Where are the others?

PLACEMAN   We believe most have fled the country by now!

SIDMOUTH   The rabble will consider that some sort of victory.

PLACEMAN   They have been outlawed. Which is tantamount to guilt. Your Majesty! *(Slight bow.)* I assure you every endeavour was made to obtain appropriate results.

GEORGE   Only three to be hanged!

SIDMOUTH   Out of almost a hundred!

PLACEMAN   A score and a half will be transported to the colonies!

GEORGE *(sour growl)*   Had these figures been reversed, it would be more to our liking.

PLACEMAN *(in a difficult situation)*   …Feelings still run very high in the matter, your Majesty. It is regrettable, but nonetheless true, that the Radicals can still call on considerable support.

SIDMOUTH   A support that should have been crushed by now!

GEORGE   By hangings!

PLACEMAN   An over-reaction might actually increase that support. I know the character of my people.

GEORGE *(peering closely at him)*   On more than one occasion we have wondered if you… loyal Scots, don't make a deliberate mystique of alleged differences in our Kingdom… *(to* SIDMOUTH:) to justify their inclusion in government, here!

PLACEMAN *(just controlled)*   Already many Scotsmen of position, are turning against us.

SIDMOUTH   Yet you maintain that three executions will subdue the rest?

PLACEMAN   I do, m'Lord.

SIDMOUTH *(blandly)*   Then your people are not so difficult to subdue as is commonly supposed. *(Moving away.)*

PLACEMAN *(stiff)*   Unlike some, m'Lord, the Scotsman is controlled by mild repression. Under too brutal a lash, his rebelliousness will merely become more obdurate.

GEORGE   Tschh! More damned mystique! *(Turns to leave.)*

SIDMOUTH   Does not your Majesty wish to give Sir Placeman specific instructions?

GEORGE   *(rudely)*   Let him get on with it!... *(Jabs a finger towards* PLACEMAN.) But be warned! We will hold you entirely responsible for the effectiveness, or otherwise, of those measures.

PLACEMAN   *(draws himself up)*   I could ask nothing more, your Majesty, *(bows)* nothing less.

GEORGE   *(to* SIDMOUTH)   With the exception of Sir Walter Scott we always did regard the Scots as a bunch of bloody barbarians. *(Exits.)*

SIDMOUTH *enjoys watching* PLACEMAN'S *unexpressed outrage.*

GEORGE   *(re-appearing briefly)*   And sometimes we're not too certain of Walter! *(Exits.)*

SIDMOUTH   Right then. *(Smiles.)* Three executions it will be.

PLACEMAN   *(quietly seething)*   Thank you. *(Turns away.)*

SIDMOUTH   But take care the rabble does not turn these three criminals into martyrs. See that they are discredited. Publicly and in every possible manner!

PLACEMAN   *(stiff, sour)*   We had already foreseen that danger for ourselves, m'Lord. *(Bows.)* The matter is in hand. *(Exits.)*

Instrumental variation on 'Such a Parcel of Rogues in a Nation'; spotlight on WILSON, *then widen to:*

Scene 8

Glasgow tolbooth. MACGREGOR, THE JAILER, *approaches. He speaks softly, with a strong Highland accent.*

JAILER   *(almost apologetic)*   Mister Wilson, the Reverend James Lapslie is here to see you.

WILSON   Is there nae sign o ma wife, yet?

JAILER   I am assured she will be here in plenty of time.

WILSON   Thank ye.

JAILER   ...There is still the Reverend gentlemen.

WILSON   Awready Ah hae seen mair o them than Ah can stomach!

JAILER   Unfortunately, whether you wish it or not, he has the offeecial permission.

WILSON   The hounds o hell, bayin at a man's heels even through his last minutes on earth.

JAILER *(quietly)* I am sorry. *(Calls.)* Mister Lapslie!

LAPSLIE *enters. Stops. His look sends* THE JAILER *on his way.*

JAILER *(uncomfortable)* I'll bring your wife up the minute she arrives.

WILSON *nods to him.*

LAPSLIE Ay, Wilson. You had a fair run for your money. *(Going to him.)* Had you not? (WILSON *looks away.*) I wonder what you're thinking now of your French Republican Principles.

WILSON Say whit you're paid t'say, then leave.

LAPSLIE *(sharp)* That's no suitable manner for a man about to face his Maker!

WILSON *(grinding it out)* It's a long time since Ah first cam across you, Lapslie; and the opinion Ah formed then is altered, only in that it is noo even lower!

LAPSLIE *(beginning to preach a little)* It is an important duty of the Pastoral Office to admonish Christians of their dangers, from any prevailing evil; whether in the church or in the world. This is not preaching politics, Wilson, this is preaching Christ.

WILSON *(bitterly)* Your Christ wad be sittin in wi the Glesca Magistrates! Offerin bribes tae informers!

LAPSLIE *(sharp)* And yours would carry a pike? 'If my kingdom were of this world, then would my servants fight!' The Lord Jesus Christ himself hath said that. *(Emotionally.)* My dear brother, as you would not ruin your own soul and break the hearts of those who really love you; as you would not madly plunge thousands into misery; as you would not bring reproach on the way of the Lord, and open the mouths of his enemies to blaspheme, let me press upon you the paternal admonition of Solomon. 'Enter not into the path of the wicked, and go not in the way of evil men. Avoid it, pass not by it, turn away from it, and pass away.'

WILSON *(puzzled)* Whit d'ye want o me, Lapslie?

LAPSLIE *(hurriedly)* Contrition. Repentance. Confession of your sins!

WILSON Get oot.

LAPSLIE Hope for eternity is as bright as ever, Wilson. Even for you; even on this your last day! It is never too late!

WILSON *(calls)* MacGreegor?

LAPSLIE *(quieter again, persuading)* Wilson! Let not a struggle about the politics of the day withdraw attentions from the precious Saviour, the one thing needful, the good part which shall not be taken away from those who have chosen it! And you *can* choose it Wilson! Even now. Even you. You can choose.

THE JAILER *has returned and is standing at the entrance unsure how to behave in this situation.*

WILSON   Get this man oot o here!

LAPSLIE   *(turns to* JAILER, *dominates him)*   Not... yet! (THE JAILER *can only obey that order.* LAPSLIE *turns his attention back to* WILSON, *who sinks back onto his bench.)* I am perfectly aware that the sentiments I express may be ascribed by some to time serving, and the fear of man; but, Wilson, I would conceive it time serving and man fearing too, on such occasions, to withhold those sentiments. (WILSON *bows his head between his hands as* LAPSLIE *paces the cell.)* Some impute the motive of self-interest to me. Yet how can it be otherwise? I along with others am a party concerned. I feel this deeply, Wilson. Where is the man who has not an interest in the peace and order of civil society?

WILSON   Ah thocht it was ma confession that wis wantit! (LAPSLIE, *annoyed, turns away from him.)* Whit's wrang? *(Very bitterly.)* Is the sicht o an honest man stirrin the maggots o doubt that must gnaw even at such guts as yours?

LAPSLIE   *(stung)*   Search for yourself the Holy Scriptures! If they teach treasons, stratagems, and spoils, then by all means shout for battle! But if, while they ascribe glory to God in the Highest, they teach peace on earth, and good will to men, then 'Let us eschew evil, and do good!' *(Thrusts some papers forward.)* Will you sign this statement, Wilson?

WILSON *reaches out for it,* LAPSLIE *snatches it back out of his reach.*

WILSON   Then Ah'll pit ma name t'naethin.

LAPSLIE   It is the statement you made to the Reverend Grenville Ewing, which you said you wished to be printed and circulated.

WILSON   Ah wantit pen an paper, that Ah micht compose ma ain thochts for masel.

LAPSLIE   That is not allowed, and you know it.

WILSON   Then why are my freens denied access t'dae it for me?

LAPSLIE   The Reverend Grenville Ewing is a friend to all sufferers. *(Decides to read from papers.)* I acknowledge that I die a patriot for the cause of freedom for my country. I hope that my countrymen will continue to see necessity of a reform in the way of the country being represented. I am convinced that nothing short of universal suffrage and annual parliaments will be of any service to put a stop to the present corrupted state of the House of Commons. Therefore, I hope my countrymen will unite and stand firm for their whole rights. *(Looks up enquiringly.)*

WILSON   *(surprised)*   That's... verra close t'whit Ah ootlined.

LAPSLIE   *(greatly compassionate)*   Then waste no more of what little time is left to you, man. *(Turns document and holds it for him to see the bottom half only.)* It requires only your signature.

WILSON *appears to give in, then suddenly snatches the document away from* LAPSLIE, *who tries to get it back.* WILSON, *hampered by the manacles, dunts him off. He finds that the document had been folded. That there is a previous part of the declaration which had been concealed from him. He needs only to scan this briefly.*

LAPSLIE *(reaching for it)*   Hand that b…

> WILSON *rips the document across, twice, then throws the pieces at* LAPSLIE'S *feet.* LAPSLIE *quickly stoops to gather up what might be incriminating evidence against him.*

WILSON *(looking down at him, trembling with rage)*   In aw ma born days, Ah never saw such hellish lies!

LAPSLIE *(bit desperate now)*   If you will not sign this, Wilson, will you sign a statement renouncing your former conduct?

WILSON *(quietly)*   No.

LAPSLIE   A statement naming your former associates?

WILSON *(louder)*   No!

LAPSLIE   A statement denouncing these former associates, who have led you to this sorry plight, but who have escaped a just punishment themselves?

WILSON *(a roar)*   No! *(Grim, burning face.)* Ah'd see the hale tribe o black coats drooned at the Broomielaw, an burn every bible ever was printed, afore Ah'd betray ma fellow man!

LAPSLIE   Be not deceived. God is not mocked. For whatsoever a man soweth that shall he also reap! *(Moving away.)* For he that soweth to his flesh shall of the flesh reap corruption, but he that soweth to the Spirit shall of the Spirit reap life everlasting!

> *Despite his determination the strain is beginning to tell on* WILSON.

WILSON *(quietly)*   Oh, God! Why? Why?

LAPSLIE   Will you not be guided by your spiritual advisors?

WILSON   No.

LAPSLIE   Will you not confess the enormity of your crime?

WILSON   No.

LAPSLIE   To free your immortal soul?

WILSON *(a bit brokenly)*   Never!

LAPSLIE *(a roar)*   Then you condemn your immortal soul to everlasting damnation!

WILSON *(drops to his knees and begins to pray quietly)*
The Lord's ma herd, nocht sall Ah want,
He maks me tae lie in green a baittle gangs;

LAPSLIE *(near the entrance)*   He is anti-Christ that denieth the Father and the Son!

WILSON   He leads me aside the quate waters.
He refreshens ma saul.

LAPSLIE   Many deceivers are entered into the world, who confess not that Jesus Christ is come in the flesh. This is a deceiver! And an anti-Christ!

WILSON   He leads mc in the path o righteousness for his name's sake.

> LAPSLIE *has left the cell. He bursts into a powerful, resonant rendering of Psalm*

twenty-six as he recedes slowly down a corridor, offstage. The reverberant acoustic, and the other voices swelling into a choir add all the authority of established institution to the sound.

LAPSLIE and CHOIR *(offstage)*   Judge me, o Lord, for I have walk'd
  In mine integrity;
  I trusted also in the Lord;
  Slide therefor shall not I.

WILSON continues to use prayer as a barrier against his persecutors. In contrast to the pompous sanctimony offstage, his words, based on folk ritual, are more a reaching out into the unknown than any expression of optimistic faith.

WILSON *(covering his ears against* LAPSLIE)
  Yea, though Ah walk thro the valley of the shadow
  o daith, Ah will fear nae ill.
  For Thou art wi me; crook and staff, they comfort me.

LAPSLIE and CHOIR *(offstage, fading)*
  Examine me, and do me prove;
  Try heart and reins, o God;
  For thy love is before mine eyes,
  Thy truth's paths have I trod!
WILSON   Thou preparest a table in the presence o ma enemies.
  Thou anointit ma heid wi oil.
  Ma cup rins ower.

THE JAILER *has appeared at the entrance.*

JAILER *(gently)*   Mister Wilson.

WILSON *has not heard.* THE JAILER *advances slowly into cell.*

WILSON   Shairly guidness an mercy sall follow me aw the days o ma life... An Ah wull dwall in the house o the Lord,... forever.
JAILER *(very quietly, sincerely)*   Amen. (WILSON, *startled, looks up.*) It is your wife and your daughter.

WILSON *rises, composing himself as best he can in the circumstances. The chains hamper his movements and the jail is damp and filthy.*

JAILER *(calls quietly)*   Would you just come up now, mistress.

MARY *enters, followed by* JANET.

134

MARY *(trying to hold herself together)* Jamie. *(Going to him.)* ...Oh, Jamie. *(He embraces her.)*

WILSON There, lass... Come, sit doon. *(Gently leads her to bench.)*

JANET *(calm, with great control)* Hoo are ye, faither?

WILSON Fine, Janet lass. *(Indicates she should sit on other side of him.)* Fine. *(To JANET:)* Are ye fendin awricht? *(His arm round MARY who has smothered her grief against him.)*

JANET There's naethin t'worry aboot... Ah'm seeing t'things.

He nods, presses his daughter's hand. Then he takes a bit of cloth from his pocket.

WILSON Wipe your e'en wi this, lass.

MARY *(almost recovered)* Ah didna want tae... Ah wantit, no t'mak it hard for ye.

He soothes her.

JANET *(softly)* ...The reprieve's been turned doon.

WILSON *(calm)* Ah never thocht it wad be otherwise, Janet.

MARY But the peteetion wis signed b'sae mony weel kent men!

WILSON It would gang the same road as aw the petitions we've pit doon t'London this thirty year past.

JANET The Provost o Glesca wad hae naethin adae wi it... and Lord Sidmouth never even acknowledged it cam intae his office.

WILSON *(quietly)* Can the Ethiopian change his skin, or the leopard his spots?

MARY Jamie.

WILSON Wheesht, Mary... *(Comforting her.)* Dinna greet, lass... Janet, there's twae things ye maun dae for me.

JANET Ay.

WILSON I dinna like t'burden ye, but wi Walter in hidin, and no a son of ma ain spared t'me... *(Leaves it unfinished.)*

JANET Tell me whit you seek, faither.

WILSON They'll no let me pit pen t'paper; but things are bein written t'slander ma name, an the cause we rose for... Dinna ye let onythin be attributed t'me that Ah wouldnae hae said.

JANET Ah'll see tae it. Whit wis the other thing?

WILSON Oh, *(less certain now)* ...it's maybe a foolish bit notion... maybe no yin Ah should be concerned wi noo..., but Ah've aye thocht ma remains wad rest in the kirkyard at the side o oor hoose yonder in Strathaven. (JANET *nods silently.*) Is that foolish, Janet? Is it foolish t'want such a thing? Is it, lass?

JANET Naw, faither, *(hoarse whisper)* it's no foolish... no foolish.

Spotlight on musicians as they play 'The Rising' slowly, hauntingly. THE JAILER, LAPSLIE, BOSWELL *and* PLACEMAN *enter to escort* WILSON *out* JANET *leads her mother to one side. She and the other women take up the song half-way through the verse.*

JANET and WOMEN *(together)*   Frae London the Judges o Law were instructed,
Tae banish oor brithers, oor faithers, and sons,
Baird, Hardie and Wilson, by cowards executed,
While privileged, corrupted, oor country still runs.
PLACEMAN *(quietly)*   To Lord Sidmouth, Secretary of State for the Home
Department, London… m'Lord. At three o'clock this afternoon James Wilson was
duly executed in Glasgow… Because of the uncertain temperament of the crowd,
it was necessary to have both cavalry and foot soldiers guarding the scaffold,
whilst the Rifle Brigade was dispersed throughout the streets of the city. Wilson
was hanged, his head struck from his body, but in accordance with what was
previously agreed his body was not quartered. This may well have been a wise
decision, for the crowd were already greatly agitated… We have not allowed
Wilson's relatives to claim his remains. We have no desire for his grave to be
turned into a shrine for the disaffected. He has been buried in an unmarked spot,
in pauper's ground, near the High Church in Glasgow.

Scene 9

Pauper's burial ground. JANET *and* CHARLOTTE *on their knees beside a low mound,
lit only by a hand lantern, held by* CHARLOTTE. JANET *is working behind the mound.*

JANET   Haud the lantern mair owre this way.
CHARLOTTE *(very fearful)*   Ye're no gaun tae open it!
JANET   There's been several buried here in recent days.
CHARLOTTE *(fearful)*   Oh, Janet. Ah dinna like it!
JANET *(urgent)*   Charlotte!
CHARLOTTE   Janet, Ah'm feart!
JANET *(takes lantern from her)*   There's naethin here t'fear.

JANET *works again below the ground.* CHARLOTTE *twists away, covering her face.
After a moment* JANET *straightens up towards* CHARLOTTE, *badly shaken.*

JANET *(hoarse)*   Charlotte. *(Shakes her arm.)* Charlotte, listen. Awa doon noo t'the
High Street an get ma kizzens. Tell them we've got ma faither an we're ready
t'tak'm back.
CHARLOTTE *(shaking)*   Ah cannae Janet! Cannae!
JANET *(quietly insistent)*   Charlotte! (CHARLOTTE *tries to turn away, becoming
upset.*) Stop that! *(Shakes her roughly.)* …Stop it!… Tell them t'bring the cairt
t'the west gate. Ah'll be waitin there.

CHARLOTTE   Ah dinna ken if I can dae it, Janet!

JANET   Ye will. Ye must!... *(Pushes her away.)* On ye go!

CHARLOTTE *(suddenly realising)*   But you cannae stey here yirsel. No here. No here, Janet!

JANET *(quietly)*   Ma faither showed me naethin but love an kindness when he wis alive. What wey wad it be different noo?

PLACEMAN   To Lord Sidmouth, Secretary of State for the Home Department, London... *(Subdued.)* M'Lord. We regret to inform you that the body of James Wilson was disinterred on the night following the execution. This was done in a secretive, and clandestine manner. Since more harm than good could come from making an issue of it, or from attempting to search out the culprits responsible, it has been deemed prudent for us to remain silent. The Press have been informed to this effect.

During this speech a slow instrumental of 'The Rising', which becomes a funeral march for:

Scene 10

Strathaven burial ground. Strathaven folk carrying a rough wooden coffin past a suggestion of old grave stones and Celtic crosses. RONY, MACINTYRE, WALTERS, HAMILTON, JANET *and* CHARLOTTE *are among those present. The coffin is laid on prepared ropes on a rostrum. The music stops. It is the time of pre-dawn. The time when the cry of an unseen whaup overheard seems to belong more to times past than to time present.*

CHARLOTTE   Davie, ye'll need tae hurry, son. The toon'll be stirrin.

WALTERS   Ay, Charlotte.

He helps the other men adjust the cords under the coffin.

JANET *(suddenly aware of the absence)*   Whaur's ma mither? (WALTERS *straightens up slowly. More urgently:)* Whaur is she?

WALTERS *(going to her)*   ...Ye'll need t'be prepared for a bit o a cheynge, Janet.

RONY   'Twas the shock of it all, lass.

WALTERS   It proved owre muckle for her.

They all become aware of MARY'S *slow, almost aimless approach. When she speaks it is in the vacant, inconsequential manner of someone whose mind is broken.*

MARY   Hello Janet. Whit're ye daein, lass? Whit are ye aw daein?

JANET *buries her face in her hands.*

HAMILTON *(very low, hurt)*   We've brocht... Jamie, hame.
MARY *(conversationally)*   Oh ma Jamie slept under that yin roof there, Rab; *(indicates nearby cottage)* every nicht since the day an oor we were merrit. *(To* JANET:) Ah kent fine he wouldna bide aw this nicht.

JANET *takes hold of her mother's shoulders to keep her from wandering off again. Holds her close.*

CHARLOTTE *(very soft)*   Pair lassies. *(Shaking her head. Breathing it.)* Pair lassies.
WALTERS *(brusque)*   Duncan, Matt. *(He stoops, hands a cord to* HAMILTON.) Here, Rab. *(The men take up their cords.)* Charlotte, will ye tak a rope's end?
CHARLOTTE *(firmly)*   Ay, will Ah. For Ah aye likit Jamie Wilson.
WALTERS *(quietly)*   Janet. (JANET *takes the sixth cord.)* Richt, then. *(They lower the coffin into the grave, in the middle of the rostrum.)*
CHARLOTTE *(disturbed)*   There should hae been a meenister here. Nae man should go withoot a word said.
JANET   ...Davie?
WALTERS *(shakes head)*   Ah cannae, Janet... *(Choked.)* Cannae.

HAMILTON *bows his head.*

RONY *(diffidently)*   I'm no good at scriptures, Janet... But there's a thing Burns wrote, an I know your father always liked it.
JANET   You dae it, Matt.
RONY *(recites quietly)*   An honest man here lies at rest,
As e'er God with his image blest,
The friend of man, the friend of truth,
The friend of age, and guide of youth:

They let the cords fall, one by one. They make a soft, dull sound on the coffin lid. Punctuating the lines of the poem.

Few hearts like his, with virtue warmed,
Few heads, with knowledge so informed.
If there's another world, he lives in bliss;
If there is none... he made the best of this.

The soft instrumental of 'The Rising' as this scene blacks out completely. A spot slowly brightens on PLACEMAN.

PLACEMAN *(subdued, and also now unhappy)* September the first, eighteen-twenty. To Lord Sidmouth, Secretary of State for the Home Department, London... M'Lord. Conditions here have largely returned to normal... a careful watch continues to be kept for outlawed Radicals, but it is known for certain that a large number of these left the country for Canada, or America... There should be no further necessity for our reports to you... We trust, m'Lord, that the government in London is at least partially satisfied with the exertion of its loyal subjects in... *(bowing his head as he capitulates completely)* North Britain.

PLACEMAN *turns away into the darkness, but not into the obscurity he now seeks. We cannot afford to let him have the obscurity he would otherwise deserve. There are too many important lessons still to be learnt from such men.*

SINGERS   The weavers o Scotland aspired tae win freedom,
They socht naethin less than the true Rights o Man;

The chorus swells as the various groups join in one after the other.

RONY, WALTERS, HAMILTON, MACINTYRE   They joined in a union, its aim was Reform.
·JANET, MARY, CHARLOTTE   A vote for each man and each woman their plan.
FALLOW, MEG, MARGARET, SHIELDS and OTHER WEAVERS   But naethin was heard o but plots and sedition!
BOSWELL, PLACEMAN, LAPSLIE, GEORGE, SIDMOUTH   High Treason, rebellion, and blasphemy wild!
EVERYBODY   Because that the people had dared tae petition,
In plain honest language, firm, manly, and mild.

Through the first part of the song a red dawn has slowly flushed up behind the Celtic crosses of the Strathaven burial ground. It warms to a burning crimson as the cast come together into one unit for the reprise.

But naethin was heard o but plots and sedition,
High Treason, rebellion, and blasphemy wild;
Because that the people had dared tae petition,
In plain honest language, firm, manly, and mild.

Curtain.
When the curtain rises again WILSON *takes his place at the centre of the group.*

WALTERS *(to* THE MUSICIANS*)*   Richt then lads! The Weaver's March!
SINGERS   Though the battle's by betrayers won,
Oor country by time servers run,
The fight has barely but begun,

For right was wi the Weavers.

Sae forward lads, step heel and toe,
In manhood bound come weel, come woe;
There's nocht but freedom we wad know
Gin we follow the gallant Weavers!

There's Placemen paid oor cause despise,
Wha seek tae stem Man's spirit rise;
But truth will stand against their lies,
We'll sing the gallant Weavers!
EVERYBODY   Sae forward lads, step heel and toe,
In Manhood bound, come weal come woe,
There's nocht but freedom we wad know,
Gin we follow the gallant Weavers!

During a reprise of the chorus the cast break and leave the stage, THE MUSICIANS
last.

Curtain.

The Burning

by

Stewart Conn

First performed at the Royal Lyceum Theatre, Edinburgh,
on 18 November 1971, directed by Bill Bryden

Stewart Conn

Stewart Conn was born in Glasgow in 1936 and brought up in Kilmarnock. He was educated at Kilmarnock Academy and the University of Glasgow. After National Service in the Royal Air Force he became a producer with BBC Radio. He was appointed head of BBC Scotland's radio drama department in 1977, where he remained until 1992 when he left to concentrate on his own writing. Through his work for the BBC he made an important contribution to encouraging new Scottish writing.

His stage plays include *Break-Down* (1961), *Broche* (1964), *Victims* (comprising *The Sword, In Transit* and *The Man in The Green Muffler)* (1967), *The King* (1967), *I Didn't Always Live Here* (1967), *A Slight Touch of the Sun* (1968), *The Burning* (1971), *The Aquarium* (1973), *Thistlewood* (1975), *Play Donkey* (1977), *Count Your Blessings* (1977), *Hecuba* (1979), *Herman* (1981), *Hugh Miller* (1988), *By the Pool* (1988), *The Dominion of Fancy* (1992), *Mission Boy* (1996), and *Clay Bull* (1998).

For television he has written *Wally Dugs go in Pairs, The Kite,* and the screenplay for a film adaptation of Neil Gunn's *Blood Hunt.* His radio plays include *Any Following Spring, Cadenza for Real, The Canary Cage,* and dramatisations of Alan Paton's *Too Late the Phalarope* and George Mackay Brown's *Beside the Ocean of Time.* His adaptation of George Mackay Brown's *Greenvoe,* set to music by Alasdair Nicolson for the BBC, was premiered at the 1998 St Magnus Festival.

As well as being a prolific playwright he has written a substantial body of poetry. His collections include *Thunder in the Air* (1967), *The Chinese Tower* (1967), *Stoats in the Sunlight* (1968), *An Ear to the Ground* (1972), *Under the Ice* (1978), *In the Kibble Palace* (1987), *The Luncheon of the Boating Party* (1992), *In the Blood* (1995), *At the Aviary* (1995), and *Stolen Light: Selected Poems* (1999). An essay on his poetry by George Bruce can be found in *Akros,* No. 40 (April 1979), and another in Iain Crichton Smith's *Towards the Human: Selected Essays* (Edinburgh: Macdonald Publishing, 1986).

His work in recent years reflects an interest in Southern Africa, which he first visited in 1984 on a Thyne travel scholarship awarded by the English-Speaking Union. In 1993 he was the overseas judge for the Amstel South African National Playwriting Competition. His plays *By the Pool, Mission Boy* (written for Theatre For Africa) and *Clay Bull* are set in Africa, and his book of poems *At the Aviary* was inspired by his African experiences and published by a South African press.

Author's Original Note

The Burning did not spring from any predisposition on my part towards Scots historical drama; but from what struck me as the theatrical potential of the theme, and its relevance today. Our own age is as 'mocking and hostile' as that of James and Bothwell; as brutal towards those caught in the middle of any battle of creeds, or for power; and as ready to identify 'evil' with the other side.

Much of the play's incident is drawn from historical sources, among them James's own *Daemonologie*. Liberties have naturally been taken with the attitudes of the characters – and with chronology. It proved necessary, during the lengthy process of revising the play, to take a committed line on the 'witches'. If any apology is due, it is to the ghost of Bothwell. (Bothwell incidentally is not the husband of Mary Stuart, but their nephew Francis Stewart-Hepburn, fifth earl and cousin to King James.)

There is no attempt at a reconstruction of sixteenth-century speech. I have aimed at the idea rather than the reality; at a hardness of diction, yet suppleness of rhythm, capable of suggesting the period and coping with the play's contemporary concepts – while remaining clearly intelligible. In speaking the lines, the use of the letter *t* should be closely observed (as in the substitution of *-it* for *-ed* in the past participle, e.g. want*it* for want*ed*, intend*it* for intend*ed*). If the language can be thought of as a leather belt, this sound provides the studs that hold it in place.

In visual terms too, any presentation of the play must resist sentimentality or over-elaborateness. Costumes should be functional, not merely decorative. I envisage the stage being as bare as possible – where practicable, completely bare.

Stewart Conn, 1973

Author's Textual Note

In one production the role of Lord Home was absorbed by that of the Herald: with a little help from Maitland in Act I, Scene 2, but through virtually a straight reallocation of lines in Act II. The Herald also took over the reading of the indictment, from the Dempster. A number of cuts were also made [indicated here by square brackets on pages 151, 156–157, 157, 167–168, 172, 174–175]. The cuts contributed both to a tightening of the action and to a reduction in the size of the cast overall. A director has the option to include or ignore the suggested cuts.

Stewart Conn, 2000

For it is written in the Scriptures, that God sendes Legions of Angells to guarde and watch over his elect.

(James VI, Daemonologie)

On this earth there are pestilences and there are victims, and it's up to us, so far as possible, not to join forces with the pestilences.

(Albert Camus, The Plague)

Toutes les choses terribles au monde commençent avec des petites lâchetés.

(Dr Adelaide Hautval)

Characters

PRIEST

HERALD TO THE KING

DAVID SEATON, DEPUTE BAILIFF

THE MINISTER OF TRANENT

JAMES VI OF SCOTLAND

LORD MAITLAND, HIS CHANCELLOR

LORD HOME

FRANCIS HEPBURN, EARL OF BOTHWELL

THE KING'S JESTER

SIM

CRAW

DR FIAN

EFFIE McCALYAN

GILLES DUNCAN

THOMAS STRACHAN, *smith*

OFFICER TO THE KING

JUDGE

DEMPSTER

SCRIVENER

WOMEN

The action takes place in the Kingdom of Scotland, towards the end of the sixteenth century.

Act One

Prologue

A raised altar, upstage. Huge candles, a cross. Two cloaked figures enter, each bearing a chalice. The chalices placed ceremonially on the altar. Other figures enter, among them a hooded PRIEST: *he takes position at the altar, while the others kneel as though praying silently. All formal, like a dream.*

PRIEST *(intones)*   sake Jesu's   swete for
    gane be will ever   Joye the me grant
    Damnatioun   endless and
    Shame wardly and   Sinne frae me keep
    Passioun bitter Thy   for Lord thou
    slae felon the   frae me keep
    Kingdome His to   dead and quick baith
    doom to there and   come us bade He
    Ghost Holy the   of gotten was
    Christe Jesu Sonne   dear His to and
    nochte of all and   Eard and Heavin baith
    wrochte that God Almychty   in trow I
    (During the responses, the figures drink in turn.)
    (Loudly.) Believe not in God

VOICES   We believe not in God
PRIEST   Nor in Christ His Son
VOICES   Nor in Christ His Son
PRIEST   But in HIM
VOICES   But in HIM
PRIEST   Ever do his bidding
VOICES   Ever do his bidding
PRIEST   Breaking not bread
VOICES   We break not bread
PRIEST   But rendering up the flesh
VOICES   Render up the flesh
PRIEST   In honour of HIM
ALL   In honour of HIM

The PRIEST'S *arms raised, as in benediction. Tableau: a mediaeval wood-cut.*

PRIEST   all you with be Christ
    Jesus Lord our of grace the

The chalices are drained.

VOICES   our of grace…
              our of grace…
                    our of grace…

The figures fan out as a WOMAN *is brought forward. She carries a* CHILD. *The* CHILD *is prepared for baptism. The* PRIEST *withdraws the cross: it is a ceremonial sword, its pommels studded. The figures weave. The* WOMAN *is held. The sword is raised. The chant reaches its climax. The sword plunges. The* WOMAN *shrieks. Blackout.*
    A spot comes up on the HERALD.

HERALD *(reads from a scroll)* PROCLAMATION –
The Royal Majestie and Three Estates in Parliament
being informit of the dire and abominable superstitioun
of Witchcraft, Sorcery and Necromancy in times
bygone against the law of God,

and for the avoidance and away-putting of all such
vain superstitioun in time to come,

it is hereby statute and ordainit by the Royal Majestie
and Three Estates aforesaid that no manner of person
of whatsoever degree is to take upon hand in any times
hereafter any manner of Witchcraft, Sorcery or
Necromancy, nor give themselves furth to have any
such craft nor knowledge thereof,

nor that no person seek help, response nor any
consultatioun at the hands of such aforesaid users,
under pain of death –

and this to be put into execution by the Justice Sheriffs,
Stewards, Bailiffs, Lords of Regality and Royalty,
their Deputes, and other Judges competent within this
Realm with all rigour having power to execute the same.

And this by Act of Parliament.

Scene 1

Near Tranent. A log bridge over a swollen stream. A thunderstorm. Looking into the water, a man in hodden grey, with a bonnet: DAVID SEATON, *depute-bailiff. A huddled figure enters: the* MINISTER. *Each has a lantern.*

MINISTER   Have you lost your senses? *(As* SEATON *turns.)* To stay out in this?

SEATON   We have dug ditches, lest the stream rise and destroy the crops, as last year. *(Looks down again.)* It is less in spate now. God be thankit. *(Pause.)* Yourself, Minister?

MINISTER   Putting up prayers for the miller's son, that is sick.

SEATON   Not the pestilence?

MINISTER   The great sweirness, more like! Causit by lying in bed past noon. Instead of giving assistance to his father.

SEATON   He will recover?

MINISTER   He is in God's hands. Already the Papists have attemptit to treat him, with their herbs and simples. *(Smugly.)* That were soon put a stop to. *(Roll of thunder, not too near. The* MINISTER *glances up.)* The storm is almost past. *(Pause.)* What is it, Master? What are you seeking?

SEATON   My... maidservant... Gilles Duncan...

MINISTER   She is never out in this?

SEATON   I fear she may be.

MINISTER   For what purpose?

SEATON   These past three weeks, she has absentit herself from under my roof, alternate nights. Most like, she trysts with some lad.

MINISTER   That were illicit. *(Pause.)* There are tales abroad in Tranent, of this Gilles Duncan's potency to heal the sick. By the laying-on of hands.

SEATON   Creditable, if scarce credible.

MINISTER   Where there is potency to heal, there is also potency to hurt. By unnatural means. If she is again absent, the Session must be alertit.

SEATON   It concerns the Session!

MINISTER   More than the Session. *(Thunder.)* Does that mean nothing? Do you not know, to what King James credits these storms?

SEATON   The King!

MINISTER   He says they are causit by witches in his kingdom. *(As* SEATON *laughs.)* Hear me out! When James set sail for Denmark, to collect his royal bride, tempests tore the canvas from his vessels, split their masts and drove them from their moorings. Crushing the hulks like tinder. Another, loadit with princely jewels, was sent to the bottom, off Leith. The ancient Greeks blamit Neptune. James accuses Satan.

SEATON   Behind the storm, witchcraft?

MINISTER   And behind that, the Black Earl.

SEATON   Bothwell!

MINISTER   So, there is significance outwith ourselves.

SEATON   She is but a lass. She would never have truck with such—

MINISTER   You are depute-bailiff. *(As* SEATON *nods.)* And would rise to bailiff? *(Pause.)* See you make your report.

SEATON   If she is innocent?

MINISTER   The Lord will look after His own.

SEATON   This is on my conscience.

MINISTER   There is also your duty. Take care the demands of the one do not blind you to the dictates of the other. Else I should not care to answer for you.

SEATON   Sir, I am prepared to answer for myself.

MINISTER   Before God?

SEATON   Before God.

MINISTER   And the King?

SEATON   And the King.

The MINISTER *exits.* SEATON *looks round, pulls his plaid about him.*

Scene 2

Holyrood. A chair of state. Banners, drapeaux. The KING *stands on the throne, a sword in his hand. Before him, an* ATTENDANT. SIM *and* CRAW *look on. The* ATTENDANT *kneels. The* KING *scratches vigorously at his codpiece. He raises the sword, lowers it.*

KING   Thou art hereby, heretofore and hereinafter ordainit, dubbit and proclaimit: Freeman of the Grassmarket, Warden of the Lawnmarket, Grandmaster of the Fishmarket, the Fleshmarket and the Saltmarket, Great Stinker of the Fartmarket, Farter of the Stinkmarket, Defender of the King's Faith, the King's Breastplate and the King's Codpiece *(he scratches)* and all that lie therein... *(He dubs the* ATTENDANT.) Arise Sir Silly Smiddy, Seigneur of Tosspots, Champion of Pishpots... It is now our kingly wish that thou shouldst kiss... our ring!

The KING *turns his back. A raspberry, as the* ATTENDANT *kicks him.* SIM *and* CRAW *jig round the throne.*

SIM   Matthew, Mark, Luke and John
Bless the wench the King lies on...

CRAW   Genesis, Exodus, Leviticus, Numbers,
Watch over King James's nightly slumbers...

The KING *joins them.*

KING   Amo, amas, amat...
    Amamus, amatis... Ah cant!

He clutches himself. Laughter. The ATTENDANT *gestures, exits. The* KING *crosses to the throne, spits on it and pretends to polish it. Sounds, off. He drops his sword, has to pick it up, trips. He giggles. He is in fact* KING JAMES'S JESTER. JAMES *himself enters: wearing a doublet with a white ruff. Well padded. Unshapely legs. With him:* LORD MAITLAND *his Chancellor,* LORD HOME, *the* HERALD, *the* OFFICER *as bodyguard.*

MAITLAND   No castle can hold him long.
HOME   Dispose of him.
HERALD   There is no proof against him.
HOME   His reputation is enough.
HERALD   He paints himself larger than life, among the gullible.
HOME   He has made attempts on the King's person.
JAMES   And that of our affectionate bedfellow the Queen... *(He toys with the feathers of his codpiece: the* JESTER, *who has with the others cleared the central playing area, mimics him and stifles a laugh, then turns away as* JAMES *continues.)* You cannot have a man put down, without proof having been found against him.
HOME   Enough is known, to incriminate him.
MAITLAND   Not just incriminate, but utterly destroy.
JAMES   Justice must be seen to be done. Else his minions will await his return. Calling his spirit corporeal. He must be treatit with the full force of the Law; his guilt held up to the light. Which he blots out, like a black spider.
HOME   But you plan to set him free!
MAITLAND   So that we can ensnare him.
HERALD   If he is the threat you say.
HOME   You defend him?
HERALD   Scarce my function. *(To* JAMES.) I bring news from Tranent. Anent a servant maid Gilles Duncan—
HOME   This is no time—

But JAMES *raises a hand, for the* HERALD *to continue.*

HERALD   She has been reportit to the session, after injunction from the pulpit. In consequence of village squabbles, guaranteeing one party injury against another.
MAITLAND   Be specific.
HERALD   There is reportit potency in healing the sick. Plus matters bordering on the miraculous.
MAITLAND   She has been interrogatit?
HERALD   Not yet.
JAMES   Tranent is near North Berwick. Where were cast those spells against our

person. *(To* HOME.) Here is the chink in Bothwell's armour, through which he will be deliverit up. Release him now, he will take advantage of the next full moon. To manipulate our overthrow. But we shall have him. *(He circles the stage.)* Bothwell is a bloody hell-bent creature, that has no care for those he drags to purgatory with him. A dark rider, on a dark mount. It befits him to perish in a desert of flaming sand – as all that are violent against God. There shall he lie, defiant in death as in life, like Capaneus obdurate under judgment. *(Sits on the throne.)* It only grieves us to think how many must perish, through him.

HERALD   Must they?

JAMES   It is in accord with Scripture. We are the Lord's anointed, and sacred the breadth of the Realm. Is there not about us a ring of stalwart servants, in whom we trust? And have done, since the unkindly murder of our mother the Queen?

HERALD   You are hard on Hepburn.

MAITLAND   Hepburn is what he is.

HERALD   He has the blood royal. (JAMES *contorts.)*

MAITLAND   But no fit claim to the throne.

HERALD   My suspicion is, he would be satisfied as second in the land.

MAITLAND   He has no right!

[HOME   His time draws near.

HERALD *(turns on* HOME)   I smell pettiness. Against a better swordsman than yourself.

HOME   How dare you!

HERALD   The last time you and Bothwell met in the High Street, did he not—?

HOME *(enraged)*   We were outnumbert three to one.

HERALD   Not the story I heard.

HOME *takes a furious step towards the* HERALD. *The* HERALD *pushes him back.* HOME'S *hand flies to his swordhaft. The* JESTER *jinks between them, with his own sword.*

JESTER   Now, now, Lordships… never nakit steel… in the King's presence… *(To* HOME.) You'll have to learn to keep your tempers, or it'll get you into trouble.

HOME *pinions him.*

MAITLAND   The King could have you hangit.

JESTER *(to* JAMES)   Never fash, Majesty… it's only made of wood… like Home's head… *(as* HOME *twists his arm)* ouch… Majesty…

JAMES   Release him… my Lord.

JESTER   You heard what the mannie said… *(Reluctantly,* HOME *obeys.)*

HOME *(to the* HERALD)   The next time, you will pay…]

JAMES   What… if Bothwell should suspect our motive?

MAITLAND   A sum will be demandit for his release.

JAMES   Substantial.

MAITLAND   He knows the state of the coffers.

JAMES   He is responsible!

MAITLAND   *(a slight glance at* HOME*)*   As are we all.

JAMES   Let conditions be drawn up.

MAITLAND   That has been done.

JAMES   All that remains is for Bothwell... to be brought... *(he rubs his hands together)* and humblit...

MAITLAND   Bothwell is here.

HOME'S *hand steals to his sword.* MAITLAND *smiles.*

JAMES   He was secure...

MAITLAND   He is secure...

JAMES   ...in Tantallon.

MAITLAND   ...no longer in Tantallon.

JAMES   Here? (MAITLAND *nods.)* In... Holyrood? (MAITLAND *bows.)* Well then... (JAMES *has to clear his throat.)* Let us... have him in! *(As the* ATTENDANTS *turn.)* Wait! *(Then with a show of casualness.)* Let us first... read the conditions... *(And the parchment is handed to him.)* Aaaah... aaaaaah... yes, excellent... He... aaaaah... is bound?

MAITLAND   Sire.

HOME   And has a gauntlet to run.

JAMES   *(loudly)*   Bring him in!

JAMES *hands back the parchment, adjusts his dress, adopts a regal posture. Tableau.* BOTHWELL *is brought in, roped. He bows.* SIM *and* CRAW *watch the scene, but without impinging on it.* BOTHWELL *breaks the silence.*

BOTHWELL   I bow to one fool, the other bows back: on one hand, the King's Fool; on the other, the Fools' King!

MAITLAND   To think the Bishop of Durham spoke of this noble's 'social graces and attainments'.

BOTHWELL   I have a complaint—

MAITLAND   Later!

BOTHWELL   *(ignores him)*   —about the porridge, in Tantallon Castle.

MAITLAND   There is a paper, his Grace would first have you sign.

BOTHWELL   Putting on weight again, cousin... or are you just well paddit?

JAMES   It is our wish—

BOTHWELL   Or your Chancellor's.

JAMES   —that you be releasit—

BOTHWELL   What surety?

JAMES   —on surety of good behaviour—

BOTHWELL   The terms?

MAITLAND   A sum will be—

BOTHWELL   You must be short of silver.

MAITLAND   I recall your promise to feed this Court at the rate of two hundred thousand crowns per annum, without expense to his Grace of one farthing.

BOTHWELL   By bleeding Elizabeth, not turning out my own pocket.

MAITLAND   Elizabeth will relish that, when next you play lapdog to her.

BOTHWELL   If I reject your offer?

MAITLAND   Your estates are forfeit.

BOTHWELL   How is my silver to be usit?

JAMES   Towards furtherance of peace throughout the Realm. Our intent is to put down all warring factions, and dominate the northern nobles utterly. To banish from our house all Jesuits and Papists, and command full obedience to our Acts of Parliament. Through Maitland here at our right hand, we treat with Elizabeth, that our enemies be deliverit into our hands. On behalf of that course we shall share common foes unto death – in despite of the Pope, and the King of Spain, and all Leaguers – and the Devil their Master.

Pause.

BOTHWELL   *(quietly)*   A costly house to put in order.

JAMES   Our position is God-given, and a divine duty.

MAITLAND   While you are but England's errand-boy.

BOTHWELL   An errand-boy who holds the key to the Border.

MAITLAND   Errand-boys should learn to serve the one master.

BOTHWELL   I do, Chancellor... I do...

Pause.

JAMES   It is right you should serve us, who rule this land by policy.

BOTHWELL   Policy demands wisdom.

JAMES   There are our councillors. Besides, the King is the true child and servant of God. Wisdom is investit in him, through heavenly grace. He has the key to the nation's safety.

BOTHWELL   A King should not shiver at the sight of steel.

HOME   It is discourteous to cite that. It was instillit in the King in the womb, when those men burst into his mother's chamber to despatch David Rizzio.

BOTHWELL   His legs got bent, at the same time!

MAITLAND   King James has a position in this Realm. He approaches the prime of his years and vigour; is alliet with a potent prince, heir to a mighty kingdom, dominant in Europe. It is not meet he be beardit in his Court by any jackanapes baron that feels himself outdone.

BOTHWELL   A pity so great a sovereign should have as Chancellor an empty puddock-stool of a knight.

MAITLAND   You forget one thing. You are in the King's power.

BOTHWELL   What power? *(He beckons the JESTER forward.)* He has but the appearance of power. Its illusion. Not power itself. Or its basis. *(He takes the* JESTER'S *wooden sword.)* Here is your illusion, cousin. It has the trappings. But lacks the ring of metal. Instead, it is soft and pliable... Able to be manipulatit, but without a cutting edge. It remains a plaything... a Fool's bauble, a wee boy's toy... or an appurtenance for ladies. Never for a grown man, far less a sovereign at the height of his vigour. You wield this Chancellor, as he wields you. You make gestures of kingship. Nothing more. You are all pageant and procession. Your monarchy is a monkey-like masquerade. The whole base of your power, a pretence, to be snappit at will.

He is about to break the sword across his knee.

JESTER   Hey!

But it is JAMES *who intervenes, takes it.*

JAMES   The weapon may be weak. In hands that wear fetters. In ours, it is investit with puissance beyond itself. The Right is on our side. In any battle we engage. You call this blade puny, and deride it? Behind it lie our birthright and the traditions of the Court. Through God's heavenly guidance, we command obeisance. This is a mighty weapon, manifest through God, and Christ our Saviour.

He flourishes the sword. The JESTER *takes it from him.*

JESTER   Here... You'll do yourself an injury...
JAMES   There are other ways to govern, than by violence. We shall rule Scotland by a Clerk of the Council, which others have not been able to do with the sword.
BOTHWELL   Wait till you draw your dagger across Moray's cheek. Or head for Hampton Court, leaving behind the stench of rotting flesh.
JAMES   You offend all decency.
BOTHWELL   It is you! With your feminine fancies and lewd lures. *(As* JAMES *grows more and more upset.)* With your scribbling... and your... snivelling...

JAMES *responds as though struck. The* JESTER *supports him.*

JAMES   You are an evil man. And you will be put down. Who are neither true Protestant nor Catholic... and have nothing... but secret and unholy ambition.
BOTHWELL   I have the one thing you lack, cousin... popularity.
MAITLAND   Easy bought.
BOTHWELL   Less easy kept. For all the fripperies you dole out. The sweetmeats and strips of land. *(To* JAMES.) Where you curry favour, I command it. Through the lealty of my people. That is my strength.
MAITLAND   It will soon change. *(To the* HERALD.) Let him hear the conditions.

HERALD *(reads)* 'On leaving this place, you are to remain in house or estate, notifying the King's Lieutenant of any journey of three miles or more abroad. Second, you will avoid public meeting-places, and all congregation of above one dozen persons. Third, you will employ as household staff not above sixteen of either sex, and these not accoutred bondsmen, but common hirelings... *(with added stress: meanwhile* MAITLAND *smiling)* ...without debt to your blood or lineage. Nor is any residence to be fortified; but remain open to inspection by the King's Lieutenant at whatsoever hour he pleases. Finally you may not linger in any public place between sunset and sunrise. Under pain of dispossession. This last being the most crucial of the terms laid down.'

The parchment is returned to MAITLAND.

BOTHWELL   That all? Last time, I was to 'prove another man in time coming.'
JAMES   Better *im*prove the one you already are.
MAITLAND   His Grace's terms are, as has been—
BOTHWELL   The style is stiltit. It could only be yours. Or that blind pedant your father's.
MAITLAND   You sound keen to return to Tantallon.
BOTHWELL   That would not do. The King must have me releasit. In Tantallon, he'd find me too hot to handle. It would demand too many soldiery. That are needit elsewhere. The freedom the King offers me, is forcit on him.
MAITLAND   You despise freedom so?
BOTHWELL   What is the exchange? From a sandstone cell six paces square, to a cage the size of Scotland, with as many bars as there are King's men! *(Pause.)* Still, I have a freedom of sorts. Freedom of thought, and sentiment. Freedom of affection. Which is a man's real freedom. That is something you could never understand, who want your subjects to conform, to support your State and attend your Kirk. To be dominatit, utterly. *(Pause.)* If you could, you'd control their dreams.
MAITLAND   Yours are your own, thank God.
BOTHWELL   *(to* JAMES*)*   Yours, cousin? No dark shadows there?
MAITLAND   Greater shadows than Bothwell. The Pope. And Philip. You have forgot to sign.
BOTHWELL   My word is not acceptit, as bond?
JAMES   *(a puny figure, in the throne)*   No.

MAITLAND *smiles, shakes his head.* BOTHWELL *sighs. He signs with a flourish.*

BOTHWELL   What will you be doing, cousin, while I am...?
JAMES   We shall repair three days hence to our fortress of Fife. From Leith, by royal barge. Complete with entourage.
JESTER   To gralloch the red deer. That cannot defend themselves.
MAITLAND   *(sees the signature)*   Take him away!

BOTHWELL   If all the fools in the world were wise men, and the wise men fools...
JESTER   It would make little difference.
BOTHWELL   At least there is one, knows his station.
JAMES   Before you go... do you frequent... the east sector of the Kingdom?
BOTHWELL   Seldom. There is a snell wind there, they tell me...
JAMES   Yes, snell...
BOTHWELL   We will meet again, cousin... never fear...

BOTHWELL *is taken out.* HOME *turns to* JAMES, *whispers urgently.*

HOME   Was it wise to say we would sail from—?
JAMES   We said in three days time. By design. We shall defeat his purpose, by
  setting out furthwith.
HOME   I dislike his being releasit.
HERALD   You heard the conditions!
JAMES   As he says, it is the freedom of the walled garden. He is a stag, and will
  soon be at bay. Like Actaeon, destroyit by his own hounds.
JESTER *(returns from having seen* BOTHWELL *depart)*   Can we come with you to
  Fife, Majesty?
MAITLAND   Beware lest we set a pair of antlers on your brow and whip you through
  the wood for sport.
JESTER   Save your rhetoric. Enough's been spilt for the one day.
JAMES   Put foot on the soil of our Court within thirty days, you will indeed be
  whippit.

JAMES *exits.*

HERALD *(holds out the parchment)*   What of this?

MAITLAND *takes the parchment, tears it across, lets the pieces flutter to the floor.
All exit, except the* JESTER. *He steps forward, and is joined by* SIM *and* CRAW. SIM
makes a ball of the torn parchment, bowls it at the JESTER *who uses his sword as a
bat.* CRAW *fields.*

SIM   A fine instrument, you have there.
CRAW   What you could cry... a comely blade!
JESTER   Or a tough tool... *(holding it in front of him)* that has done sturdy work in
  its day.
SIM   Sturdy or turdy?
CRAW   Careful, you'll give her a skelf!
SIM   I hope you find a clean scabbard for it.
CRAW   Look who's talking.
SIM   Craw doesn't mind where he planks his. Do you, Craw?
[CRAW   As bad as that Bothwell... they say he doesn't even stop to dry it in atween.

JESTER   In atween what? *(Laughter.)*

SIM   Mind you... a man has to stop some time... or he'll do hissel an injury...

JESTER   Don't you believe it. Craw's been at it steady for the past ten years.

SIM   Aye, and look at him!

CRAW   You're just jealous.

SIM   Could give you six inches of a start.] Seriously, though... I mean... they say Bothwell has a... superhuman capacity.

JESTER   That's why his Kingship gets so upset. He doesnae have a look in.

CRAW   Doubt if he ever gets anything else in, either. They say... *(looks round)* he's got... a carbuncle on it. That's why he keeps... *(Scratching gesture.)*

SIM   His isnae big enough to haud a carbuncle!

JESTER   One day he'll waken up and find it's disappeart.

SIM   Fell aff, more like!

JESTER   I'm telling you—

SIM   Who's asking?

JESTER   —there's more to that Bothwell, than meets the eye.

CRAW   Exactly.

JESTER   He doesnae scare easy, for a start.

[CRAW   More than you can say for his Prissiness.

SIM   Say that again.

CREW   More than you can say for—]

SIM   *(to* JESTER*)*   Hie... you're not thinking of...

JESTER   Thinking of what?

SIM   ...well, taking up with Bothwell, are you?

JESTER   No me. I ken whit side my bread's buttert!

They sing.

Song: The Bauld Winds Blew

The bauld winds blew, the fire-flauchts flew,
   The sea ran tae the sky,
For the thunder growled, the sea-dogs yowled,
   As they gaed scourin by.

For storms blew up, and rains cam doon,
   On King James and all his men;
But whether sent by witches or no,
   They honestly didna ken.

The King's bark crossed the pearly Forth,
   Wi whitna pearly prow;
When it couldna speil the brow o the waves
   It needled them through ablow.

O the King frae regal seat was tossed
   And piteously did roar;
For a vulgar part o his bodie
   Cam thud upon the floor.

Yet soon the Fifeshire coast was won
   And he mounted his steed o wind;
And he headed him to fair Falkland
   And left the shore ahint.

So in the fertile land o Fife,
   They rade to catch the deer...
(last couplet spoken)
While in the village o Tranent
   David Seaton had things to speir.

Scene 3

Outdoors, Tranent. The MINSTER, SEATON. *Birdsong. The* MINISTER *carries a Bible.*

MINISTER   You have actit wisely, Master.
SEATON   In whose eyes?
MINISTER   All. Including your own.
SEATON   If we are in error?
MINISTER   That will be revealit, at the questioning. Evil must be brought to book.
SEATON   You make her out to be already guilty.
MINISTER   So she is. Till and unless her innocence shine like a light.
SEATON   She is of honest parentage.
MINSTER   There is an evil in this land, that propagates in every shire, never showing its face but undermining the structure of the state, like a warren.
SEATON   She... attends the Kirk.
MINISTER   Did not Antide Colas confess she did attend midnight prayer on Christmas eve, then go to a profane meeting, only to return to break holy bread at dawn? No wonder the Inquisitors have been sore exercisit in dealing with such gross offence, when it matures within the marrow of the body politic, the very kernel of the Kirk.
SEATON   We deal with a simple country lass.
MINISTER   We deal with a Beast. Foreign to the laws of God's kingdom. And the decencies of His people. God is so vigilant for the weale of His own, that he disappoints the will of those that conspire against His holy throne. By this same power have been put down of late, here in Lothian, a number of ungodly creatures

little better than devils. That have arisen in guise of innocence, like this 'simple lass'. They have entert into league with the Devil, in their souls' despite.

SEATON   It is surely never God's will that—

MINISTER   It is not for you to question God's will. *(Pause.)* She is... shapely... this Duncan? Full-breastit?

SEATON   She has apples in her cheeks.

MINISTER   Look out on your own account. Lest it be said you protect her out of lust.

SEATON   You wrong me.

MINSTER   Listen! Are there marigolds on your land?

SEATON   Marigolds?

MINSTER   Marsh... marigolds... on your ploughgate?

SEATON   I fail to—

MINSTER   For each marsh marigold found, the fine is?

SEATON   One sheep.

MINISTER   How much greater penalty, to harbour under your roof-tree a spiritual weed, a festering and infectious growth, a canker.

SEATON   What would you have me do?

MINISTER   See she names names.

SEATON   If she cannot?

MINSTER   She must. To clear her own. There is Justice left in this world, Master. But first, lay bare the Truth. By whatever means you will. For your own good name, as much as hers. Then will the Session take matters into its own scrupulous hands. It is the Lord's work, Master, and brings glory!

Pause.

SEATON   If I fail?

MINISTER   It were better you did not.

Scene 4.

Effie McCalyan's home: the bedroom. Bed, futegang, velvet stool, tapestry, a chamberpot. A table, with FIAN'S *wares.* EFFIE *wears an embroidered gown;* DR FIAN *alias* CUNNINGHAM, *school-master of Saltpans.*

FIAN   This phial contains a secret philtre, comprisit from rare juices of the Orient. I receivit it only after great effort, from a merchant who exchanges local salt for timber, in the German ports. He had it from a sea-captain, a Hollander, whose wares are claimit never to fail. In that he secures substances from Samarkand and beyond. He once had one from snake-juices could kill instant.

EFFIE   This... is not to kill?

FIAN   No, ladyship... this is... for the other.

EFFIE   Is potent?

FIAN   It will bind the recipient to yourself, so long as you please. See... three drops in the evening... either in ale or wine... the latter being less destructive to the desires... nightly upon requirement, till the potion be done.

EFFIE   Nothing else?

FIAN   But womanly wiles...

EFFIE   I am in your debt.

FIAN   Never reveal the source. *(Pointedly.)* I am only sorry your ladyship's husband Patrick is abroad these months, that you cannot put it into practice straightway...

EFFIE   *(muses)*   Yes, it will be some time... before I can—

FIAN   You have not heard?

EFFIE   Heard what?

FIAN *(confused)*   I... that is...

EFFIE   Out with it!

FIAN   It was... our next meeting... the night is almost upon us, and... there are no instructions, as to the addit matter we were to—

EFFIE   How could there be?

FIAN   I had hoped perhaps... he might... the Earl might...

EFFIE   When he is in Tantallon? Stop talking in riddles.

FIAN   The King has had him releasit. Under condition—

EFFIE   When?

FIAN   I have newly—

EFFIE   No, when did the King—? *(Three heavy beats, as with a staff on the ground, off. They freeze, then* EFFIE *takes* FIAN'S *arm.)* This way, quickly... *(As she shows him out.)* Stand by, to be summonit.

FIAN *exits. Pause.* BOTHWELL *enters, upstage. Pause, then:*

BOTHWELL   Madam!

EFFIE   My noble Lord!

BOTHWELL   I bring greetings from the Court... to yourself... and your husband...

EFFIE   My husband... is from home...

BOTHWELL   Then our affection... is yours, entire...

EFFIE   I would have it so!

They eye one another. BOTHWELL *bows elaborately.* EFFIE *curtseys. Suddenly they drop the pose. She throws herself into his arms.*

EFFIE   How I have missed you.

BOTHWELL   I came as soon as I was releasit.

EFFIE   Maitland did not have you followit?

BOTHWELL   I gave them the slip.

EFFIE   You are quite safe?

BOTHWELL   But for a stiffness in the limbs; a stiffness that will soon turn... to advantage.

EFFIE   I have told Fian to stand by.

BOTHWELL   The more that congregate in the King's despite, the more we shall have him in a flurry. It also leaves us... free to breathe...

EFFIE   It is good to see you again... after these months.

She puts her arms round his neck.

BOTHWELL   What is this?

He takes the phial.

EFFIE   Three drops each night, Fian said... rare juices from the Orient.

BOTHWELL   Rare juices! One part brose, three parts water of Leith.

EFFIE   You do not trust it?

BOTHWELL   I do not require it. *(He sniffs the phial, pours the contents into the chamber-pot.)* As if we lacked pull in our own bodies, that we should need philtres and 'rare juices'.

EFFIE   I have criet out for you, in your absence. My body longs for yours.

BOTHWELL   And mine, for yours... My blood is firit by your thighs, your warmth, your glow... *(He kisses her, draws her on to the bed.)* By the magic potion that runs in your veins... and beats in your breasts... and makes our bodies one...

He starts to unclothe her. The lights go down.

Scene 5

A smithy. Tools of the trade. DAVID SEATON *questions* GILLES DUNCAN. THOMAS STRACHAN, *smith, listens.*

SEATON   You must tell me, which farm?

GILLES   I have telt you. On the Craigs.

SEATON   Where there was a sick bairn? *(She nods.)* That is sick no longer? *(She nods.)* You have curit this bairn?

GILLES   I but cradled him in my arms, Master.

SEATON   By whose grace then?

GILLES   By God's good grace, what else?

STRACHAN *(aside)*   Satan's.

SEATON   How often have you usit this... power, Gilles?

GILLES   I have no power. Had the bairn died, would I have been liable?

161

STRACHAN   Yes!

SEATON   Enough!

STRACHAN   There are tales of sick-making.

GILLES   I have healit only.

STRACHAN   What of the miller's son, that died in the night?

SEATON   It is I who am chargit to put these questions. I am instructit by the Minister.

STRACHAN   *(spits)*   The Minister!

GILLES   They say God favours them that love him, and obey His commandments.

SEATON   And them that break them? Does God not chastise?

GILLES   *(simply)*   Master, I am in your hands.

SEATON   You must account for... these other nights. *(Pause.)* Is there not... some lad?

STRACHAN   *(straightens up)*   What lad would touch her? When half the village has been up her, afore him? *(As she protests.)* Look at her, Master... smell her... she's sticky with it.

GILLES   Not true!

STRACHAN   Bare-facit bitch!

GILLES   He says this, because I preventit him, every time he wantit me. *(Appeals to* SEATON.) He has tried to take me, Master... to force me.

STRACHAN   Whoor!

SEATON   I forbid this... wantonness of tongue... Things must be done... in a seemly fashion... without violence or abuse... *(He takes* GILLES' *wrists.)* Gilles... you must loose your tongue... else it will be loosit for you... I speak in your own interest... What persons have you been with? *(As she turns her head away.)* Please, Gilles... *(His speech is punctuated by* STRACHAN'S *hammering. Shouts:)* Stop that! (GILLES *has snatched her hands away, pressed them to her ears.* SEATON *takes them again.)* For your own sake, speak... Gilles... before it is too...

He turns resignedly to STRACHAN, *who steps forward – a length of rope in his hands.* STRACHAN *loops the rope round her forehead. She struggles.*

STRACHAN   I'll give her a... taste of what... her hands, Master... hold her hands...

SEATON *obeys.* STRACHAN *tightens the rope.* GILLES *screams.*

SEATON   Loose the rope! Loose it. (STRACHAN *does so, reluctantly.)* That is but a foretaste... of what we must do... if you still refuse.

GILLES   I have nothing... to tell...

STRACHAN   What of Fian?

SEATON   What of him?

STRACHAN   Ask her.

SEATON   Gilles? Fian?

GILLES   Nothing...

Again they take her. Slowly, rhythmically, the rope eats in.

SEATON   Please, Gilles... please... please...

GILLES   Slacken the rope... my head... my skull... it is being split... in two...

STRACHAN   Fian? Sampson? Napier? No?

He gives a final twist. She shrieks.

GILLES   Fian! Yes... Fian... yes... yes... yes...

STRACHAN   Sampson?

GILLES   Yes... Agnes Sampson... and Napier... with her...

STRACHAN   And others? Name the others!

GILLES   I will tell you... please... my brain... you bite into... my brain... I will tell you... if... please...

STRACHAN   Agnes Sampson?

GILLES   Midwife...

STRACHAN   *(to* SEATON*)*   There is always a midwife...

GILLES   Barbara Napier... and others...

STRACHAN   Who else?

GILLES   Janet... Janet Blandilands... and another Agnes, yes Agnes Thomson... then John Ker... also George Mott's gudewife, that dwells in Lothian... then the... the potter's wife at Seaton...

SEATON   Seaton!

STRACHAN   Soon enough for a coven!

GILLES   *(incredulous)*   No! No, we but met... never that, you never think it was... no...

SEATON   You see the gravity? Who was the prime mover?

GILLES   I... no, I... there was never any...

STRACHAN   Again?

SEATON   Gilles?

GILLES   *(as the smith takes her)*   Effie... McCalyan... yes, her... the same whose godfather died...

STRACHAN   She has conspirit?

GILLES   Conspirit!

STRACHAN   Conspirit what?

GILLES   *(lost)*   That she...

She collapses. STRACHAN *dashes water at her.*

SEATON   You take over much pleasure in this.

STRACHAN   Every man should take pleasure in his work, Master. The same could turn on you, if the Session wantit. *(The* MINISTER *appears. He stands silently, watching.* GILLES *comes round.)* Ask her... where do they meet?

SEATON   Where, lass? Where do they meet? Tell us, for your soul's sake...

STRACHAN *(aside)* For her white body's sake...

GILLES Then no more harm will come to me? No more pain? *(As he nods his head.)* None, at all? *(But she suddenly shakes her head.)* No... it is no use...

SEATON Tranent?

GILLES Not Tranent...

STRACHAN *sees the* MINISTER. *The* MINISTER *makes a slight gesture, so that* STRACHAN *gives no indication of having seen him.*

SEATON Where, lass...? If not Tranent...?

GILLES The kirkyard... of North Berwick...

STRACHAN This is what we have been seeking. They are trappit now, them and their foul horde. That seek pleasure in themselves, and deny it to others...

SEATON This child, to have been so usit...

GILLES I may go, now?

SEATON You may go.

STRACHAN But—

SEATON I have been given that assurance. Stand aside.

STRACHAN *glances past* SEATON, *and receives a look of approval from the* MINISTER. STRACHAN *steps aside. The* MINISTER *exits, silently.*

STRACHAN I wonder whiles, Master, what goes on under your roof... Witch that she is!

GILLES *(turning)* Good Master... witch is false... witch is... false...

SEATON I pray to God it may be.

GILLES I have your word, Master... you have given me your word.

Song: Gift of Marigold

Frae the skies cam drizzling rain
On the eard and on the stane
Frae the skies cam sizzling sun
Dries the black eard up again.

Seedlings plantit raw on raw
Turn to stalk and then to straw
Turn to yellow where land was sowed
Each ploughgate a strip of gowd.

I bind marigolds in your hair
Draw them tight and hold them there,
Gift of marigold maks you proud
Of your yellow tresses, rope of gowd.

Binding sunflowers in your hair
Yellow crops, gowd tresses there:
But set them alight and raw on raw
Rats come running frae the straw.

Faster and faster see them come
Each rat trailing a burning plume
Eyes like beads and sizzling skin
See how fast their colours run.

Some will die by stick or stane
Crushed in the black eard one by one,
Others in the ditch or in the pyre
Will die by water or by fire.

Scene 6

BOTHWELL'S *house, Leith. A large chest, a table.* BOTHWELL, EFFIE, FIAN. *They drink from pewter mugs, which* BOTHWELL *refills.*

FIAN *(to* EFFIE)   You have access to a black cat?

EFFIE   I do.

FIAN   Black from snout to tail. Castrate it, and do on it the marks of thy will. Christen it, then attach to it the chief parts of a dead man. The joints of the body to be broken apart and attachit. Then the beast cast into the full flood. At such time as James sets sail for the further shore. That he fall utterly. Repeat to me the instructions for the beast, which you will pass on.

EFFIE   Two of them to hold a finger, one on each side the chimney-cruik, the two nebbes of their fingers meeting together. Pass the beast through the links of the cruik, thereafter under the chimney. Still at the house, knit the four feet of the beast to the joints of the dead man. Then fetch it to the shore at Pittenweem, it being midnight for our cause. Then cast the burthen into the sea.

FIAN   Your words being?

EFFIE   'See that there be no deceit among us'.

FIAN   After which the boat should perish. *(To* BOTHWELL.) To the same end we meet tomorrow.

BOTHWELL   Your task is to vest the image.

BOTHWELL *opens the chest.* FIAN *brings out garments.*

FIAN   Ample... ample... So I may assure them his Excellency will be there?

BOTHWELL   He will indeed. In true garb. There are other things, there, you may dispose of at will.

FIAN *eyes the contents of the chest greedily, stuffs his pouches with what he can: buckles, ornaments, brooches.*

FIAN   This must have a speedy conclusion.
EFFIE   Why must it?
FIAN   They say the Session has startit to smell out folks' business.
EFFIE   To what effect?
FIAN   Some servant-lass has been questionit.
BOTHWELL   I have been questionit by the King. It aidit him little.
EFFIE   Too much is at stake, to call a halt.
FIAN   I hope I may... give your ladyship... every satisfaction.
BOTHWELL   You will be well rewardit.

FIAN *exits.*

EFFIE   *(looks up)*   To cast a dead cat into the sea! To drown a King! Fian is a schoolmaster, yet deludit like the rest.
BOTHWELL   James is deludit also. Why should not Fian claim he can, by his devices, harm the King – when James himself credits it? Who dare say we are mistaken, when James attributes storms to black cats, the scarts on his skin to the scratching of witches' pins?
EFFIE   Their acts can never be proven.
BOTHWELL   Neither can they be disproven. This is a strong string to our bow.
EFFIE   If Fian accomplishes what we have set him to do?
BOTHWELL   A triumph. Yet leave us in the clear. No proof possible. Even if he does not, he still creates an unease throughout the shires. A confusion, in the land. Only thus may we change the larger climate of the times.
EFFIE   Does James suspect?
BOTHWELL   He jumps at his shadow.
EFFIE   Maitland, then? More girth to him?
BOTHWELL   As Chancellor, he is intent on private feuds. He claims estates for the Crown, to milk them himself.
EFFIE   As my father could testify. Three times Maitland attemptit to seize our lands. I shall not forgive him, for what my father went through.
BOTHWELL   Where Maitland keeps a festering stank, I shall create a lilypond.
EFFIE   The King would destroy your lilypond. And you in it.
BOTHWELL   He would like to. But he cannot. Because I am his pike. And pike have teeth.
EFFIE   Why not use them?
BOTHWELL   My aim is not self-advancement, but the renewal of the Kingdom.
EFFIE   When James ceases to be King?

BOTHWELL   There will be another.

EFFIE   There will always be Kings? ·

BOTHWELL   Then there will always be need for you and me, my love… and for dragon's teeth, to sow.

EFFIE   It is you I think of.

BOTHWELL   They are indivisible, what I am and what I am to do.

EFFIE   So are we indivisible… you and I… I am your lilypond… and you… are my pet pike.

She snaps at him.

BOTHWELL   I hope I may give your ladyship… every satisfaction.

EFFIE   You will be well rewardit.

EFFIE *exits.*

BOTHWELL   May she burn like coal, this night… May she burn like coal, as has been ordainit.

To Black.

Song: Berwick-Brigge

When the grey howlit has three times hoo'd,
When the grinning cat has three times mew'd,
When the tod has yowl'd three times in the wood,
At the red mune cowerin ahint the cloud,

When the stars hae cruppen deep in the drift,
Lest cantrips had pyked them oot of the lift,
Up horses a', but mair adowe:
Ryde, ryde, for Berwick-Brigge Knowe…

                    *

[Cummer, gae ye afore, cummer gae ye,
Gin ye winna gae, cummer let me,
    Ring-a-ring-a-widdershins,
    Linkin lithely widdershins,
Cummers carline crone and queyn
        Roun gae we:

Cummer gae afore, cummer gae ye,
Gin ye winna gae, cummer let me,

> Ring-a-ring-a-widdershins,
>   Loupin lichtly widdershins,
> Kiltit coats and fleean hair
>   Roun gae we:
>
> Cummer gae ye afore, cummer gae ye,
> Gin ye winna gae, cummer let me,
>   Ring-a-ring-a-widdershins,
>   Whirlin, skirlin widdershins,
> And De'il tak the hindmaist
>   Whae'er she be!]

Scene 7

North Berwick Kirkyard. Tombstones, trees, candles. Masked figures. In the background a naked form gyrates. FIAN, *in an animal-skin, has a staff in his hand. He leads them.*

FIAN   Oh put thy trust in HIM
ALL   We put our trust in HIM
FIAN   That will appear before thee
ALL   That will appear before us
FIAN   And not in God the Father
ALL   Not in God the Father
FIAN   Nor his Son
ALL   Nor His Son
FIAN   Who neither answer
ALL   Who neither answer
FIAN   Nor appear on thy call
ALL   Nor appear on our call

FIAN *strikes the ground, three times.*

FIAN   Benedicite!
                Benedicite!
                        Benedicite!
ALL   Glory!
            Glory!
                Glory!

BOTHWELL *appears, as the* DEVIL: *black-masked and cloaked.*

BOTHWELL   I adjure ye, worship only me!

ALL   With full allegiance.

BOTHWELL   My servants shall neither want nor ail anything, nor shall I let a tear drop from their eyes so long as they serve only me. Now spare not to eat, drink and be blythe, taking rest and ease. For I shall raise thee up at the latter day gloriously. Eat ye… drink ye…

Moaning, keening from the WOMEN.

ALL (FIAN *leading)*   We eat this meat in the Devil's name
With sorrow and sych and meikle shame
We shall destroy house and hald
Baith sheep and goats intil the fald
Little good shall come to the fore
Of all the rest of this little store.
(He touches them in turn.)
(FIAN *leading.)*
And the more to prove our allegiance true
   Like to vassals good and leal
He has brandit our banes wi his Devil's mark
   And our flesh wi his privy seal.

A wax model of KING JAMES *is unveiled.*

BOTHWELL   May winds rise and grow, that they destroy the false King and Queen.

EFFIE   Why dost thou bear such a grievance against the King?

BOTHWELL   For reason he is the greatest enemy we have in this world.

FIAN   Let the King perish.

ALL   Let the King perish.

Skewers are thrust into the wax image. BOTHWELL *has gone.*

FIAN   Let King James perish

EFFIE   Molten by blue fire

AGNES   And wastit by degrees

FIAN   Let him perish by water

EFFIE   By fire

AGNES   And air

FIAN   By conjoinment of the elements

EFFIE   In his despite

FIAN   By fire and water

ALL   And fire agen

FIAN   So let him burn

ALL   Until Amen

FIAN   By fire and water

ALL   And fire agen

FIAN   So let him burn

ALL   Until Amen

FIAN   So much for King James the Sixth, ordainit to be consumit at the instance of a noble man! *(Slow dance.* GILLES *enters, sees the skewered image, screams.)* Who is she?

AGNES   Gilles Duncan. From Tranent.

FIAN   The one that has been interrogatit?

GILLES   Who is that… that man… good Master… I came…

AGNES   That is no man. That's the King.

GILLES   My head… is split… my good Master…

FIAN   I have a mind to silence her.

EFFIE   She's but a silly chicken.

FIAN   She may give away our meeting-place.

EFFIE   We shall soon find another.

GILLES   I have come… to warn you.

A skewer is held out to her. She thrusts it away, runs. She is stopped in her tracks.

OFFICER   Stand, in the King's name!

1st SOLDIER   In the name of King James of Scotland, stand!

SOLDIERS *enter,* STRACHAN *with them. Torches, drawn swords. Panic, milling figures. The wax image is knocked over.*

2nd SOLDIER   No you don't, my wee burdie…

OFFICER   *(indicates* FIAN, *still masked)*   There he is. Our chief prize. He is wantit alive. Do not let him slip!

FIAN *flees, pursued by* SOLDIERS. STRACHAN *takes* GILLES.

STRACHAN   Bite, would you? I'll give you something to bite about.

3rd SOLDIER   Feel like having a go?

STRACHAN   Bloody split her in two!

EFFIE   The lass has done you no harm. Do her none.

OFFICER   So you speak, do you? Superior tones, and all. Come on, we'll see how you take to a good… plucking… *(As the* WOMEN *are roped,* FIAN *is brought in.)* So this is the Black Earl, is it? You may worry King James, sonnie, but you don't fricht me.

FIAN   I am the King's man.

OFFICER   The King of Darkness, belike. You are as black as the Earl o' Hell's waistcoat. And by God, you'll pay dear for it. We'll have your marrow running like candle-wax.

He tears off FIAN'S *mask.*

FIAN   You are mistaken.

The OFFICER *looks at him, enraged, then strikes him.*

OFFICER   Where… is… Bothwell?

Silence. As FIAN *turns his head away, the* OFFICER *clubs him to the ground.*

3rd SOLDIER   I kent fine that wasn't Bothwell!
OFFICER   Get a move on. We haven't all bloody night. *(The roped* WOMEN *are removed.* FIAN *is dragged off.)* You, bring up the rear. *(He indicates the wax image.* 2nd SOLDIER *lifts it, hesitantly.)* It's only a bloody doll!

The SOLDIER *exits, with the image. The* OFFICER *looks round, follows. Only wreaths of smoke remain.* BOTHWELL *appears. He looks after the* SOLDIERS, *raises his head, eyes closed.*

Act Two

Proclamation

[HERALD   When SATAN taks a woman for wife,
　　She comes to sorrow and meikle strife,
　　For that her bodie be burnt whole
　　For good of her immortal soule.

　　What woman taks SATAN for husbande
　　Be helde for scorne throughout the land,
　　And she must drink frae a bitter cup
　　For fear her soule be rendered up.

　　Thus hath this present PARLIAMENT
　　A ledger to the DEVIL sent,
　　Fully empowred to treat about
　　Finding revolting WITCHES out.]

Scene 1

Falkland Palace. A courtyard, its centre flags set out as a chequer-board: red and white squares. The chequers moved by poles. Birdsong. JAMES *and* HOME *stand on either side of the board. Extremely long pause. Ultimately* JAMES *makes a move.* HOME *takes a chequer.* JAMES *retaliates.*

JAMES   Pre... cipi... tate!
HOME   Two can play at that... game...
JAMES   The essence of statecraft: to look as though you are headit in the one direction – then loup in the other.
HOME   No-one more adept than your Grace.
JAMES   No news of Maitland? *(As* HOME *shakes his head.)* His transactions in the city take ower long.
HOME   He's scared Edinburgh Castle slides into the Norloch when he's not looking.
JAMES   He is a trusty Chancellor, for all his foibles. And sets good store on the royal coffers. Whereas there are some that... line their own pockets...

He shoots a look at HOME.

HOME *(coolly)*   Surely never… prelates exceptit.

JAMES   It has been said…

HOME   Tut tut, your concentration's slippit… *(This as he takes a chequer.)*

JAMES   Tut tut tut… *(As he takes* HOME'S.*)* Not so much a matter of concentration, as of having it up here! *(Taps his head.)*

HOME   Just so! *(He takes another.)*

JAMES   Aye… just so! *(He retaliates.)*

HOME   An ambitious piece… that seeks a crown.

JAMES   They are not… easy come by…

The JESTER *enters.*

JESTER   Weel playit, Majesty! *(To* HOME.*)* Is that him won again?

HOME   We've not finished yet.

JESTER   Best cry it a draw. Here's the rain. *(With a sly look at* JAMES.*)* Think there'll be more thunder?

JAMES   *(a hand to his ear)*   Do not mention it.

JESTER   Aw, I forgot… *(To* HOME.*)* His Majesty can't stomach the lightning… it brings him out in spots.

JAMES   How about crying it a draw? Time we were in the saddle.

JESTER   A saddle'll do you little good, if you haven't a horse.

JAMES   The horse are stablit.

JESTER   *(shakes his head slowly)*   That's what I've come to tell you. They're gone.

HOME   Gone!

JAMES   If this is a prank, or Nicol hasn't boltit his gates, we shall—

JESTER   No, it's the horse that's boltit.

HOME   They were lockit in, good and proper.

JAMES   Maybe they broke their tethers…

JESTER   They were untyit.

JAMES   *(it dawns)*   Bothwell! Bothwell has spiritit them away. Praise God our own life has been sparit, through God's mercy.

JAMES *falls to his knees, in thanks.*

HOME   Are they *all* gone?

JESTER   No, just the chestnut and the roan.

HOME   Why did you not say?

JESTER   I couldn't get a word in.

JAMES *is on his feet in a flash.*

JAMES   Nothing but the old nags? Scarce fit for tallow. Serve him right! *(He tosses his head.)*

HOME   So we can ride, after all.

JESTER   Unless the deer have been spiritit away by Bothwell.

JAMES *crooks a finger. The* JESTER *approaches him.*

JAMES   You were forbidden our court for thirty days, under pain of a whipping.
JESTER   I'm... a little hard of hearing, Majesty... I didn't...
HOME   Cut off his ears instead. He'd not miss them.
JESTER *(covers his ears)*   I heard that! *(To* JAMES.) Look, Majesty... you said, if I set foot on the soil of your court... well, this isn't your court. Since you gave it to the Queen, for her wedding... by way of dowry...
JAMES   Man and wife are one. That will not save your hide.
JESTER   Maybe this will! *(The* JESTER *sits on the chequer-board, removes one shoe and then the other, and pours sand from them.)* 'If I set foot on the *soil...*' I haven't... I've been walking on Queensferry sand, fresh frae the firth of Forth.
JAMES   Would Papistry take root in't?
JESTER   Tis lustratit by Protestant seas. Am I forgiven?
JAMES   Better than you deserve.
HOME *(puts a finger to his nose)*   Put your shoes back on, quick...
JESTER   Your nose is too near your arse.

The JESTER *tries to put on his shoes.* JAMES *and* HOME *prod him, with their poles. He skips over the chequer-pieces. A touch of cruelty in their fun.*

HOME   Dance! Dance!
JESTER   Help! Help!
JAMES   Dance! Dance!
JESTER   Aw... naw... *(The* JESTER *is on the ground, covering his head.* SIM *and* CRAW *enter.* JAMES *and* HOME *hand the poles to them, and exit.* SIM *and* CRAW *beat the ground, round the* JESTER.) Naw... aw... let's cry it a draw, Majestie...

From their laughter he realises it is SIM *and* CRAW. *He shakes his fist at them. They come forward. The* JESTER *puts his shoes on, rubs his bruises.*

JESTER   I wish Bothwell *had* spiritit away the horses.
CRAW   Why?
JESTER   Why do you think?
CRAW   Thinking isn't his line.
JESTER   No more than galloping round the countryside's mine. I've a sore enough backside, as it is.
[CRAW   Hear that: he admittit it!
SIM   Admittit what?
CRAW   That he's a pain in the arse.
JESTER   If it comes on buckets, that'll make it even worse.
SIM   It's healthy... keeps you in trim... develops the muscles.

JESTER   What for?

SIM   I'm open to suggestions.

JESTER   Only thing you're open to is ridicule.

CRAW   Depends on your sense of humour. *(To* SIM, *indicating the* JESTER.) Not that he's got one.

JESTER   Not surprising, the company I keep. *(As they are about to strike him, he drops to his knees, intones:)* Semper ibi oh pudendum
Bonum vinum ad bibendum!

CRAW   What does that mean?

JESTER   A Master of Art
Is not worth a Fart!

Hunting horns loudly, off.

SIM   Come on!

CRAW   We're off!

They exit. The JESTER *rises.*

JESTER   I'm famisht... and I can't stand venison...]

He exits.

Scene 2

Falkland. JAMES'S *hunting party.* JAMES *in green doublet with velvet trimmings; and crimson almost to the waist.* HOME, ATTENDANTS, *dabbing themselves clean.* MAITLAND, *apart. Also* SIM *and* CRAW. *Hounds.*

JAMES *(pettedly)*   You obstructit the field. Else we had another stag. Your horse cut across.

HOME *(heatedly)*   No need to cry off the hounds.

The JESTER *enters, wearily.*

JAMES   There was no scent. Too much rain has made the dogs' noses dull.

HOME   Too much rain! Kilbuk and Ding-dew are past it!

The HERALD *enters, wearily.*

HERALD   Your Grace... (JAMES *pays no attention. The* HERALD *addresses*

MAITLAND.) His Grace…

As he pauses expectantly, the JESTER *cuts in.*

JESTER   Has been picking raspberries!

MAITLAND *(to the* HERALD)   His Grace's physician has ordert him to dip his legs in the belly of a slaughtert stag, to strengthen his sinews.

JESTER   Nae need to go paddlin'.

HERALD   Bothwell has been let slip.

JAMES *and* MAITLAND *freeze.*

JAMES *(in fury)*   Escapit! Bothwell escapit! Out of your grasp. When you might have had him.

Pause.

HOME   Was there any doubt he was there?

HERALD   There was—

JAMES   —no circumstantial doubt. His presence will be confirmit. Who was taken?

HERALD   The most base would appear to be one Cunninghame, schoolmaster of Saltpans, alias Dr Fian. Whom the Officer mistook for Bothwell.

MAITLAND   And?

HERALD   Sundry women, of varied degree.

MAITLAND   The highest?

HERALD   One Eupham McCalyan.

MAITLAND   Daughter of Lord Cliftonhall. Hence of pedigree. We shall see how she takes to interrogation.

HERALD   The charge?

MAITLAND   Witchcraft.

JAMES   A witch is a person that has conference with the Devil, to take counsel or do some act. For this, the Devil's bodily presence must be proven. Then the facts of the conference. Finally, the taking of counsel, and the act itself.

MAITLAND   Were devices taken?

HERALD   A wax image.

JAMES   What sort of… likeness?

HERALD   Crude.

MAITLAND   In whose possession was it?

HERALD   This Fian.

JAMES   Put him to the test. He appears the major instrument. The powers of darkness are fell, that make the royal hand shake. Yet we must defy him. Till our marriage with Anne bear issue. To maintain the line. Bothwell is a black stag.

HERALD   And the hinds? What of them?

JAMES   Proven agents must be put to death, in accord with the laws of God.

HERALD   What manner of death?

JAMES   Kindless. As is commonly usit by fire.

HERALD   Ought then neither sex nor rank to be exemptit?

JAMES   It is the highest point of idolatry, wherein no exemption is admittet.

HERALD   Bairns not to be sparit?

JAMES   Not a hair the less of my conclusion.

MAITLAND *(impatiently)*   His Grace condemns all that are of counsel of such crafts.

HERALD   Surely, since this crime be so severely punisht, Judges must beware condemning any, but as are truly guilty?

JAMES   Judges ought indeed. For it is as great a crime – as Solomon hath said – 'to condemn the innocent, as to let the guilty escape free'. Neither ought the report of one infamous person be admittit as sufficient proof, which can stand of no law.

HERALD   What of the guilty confessions that may work against one so accusit?

MAITLAND   The assize must serve for interpreter in that respect.

JAMES   But in our opinion, since in matter of treason against the Prince wives and bairns may serve as sufficient proof, it would seem the more adequate in matters of high treason against God. For who but witches can witness the acts of other witches? Further proof rests in the finding of witches' marks, and also in their fleeting by water. Together with the gushing of blood from the carcass of one destroyit by them. These are God's supernatural signs. Which we interpret as we may.

MAITLAND   They are familiar with the water-test, at Berwick?

HOME   They soon will be.

JAMES   The method straightforward: stripping and binding, then the tying of the thumbs to the toes. *(Pause.)* There is to be an innovation. The right thumb is now to be tied to the left great toe, and vice-versa. Thus making the sign of God's holy cross. *(The* JESTER *has mimicked the position.)* If she sink she be innocent. If she float, guilty – and treatit according.

HERALD   By what reasoning?

JAMES   Water rejects the flesh of witches, baptisit as they have been in unholy liquid.

JESTER   In other words, we're a Christian nation! *(As the others turn angrily, he raises an arm.)*

Full moon and high sea

Shall not touch thee.

Dark dawning, stormy sky,

King James shall never die.

JAMES   It were best not, in that he is God's instrument in this place, against the lawlessness that shakes loose the commonweal. It is God's cause, that we are fighting.

MAITLAND   There are papers to be preparit.

HOME   And apparel to be changit.

JAMES   Only by earnest prayer to God and his Angels of Light can this disease be curit, and darkness driven from our shores. The causes are manifest, that make them rife. For the wickedness of the people on one hand procures this defection, whereby God punishes sin, by a greater iniquity. On the other part, the consummation of the World and our deliverance draw near, making Satan to rage the more at the imminent o'erthrow of his instruments. *(To* HERALD.) Prepare a writ, to have Bothwell declarit outlaw. Have it proclaimit thrice at the Mercat Cross, and throughout the land. To this effect: it is for every law-abiding citizen to apprehend him and bring him to justice, giving respect neither to him nor his property. Return post-haste, with notice of our imminent arrival. *(To* HOME.) Let there be a good meat on the spit, and flagons of red wine. Thereafter we depart for the palace of Holyroodhouse, and from thence to the Toolbooth. There to stamp the bloody seal upon this affair.

Scene 3

Tranent. MINISTER *and* SEATON.

SEATON   You said she would be releasit.
MINISTER   So she was.
SEATON   As bait. For Bothwell.
MINISTER   Who denies King James all dignity.
SEATON   And can look after himself. Which she cannot.
MINISTER   These are confessit witches. They are altogether different.
SEATON   Different?
MINISTER   Defilit.

   Pause.

SEATON   You say… there is no cure?
MINISTER   Only the grave. As for hunchbacks.
SEATON   If I could speak for her.
MINISTER   A great wheel is set in motion, that would crush you.
SEATON   She is innocent.
MINISTER   She has confessit.
SEATON   Under duress.
MINISTER   The Godly remain firm in their resolve. It is Satan's own, that reveal their true colours.

   Pause.

SEATON   What have you… against this Bothwell?
MINISTER   Till he is put down, the King cannot turn his attention to the dissolution

178

of the Popish lords who disdain the true faith.

SEATON   The Kirk's job is to save souls, not abjure them.

MINISTER   Say no more. As for the creature Duncan, her bodily comforts will be seen to, never fear.

SEATON   You... will do nothing?

MINISTER   I will overlook this meeting.

Scene 4

BOTHWELL'S *house, Leith. The* HERALD *enters.*

BOTHWELL   I expectit you sooner.

HERALD   I had to be careful, not to be interceptit. I have come to warn you.

BOTHWELL   Has Maitland turned into the Fox he is?

HERALD   James has had you proclaimit outlaw. (BOTHWELL *turns to face the* HERALD.) Your armorial bearings have been torn, at the Mercat Cross.

BOTHWELL   I terrify him so!

HERALD   He blames you, for raising storm.

BOTHWELL   If he catches the croup, he blames me.

HERALD   Soldiers are on their way.

BOTHWELL   Why not sooner?

HERALD   The last place they'd think to find you, is your own hald. There is still time. Head for the Borders.

BOTHWELL   Something I must do, first.

HERALD   You mean... the Lady...

BOTHWELL   Lady?

HERALD   McCalyan.

BOTHWELL   What of her?

HERALD   It is too late... to save her.

BOTHWELL   Why should I save her?

HERALD   I... had heard.

BOTHWELL   Heard what?

HERALD   They say she... has been... seducit.

BOTHWELL   She is a marrit woman. How then, seducit?

HERALD   That she... well... has been led astray... usit.

BOTHWELL   By me? *(The* HERALD *nods, hesitantly.* BOTHWELL *pushes him into a chair.)* 'Led astray... usit...' A mealy mouth, to be a King's Herald. *(He laughs.)* Bothwell, to seduce... a woman of high degree... daughter of a noble lord... It is kitchen wenches that get themselves seducit... not ladies of style, and pedigree, that wear silks and satins next their skin... Such ladies know best how to... raise the Devil... in a man... how to tempt the flesh... and make it rise... We are not

Devils in ourselves, but that women make us so. What is a man to do, but take
what is offert him? On a silver platter? Or a paddit couch?

But make no mistake, Herald... it is not Bothwell that seduces... but he who is
seducit... time and again, it has been so... Never was Earl so put upon, as this
poor fellow that stands before you... whether he wantit it or no, there was little
option, no politic escape... this poor woman's tool, that now confronts you... *(As
the* HERALD *rises.)* And listen, Herald... when they are done, or undone as you
would have it... it is their own look-out...

But you are not a ladies man... I forgot... you are a most moral Herald... and
servant of the King... I can tell by your stance you disapprove... a most moral
Herald... whose only sin... is to betray his Master...

HERALD *(vehemently)* No!

BOTHWELL He may see it in that light. When you come to the Borders.

HERALD No.

BOTHWELL You will not join me?

HERALD I have a wife, and duties at Court.

BOTHWELL And set surface glitter against our cause?

HERALD I am for peace. And always have been. I was not against James, but his
excesses. And aimed at unity, to hold these in check. But each faction has gone its
own gate. While James is grown more mature in statecraft.

BOTHWELL In dissimulation.

HERALD I believe he should retain his throne. And in due course align it with
England's.

BOTHWELL He still acts in excess.

HERALD Not to the extent you do. I can no longer stomach your desperate ways.

BOTHWELL Who have a wife, and duties at Court! *(Pause.)* So you side with James,
against me.

HERALD Not against you. Or I would not be here. But with James, yes. Because he
will win through.

BOTHWELL Why?

HERALD Because he is the King.

BOTHWELL And legitimate.

HERALD That too.

BOTHWELL But for my impediment, the crown could have been mine.

HERALD Or Moray's.

BOTHWELL They say Moray and the Queen... are at it.

HERALD I do not know.

BOTHWELL And if you did, you would not tell! *(Pause.)* As for McCalyan, you are
mistaken. That has nothing to do with me. Maitland had her taken, because he is
after the lands she inheritit from her father. It is not his first try.

HERALD I must go.

BOTHWELL *holds out his hand. The* HERALD *takes it.* BOTHWELL *snatches the*
HERALD'S *dagger.*

BOTHWELL   Is this a plot? A subterfuge? Is some trap set, between here and the
Borders?

HERALD   Not that I know of.

BOTHWELL   Prove your good faith.

HERALD   How?

BOTHWELL   There is a Lady… by whom I would dearly like… to be seducit!

HERALD   That is no concern of—

BOTHWELL   She has a chamber… in the palace of Holyroodhouse… which
chamber… has a key.

HERALD   My honour forbids that I—

BOTHWELL   Your honour! That wear one colour on your front, another to the rear?
(Pause, as he toys with the dagger.) James wants me alive? What if Bothwell were
found, with in his breast a dagger… and on its hilt, the initials of the King's
Herald? Or in the breast of some other… convenient corpse? *(Pause.)* The Lady
Atholl… has a chamber… in Holyroodhouse…

HERALD   No!

BOTHWELL   When the key to that chamber… rests in this palm this dagger will be
returnit to the King's Herald… who has his wife… and duties, at Court.

Pause.

HERALD   You revolt me! You are… a bee at a honeycomb.

BOTHWELL   You disapprove?

HERALD   I merely wonder at it.

BOTHWELL   What wonder you? I shall give you occasion to wonder!

BOTHWELL *raises the dagger. He seems about to stab the* HERALD. *Instead he
plunges it into his own belly. He falls to the ground, with a howl. The* HERALD
stands petrified. At last he stoops to touch BOTHWELL. BOTHWELL *squirms aside
and rises to his feet, laughing. He holds out the dagger.*

BOTHWELL   Here… take it! *(The* HERALD *takes the dagger. He exits, without
speaking.* BOTHWELL *looks after him.)* Such sleekit pawns… are needit… in the
game we play… *(Suddenly:)* McCalyan! What is McCalyan… to me? Nothing!
She is past… and done with… It cannot be… otherwise… But must… be so…
Past… and no more… to me… or anything… in this stinking pit of a world… this
rotten cell… where kings smile… and strut… *(His tone changes:)* God help her…
God help them all… for no-one else will…

Song: The Badger's Fur…

The badger's fur is black and white
I make a money purse out of it.

Wild boar has a bristly pelt
Slice it into a yellow belt.

Russet-coloured fox is fine
Ladies like him next their skin.

In winter tak the weasel and stoat
Turn them into an ermine coat.

The beardit buck upon the brae
Will come upon an evil day:

They will be catcht in subtle traps
Ladies will wear them on their laps.

Not even the lavrock will escape
Whose feathers deck a nobleman's cape.

However sweetly she has sung
The philomel will lose her tongue.

Lion's the one we all adore
In one hand water, in one hand fire.

Yet see him put his head atween his knees
And pass the time scratching for fleas.

Scene 5

The Tolbooth. McCalyan's trial. The Indictment. EFFIE, *centre-stage, in a white shift,
her hair shorn, ankles tied. The* OFFICER *by her.* JAMES *plays nervously. With him,
the* HERALD *and* HOME, *the latter with a flippant air.* MAITLAND *as Interlocutor.*
JUDGE, DEMPSTER, SCRIVENER, SOLDIERS, *others. The* MINISTER *and* SEATON.

DEMPSTER *(reads)* '…indictit of bewitching by your airt of Sorcery, John
Johnston, Miller's son of Tranent, being of 17 yrs of age, by the which witchcraft
he died; and thereby for the cruel slaughter and murder of him;
'Item the twelfth, indictit with consulting with Agnes Sampson aforesaid and
ither divers witches for the treasonable staying of the Queen's homecoming by
raising storm and wind, to that effect, or else the drowning of her Majestie and her
company by conjuring of catts and casting them in the sea at Leith, at the back of

Begie-Todd's house, also criet Rbt Grierson;

'And generally you are indictit for common witch, having usit and practisit these sorceries and witchcrafts, divinations and charms, as is particular above-written, and giving yourself furth to have such knowledge, to the abuse of the people. And to the detriment of the King's Majestie within his Realm – in the furthering of the work of the Devil your Master. And ought to be judgit to death thereof and in dry exemplar to ithers to do the like'.

Here endeth the indictment.

The scroll is handed to the JUDGE. JAMES *beckons for it, glances at it, and returns his attention to* EFFIE. MAITLAND *bows to* JAMES, *and to the* JUDGE.

The Interrogation.

MAITLAND   Have you ever intendit the death of the King?
EFFIE   Never.
MAITLAND   You have had no illicit liaison, to put this into practice?
EFFIE   Never.
MAITLAND   You would renounce all such claims against you?
EFFIE   I would truly.
MAITLAND   What of Gilles Duncan, servant to David Seaton, Depute-Bailiff of Tranent, of this Kingdom?
EFFIE   I have never met Seaton.
JAMES   Satan, more like.
MAITLAND   What of Agnes Sampson?
EFFIE   I have no business with her.
MAITLAND   She has had business with you. She has confessit taking a black toad, hanging it by the heels three days to let the venom drip out, that she collectit the venom in an oyster-shell, till she could find a piece of linen cloth belonging to his Grace, which she would obtain by the service of one John Ker, an attendant in his Majesty's chamber. This same Ker refusit to help her, and reportit the same.
JUDGE   To the saving of his soul.
MAITLAND   The said Agnes further confessit that, had she obtainit any single piece of linen cloth worn by the King, she would have bewitched him instant to death by extraordinary pains, as if he had lain among thorns. You had no part in this? Or in taking a tom-cat christent with ceremony, thereafter conveying the beast into the sea?
EFFIE   You wrong me.
MAITLAND   This done, there arose great storm. Causing the foundering of a boat bound from Bruntisland to Leith.
JUDGE   True or false?
EFFIE   False.
MAITLAND   Sampson said false. Till she was strippit, and the Devil's mark found on her privates. She did straightway confess.

EFFIE   I am an honest woman.

MAITLAND   Greymeal?

EFFIE   Greymeal?

MAITLAND   Barbara Napier?

EFFIE   You have found nothing against her.

JUDGE   Not yet.

MAITLAND   It is further statit you did dance in the kirk-yard of North Berwick. The major aim being to harm your King.

EFFIE   Cannot friends meet, for simple pleasure?

MAITLAND   Simple pleasure? To destroy a King? By conspiracy?

EFFIE   Conspiracy travels on tiptoe, a finger to its mouth. Not openly with song and dance.

MAITLAND   You were in the abandonment of your lusts.

EFFIE   We were all women.

MAITLAND   Fian was there. Who has been since broken on the rack.

EFFIE   I did not see him.

MAITLAND   He did not incite you against the King?

EFFIE   Why should he, as a leal subject?

JUDGE   You answer questions, not put them.

MAITLAND   You were their leader?

EFFIE   No.

MAITLAND   Intermediary then? Between them and the Unknown? You deny it?

EFFIE   How can I deny what is unknown?

MAITLAND   You confirm, then?

EFFIE   I did not say so.

MAITLAND   Gilles Duncan was of your company?

EFFIE   No, she… she is but a lass, and of no significance.

MAITLAND *looks up at the* JUDGE.

JUDGE   Bring Duncan.

GILLES *is dragged into Court, shorn and bound. She falls to the ground.* HOME *sniggers.*

MAITLAND   Gilles, tell us once more… of that night at Berwick-Brigge. When you were with the others… His Grace would be glad to—

GILLES   Grace… I beg for Grace… my lord…

EFFIE   Leave her in peace. She is innocent of—

MAITLAND   Innocent? After your foul play? Your singing and jigging…

GILLES   Ring-a-ring-a-widdershins… round gae we… Linkin blithely… to the sweet… the sweet…

MAITLAND   Were you one of them, Gilles?

GILLES   No… never one… my lord… my good Master… never one…

184

EFFIE   There is your answer.

MAITLAND   But you were going to be, is that not right, Gilles? Soon?

GILLES   Soon, they were… going to receive me… into their arms… and let me lie there… please… only sleep…

MAITLAND   *(close to her)*   Who was going to receive you?

GILLES   Effie… with all her riches… the kindest… my lady…

JUDGE   To what end? Were they going to receive you?

MAITLAND   Tell us, and then you may sleep.

GILLES   That I may… sleep… sound… *(She looks up suddenly.)* Why, they were going to make me a witch!

Sudden blackout.

The Interrogation (contd.)

MAITLAND   I put this to you. That you were not merely witch, in attempt to smear others; but yourself actit in accord. In devising means of harming his Grace. That his body waste away, his image be consumit by flame, that he be in agony thereby.

EFFIE   His Grace looks fit enough.

MAITLAND   Not through your efforts, but in their despite. Do you recall these rites? *(As she shakes her head.)* I shall refresh your memory.

A cover is removed from the wax image.

EFFIE   It is little like the King, to me.

JUDGE   Such remarks do not improve the standing of the Panel.

MAITLAND   There is further evidence that certain pins, removit from that effigy, had been seen at your home. Pins of silver, and gold. In keeping with your station.

EFFIE   A costly pastime.

MAITLAND   Yet cheap, to do away with a King.

He is handed down pins, by the DEMPSTER.

EFFIE   You cannot catch me on that score.

MAITLAND   *(to* EFFIE*)*   You have never seen these pins before?

They are held before her.

EFFIE   Never.

MAITLAND   Bring in Duncan.

EFFIE   This is kindless. How can she—?

OFFICER   Shut your mouth.

GILLES *is dragged in. She is shown the pins.*

MAITLAND   Tell us, where have you seen these before? Whose are they?
GILLES   The dew is like diamonds… on the grass… these are… such fine… my
  Lady…
MAITLAND   You have nothing to fear, on her account.
GILLES   I have seen them…
MAITLAND   In a home?
GILLES   In the home… of Effie McCalyan… there… she is a fine Lady…
EFFIE   This child has never been to my house.
JUDGE   Do not interrupt.
MAITLAND   How else have you seen these pins usit?
GILLES   She had such lovely… tresses… so like a Lady… of noble birth…
MAITLAND   Where else, Gilles?
GILLES   They were… stickit in that man there.
MAITLAND   What did you stick pins in him for?
GILLES   Never I… what would a good lass do the likes of that… I was busy,
  besides…
MAITLAND   Busy?
GILLES   I was playing my tune… my Lord…

JAMES *has leaned forward, cupping an ear so as to make out what she is saying.*

JAMES   Was there an instrument? With her?
MAITLAND   There was.

MAITLAND *lifts a jew's harp.* JAMES *steps forward, takes it gingerly. He gives it to*
GILLES, *encourages her.*

JAMES   Let her… give us… here you are… lass… play on it, to your heart's
  content…

She plays. JAMES *is enraptured.*

MAITLAND   The womenfolk jigging the while… this to provide the beat… so she
  says…

JAMES *claps his hands.*

EFFIE   A drear tune, to jig to.

A voice from the back of the Court: SEATON.

SEATON   Your Majesty.

JUDGE   Silence!

JAMES   Let him speak.

SEATON   Stop her.

SEATON *comes forward.*

JAMES   This may well be her last tune on earth. Would you deprive her of it?

SEATON   I protest. She is not acquaint with the—

EFFIE   Never fear Master, she does not sense it. They have already done their work on her.

JUDGE   Your name, Master?

SEATON   David Seaton, my Lord.

MAITLAND *(to* JAMES)   The depute-bailiff. From Tranent.

SEATON   I am her Master, Sire. I must... protest at this treatment of her...

JUDGE   Her treatment is in keeping with her sins.

SEATON   Spare some pity for her in her distress.

JAMES   Pity a witch!

SEATON   I beg she be sparit. Instead of what... you have in store.

JUDGE   We would save her soul.

SEATON   She cannot defend herself.

JUDGE   Tell us Master, do you plead for all, or only this one?

SEATON   She is the only one, my Lord. The only one I'd defend.

JUDGE   Defence amounts to defiance.

SEATON   Intercede, then.

JAMES   A witch must have no-one in this world.

SEATON   She is no witch. I swear it.

JUDGE   Can you prove it? At law?

SEATON   She has been a constant comfort to the sick. Not even the Minister could deny she—

JAMES   'Satan can transform himself into an Angell of Light': Second Corinthians, eleven and fourteen.

SEATON   Say... some folly came over her... for a spell...

JAMES   As Christ says, 'It is not anything that enters in that defiles, but only that which precedeth and cometh out.'

SEATON   I speak out of no disrespect to your Grace... or towards this assize... but because... *(He is lost for words.)* Let her return to Tranent. I shall answer for her. And act as surety, however the Court command... keeping a careful eye... on her behaviour. *(He looks up.)* The Minister there... can supervise... in matters of... *(But the* MINISTER *stiffens, turns his head away.)* My Lord... we have walls to big, ditches to be dug... but there is also women's work... fruit to pick, cream to skim, water to be drawn from the well... These tasks she can fulfil... the stitching of garments... and much else besides... *(He appeals.)* My Lord... Please...

JUDGE   Enough of your prattle.

SEATON   I see no logic, in her suffering.

JAMES   If an arm offend thee, cut if off. If an eye, cut it out. That the remainder of the body be whole. There is logic. Not logic mere, but *Logos*, the Word. Would you give free rein to them that would tear down God's Kingdom?

GILLES *starts to strum on the harp.*

SEATON   Gilles... Gilles...
MAITLAND   Do you not see, she does not know you.
SEATON   Gilles, lass...
JUDGE   We await your decision.
SEATON   I am torn...
MAITLAND   And may well be.
EFFIE *(to* SEATON)   It is too late, Master...
SEATON *(after a pause)*   Forgive me... I wish to God I had more courage...

SEATON *exits. At a sign from* HOME, *two soldiers follow.* GILLES *plays the jew's harp.*

MAITLAND   Courage enough... *(To* GILLES.) One thing more, then that is all. Who was it, led the circle round the image?
JUDGE   She has said, the Panel.
MAITLAND   Then what was said, Gilles? What did they say?
GILLES   They said... the blackthorn and the may... the laverock and the merle... the coushat and the philomel... all on a sweet summer's day... the fulmart and the fox... with busy bears and brocks... did... all did together... did together... play...
MAITLAND *(gently)*   Can you remember? Tell his Grace... and he will be well pleasit.
GILLES   I would always please his Grace... my gracious Master... has gone...
MAITLAND   Yes.
GILLES   I am all alone.
MAITLAND   We are with you. Was it... about King James the Sixth?
GILLES   Yes... that is right... they said...
JUDGE   Speak up, child.
GILLES   'This is James the Sixth, orderit to be consumit at the instance of a noble man.'
MAITLAND   What noble man?
GILLES   Of breeding... the highest...
MAITLAND   Fian?
GILLES   Higher...
MAITLAND   Did you see him?
GILLES   The once.
MAITLAND   Was he dark, or fair?
GILLES   Fair.

188

JUDGE   Not Fian. The... Other...

GILLES   Oh... dark...

MAITLAND   Did you touch him?

GILLES   No. But he touchit me.

MAITLAND   Was he... hot? Or cold?

GILLES   He came, and causit all the company to kiss his hinder parts... which
were... as cauld as ice... His body as hard as iron... his face terrible, his nose the
beak of an eagle, great burning eyes... that did leme of licht... claws to his
hands... his feet... hairy... like a griphon...

JAMES   *(sotto)*   Hepburn is hirsute.

MAITLAND   His voice?

GILLES   Was soft... low and soft... like the wind in the corn... at twilight... but so
cold... so cold... like the time in the mill-stream... when I fell in, as a child...
under the ice...

MAITLAND   He kisst you?

GILLES   I cannot recall... whether he... he kissit me... he kissit... he kissit me...
and his body was cauld, but oh his kiss was warm... like blood... on my lips...
Have I done well, my lord?

MAITLAND   Did he give himself a name?

GILLES   I scarce remember... it was soon morning... the world full of throstles... a
dewy cage...

MAITLAND   What was his name?

GILLES   The... the Earl... the Black Earl... but it was others that he kissit, my
lord... I am a good girl... a good girl, Master... in my dewy cage... of grass...

Sudden Blackout. A spot, for:

Song: *That she was a Witch*

That she was a witch, that she was a witch,
    They had nae shadow of doubt,
They prickit her body frae head tae heel
    To find the witch-mark out.

That he was a witch, that he was a witch,
    They had nae shadow of doubt,
So they gave him the rack, they gave him the screw,
    And then they gave him the boot.

That she was a witch, that she was a witch,
    There was nae shadow of doubt,
So they gave her the test, the water test,
    And then they fishit her out.

That they were all witches, that they were all witches,
    Was took for grantit quite,
So they strung them up wi' tarry ropes –
    And then they bade them goodnight...

The Interrogation (contd.)

EFFIE   Why must the answer always be witchcraft? To anything that frights you? When Bothwell was chasit to the Tyne, your Grace's horse was seen to stumble. Your Grace was heard to cry out, 'Witchcraft!' That was not witchcraft!

MAITLAND   What then?

JAMES *(to* SCRIVENER)   Note this.

EFFIE   A rabbit hole.

MAITLAND   The ways of witches can be simple. Crude, as well as complex. This Fian has been seen flying through the air. Over walls and biggins. No horse near.

EFFIE   Many's the man sees his companions fleeing, at night. And forgets it next morning, when he's sobert up.

MAITLAND   Yet things exist in the land, to do evil.

EFFIE   They say there are black bogles in Loch Morar, that blow out steam, and eat men.

JAMES *(to* SCRIVENER)   Register that.

MAITLAND   You are happy in this land?

EFFIE   Happy?

MAITLAND   These things and persons we speak of, are an attempt to o'erthrow Law and Order. To do away with true Government, that Another may rule in its stead. Letting the Government, as has been said, go to the Devil.

EFFIE   I suspect it is there already, from the misery around.

MAITLAND   You have an interest in Government?

EFFIE   Not I.

MAITLAND   But your Master has.

EFFIE   My Master?

MAITLAND   Bothwell.

EFFIE   He is not my Master.

MAITLAND   Help us trap him, you will earn the King's lasting pleasure.

EFFIE   I have heard the King's pleasure is seldom lasting.

MAITLAND   Bothwell has assuredly led you in unholy worship.

EFFIE   Led who?

MAITLAND   Those we have spoken of. Fian, and Sampson, and—

EFFIE   Whom you torture, for your own satisfaction. You dream up devils, so that you can put them down. What purpose does such cruelty serve? Or is it because we are Catholics, that we are treatit so?

MAITLAND   Not because you are Catholics. But to show our Kirk is as vigilant as yours, in its zeal against the powers of Darkness. (JAMES *signs to* MAITLAND. *They whisper together.* MAITLAND *resumes his stance.* JAMES *is attentive.)* You know the penalty for Treason? And that it is Treason to support a rebel? An outlaw, against the throne?

EFFIE *(wearily)* Yes.

MAITLAND You still say Bothwell is nothing to you?

EFFIE How could he be?

MAITLAND Then he is without a friend in this land. His proper place is in the Tolbooth. But he has a hide-out. The court would favour anyone... that would reveal that hide-out.

EFFIE You needn't try to bargain with me.

MAITLAND You protect him still?

EFFIE I am exhaustit.

MAITLAND You protect him, at your peril.

EFFIE We have been over this.

MAITLAND And must continue to do so.

EFFIE I am in no position to—

MAITLAND It is treason to protect a traitor.

EFFIE Will this business soon be—?

MAITLAND Bothwell is a traitor.

EFFIE Why 'Bothwell' me?

MAITLAND He is nothing to you?

EFFIE Nothing.

MAITLAND Nor you to him?

EFFIE Nor I to him.

MAITLAND That I accept. *(Pause.)* Or he would be here, to protect you.

JAMES He would have appearit—

MAITLAND —on a shining stallion—

JAMES —at the head of a glittering troop—

MAITLAND —and made a triumphal exit—

JAMES —whereas he has gone to ground—

MAITLAND —to save his skin—

JAMES —at the expense of yours—

MAITLAND —which he would not have done—

JAMES —had you meant the least thing to him.

EFFIE You toy with me!

JAMES We shall tell you why he has not come. Because he lies with his whoors. In a secret bed. Under a greasy coverlet, arm in arm.

EFFIE This is obscene.

JAMES Not so obscene as their posture. You cannot bear the thought, who bear his seal upon your privy parts.

EFFIE I have never lain with him.

JAMES Others have! His presence has been notit. And provit. He leaves a mark on a woman. Between her thighs. Like a great fish, with silver scales.

EFFIE Please...

JAMES   We see it, before our eyes. Bothwell taking these filthy creatures, baring their flesh, thrusting their legs apart... then doing his will.

EFFIE   No!

JAMES   One after another on beds of straw... beneath his embrace... or lying on velvet, like liquid gold...

EFFIE   Never!

JAMES   Can you not imagine? Do you not envy them? Think of it! Your flesh, one with his. As he prises your body, and takes his fill... Bothwell on top, yourself working below... panting and huffing, his body making its mark... breath fiery, as he splits you... your breasts like petals, beneath his thrust... opening to him... love swelling and rising... limbs entwinit and threshing... his seed spilling, your juices commingling... soft flesh worked to a frenzy, as he rides you and rides you... festooned in your lust! *(She shrieks, tries to cover her ears.)* You! And Bothwell your Master!

EFFIE   I have no Master.

JAMES   Every woman has a Master.

EFFIE   Not Bothwell.

JAMES   He has ridden you.

EFFIE   No!

MAITLAND   Not Bothwell?

EFFIE   Not Bothwell.

MAITLAND   Whom, then?

EFFIE   Whomsoever you wish.

MAITLAND   The Black Devil himself!

EFFIE   The Black Devil himself... if you would have it so... *(She is reeling.)*

JAMES   'Thou shalt not suffer a witch to live!'

MAITLAND   Not treason. But sorcery. In professit presence of Satan, her hideous Master.

JAMES   We have taken not Bothwell, but an Other.

EFFIE   This is a trick... your subtle words... and images... have upset my senses...

MAITLAND   You are deliverit up in accordance with God's will. I call the indictment proven.

EFFIE *collapses.* JAMES *faces the Court.*

JAMES   This corruption here, bairns suck at the pap. Our conscience doth set us clear in this instance, as did the conscience of Samuel – that did say unto Saul: 'that disobedience is as the sinne of witchcraft': to compare to a thing that were not, were too absurd.

So as we have begun, we plan to go forward. Not because we are James Stewart, and can command so many thousands of men – but because God hath made us King and Judge, to make righteous judgement.

Witchcraft, a crime known to be common amongst us, we call an abominable sin, and that most odious: *Maleficium* or *Veneficium* – an ill or poisonable deed.

We have spent three quarters of a year sifting out those that are guilty of the same. And by God's law punishable by death. For them that are found guilty, they must be rendert up in accord with the law.

And so demand a verdict in this case.

The Verdict. EFFIE *dragged upright.*

JUDGE   We find dealings with the Devil, and the Devil's bodily presence, proven. Second, full conference with the Devil, proven. Finally, the taking of council and study of the act itself, proven. That being the true verdict of this Court. *(To* EFFIE.) This day, Eupham McCalyan, spouse to Patrick Moscrop, alias McCalyan, being presentit here on Panel, as she that was convictit in Court of Justiciary here held in Edinborough the 15th day of June, 1591; and in view and due consideration of the articles heretofore indictit and read, and on her own confession before the Court and in presence of his Grace, is hereby given to sentence, by the mouth of Wm Grey, Dempster:

All rise.

DEMPSTER   'That the said EUPHAM McCALYAN, as culpable and guilty thereof, be taken to the Castel-Hill of Edinborough, and there—
EFFIE   Not stranglit... never stranglit...
OFFICER   Shut your mouth.
DEMPSTER   '—The Castel-Hill of Edinborough, and there bound to a stake and burnt alive to ashes. And all her lands, steadings, heritages and cattle to be forfeit. Which I, Dempster to this Court, do hereby give for doom.'
EFFIE   Sweet Christ... to be burnt alive... never to be... have pity on a poor child in Christ... sweet Jesu, have pity...
JAMES   There can be no appeal. It is not we that do this thing, but Christ God; in that we are the Lord's anointit, and true servant and child of God, while thou art a vessel of His wrath.
EFFIE   He will save me... he will rescue me... never fear...
JAMES   Thus perish all Infidels!
EFFIE   No... you will never... I defy you... I defy you, to the uttermaist, and your vicious ways... I glory in it... I glory... glory... glory...

EFFIE, *arms outstretched, is removed bodily by the* OFFICER. *Blackout.*

Song: The Burning

They trailed her to the high Castel-Yett
    And hemmed her about,
And they smeared her ower frae head tae heel
    To drive the witch-mark out.

They harled her to the Castel-Court,
    And smeared her ower wi tar,
And they chained her to an iron bolt
    An eke an iron bar.

They biggit a pile aboot her bodie
    Twa Scots ells up and higher
Then the hangman cam, wi a lowin torch,
    And kindelt the horrid pyre.

Flames met and broke, in seikly smoke,
    A red ball in the sky;
And then it turned, and then it fell
    To ashes suddenly.

The King transfixt in wonder stood
    And scarce believed his e'en,
And all aghast the courtiers cowerd
    As spell-bound they had been.

But that ae night, his Majestie
    As in his bed he lay
(Last couplet spoken.)
Did find his thochts did wander to
    Anither Judgement Day…

Scene 6

JAMES'S *bedchamber, Holyrood. A carved four poster. Early morning.* JAMES *snores. Slight sounds, whispers, off. A break in the rhythm of the snoring. A gleam in the shadows.* JAMES *stirs in his sleep. Suddenly he sits bolt upright, rubs his eyes.* BOTHWELL *emerges from the shadows, with a drawn sword.*

JAMES *(screams)* Treason… Treason… (BOTHWELL *approaches the bed.)* Help! Help!
BOTHWELL No-one will answer.
JAMES The Guard? My gentlemen of the bed-chamber?
BOTHWELL Taken care of.
JAMES How… how did you…? Treason! (BOTHWELL *throws a key on the bed.)* We shall have you hangit!

194

BOTHWELL *plucks the bed-clothes with the sword.* JAMES *shrinks back, then leaps out of bed: ungainly in cap and nightshirt.* BOTHWELL *in black,* JAMES *in white.*

BOTHWELL   Who'll do the hanging? When the King's on the floor of his chamber, a sword through his—

JAMES   *(cringes, wrings his hands)*   So... after all your intrigues... and affairs... it is come to this... to play assassin... by moonlight... to soil your hands, with... *(He challenges.)* Did your covens not work? *(No reply.)* Aaaah... that's why you're... to avenge them, is it? Aaaaah... It'd have done... them more good, if you'd come to treat for them... while they were still alive.

BOTHWELL   Why should I do that?

JAMES   You were guilty of their deaths.

BOTHWELL   No more than you, who passed sentence on them, and had them executit.

JAMES   You are a force for evil. I for good.

BOTHWELL   You delude yourself. You call evil, what it suits you to call evil. There is no such thing as black and white, in these matters.

JAMES   Through you, they treatit with the Devil. Were made contaminate.

BOTHWELL   All that concerns you is policy... and your own preservation.

JAMES   They were consignit to the flames, by God's Law.

BOTHWELL   Do you not have them on your conscience?

JAMES *on the bed.*

JAMES   You should have been there. To hear their cries, as the flames lickit at their feet. To hear her scream, and beg for Grace. Yet refuse to confess out of lealty to you. To the peril of her soul. Can you see her, at the stake? Atoning for what you made her do? Can you not feel for her? Feel the flesh burn, the fats sizzle and cinder, as the faggots fume? Her lush muscles shrink, sinew shrivel and crack? Her parts of womanhood—

BOTHWELL   She was a lamb let to the slaughter.

JAMES   Through you!

BOTHWELL   Through you!

JAMES   *(holds up a Bible)*   'Put on the whole armour of God, that ye may be able to stand the wiles of the Devil' – Ephesians six and eleven.

BOTHWELL   *(strikes the Bible with his sword)*   You're pretty nakit at the moment.

JAMES   I worship the Lord God of Hosts. While I have heard... your minions make obeisance... in a ritual... one degree more obscene than the kissing of the Papal great toe.

BOTHWELL   It is no great matter which God we worship. The world remains a parchit place.

JAMES   By your pestilence.

BOTHWELL   When there should be more in it to admire than despise.

JAMES   Pestilence is to be despisit. And burnt out.

195

BOTHWELL   To burn houses will not destroy the plague.

JAMES   That will be arrivit at.

BOTHWELL   Root out one pestilence, you make room for another. And end, never seeing the truth.

JAMES *goes to* BOTHWELL.

JAMES   We are the Truth. You do Devil's work. And are now come to seek your King's life. I am wholly in your power. Better die with honour, than live in shame. I am ready to die. Take my miserable life. But before God, I swear thou shalt not have my soul. (JAMES *bares his chest, closes his eyes. Instead of striking,* BOTHWELL *kneels at* JAMES'S *feet.* JAMES *opens one eye.*) Kneel not, adding hypocrisy to treason. Is the manner of your entrance that of a suppliant? I am no longer a boy or a minor, to be treatit as a fool. You, Francis Hepburn, have plottit my death. I call on you, discharge your dishonourable purpose. I will not live a prisoner, and dishonoured. I am ready!

But BOTHWELL *kisses his sword, renders it up.*

BOTHWELL   I harbour no ill-will toward your person. You are my sovereign, and I your subject.

JAMES   Then what on earth... is it you...? *(He scratches.)*

BOTHWELL   Stop playing with yourself!

JAMES   *(a scream)*   What is it you want?

BOTHWELL   Annulment of outlawry. Repeal of the edict against me. Full remission of all bygane offences, and restoration of offices, properties and titles; the same to be ratifiet by Parliament at Linlithgow. Your word to act as surety meantime.

JAMES   Is that all?

BOTHWELL   That is all.

JAMES   What makes you think... *(He breaks off, clenches his fists. He controls himself.)* If I were to refuse?

BOTHWELL   In that courtyard are three hundred men from the Borders. If by dawn, they have not had the signal, they take this palace and put everyone in it to the sword.

JAMES   The signal?

BOTHWELL   From you. 'God save King James of Scotland, and his belovit cousin the Earl of Bothwell!'

JAMES   Three hundred...

BOTHWELL   Oh, I forgot. There is one other thing. My position at Court.

JAMES   Was forfeit.

BOTHWELL   I would like it back.

JAMES   You belong in a dungeon.

BOTHWELL   You had me releasit.

JAMES   But Maitland... he would never consider... it is too much for...

JAMES *is distraught.*

BOTHWELL   Maitland can go.

JAMES   He is my Chancellor.

BOTHWELL   Find another. I want him removit. It is a small price to pay. For life and liberty.

JAMES   You have no right!

BOTHWELL   You see yourself as the one and only true power. Absolute. And any force opposing you, not power but violation of power. Mere violence. In time to come you will realise you are but an infringer of power. Already there are movements afoot. To make rulers act in accord with the will of their people, not their own whim.

JAMES   That would be chaos. Men must be governed.

BOTHWELL   So must monarchs. That men may be free in themselves.

JAMES   Who are you, to think yourself so superior?

BOTHWELL   Your dark shadow, whom you cannot go without.

JAMES   I say you are in league with the Devil.

BOTHWELL   There are many Devils, cousin.

JAMES   I mean Satan.

BOTHWELL   I know his haunt.

JAMES   *(approaches him)*   Tell me. That I may burn him out.

BOTHWELL   He is in this chamber.

JAMES   Where, in this chamber?

BOTHWELL   Why here, cousin…

BOTHWELL *taps himself on the chest.* JAMES *gapes.*

JAMES   You… openly confess it!

BOTHWELL   And here… *(touching* JAMES *lightly on the chest)* …as much as anywhere. (JAMES *is speechless, hand on heart.)* You seem to recognise his haunt at last. *(Pause.)* We are the upper and nether millstones, you and I. One way or another, it is those trappt in the middle, must pay the price.

JAMES   *(indicating* BOTHWELL'S *sword)*   And this?

BOTHWELL   The King's. If he will have it.

JAMES   Sheathe it.

BOTHWELL *does so.*

BOTHWELL   But remember, my dearie… one day will come the time of the real burning! *(Pause.)* It is almost light.

BOTHWELL *supports* JAMES *as he crossed slowly and unsteadily.*

JAMES   *(calls, off)*   Long live King James! And his cousin… And… his… belovit cousin… the Earl of Bothwell…

A great cheer, off. BOTHWELL *exits. Pause.* JAMES *appears, looks round. He is overcome. He crosses to the bed, kneels by it. A single spot on him.*

I trowe in Almychte   God that wrochte
Baith in Heavin and Eard   and all of nochte;
And to His dear Sonne   Jesu Christe,
Was gotten of   the Haly Ghaist.
He bade us come   and there to doom
Baith quick and dead   to His Kingdome.
O keep me frae   the felon slae.
Thou, Lord, for Thy   bitter Passioun
Keep me frae Sinne   and warldly Shame,
And endless Damnatioun.

Grant me the Joye   never will be gane
For sweete Jesu's sake…
                              Amen.

The town bell has started to toll. The spot on JAMES *dims, slowly, to blackout.*

The Jesuit

by

Donald Campbell

First performed at the Traverse Theatre, Edinburgh, on 4 May 1976,
presented by The Heretics and directed by Sandy Neilson

Donald Campbell

Donald Campbell was born in Wick, Caithness, in 1940. In 1947 his family moved to Edinburgh, where he has spent most of his life. After serving an apprenticeship with the Bank of Scotland, he spent a few years in London in what he has described as 'a succession of dead-end jobs'. Returning to Edinburgh in 1967 he worked as a cost accountant for seven years, writing poetry, drama and essays in his spare time. He became a full-time writer in 1974, since when he has been active as playwright, theatre historian, stage director, script-writer and poet.

His first stage play, *The Jesuit,* was written in 1971 and produced in 1976. He has gone on to write more than a score of plays. He considers the most successful of them to be *The Jesuit, The Widows of Clyth* (1979), *Blackfriars Wynd* (1980), *Till All the Seas Run Dry* (1981), *Howard's Revenge* (1985), *Victorian Values* (1986), *The Fisher Boy and the Honest Lass* (1990), *The Ould Fella* (1993), and *Nancy Sleekit* (1994). Three of his plays have won *Scotsman* 'Fringe Firsts' at the Edinburgh International Festival. In 1995 he was awarded a Scottish Arts Council Playwright's Bursary to write *The Herring Queen,* and in 1996 was commissioned by the Edinburgh Festival Society to write *These Fifty Festival Years* in celebration of the Festival's fiftieth anniversary. *Glorious Hearts*, a musical on Heart of Midlothian Football Club, for which he wrote the book and lyrics, was staged in 1999.

He has written some fifty radio programmes, a number of which have won international awards: *A Clydebuilt Man* (New York, 1983), *The Miller's Reel* (Sydney, 1987), and *The Year of the Bonnie Prince* (Monte Carlo, 1996). For television he scripted *The End of an Auld Sang* (1980), *The Old Master* (1984) and episodes of the drama series *Strathblair.* In 1986 he made his directorial debut with John McGrath's *Plugged into History.* Since then he has directed, among other work, some of his own plays and adaptations.

Donald Campbell has published a substantial body of poetry. Poems from his six volumes of verse are included in his *Selected Poems: 1970–1990* (Edinburgh: Galliard, 1990). His poetry is discussed in Leonard Mason's study, *Two Younger Poets: Duncan Glen and Donald Campbell* (Preston: Akros, 1976). He has also published essays on literature and theatre, as well as two books on Scottish theatre history: *A Brighter Sunshine: A Hundred Years of the Edinburgh Royal Lyceum Theatre* (Edinburgh: Polygon, 1983), and *Playing for Scotland: A History of the Scottish Stage 1715–1965* (Edinburgh: Mercat Press, 1996).

He was Writer-in-Residence to Lothian Schools (1974–77), Resident Playwright at the Royal Lyceum Theatre (1981–83), Fellow in Creative Writing at the University of Dundee (1987–89), Writer-in-Residence in Dumfries and Galloway (1990), and William Soutar Fellow in Perth (1991–93). He will be Royal Literary Fund Fellow at Napier University from 2000–2001.

Author's Original Introduction

We live in an age of disillusionment and desperation, an age which is characterised by a conspicuous absence of goodwill. All over the world, confrontations of one kind or another have reached the point of impasse, their participants having discarded peaceful means in favour of the apparently more persuasive arguments of the gun and the bomb. Social conflict – whether we call it 'urban terrorism' or 'freedom fighting' – has become part and parcel of a way of life for a great many people.

With so much blood being spilled to so little purpose, it all seems so hopeless. Yet the instigators of this violence are not evil. Mostly they are honourable men – intelligent, courageous, totally dedicated to the service of their chosen cause, men who are moved to oppose what they see as injustice, and who are prepared to carry that opposition to the point where they will sacrifice their very lives. No matter how honourable, however, they cannot expect to escape unscathed from the consequences of their desperate actions. Just as excessive violence has an ultimately brutalising effect, so too does extremism breed its own form of debilitating cancer – a certain attitude of mind which rejects all other attitudes and despises the people who hold them. Whenever a man resorts to desperate measures – in no matter how worthy a cause – he is in danger of succumbing to this life-denying (and, ultimately, self-destructive) attitude. The play you are about to read concerns the fate of one such man – he lived and died over three hundred and sixty years ago and his name was John Ogilvie.

John Ogilvie was no villain. On the contrary, the Roman Catholic Church, with every justification, have proclaimed him to be a saint. But did he really have to die that day in March, 1615? Was the Catholic faith really served by his death? Or did he offer up his life as a ritual sacrifice to a dogma which had become, for him, the only true reality? Did he cheapen his faith by putting its rituals before its teachings? Although I have my own opinions on this matter, I realised from the outset that my opinions must inevitably be coloured by my own – Presbyterian – background and I have tried to be as objective as possible. I therefore leave my readers to answer the above questions for themselves.

The Jesuit was written in October, 1973. At the time, I had no idea of Ogilvie's impending sainthood and I doubt if it would have made much difference to the writing of the play if I had. I certainly made no amendments to the script because of the canonisation. The fact that the news broke at almost exactly the same time that *The Jesuit* opened was nothing less than pure coincidence. However gratifying this coincidence may have been for me personally, there is one aspect of it that ought to be mentioned in this introduction.

As is the case with most first plays, it was very difficult to persuade theatre managements to consider staging *The Jesuit*. Most agreed on its merits, but felt that it was too risky to produce on the grounds that it seemed to lack topicality and would not attract audiences. I myself had all but given up ever seeing the play on the stage. Then, one day in August, 1975, I bumped into Sandy Neilson and mentioned *The Jesuit* to him. From the moment he read the play, Sandy committed himself to it utterly, not only as Director but also taking over the very demanding part of Spottiswoode when Henry Stamper, due to personal circumstances, was forced to drop out of the production. Sandy's involvement, no less than my own, pre-dates the announcement of Ogilvie's canonisation and he deserves as much (if not more) credit as I do for the acclaim that *The Jesuit* has received.

Others, too, ought to be mentioned. Robin Lorimer, who gave me both his encouragement and the resources of his very considerable personal library when I was researching the play: David Campbell, who read the first draft, discussed the stage-craft with me and proclaimed his enthusiasm for the play long before it had reached the production stage: most of all, my wife Jean (to whom this play is dedicated) who had the unenviable task of living with me throughout all the ups and downs that *The Jesuit* underwent. Lastly, there was George Brown, who, with no thought or possibility of personal gain, worked and wrangled and worried his way through God only knows how many sleepless nights to get the production off the ground. To those – and many others too numerous to mention – I can only offer my undying gratitude.

Donald Campbell, Edinburgh, June 1976

Editor's Note: The text of *The Jesuit* published in 1976 showed some passages of dialogue enclosed within square brackets. These indicated cuts that were made when the play was first performed at the Traverse Theatre in 1976. At Donald Campbell's request, the square brackets have been removed in this present edition and all of the bracketed dialogue has been retained, with the exception of a few cut sentences as follows (the page references are to the 1976 edition): 'You're the one.' (p. 43); 'The worst, the very worst of the lot.' (p. 43); 'Sandy – poor Sandy – Sandy is a bore.' (p. 44); 'You are always this way. You hardly say a word.' (p. 45); 'Andrew, when Wat was tapping in the nails – the nails into my fingers' (p. 46).

It has plesit God to cast in my hands a Jesuit, that callis himself Ogilvie ... In his bulget we haif found his vestementis and other furniture for the masse with some bookis and reliques of S. Ignatius, S. Margaret, S. Katherin and other thair saints; also some writtis amongst qhiche the principal is a Catalogue of things left be Father Anderson, a Jesuit in Scotland qho semis to be furth of the countrey. Thairby your Majestie wil persaif the furniture of bookis and vestementis thai haif in store against the day they looke for, and sum of thair freindschip with qhom the samin is reservit.

Archbishop John Spottiswoode to James VI, October 1614

If nothing could be found but that he was a Jesuit and had said Mass they should banish him the country and inhibit him to return without licence under pain of death. But if it should appear that he had been a practiser for the stirring up of subjects to rebellion or did maintain the Pope's transcendent power over kings and refused to take the Oath of Allegiance they should leave him to the course of law and justice.

King James's reply

If the King will be to me as his predecessors were to mine I will obey and acknowledge him for my King but, if he do otherwise and play the runagate from God, as he and you all do, I will not acknowledge him more than this old hat.

Father John Ogilvie S.J., speech at his trial, March 1615

Characters

FATHER JOHN OGILVIE

JOHN SPOTTISWOODE, *Archbishop of Glasgow*

LADY RACHEL SPOTTISWOODE

Soldiers in Spottiswoode's service:

ANDREW

WILL

SANDY

WAT

A DOCTOR

A HANGMAN

Notes on the Language

OGILVIE speaks English with an officer-class accent.

SPOTTISWOODE speaks Scots, although I have used conventional English spelling for many of the words. This is to allow the actor freedom to modulate the degree of Scots in Spottiswoode's speech at different points in the play. For the sake of uniformity, I have used a similar orthography with Lady Spottiswoode.

THE SOLDIERS all speak an Edinburgh dialect of Scots.

Act One

Scene 1

Glasgow 1614. An ante-room in the provost's house at four o'clock on a bitterly cold October afternoon. The room is small, furnished only by a table, a chair and a short bench. On the table (which is on the left side of the room) is a decanter, two goblets and a jug of water. Opposite the table is a small fire-place in which a freshly-lit fire is blazing. The bench is between the fire and the table, lying along the wall beneath the window. The window is open and the howling of an angry mob can be heard outside.

WILL *(off)*   Come on, man! Get aff yer knees! Get a move on!

ANDREW *(off)*   Dinna talk tae him, Wullie! For Christ's sake, dinnae jist talk tae him! If he winna move, gie him yer fuckin buits!

ANDREW, OGILVIE and WILL enter from the right. The soldiers are contrasting types – ANDREW is a grizzled veteran, WILL a raw recruit. Both are plainly frightened but disguise their fear in different ways – WILL takes it out on OGILVIE and ANDREW takes it out on WILL. OGILVIE is a fair-complexioned man in his middle thirties. He has had a bad mauling from the mob – his face is a mass of scratches, his shirt is torn and open at the waist and a swordless scabbard is twisted round his back. He grips his cloak rather desperately in his right hand. He takes two steps into the room and falls, exhausted, flat on his face.

ANDREW goes to the window and pulls it shut, blocking off the noise of the mob which is, in any case, beginning to die away.

WILL   Aw Jesus Christ! *(Kicks OGILVIE in the kidneys and spits on him.)* Ye papish bastard! Damn ye…

OGILVIE groans and tries to rise, but cannot manage it. WILL kicks him again and ANDREW, hurrying across the room, shoulders WILL out of the way.

ANDREW   Jesus Christ, laddie, ye've nae fuckin idea have ye? *(Stepping across OGILVIE's body, he turns him over and tries to lift him but cannot manage it. He grunts, straightens, and turns on WILL in a fury.)* That's right, Wullie, that's right! That's whit ye draw yer fuckin wages for – staunin there like a spare prick at a hooer's weddin! For Christ's sake, laddie, catch a grup at the ither end afore I catch a grup o you!

WILL comes forward and together they lift OGILVIE on to the bench. He half-sits, half-lies there, shivering in a semi-conscious condition. They stand back and look at him for a moment, wiping their brows and spitting and generally assuming the

205

attitude of men admiring a finished job. ANDREW *turns and picks up* OGILVIE'S *cloak (which he dropped when he fell) and throws it over* OGILVIE'S *body.* ANDREW *then turns to the table and pours himself a stiff drink.*

WILL   Hi, hi, ye cannae dae that!

ANDREW   Cannae dae whut?

WILL   That's the Airchbishop's drink…

ANDREW   *(smouldering)*   The Airchbishop – can get *stuffed! (Takes off the drink.)* Bluidy man, he can take a runnin fuck at hissel! And I'll tell him that when I see him anaa, you see if I dinna! Jesus Bluidy Christ, he's aff his fuckin heid! *(Pours another drink and takes it immediately.)* Twa men – twa men. A haulf-airsed wee laddie and a buggered auld man, no even twa real men tae tak a prisoner through thon rammy! Wullie, the man's a heid-case!

WILL   Aye, it was a haurd ane, richt enough! The mood thae folk were in – tae tell ye the truth, Andro, I didnae think we were gaun tae make it! Naw! Christ, I dinnae mind tellin ye, Andrew, I was a wee bit feart gettin…

ANDREW   Aw, ye were, were ye? Well, thanks for tellin me pal! Thanks a lot! Because wance or twice oot there, I was gettin the distinct impression that you were aa set tae shoot the craw and leave me on my jaxy!

WILL   Aw, come off it, Andro! I wadnae dae that!

ANDREW   Too right ye wadnae! Too fuckin right ye wadnae! *(Turns his attention to* OGILVIE.*)* Look at him! *(Laughs.)* That's him! That's the lad! That's the lad that sterted aa the trouble! *(Laughs again.)* Christ, if this wasna sae serious, ye could piss yersel laughin at it! Whit that mob werenae gaun tae dae tae that puir bugger lyin there! And whit for? Whit for, eh?

WILL   *(with some embarrassment)*   Hi, Andro, screw the nut eh?

ANDREW   Eh?

WILL   Ye ken fine!

ANDREW   Aw I dae, dae I? Well, I'm sorry, son, but I'm no shair that I dae. I'm no shair that I ken whit this boy's done – whit *ony* man could hae possibly done – tae turn the fowk o this toun intae a gang o fuckin animals. Because that's whit…

WILL   Aw come aff it, Andro, come aff it! Ye yen fine whit that oot there was aa aboot! That bugger there's a Pope's man!

ANDREW   A Pope's man? A Pope's man! The Pope, is it? Bugger the Pope! I didnae bring the Pope through thon rammy. I didnae risk my life for the Pope. And gin I did, son, and gin I did, they'd hae as little reason for it as they had wi this ane!

WILL   Aw, for Christ's sake, Andro! Whit's the matter we ye? Here, ye're no gonnae stert feelin sorry for him, are ye? He's a dangerous Jesuit priest! He's been sayin the Mass aa owre the place!

ANDREW   The Mass? Dae ye tell me that? *(Whistles through his teeth.)* Ha, that maun be a gey wanchancy thing tae dae, eh? Dangerous man, that. Aye, oh aye! Masses, eh? Jesus Christ. Dearie me. They'll shairly hing him for that.

WILL   *(ignoring* ANDREW'S *sarcasm)*   Serve him right anaa! B'Christ, hingin's owre guid for the like o that! See if it was me, I'd burn him. I'd pit the bastard on that fire here and nou! Papes, they're bastards! Bastards! I'd pit every fuckin pape in Scotland on that fire gin I had my wey; every fuckin pape in Scotland...

WILL advances towards ANDREW *as he speaks, aimlessly wandering about the room.* ANDREW *seizes him by the lapels of the tunic and pulls him to his* (ANDREW'S) *face.*

ANDREW   Ye little... *(He is so full of anger that he can say no more. He pushes* WILL *away from him with a gesture of contempt.)* I'm sorry tae disappoint ye, son. He'll no hing. No for sayin masses.

WILL   *(bewildered by* ANDREW'S *assault, has all but lost interest)*   Naw? Will he no? *(Suddenly realises the import of what* ANDREW *has said.)* Whit for no?

ANDREW   Because it's the law! This is his first offence – he'll maybe no even get the jile. Likely he'll get off wi a fine.

WILL   A fine! Christ, dae you mean tae tell me...

ANDREW   Aye. We brocht that man *(points to* OGILVIE *who has now recovered sufficiently to be able to sit up and take an interest in the conversation)* through aa that – and aa he'll get is a fine.

WILL   A fine! It's no right, Andro, it's no right! *(Pauses and thinks before he says any more.)* Listen, Andro, if his kind got back, if the papes got the pooer...

ANDREW   Wullie, Wullie, Wullie! *(Gentler.)* Wullie! Hou often dae I hae tae tell ye, son? Gin ye're gonnae be a sodger, gin ye're gonnae be ony kind o sodger – for Christ's sake, son, dinnae tak onythin tae dae wi politics!

WILL   *Politics?* Whae's talkin aboot politics? This is religion!

ANDREW   Politics, religion, whit's the fuckin difference in this day and age? *(Suddenly weary, he passes his hand across his eyes and looks about him.)* Whaur the hell has Spottiswoode got tae? Gode, I swear that man'll be the daith o me yet! He'll drive me tae the grave, b'Christ he will. See you that's talkin aboot Pope's men and religion? Well jist you keep an eye on the guid Airchbishop, that's aa! God, I whiles think he's hauf-roads tae bein a Pope's man himsel – and if we ever get anither Catholic King, I'll gie ye three guesses whae'll be the Airchbishop o Glesca! See if you want tae keep yer job...

WILL   Shote!

Slow, heavy footsteps are heard outside on the stair. ANDREW *throws the dregs of his goblet on the floor and tries to dry the goblet on the tail of his tunic while* WILL *tries to straighten* OGILVIE *on the bench and bring him round by slapping his cheeks.* OGILVIE, *who is fully conscious by this time, pushes* WILL *away.* SPOTTISWOODE *enters. He is a biggish, heavy-set man in his middle age. He wears a long black cloak and a tight-fighting skull cap. Apart from the merest hint of a smile his face is quite expressionless. Both soldiers go to him and kiss his hand.* SPOTTISWOODE *never takes his eyes off* OGILVIE *from the moment he sees him.* OGILVIE *rises to his feet as soon as* SPOTTISWOODE *enters.*

SPOTTISWOODE *(a statement rather than a question)*   This is the man.

ANDREW   Aye, m'lord. *(Clears his throat.)* We had a bit of a job bringing him owre, m'lord. The mob were – eh – unco coorse. We very near didnae manage…

SPOTTISWOODE *has been gazing thoughtfully at* OGILVIE *and listening to* ANDREW *with the slightest of attention. He now turns to* ANDREW *with a nod.*

SPOTTISWOODE   No doubt it went sair with ye. *(Looks at* ANDREW *expectantly.)*

ANDREW   *(sighs and takes a small pouch and papers from the inside of his tunic)* We fund this at his ludgins, m'lord.

SPOTTISWOODE   *(taking the pouch and papers with a cursory glance)*   Guid. *(Thoughtfully, with a dismissive shake of his head.)* Attend me.

ANDREW *and* WILL *begin to leave. As they reach the door,* SPOTTISWOODE *suddenly, without turning, calls after* ANDREW.

SPOTTISWOODE   Andro!

ANDREW   M'lord?

SPOTTISWOODE   Gif ye think it is necessary to bawl at the top of your voice anent sic matters as the richts and wrangs of the orders I see fit to give ye – will ye please make an effort to moderate your language? It is – nocht seemly for the Airchbishop's man to be heard effing and blinding aa owre the Toun House of the Provost of Glasgow. *(He turns his head to look sternly over his shoulder at* ANDREW.)

ANDREW   *(without expression)*   M'lord.

SPOTTISWOODE *waves the soldiers away. When they have gone, he suddenly smiles warmly and shakes his head. He returns his attention to* OGILVIE, *going to the table, taking off his cloak and draping it over the chair. As he is taking off his cap, he speaks to* OGILVIE.

SPOTTISWOODE   Captain Roderick Watson, is it no?

OGILVIE *(somewhat shakily)*   I think – perhaps it would be better to dispense with that name. It is a completely false one and to continue the pretence further would serve little purpose. My name is…

SPOTTISWOODE   Ogilvie. John Ogilvie. *(Drops his cap on the table.)*

OGILVIE *(biting his lip)*   That is perfectly correct. You have the advantage of me, sir.

SPOTTISWOODE *(amused)*   Just so, Master Ogilvie. Just so. *(Rubbing his hands together.)* Nou. Would ye take a dram? Ye look in sair need of it?

OGILVIE   That is very kind of you. I would be most grateful.

SPOTTISWOODE *picks up the goblet that Andrew has used, examines it for a moment, purses his lips and looks sceptically towards the door. He tosses the goblet in his hand, lays it aside and pours* OGILVIE'S *drink into a fresh goblet.*

SPOTTISWOODE   Water?
OGILVIE   Please.

SPOTTISWOODE *pours some water into the drink and hands it to* OGILVIE.

OGILVIE   Thank you.
SPOTTISWOODE   And you are of noble bluid, I understand?
OGILVIE   I am – and all my people before me.
SPOTTISWOODE *(conversationally)*   Sir Walter Ogilvie of Drum?
OGILVIE   My father.

SPOTTISWOODE *smiles and, sitting down, turns his attention to the papers. He begins to read, then looks up solicitously.*

SPOTTISWOODE   Sit ye doun, Master Ogilvie, sit ye doun. There is no need for you to stand.
OGILVIE   Thank you – but I prefer it.
SPOTTISWOODE *(with a slight shrug)*   As ye please.

SPOTTISWOODE *reads one paper, lays it aside with a sharp sniff of breath and frowns up at* OGILVIE. *He picks up the second paper and asks his next question casually as he spreads it out.*

SPOTTISWOODE   And you have been saying masses in the City of Glasgow?
OGILVIE *(mildly)*   If to do so is a crime, then it will be necessary to prove it – with witnesses.

SPOTTISWOODE *leans back in his chair and regards* OGILVIE *with a kind of stern speculation before he speaks.*

SPOTTISWOODE   To say the mass in His Majesty's Dominions – ye maun be maist siccarly assured – is a crime. *(Leans forward and re-commences his study of the paper.)* And I have any amount of witnesses.

SPOTTISWOODE *spends little time with the second paper, laying it carefully on top of the first. He picks up the pouch and empties the contents on to the table. There are a number of bones and a small hank of grey hair.*

SPOTTISWOODE   Oh aye. Relics. *(Picks up the hank of hair rather gingerly between his thumb and forefinger and glances enquiringly at* OGILVIE.)
OGILVIE *(crosses himself)*   A lock from the head of the blessed St Ignatius.
SPOTTISWOODE *(nods without comment, lays the hair down and leans back in his*

chair with interlocking fingers)   I am given to understand that ye have been furth of Scotland this long while – twenty-two year, to be exact, the maist of your days?

OGILVIE   You appear to be remarkably well informed.

SPOTTISWOODE   Master Ogilvie, what garred ye return?

OGILVIE   My vocation.

SPOTTISWOODE   Which is?

OGILVIE   To save souls. *(Proudly.)* To unteach heresy.

SPOTTISWOODE   Indeed? Sic a michty vocation would of necessity – require a michty authority. But where is yours, Master Ogilvie? Since ye did not get it from the King or from any of his bishops…

OGILVIE   The King is a layman – as are all his so-called bishops. None of them are competent to place authority, spiritual authority that is, on any man.

SPOTTISWOODE *(slightly mocking)*   The *King* is a layman?

OGILVIE   He has not had his first tonsure – and he is certainly not a priest!

SPOTTISWOODE   And you are?

OGILVIE *gives a little start, hesitates, then laughs.*

OGILVIE   Since you are so certain that I have been saying masses, you must be positive that I am a priest!

SPOTTISWOODE *(acknowledging the point with a faint smile and nod)*   Aye. But let us return to my original question. From where do you derive your authority?

OGILVIE *pauses, looks seriously at* SPOTTISWOODE, *finishes his drink, and lays the goblet carefully on the table. Taking a deep breath, he delivers his next speech as if he were giving a lecture.*

OGILVIE   Christ's sheep were committed to the charge of Peter. Any man who would feed them must first seek his authority from the Apostolic See. Preserved there – through an unbroken line of succession – is the authority and power given in the first instance to the Prince of the Apostles. 'Thou art Peter and upon this rock I will build my church; and the gates of hell shall not prevail against it!' *(Pauses and lets the passion of the quotation subside.)* Thus was Simon, son of John, made the strong rock of the Church that he might be Cephas and be called Peter. By the simple method of working back through all the Pontiffs, I can trace my authority to him – and through him to the Lord Jesus Christ.

There is a short silence between them.

SPOTTISWOODE *(with a sigh)*   Aye. The Petrine Claim.

OGILVIE   The Truth.

SPOTTISWOODE *(sternly)*   That, Master Ogilvie, is treason!

OGILVIE *(equally sternly)*   That *Master Spottiswoode*, is faith!

SPOTTISWOODE *(snapping)*   And ye would sign a declaration to sic effect?

OGILVIE *(hotly)* In my own blood if need be!

SPOTTISWOODE I hardly think so. *Faither* Ogilvie. I hardly think so. I hardly think that that will be necessary. Plain ink, no doubt will do just as well! *(Pushes his chair back savagely and walks a few steps away from* OGILVIE *before swinging round to address him again.)* It is the law of the land – the law of this realm – that the King – His Sovereign and Maist Gracious Majesty King James the Saxt – demands and is entitled to the allegiance and lealty of his subjects – of aa his subjects – in aa matters touching their lives. Aa matters – temporal *and* spiritual. That is the law. Did ye ken that?

OGILVIE The law of the land is the law of man. The laws of God are not to be changed so readily.

SPOTTISWOODE Maybe no. The fact remains that ye deny allegiance to the King in this matter and in aa religious matters?

OGILVIE I do.

SPOTTISWOODE And would render up sic allegiance to the Pope?

OGILVIE I would.

SPOTTISWOODE And if the Pope took it into his head to depose a king on the grounds of heresy, ye would uphold and support the Pope's richts in the matter?

OGILVIE *(guardedly)* I do not know whether the Holy Father has, or would claim such a right. It is true that many learned doctors of the Church have asserted that this is the case...

SPOTTISWOODE Never mind the doctors of the Kirk, Faither. I'm speiring at you!

OGILVIE It is not an article of faith. If and when it becomes so, I will die for it – and gladly. Until then, I do not need to pass an opinion to anyone – and certainly not to you. You have no right...

SPOTTISWOODE Aye, Aye, I ken. I'm a layman. No had my first tonsure. I've no bloody rights ava! *(Pauses, looks seriously at* OGILVIE.) I must warn ye, Faither Ogilvie, that sooner or later, ye will be forced to answer that question. Your very life micht weill depend on the answer ye give. So. Aince mair. Gif the Pope took it into his head to depose a king on the grounds of heresy, would ye uphold and support the Pope's richts in the matter?

OGILVIE *(with some hesitation)* I assume you are asking me whether or not I would condone regicide. I fail to see why you cannot ask me the question straight out. I am opposed to regicide, Master Spottiswoode, I am opposed to murder – the murder of a king or the murder of a beggar. As a Christian and as a Catholic, that is the only answer I give you.

SPOTTISWOODE And gin I asked ye as a Jesuit, what answer would ye gie me then?

OGILVIE What do you mean by that, sir?

SPOTTISWOODE Let us get doun to specifics, Faither Ogilvie. There are others in your order who have less scruple when it comes to murder.

OGILVIE I haven't the faintest idea what you are talking about.

SPOTTISWOODE Oh, have you not? Perhaps I am being less than plain. Does not the name of Henry Garnett mean anything to you? Faither Henry Garnett and the Gunpowder Plot?

OGILVIE   That is a monstrous slander! Father Garnett was a good and holy man!

SPOTTISWOODE *(snorting)*   Holy man! Garnett was a traitor, a willing accomplice to the attempted murder of his king!

OGILVIE   That is a lie! Father Garnett was executed by the English for refusing to betray a penitent – and he was not obliged to do that for anything in the world.

SPOTTISWOODE   Ha! Was he no? Let me tell ye, Faither Ogilvie, that if any man was to confess sic a crime to me, I'd no lose much time in turning him in.

OGILVIE   Nobody should confess to you.

SPOTTISWOODE   Maybe no! But the fact remains that there was a Jesuit priest involved in the Gunpowder Plot. I ken that and so do you…

OGILVIE   I know no such thing!

SPOTTISWOODE *(scornfully)*   Ach, he was up to his oxters in it! What's more, barely a year of his Majesty's reign has gone by without some plot or intrigue or some scheme or other of a traitorous and seditious nature being uncovered. And on every single occasion there's been a Jesuit at the foot of it! And nou here you come owre from France with your English manners and your assumed name and *(snatches up the papers in his fist)* this neiveful of sedition in your kist. At this very minute…

OGILVIE   This is preposterous! What are you charging me with? If you're looking for traitors, why don't you try Robert Bruce? I'm told he lives near here and you have plenty of evidence…

SPOTTISWOODE *(ignoring the question)*   At this very minute there are twenty-seven…

OGILVIE   Are you afraid to answer me then? Why don't you arrest a presbyterian traitor? Why don't you…

SPOTTISWOODE *(shouting him down)*   Jesuit priests working against the well-being…

OGILVIE   What about the seventeenth of September riots? Why don't you drag Robert Bruce in here?

SPOTTISWOODE   …and security of this nation.

OGILVIE *(shouting almost into* SPOTTISWOODE'S *face)*   What about Robert Bruce? What about Robert Bruce? Answer me, you imposter, answer me you *God-damned king-worshipping Heretic!*

SPOTTISWOODE *knocks* OGILVIE *down with a full-blooded punch to the jaw. He stands over him, panting with rage.*

SPOTTISWOODE   At this very minute, there are twenty-seven Jesuit priests working against the guid-keeping and security of this nation of Scotland – and I am Airchbishop of Glasgow and hae no need to answer to any one of them! *(Turns to the door.)* Andro! Andro!

ANDREW *and* WILL *enter at the double.*

SPOTTISWOODE   Take this man out of my sight!

ANDREW   Aye, aye, m'lord! Whaur tae?

SPOTTISWOODE   *(angrily)*   The Castle, ye fool! Where ither? Get me lowse of him!

OGILVIE *rises slowly to his feet as the soldiers advance. He stares at*
SPOTTISWOODE *who has turned his back on him.*

OGILVIE   Who made you my executioner? *(Spits on the floor at* SPOTTISWOODE'S
feet.) And who made you Archbishop? Better butcher than bishop!

SPOTTISWOODE   *(without turning)*   Get him away!

The soldiers lead OGILVIE *out.*

SPOTTISWOODE *goes to the table and pours himself a drink. He gathers the papers
together carefully, re-dons his cap and picks up his cloak. Finishing his drink, he
sighs and stares into space for a few moments.*

SPOTTISWOODE   Robert Bruce – oh damn Robert Bruce! *(Hurls the empty goblet
into a corner of the room.)* God damn him!

SPOTTISWOODE *stamps out.*

Scene 2

The following January. A corridor in the Palace of the Archbishop of Glasgow.
ANDREW *is on his own, happed up for a journey and carrying a shield and spear. He
looks distinctly cheesed off as* WILL, *similarly attired, enters briskly.*

WILL   Nae sign o them yet?

ANDREW   No chance!

WILL   Sandy's got aathing organised at the gate and Wattie and the ither lads are
staunin by with the horses.

ANDREW *(nodding)*   Guid.

WILL   Here, though. Gin we dinnae get a move on, we'll hae a job winnin awa.
There's a fair crowd buildin up ootby.

ANDREW   Ach, the Airchbishop's no bothert! No him! No wi *us* ridin aside him tae
tak aa the stanes and glaur they'll be chuckin at *him*. Och! I'm fair wrocht tae
daith wi aa this ditterin aboot!

WILL   Whit are they jawin aboot, onywey? They've been in there for mair nor an
'oor!

ANDREW   Christ knows! Ogilvie'll be argyin the toss again, I shouldnae wonder.

WILL *(laughing)* Weill, I hope the Airchbishop disnae lose the heid and thump him this time! Oh he's a funny ane that Ogilvie!

ANDREW Funny's no the ward. Bluidy bampot if ye ask me.

WILL Christ, no hauf! Tellt me aince – when I brocht him in his meat like – tellt me aince that he didnae mind the jile! Nae kiddin, aye! Said he was servin his destiny, fulfillin his destiny – I cannae mind right what he said but it was somethin aboot his destiny. And he's aye crackin bawrs and laughin, ken? Aye that cheery. Damn shair I wadnae find muckle tae be cheery aboot gin I was in he's place! Christ, ye ken whit it's like in there, Andro?

ANDREW Aye. Oh aye.

WILL He's no been oot of that place for geynear three month. It's cauld and it's damp and it's pitch-black and fair crawlin wi rats. And there's this muckle iron beam at the fit o the bed. Ogilvie's chyned til it by the ankles and it's a gey short chyn! He gets naethin but parritch tae eat and water tae drink. If he's aff his heid bi nou, it's nae wonder!

ANDREW He was aff his fuckin heid afore he gaed in there if ye want my opinion.

WILL Aye. Maybe he was anaa! *(A thought strikes him.)* Here but! I didnae tell ye aboot this mornin. *(Laughs at the recollection.)* I gaed in there aboot – och, echt o'clock it wad be – brocht him in his parritch and some clean claes and that. *(Laughs again.)* He's lyin there, aa clairty and bleary-eyed among the rats and the shite *(laughs)* and his feet're stuck hauf-roads up tae the ceilin wi this bluidy chyn! I gets in there and I says tae him I says 'Hello there, Faither! Hou're ye daein the day?' And ye ken whit? He's lyin there *(laughs and shakes his head)* and he says tae me, he says 'Oh Will' he says – aa englified ken? – 'Oh Will!' he says 'It's past joking when the heid's aff!'

They both laugh.

ANDREW Christ, that'll dae!

WILL Past joking when the heid's aff! Oh Jesus – Andro, I geynear creased mysel! It was the way he said it, ken? Aa English and that *(mimics)* 'Past joking when the heid's aff,' Aw Christ!

ANDREW *(serious again)* I wonder – maybe his heid'll really be aff efter they've done wi him in Embro.

WILL Here, when we get hame – tae Embro like – what's the chances o a couple o days aff? I'd like tae get up the road – see my Maw.

ANDREW *grins broadly and chuckles to himself.*

WILL What's the joke? Whit are ye laughin at?

ANDREW Naethin. Naethin. It's jist – eh, want tae see yer Maw, eh?

WILL Aye! I've no seen her for a while and – weill, I mean tae say, she's no gettin ony younger. Whit's the maitter wi that?

ANDREW Naethin. Naethin at aa! *(Wipes the smile from his face.)* Aw, never mind,

Wullie. Never mind, son. It's jist my sense o humour. I daursay we'll get some time away when we're in Embro – tae stert wi onywey. Later on, I'm no sae shair.

WILL   Later on? Are we gonnae be in Reekie for a while then?

ANDREW   A few weeks, I reckon. Depends.

WILL   Depends on whit?

ANDREW   Depends on hou muckle trouble they get frae Ogilvie. Ach Ogilvie! Buggers like him gie me the boke, so they dae!

WILL   The Papes?

ANDREW   Naw! The nobility – nobility like thon! Rich men wi bees in their bonnets! Ach, they scunner me! I tell ye this, Wull – I've seen Ogilvie's like afore nou! He can caa hissel a Jesuit, a pape or whitever ye like – at the hinner end, he aye minds that he's Sir Wattie Ogilvie's son. And nae matter whit he's suffered here in Glesca, he kens up here *(taps his temple)* that the men that'll be sittin in judgment o him in Embro are his ain kind – gentlemen like himsel! Sae he argies the toss, stands up tae the Airchbishop – aw he's the brave, brave boy richt enough! Crackin jokes and aa the rest o it! But aa the time, Wullie, he kens that he can say the ward and walk oot o here free as air! And he thinks that efter he's been in Embro and aa the talkin's done, that's jist exactly whit he's gonnae dae! But that's jist where he's mistaken, son. When we get tae Embro...

SPOTTISWOODE   *(off)*   Andro! Andro!

ANDREW   At last! Christ, dinnae tell me... Come on, Wullie!

WILL   *(taking* ANDREW'S *arm)*   Andro, whit were ye gonnae say? Whit'll happen when we get tae Embro?

ANDREW *looks at* WILL *and grins.*

ANDREW   Och, ye'll mebbe get tae see yer Maw! Come on, son. We're aff!

Both exit.

Scene 3

Edinburgh a few days later. OGILVIE'S *room in* SPOTTISWOODE'S *house in the Canongate. A barely furnished room containing no more that a bed, a table and two chairs.* OGILVIE *is seated at the table, writing. An empty chair is opposite the table.* SPOTTISWOODE *enters.* OGILVIE *glances up briefly but continues to write.*

SPOTTISWOODE   Guid afternoon Faither. And hou are ye the day?

OGILVIE *(continues writing, finishing with a flourish of his pen)*   As well, my Lord Archbishop, as can be expected. Really Spottiswoode, these questions that you ask me are ridiculous!

SPOTTISWOODE *(raising one eyebrow)*   It is your answers which interest me,
Ogilvie – no your opinion of the questions. *(Indicates the paper on which* OGILVIE
had been writing.) Ye have finished?

OGILVIE *rather sourly pushes the paper across the desk and walks away.*
SPOTTISWOODE *seats himself on the empty chair and begins to read the paper.*

SPOTTISWOODE *(reading)*   'Whether the Pope be judge and have power *in*
Spiritualibus over His Majesty, and whether that power will reach over His
Majesty even *in termporalibus* if it be *in ordine ad spiritualia* as Bellarmine
affirmeth.' Aye. Well, we aa ken the answer to that ane. Nane of us has the power
to speir sic a thing of ye.

OGILVIE *(turning)*   Nor I to answer such a question! Let us be quite plain about this
– just what is it that you are asking me to pronounce on? This matter has been
hotly contested by two of the most brilliant minds in Europe – namely King James
and Cardinal Bellarmine. Father Francisco Suarez has also written on the subject
and I, as a Jesuit and a good Catholic, naturally incline to the Jesuit and Catholic
point of view – but, my good Spottiswoode, I am a very junior and unimportant
Jesuit and it would be hardly fitting for me to enter publicly into such a
controversy. Besides, what possible purpose could be served by any answer I
might give? It would affect the issue neither way.

SPOTTISWOODE *(sighs and shakes his head incredulously)*   Faither Ogilvie, whiles
ye bumbaze me! Never mind. *(Reads on.)* 'Whether the Pope has the power to
excommunicate kings (especially such as are not of his Church) as His Majesty?'
Hmm. Faither Ogilvie, I fear that I am unable to understand your answer. The
Pope, ye say, can excommunicate His Majesty? I do not understand that.

OGILVIE   What is there to understand? Of course the Holy Father has the power!

SPOTTISWOODE   But – by your own argument – His Majesty is a heretic. And if His
Majesty is a heretic, he cannot be a Catholic.

OGILVIE *(with a long-suffering sigh)*   A simple analogy. An outlaw is outside the
law as far as the protection of the law is concerned – but he can be apprehended
and tried and convicted by and according to the law. In just the same way, a
heretic is outwith Mother Church as far as her blessings are concerned but is still
subject to her justice – and to her punishment.

SPOTTISWOODE   I see. We are aa spiritual outlaws then?

OGILVIE   Yes.

SPOTTISWOODE   Even the youngest bairn baptised the day by a Calvinist minister?

OGILVIE   Yes. Yes. The Pope acquires his authority over man by baptism. Man
enters Christ's flock through baptism and the Pope is the shepherd of that flock.

SPOTTISWOODE *(sighs)*   Man, d'ye ken what ye're saying? There's scarce a man in
Scotland 'd have his bairn baptised under sic conditions!

OGILVIE   That is a matter of opinion. It may be true of those who despise Christ and
serve the Devil – it is certainly not true of the faithful. And there are many more
of these in Scotland than you, perhaps, imagine.

SPOTTISWOODE *(sighs again, reads on)* 'Whether the Pope has power to depose kings by him excommunicated? And in particular whether he have the power to depose the King, His Majesty.' Aye. Aye. The auld sang. Nane of us has the authority.

OGILVIE No.

SPOTTISWOODE 'Whether it be no murder to slay His Majesty, being so excommunicated and deposed by the Pope?' And here we are again! No spiritual jurisdiction! Can ye no, in aa conscience, give your opinion?

OGILVIE No.

SPOTTISWOODE Ye gave it to me! Ye told me that ye despised murder! Why could ye no have said the same to the Commission?

OGILVIE You have my answer there. You'll have to be satisfied with that.

SPOTTISWOODE *(reading on with a withering look in* OGILVIE'S *direction)* 'Whether the Pope has power to assoyle subjects from the oath of their borne and natural allegiance to His Majesty?' *(Sighs deeply.)* With your customary arrogance, ye condem the Oath of Allegiance. *(Lays the paper aside.)*

OGILVIE I most certainly do.

SPOTTISWOODE *bows his head wearily, rubbing the bridge of his nose between his thumb and forefinger. After a moment, he looks across at* OGILVIE.

SPOTTISWOODE Faither, d'ye ken wha framed these questions?

OGILVIE No.

SPOTTISWOODE Ye have no idea?

OGILVIE No. I assumed that it was a joint decision – yourself and some, perhaps all, of your colleagues on the Commission. Is it not so?

SPOTTISWOODE *shakes his head, taps the table, rises. He walks about a little, folds his hands purposefully behind his back.*

SPOTTISWOODE Faither Ogilvie, I'll leave ye without any doubts. The answers ye have given to these questions will send you to the gallows. You are going to hang.

OGILVIE I am not afraid to die.

SPOTTISWOODE Aye, I thocht ye'd be pleased! *(Loses his temper momentarily, leans over the table towards* OGILVIE.) But I am nocht concerned with the smaa-boukit ambitions of your vanity! *(Turns away and faces about until his temper is under control.)* These questions are speired at you by no lesser person than His Gracious Majesty King James the Saxt of Scotland and First of England! *(Pauses to glower at* OGILVIE.) When ye were arrested in Glasgow – on that same night – I scrieved a letter to the King. I thocht – and still think – that ye were involved in a plot to murder His Majesty. Oh Faither Ogilvie, ye have been used in a maist merciful manner! *I* would hae given ye the boots – and micht yet! But His Majesty thocht otherwise. These questions were put to ye in order that ye micht have the chance to prove your lealty and allegiance to your King! Well, they have disproved it! They demonstrate quite clearly how small a value ye place upon your King and your country – the insolence and provocative nature of these answers will put a rope about your thrapple! Mind on that when ye mount the gallows!

OGILVIE   I do not know what you want of me. I have given the only answers I possibly could. I have replied with all the honesty and sincerity that I could muster.

SPOTTISWOODE   Certes, man! It's not a question of honesty or sincerity but of tact! There's little wrong with the substance of your answer – it's the manner of the replies! Have ye read what ye hae scrieved? In every single instance – forby the ane anent the Pope's power of excommunication – ye deny the authority and jurisdiction of the King's Commission!

OGILVIE   Do you expect me to affirm it?

SPOTTISWOODE   Ye are no required to affirm or to deny! Aa ye had to say – aa ye *hae* to say is that ye do not ken! Ye'll get away with your answer anent excommunication – the King and the other Commissioners'll be as bumbazed as I was by it, but they'll no pay it muckle heed. As for the others, ye can just say what ye've just this minute said to me – ye are only a humble priest, no very important, and ye have no opinion in the matter.

OGILVIE   And such a reply would release me?

SPOTTISWOODE   No from the King's Justice. There's aye the matter of the masses ye have said – ye maun be tried and punished for that. But ye'll no hang for saying masses.

OGILVIE   I see. *(Thinks about it for a moment.)* You are, of course, aware that I have yet to stand trial?

SPOTTISWOODE   *(irritably)*   Ye'll stand trial when the nature of your crime can be determined. It is the purpose of the King's Commission to gather evidence for the trial. This *(indicates the deposition)* would make any trial for treason a formality!

OGILVIE   And if I answer as you advise?

SPOTTISWOODE   In any trial for treason, the process of law would be open to ye. In practice, I doubt very much whether sic a charge would be brocht.

OGILVIE   But I would be charged with saying masses?

SPOTTISWOODE   Of course. Charged, convicted and banished from His Majesty's dominions.

OGILVIE   You seem remarkably sure of the outcome!

SPOTTISWOODE   These are troubled times we live in, Faither Ogilvie.

OGILVIE   Indeed they are, Archbishop, indeed they are! *(Pauses thoughtfully.)* Why are you doing this, Spottiswoode?

SPOTTISWOODE   I beg your pardon?

OGILVIE   Why are you doing this? Why are you trying to persuade me to change my deposition? After all, you said just now that you believed me to be involved in a plot to murder the King. You are quite mistaken but I shan't argue about it – you are obviously persuaded otherwise. In your eyes, I am a potential assassin. Why should you seek to allow me to escape with my life?

SPOTTISWOODE   There are larger issues at stake.

OGILVIE   Larger than the King's safety?

SPOTTISWOODE   Larger than the life of one extremely ineffectual conspirator! Look, Ogilvie. If you are banished, I will be quit of ye – alive or dead, it's aa the same to me!

OGILVIE   *(with a deep breath)*   Then I am afraid that it will have to be dead. For I cannot and will not change my deposition.

SPOTTISWOODE   Certes, man, are ye wyce?

OGILVIE   Wise or foolish, I will not change my deposition.

SPOTTISWOODE   Damn you, John Ogilvie, for a bloody fanatic! What on God's earth d'ye hope to gain from this?

OGILVIE   Gain? I have no thought of gain. I am as in love with life as any man – but I will not change my deposition!

SPOTTISWOODE   But why, man, why? After aa I hae tellt ye?

OGILVIE   There are too many considerations. Far too many.

SPOTTISWOODE   Considerations? Certes, man – there maun be plenty of considerations to gar a man die for his faith – there's nothing byordnar about that! But this is phraseology, a trick of speech, no mair nor that! With just a wheen changing of words, ye micht be as free as air! My God, man – ye cannae die for an attitude, a pose! Hou in the warld can sic a thing be justified?

OGILVIE   It can be justified because I justify it! That is enough.

SPOTTISWOODE   Pride!

OGILVIE   Not pride but dignity! The dignity of Mother Church. *(Sighs.)* You can neither understand nor sympathise. How can you when you do not know what dignity means? We speak in different tongues, Spottiswoode. You and I, we speak in different languages. When you accuse me of attitudes and poses, you do no more than judge me by your own standards. You call yourself Archbishop of Glasgow – what is that but a pose? What is that but a cynical attitude towards a noble and ancient office? You are no more Archbishop of Glasgow than I am – but it's little you care about that! You are quite happy to be an imposter as long as it serves your purpose. So I can expect nothing from you. *(Suddenly angry.)* But I know very well what you expect from me! You would have me go before this illegal commission and – what's the expression – play the daft laddie! That's it, isn't it? That's what you want. Then you would spank the daft laddie's bottom and kick him out of the country – kick *me* out of my own country – hoping, no doubt, that Catholicism would go with me! Oh My Lord Archbishop, how mistaken you are! I may not be more than a priest – and not a very significant one at that – but when I take my place before that court, I will be the respresentative of the Church of the Risen Christ! And if my faith is to be defiled and humiliated in this land, this will not be the hand that does it! I will not change my deposition.

SPOTTISWOODE   *(stonily)*   Then ye maun take the consequences.

OGILVIE   Do you think I'm not ready for that?

SPOTTISWOODE   It will mean daith – and worse than daith!

OGILVIE   *(scornfully)*   Oh Spottiswoode, what a wonderful hangman you'd make!

Do you think that I care in the least for your threats? I haven't asked you for any favours and I never will. I despise you, Spottiswoode. I despise you and your threats and your damned heretic malice! Do what you can and see if it makes any difference to me! I'll willingly suffer more in this cause than you and your henchmen can ever inflict!

SPOTTISWOODE   Will ye suffer the boots?

OGILVIE   Oh stop making those threats! Whatever you are going to do to me, do it! You won't frighten me with threats! I'm not a hysterical woman, you know. You don't frighten me! All you do is to give me fresh heart – your threats are like the cackling of so many geese! Do what you have to do, Spottiswoode! Do not talk about it! I am not afraid. When are you going to understand that? *I am not afraid.* All I ask is that, whatever you do, you do quickly.

SPOTTISWOODE   The boots'll no be quick.

OGILVIE   Damn your boots! I am not afraid of your boots!

SPOTTISWOODE   Are ye no? *(Looks at* OGILVIE *thoughtfully for a moment, then turns to the door. He looks once at* OGILVIE'S *back before calling out.)* Wattie! Are ye there? Come in a minute. I want ye!

WAT *is a middle-aged man of medium height, rather squat in appearance and wearing a perpetually dour and surly expression.*

WAT   M'lord?

SPOTTISWOODE *(to* OGILVIE)   Wat is a great authority on the boots, Faither Ogilvie. *(*OGILVIE *glances over his shoulder at* WAT, *then looks away.)* I'll let him take a look at ye and then he'll maybe be guid enough to explain to ye just exactly what is entailed. Wat?

Hands on hips, WAT *walks slowly round* OGILVIE, *keeping a distance of approximately six feet between himself and the priest. He is carefully examining* OGILVIE'S *legs, behaving rather like a tradesman who has been asked to measure for a job of work and is making a preliminary inspection. Eventually he stops and addresses himself to* SPOTTISWOODE.

WAT   I'll dae the richt ane first, m'lord. That's the usual. *(Squats beside* OGILVIE'S *right leg.* OGILVIE *eyes him apprehensively all the time.)* Generally get mair purchase on that leg. Mair muscle, ye see.

SPOTTISWOODE *(nodding)*   Aye.

WAT   Fower splints, m'lord. Ane here, *(indicating the inside of the leg)* ane here, *(indicating the outside of the leg)* ane here *(indicating the back of the leg)* and ane here *(indicating the front of the leg).* Fower tichteners. Ane at the ankle, ane on the shin – jist ablow the knee – ane on the thigh – jist abune the knee – and ane on the thigh again, jist ablow the hip. *(Stands up and stretches.)* There's been a wheen airgument aboot the best place tae drive in the wedge – Oh! *(Takes a wooden wedge from the inside of his tunic and holds it up for them both to see.)*

This is the wedge. As I say, there's been a bit o airgument aboot the best place to drive it in. Some say that ye're better wi the ootside o the leg *(laughs)* – I think that's daft. I mysel prefer to drive the wedge in on the inside. Ye get mair purchase, m'lord. D'ye understand? *(Demonstrates on his own leg.)* The wedge has got mair tae drive intae. *(Sniffs speculatively.)* Purchase is the secret in this game, m'lord. Gin the wedge was big enough and I could get the purchase, I could drive it frae the tap o the hip-bane aa the way through tae the sowls o the feet!

OGILVIE *(hoarsely)*   And how far will you drive it in my case?

WAT *(addressing* OGILVIE *directly for the first time)*   Depends. Depends mainly on the Airchbishop but it depends on yersel anaa. I'll be hammerin awa wi the mallet richt up til the minute I'm tellt tae stop.

SPOTTISWOODE *(all but crying out to* OGILVIE)   Three blows of the mallet will gar the marrow spurt from your banes!

WAT *(with some relish)*   Jist sae, m'lord. Jist sae.

SPOTTISWOODE   That will be enough for nou, Wat. Away ye go.

WAT *(taking his leave)*   Thank ye, m'lord. *(Grinning wolfishly at both of them.)* I'll be at yer service whenever ye need me.

Exit WAT.

SPOTTISWOODE   Well. Nou ye ken what's in store for ye.

OGILVIE   I certainly do.

SPOTTISWOODE   And ye will not change your deposition?

OGILVIE   No.

SPOTTISWOODE *(exasperated)*   Ogilvie, ye are beyond me! I swear your perversity leaves me speechless! Ye would thole sic a torment as thon rather than make a reasonable deposition.

OGILVIE *(incredulously)*   Reason? What are you talking about? The boots are hardly instruments of reason!

SPOTTISWOODE   There would be no need for the boots – nor, indeed any other method – if ye would but purge the arrogance and pride from this deposition! Ogilvie, I beseech ye – in the name of the Lord Jesus Christ I beseech ye – do not make me do this thing to you. Change your deposition! For the love of God, man, have some sense!

OGILVIE   Sense? Who are you to talk of sense to me? We are beyond that now. Good Lord, Spottiswoode, even if I had been willing before to do as you ask, I cannot do so now. Can't you see that? If I did, I would seem to have been moved and led by feeling, like a beast – and not by reason, like a man. You cannot move me by reason and you will not move me by feeling. But try your boots, Spottiswoode! Try them and see how far you get! Try your boots and I'll show you that, in this cause, I care as much for your boots as you for your leggings! For I know myself born for greater things than to be overcome by *sense!* I put my trust in the Grace of God and you can do whatever you like! I will ask you for nothing – and I will neither alter nor add to anything I have said!

SPOTTISWOODE *(turning to leave)*   Ye won't? Very well. Only mind on this – the pain ye suffer wilna be the pain of the martyr. Ye maun think what ye like – you are no martyr, John Ogilvie, and aa the suffering in the warld winna make ye ane!

Exit SPOTTISWOODE.

Somewhat shakily, OGILVIE *goes to the table and takes his seat. He draws a piece of paper towards him and begins to write. Before he has written two words, he breaks down and weeps uncontrollably. He beats his fist on the table repeatedly.*

OGILVIE   I am not afraid! I am not afraid! I am not afraid!

Scene 4

That same evening in the soldiers' quarters. The dining room or, more accurately, the room in which the soldiers eat. There is a longish table with benches on either side. On the wall, there is a rack where the soldiers hang their coats, swords, etc. WILL *is at the table taking a meal. His sword and helmet are on the rack.* ANDREW *enters, whistling, a plate of food in one hand, a mug of beer in the other.*

ANDREW   Ye got back then?

WILL   Aye.

ANDREW *lays his food and drink on the table and talks to* WILL *as he unbuckles his sword and hangs it up, placing his helmet on top of it.*

ANDREW   Hou'd ye get on, well? *(Grins.)* See yer maw?

WILL   Aye.

ANDREW *(coming forward and sitting down)*   Faimly aaricht?

WILL   No sae bad. Whit's the joke?

ANDREW   Joke?

WILL   Aye, ye're laughin aa owre yer ugly face. Whit's the big joke?

ANDREW   Nae joke, Wullie. Nae joke. Honest.

WILL *looks unsure, but does not pursue the matter.* ANDREW *grins and begins to eat. He eats quickly with plenty of noise but no talk. When he is finished, he pushes back his plate, picks up his mug and grins at* WILL.

ANDREW   Come on well, let's hear it! Gie's aa yer news!

WILL *(surly)*   Naethin tae tell, Andro.

ANDREW *(with look of disappointment)*   Aw here! Dinnae tell me! Dinnae tell me ye didnae get yer hole?

WILL *(choking with outrage)*   Whit's that tae dae wi you?

ANDREW   But here I thocht we were gonnae be pals, you and me! *(Tongue in cheek.)* Comrades-in-arms, like?

WILL   There's some things ye keep tae yersel.

ANDREW   Aw haw! So ye did get yer hole?

WILL   Naw! I mean if I did – whether I did or didnae – I wadnae tell you!

ANDREW *(shrugs)*   Suit yersel! *(Takes a slug of beer, grins wickedly.)* I did.

WILL   Eh?

ANDREW   I did.

WILL   You did what?

ANDREW   Got my hole.

WILL   Aw – ye did, did ye?

ANDREW   Oooh Aye! *(Stretches himself in reminiscence.)* Had tae pey for it like! Cannae expect onythin ither at my age. But, oh Jesus…

WILL *(sighs, pulls a long face)*   Ye clairty auld tyke! And did ye no dae onythin else?

ANDREW   Och, jist the usual! Gaed oot and got fou, got intae a fecht, got a hooer and got my hole. Whit else is there for an auld sodger? And forby – the toun's no the same.

WILL *(without much interest)*   Naw?

ANDREW   Naw! Ye'll haurdly credit this, Wull, but there was a time I could walk through the Gressmerket and get stopped by every second bugger I met. They were aa my friens, I kent them aa. And nou? Nou they're aa deid – deid or no able tae get oot. I haurdly ken a saul in Embro nou, son. See whit ye're comin tae? *(Takes another drink.)* Wha'd be a sodger, eh? Wha'd be a sodger?

WILL *(smiles)*   Come aff it, Andro. Ye wadnae cheynge it!

ANDREW   Huh? Dae I hae ony option? Still. Ye're richt, I suppose. It's been my life. And it's no sae bad in a job like this – nae action tae speak o, forby the bit dunt wi the flet o the sword ye whiles dole oot jist tae keep yer haun in. Protectin his Lordship's presence frae the blandishments o a worshippin Glesca population! Huh! Staunin gaird on heidcases like Ogilvie!

WILL   Here aye! The Faither! Hou's he gettin on?

ANDREW   Ogilvie? Ach, the sooner we're shot o him the better! I dinnae ken whit wey they dinnae jist hing the bugger and be done wi it!

WILL *(troubled)*   Been actin up again, has he?

ANDREW   Ach, ye've nae idea! Still, he'll soon be sortit!

WILL   Hou's that?

ANDREW   I reckon he's for the buits. The buits'll brak him.

WILL   The buits? I've heard o them! Are they awfy…

ANDREW   Aye they're a sair thing, laddie. An awfy sair thing!

WILL   Ach, it's a shame! The Faither's no sic a bad sort o cheil, ye ken! It's an awfy pity! Ach, whit wey dae they hae tae torture him, onywey? They ken he's a priest,

223

a Jesuit! That should be mair nor enough tae hing him! Whit wey dae they hae tae
gie him the buits?

ANDREW   Politics, Wullie. I've tellt ye afore. Naethin tae dae wi us. Mair nor likely,
Ogilvie kens somethin and Spottiswoode wants tae find oot. Politics.

WILL   Well, I think it's a fuckin shame! Gin his Lordship was gonnae gie the Faither
the buits he should hae done it months ago, b'Christ! This is bluidy awful!
(Pauses obviously upset by the news.) Will they get somebody in?

ANDREW   What for?

WILL   For the buits! Will they get somebody in tae gie them tae him?

ANDREW   Ye're jokin!

WILL   Well, wha gies him the buits then?

ANDREW   I'll gie ye three guesses!

WILL   *(jumping to his feet)*   Here, here, jist a minute! Screw the nut, eh? Screw the
fuckin nut! I didnae sign on for that.

ANDREW   Ye're in the airmy nou, boy. And in the airmy – even this yucky wee
airmy – ye dae whit ye're tellt! Which reminds me – ye better get awa up and
relieve Wattie. The puir bugger'll be starvin bi nou!

Rather reluctantly, WILL *goes to the rack and takes down his sword and helmet.*

WILL   That's aaright, Andro, but I signed on for a sodger – no a bluidy torturer!

ANDREW   *(wearily)*   Forget it son! Forget it for nou! It wadnae be you that'd be
rammin the wedge intil his leg in ony case…

WILL   Maybe no, but it's oot the bluidy box for aa that!

WILL *goes to the door, pauses, hitches up his sword.*

WILL   Ye'll be on the nicht watch?

ANDREW   *(absently)*   Aye.

WILL   See ye the morn then!

Exit WILL. ANDREW *sits staring into his drink. Eventually, he drains the mug and
stands up.* SPOTTISWOODE *enters.*

ANDREW   *(turning)*   M'lord.

SPOTTISWOODE   *(raising his hand)*   It's aa richt, Andro, it's aa richt! Ye can stand
easy! I'm sorry about this – hae ye finished your dinner?

ANDREW   Aye, m'lord.

SPOTTISWOODE   Guid. Well, get armed then and come on up the stairs. I want a
word with ye. *(As* ANDREW *gets ready.)* Ogilvie, Andrew. It's about Ogilvie. What
d'ye think?

ANDREW   *(belting on his sword)*   He'll brak gif ye gie him the buits, m'lord. Shair
as daith!

SPOTTISWOODE   Mm. Ye dinnae care for the boots, do ye Andro?

ANDREW   I'm a sodger, sir. It's aa in the days wark.

SPOTTISWOODE   Aye, aye, aye. But ye dinnae care for them, do ye. Yersel, I mean! It's no a job ye like?

ANDREW   Wattie's yer man for the buits, m'lord. No me. *(Hesitates.)* As I say, I'm a sodger – I'm trained tae fecht, no torture. Naw sir, I dinnae care for the buits.

SPOTTISWOODE   I'll be frank with ye, Andro. Neither do I. And in this case – in this case I question their effectiveness. I'm thinking that it micht be better to consider something else.

ANDREW   *(all ready)*   Whatever ye say, m'lord.

SPOTTISWOODE   Come away up the stair. We'll hae a blether aboot it.

Exit SPOTTISWOODE, *followed by* ANDREW.

Scene 5

OGILVIE'S *room, nine days later. The bed has been removed and* OGILVIE *is seated at the table. He is a terrible sight. His shirt is torn to shreds, his hair is in disarray, there are enormous black rings about his eyes and scratch-marks and streaks of blood all over his hands and arms. He has been denied sleep for the past eight days.*

It is four o'clock in the morning. ANDREW, *on the night watch, is seated on the edge of the table. He has shed his sword, helmet and tunic and has no other weapon except for a dagger which he keeps in a leather sheath strapped to his bare arm.* OGILVIE'S *head falls on his chest and his eyes close.* ANDREW *slaps him hard across the face several times.*

ANDREW   Come on, Faither, come on! Ye ken ye cannae get tae sleep! (ANDREW'S *slapping has had no effect so he draws the dagger and jabs at* OGILVIE'S *shoulder several times.)* Wake up, man, wake up, wake up!

OGILVIE *staggers back out of his chair like a startled beast. He stumbles once or twice but eventually manages to stand up fairly steadily, albeit in a stooped position.*

OGILVIE   *(peers in* ANDREW'S *direction, shading his eyes with his hand)*   Who – who is it this time? Andrew? Is it you, Andrew? You'd never believe... Is it you, Andrew? Yes. Yes, it *is!* It *is* you, Andrew. I know it is. You're the one who never says anything. You never say anything. Well, very little anyway. So it must be you, Andrew. It must be...

ANDREW   Aye, Faither, it's mysel.

OGILVIE   Oh. Oh. I knew it. I knew all the time that it was you. I knew it but I hoped – oh, never mind! I hoped – I hoped it might be one of the others Because you're the worst, Andrew, did you know that? The very worst *(laughs)* of a bad, bad lot! *(Laughs louder.)* The Praetorian Guard of His Heretical Holiness! *(Bitterly.)* Bunch of workshy know-nothings and broken-down has-beens! Sandy – God, Sandy's bad enough! He talks and talks and talks and talks. He hardly stops for breath. His tongue chisels away all the way into the farthest extremities of my brain! Oh, I know all about you, Andrew – what a great warrior you were, all the battles that you fought! Sandy makes it sound like some great legend *(laughs)* – a great legend that goes on and on and on and on! *(Shakes his head.)* But he's not the worst – no, no, not by a long chalk he's not the worst. Neither is Will – oh my God, Will, Will, what am I saying? Will's the best! The only one of the whole damned lot of you with a morsel of charity in him. He's a good boy, Wullie – a very good boy. Now don't mistake me! Don't misunderstand! He does his job, he keeps me awake – nothing else you hear? *(Softer.)* But he's kind. He's considerate. He talks to me – he talks to me without shouting, without argument, without – without – without… oh dammit, what's the word, what's the word! What I mean to say is that, when he talks to me he listens to what I say, there are no barriers between us, no implacable stone walls! I have not talked to another living being, the way that I sometimes talk with Will, for many a long, long day. And perhaps I never will again. And if he could just – if I could get him to – Oh, no, no, no, it's useless, useless! He will not listen. He's a heretic, another damned heretic just as you… just as you *(gives* ANDREW *a shifty suspicious look)* all are! *(Whispers.)* Andrew? Andrew? Is that right? Are you a heretic?

ANDREW   Eh?

OGILVIE   A heretic. I asked you if you were a heretic. Are you a heretic?

ANDREW   If ye say so, Faither.

OGILVIE   No! *Not* if I say so! *I* am not *you!* It's not for me to tell you whether or not you are a heretic. It's not for me to say! It's for you. You. It's your own decision! The facts are before you, you can make up your own mind. You don't *have* to be a heretic, you know. You don't have to be! *(Suddenly weary, he passes his hand across his eyes.)* I was a heretic once, did you know that?

ANDREW   *(more to himself than to* OGILVIE*)*   Wadnae surprise me, Faither.

OGILVIE   Eh? What was that? What did you say? It wouldn't surprise you. It wouldn't surprise you, eh? Why not? Why not, pray? Do I look like a heretic! Do I sound like a heretic! Do I behave like a heretic? What am I doing here if it would not surprise you?

ANDREW   *(uneasily, not really wanting to talk)*   Jist passin a remark, Faither. Didnae mean ocht by it.

OGILVIE   No? No? It occurs to me Andrew, that you do not care for heretics. Is that right? (ANDREW *says nothing.)* Now Andrew. I asked you a question. I want an answer. I get the distinct impression that you do not greatly care for heretics. Andrew, am I right. *(Again* ANDREW *says nothing.)* Andrew, I am talking to you! I am asking you a question and I want an answer right now. Do you or do you not care overmuch for heretics? *(Still* ANDREW *says nothing.* OGILVIE *bunches up his fist and shakes it at him.)* You! You! You! Oh you! I might as well try to communicate with a rock as bother with you! Sandy speaks too much and you speak too little and Wat *(recoils as if in pain).* Wat! Oooh that twisted pig, Wat! *(Holds out his hands to* ANDREW.) Have you seen this, Andrew? Have you seen Wat's latest? Clever wee Wattie's latest trick to torment Father Ogilvie? He took ten nails, Andrew, ten nails and drove them – one at a time, with his mallet – right under my fingernails! Oh, the cunning little bastard, why did he have to do that! His ingenuity, his bestial ingenuity knows no bounds! *(Pauses to recover his somewhat fragile composure.)* And yet and yet, I'll tell you something – I prefer, I *much* prefer Wat to you. Yes. Yes. His torture, his physical torture, is far more bearable than the torment that your silence inflicts on me! *(Pauses to gather his thoughts and put them into words.)* Wat enjoys himself you know – he *enjoys* himself. You'd never guess it from his expression – that dour, heretical, swinish little face – but he *does* enjoy himself. Everything he does – every new source of pain that he invents comes from up here. *(Taps his head.)* Nobody tells him. Nobody gives him orders – how he must think and rack his brain for originality! He brings his tortures to me with all the enthusiasm and delight of a devoted father with gifts for his new baby! Mind you, there's nothing personal in it! It has nothing to do with *me!* But I am a Catholic, you see – and Wat is strong, strong against the papes! Oh aye! So he doesn't worry about me at all – and he enjoys himself. But Andrew – it works both ways. D'you understand what I mean? D'you understand? D'you understand what I'm trying to say? Wattie doesn't think of me as a human being at all – that's why he can approach his work with so much equanimity. But, you see, it works both ways – I don't think of him as human either! No! And when he was hammering those nails into my hands, there was a part of me – not all of me, I admit, just a part, a small part – that was enjoying it every bit as much as he was! Can you understand that? Eh? (ANDREW *looks sceptical but says nothing.* OGILVIE *laughs.)* You don't believe me, do you? You don't believe that anyone could enjoy it! *(Thrusts his hands in front of* ANDREW'S *eyes so viciously that* ANDREW *recoils, reaching for his dagger.)* But I did, I tell you – I did. You see, there were no complications, no extraneous considerations. There was a confrontation going on, a divine confrontation, that had nothing to do with Wat or myself, with the logic or wisdom of my beliefs or the logic or wisdom of his, with his cruelty or my pain. No, no, it was more than that, much more. We were only the instruments, we were only the instruments, the weapons of a conflict that was ultimately between the Almighty on my side and the Devil on his. Now do you understand why I hate you more than the others? Now do you understand why I asked you that question? Now do you understand why I *must* know what you feel about heretics? *(He has wound himself up almost to breaking point and now begins to weep).* Why don't you answer me? Why don't you say something? Why do you just stand there and smirk?

ANDREW   Naethin to say, Faither!

OGILVIE   That's what you always say! *(Mimics.)* 'Naethin to say, Faither'. Don't try to fool me, Andrew. Don't try to pretend to me that you are a man of few words – because I know different! *(Turns wearily away, worn out by his fury but turns back almost immediately in a more composed, if intense, vein.)* Andrew. I am not a fool. I'm not a child. Eh? I know, you know. I know why you won't talk to me. I know. You will not talk to me, you refuse to talk to me, you are afraid to talk to me because you *(points)* are a Catholic!

ANDREW *gives a scornful, embarrassed laugh but says nothing.*

OGILVIE   How long have I been without sleep, Andrew. How long? Must be – a week? Must be. Eh? Is it a week? It must be that at least! Even so. Even so, Andrew, after all this time, after all this time without my natural rest – even so, there are periods, there are short spells when I have complete, absolutely complete lucidity. There are periods when I am as awake and as aware as ever I was. And believe me, Andrew, I am fully awake now! *(Goes quickly to* ANDREW *and takes him by the shoulders.)* Andrew, I am going to ask you a question. I am going to put a question to you. And if you refuse to answer – or if you should answer falsely – Andrew, oh Andrew, Andrew you will surely be damned! *(Takes a deep breath.)* Now. Tell me. Are you or are you not a Catholic?

ANDREW   *(hesitates, looks* OGILVIE *in the eye, turns away)*   That was a while syne. A lang while syne.

OGILVIE   *(exulting)*   You are! You are! I knew it! I knew it! You are a Catholic. Heaven be praised!

ANDREW   *(angry and embarrassed and evasive all at the same time)*   My faither was! My mither was!

OGILVIE   *(without noticing the evasion)*   Your mother – your mother was a Catholic? Is that right? Is that right now, Andrew? *(Turns away as if in a dream.)* So was mine, Andrew. So was mine. Oh Andrew, it is the Catholic women who are the backbone of our faith – the Catholic women. There are many – I myself have known many, a great many men who were holy, truly holy. But I never met any man who was as holy as my mother. *(Closes his eyes as if in prayer.)* Oh you are a woman of great faith. What you have desired will be accomplished for you. *(Turns again to* ANDREW.*)* Tell me, Andrew. Where do you worship?

ANDREW   *(amused)*   Worship, Faither?

OGILVIE   Worship. Yes. Where do you worship? Where do you receive the Mass.

ANDREW   *(shaking his head)*   I never worship, Faither.

OGILVIE   *(shocked)*   Never.

ANDREW   Naw!

OGILVIE   Then how… how do you serve your faith?

ANDREW   Faither, *(with some hesitation)* I hae nae faith.

OGILVIE   No faith? No faith? This – what d'you mean, you've lost your faith? Is that it? Have you become a heretic? (ANDREW *turns away, says nothing.)* Answer me, Andrew. Answer me. You're not going to turn dumb again, are you? Just when you've started to talk? Don't you understand, Andrew? Don't you understand that I cannot bear those silences? I cannot bear your terrible silences!

ANDREW   *(savagely)*   Faither, I hae nae faith. Leave it at that!

OGILVIE   But Andrew – a man cannot live without faith!

ANDREW   *(turns savagely once more, suddenly smiles gently)*   Faither, I am forty-twa year auld.

OGILVIE   Oh Andrew. Oh Andrew, Andrew, Andrew. Oh – Oh Scotland. What kind of country have you become? What depths of barbarism have you reached? When a man can stand before his priest without shame and tell him that he has lost his faith! *(Turns to* ANDREW *again.)* So. You are beyond even the evil sin of heresy. You are a pagan. You have lost your faith. *(Suddenly savage.)* Well, I have not lost mine! That is why I am here. That is why I am enduring this – this torment! That is why I will endure all this and more! Spottiswoode – did you know that Spottiswoode threatened me with the boots. Yes. The boots. *(Smiles and shakes his head.)* I think he broke poor Wattie's heart when he decided not to use them. And he told me – Spottiswoode did – he told me, he said to me that I was lucky. Lucky! *(Mimics.)* 'Ye hae been used in a maist merciful manner, Faither Ogilvie'. *(Laughs bitterly.)* You're all fools, do you know that? *(Slaps his leg.)* What's this. Eh? It's a leg. That's all. A leg. What good is a leg to a priest? To carry him into chapel, that's all. To carry him into chapel. *I can be carried into chapel!* Don't you understand? Take my leg, take both my legs! Take my arms! I do not need them, they are of no use to me! But you, you...

Suddenly he screams and staggers about with his head in his hands. ANDREW *stands by, aghast and helpless, looking towards the door every now and again as if unsure about going for help.* OGILVIE *turns on* ANDREW *forcing him up against the wall and ranting at him in a voice that seems stretched to breaking point:*

OGILVIE   You, you you, what are you doing? What are you doing to me? What are you doing? You are driving a wedge into my mind! You are crushing my brains and my reason is running from my skull in rivers of grey! *(Pushes himself away from* ANDREW *who now seems considerably alarmed.)* You are driving me mad! You take my mind, you take my body, you take my reason, you take my comfort. Very well, then! Take it – take it all! I have no use for it, for any of it! I tell you only this: *(gathers himself together in one last defiant bellow)* you shall not have my faith!

OGILVIE *collapses.* ANDREW *rushes to him and tries to bring him round, without success. He goes to the door and bangs on it repeatedly.*

ANDREW   Sandy! Sandy! Whaur are ye, ye donnert bugger! Wake up, for Christ's sake! I want ye!

SANDY *(off)*   Is that yersel, Andro?

ANDREW   Whae the bluidy hell d'ye think? Come in here, for Christ's sake! I'm needin ye!

The door opens and SANDY *enters. He is a wiry little man, extremely talkative and of roughly the same age as* ANDREW.

SANDY   Is it the Faither? I heard aa the rammy. Away again, is he?
ANDREW   Aye. Come on, gie's a haun wi him.

> ANDREW *bends over* OGILVIE'S *body, taking him by the armpits.* SANDY *follows, dithering and talking all the time.*

SANDY   My my my my, Andro, I'll tell ye straucht. I cannae be daein with this wey
o warkin. I tellt the Bishop, I says tae him, I says…
ANDREW   Shut yer bluidy face and get on wi it!
SANDY   *(unperturbed)*   …this offends my sense o professional decorum…
ANDREW   *(struggling with* OGILVIE*)*   Jesus Christ, Sandy! Get him up! *(Together
they manage to get* OGILVIE *to his feet.)* Right. Twice roun syne let him faa. Come
on.

> *They half-walk, half-drag* OGILVIE *twice round the room.* SANDY *keeps on talking.*

SANDY   They'd hae been far, far better wi the buits – far far better. I've said frae the
start that this was a daft-like wey o warkin – wastin aa this time and no even a
cheep of whatever it is the Airchbishop wants. Ye can say whit ye like, Andro. Ye
can say whit ye like. It's jist no right that professional sodgers like you and me
should be asked tae tak on duty like this. This is Wattie's game, this. The torture
tredd. It micht be aaricht for Wattie – aye, it micht be aa very weill for Wattie! No
for me. I ken wappins, I tellt the Bishop, I ken wappins, been a sodger aa my days,
that's *my* tredd. I says tae Spottiswoode I says…
ANDREW   *(with long-suffering patience)*   Are you fuckin finished?

> *They have once more reached the centre of the room.*

SANDY   *(slightly cowed)*   Weill, ye ken whit I mean.
ANDREW   Dae I? Jesus Christ, I sometimes wonder if ye ken yersel! Have ye got
him?
SANDY   *(taking a firmer grip on* OGILVIE'S *arm)*   Aye.
ANDREW   Are ye ready?
SANDY   Aye.
ANDREW   Right. Wan. Twa. Three.

> *They stand back and allow* OGILVIE *to keel forward on his face.* OGILVIE *rises to
his hands and knees and shakes his head.*

OGILVIE   *(rising)*   My God. Oh My God. *(Shouting.)* My God! I have kept my
promise! I have made you known to the men you gave me! I have given them
your word and they have received it! My God, My God, I pray for them, these

men. I pray for them and them alone because these are the men you gave me. Let
them be with me, Oh Lord! Let them be with me in my hour of glory. Let them be
with me in the glory you will give me! Let them be with me that they might see,
that they might know that the glory that is mine is the glory of Almighty God!
Father, the world does not know you as I know you… the world does not know…
Father… the world…

He is reeling and tottering and obviously about to fall over again.

ANDREW   Watch him!

ANDREW *and* SANDY *manage to catch* OGILVIE *safely but his falling weight makes
both of them stagger back. They stand, holding* OGILVIE, *and panting for breath.*

SANDY   Jesus Christ! Andro, he's weill awa nou. Did ye hear whit he was sayin?
He's haverin nou – we'll no get onything oot o him gin we keep this up! He'll no
last the nicht. Aw Andro, when I think o aa that you and me hae been through
thegither – I never thocht I'd see the day that…
ANDREW   Shut up, Sandy! Shut up! Gie yer fuckin erse a chance, will ye? Christ, ye
never stop!
SANDY   *(hurt by* ANDREW'S *rebuke)*   I'm sorry, Andro. I didnae mean tae… Will we
tak anither turn?
ANDREW   Naw, naw, it'll dae nae guid. We'd jist tire ane anither oot. We'd better
gie the drap anither try tho. Are ye ready?
SANDY   Aye.
ANDREW   Richt. Wan. Twa. Three.

OGILVIE *keels forward again.* ANDREW *and* SANDY *go to him.* ANDREW *kneels
down and listens to his heart.*

OGILVIE   You're damned, Andrew! You are going down to the burning fires of hell!
You have thrown away your faith and you cannot be saved or released from your
damnation! God is not mocked, Andrew, God will not be mocked. I know where
you are, I know where you live. I know the spirit that burns within you, the flame,
the dying flame, the dying flame which yet might live! Wake up, Andrew, before
it's too late and the fire consumes you. Wake up, wake up, wake up! Feed that
flame that it might not die! There are few here in Scotland who have kept their
clothes clean – but wake up, only wake up and I tell you that you will walk with
me dressed in the purest of white raiment. You will walk with me dressed in the
raiment of the blessed of Christ. Oh, I know you do not love me as you must have
done once – I know you do not love me now as you did then. Only turn from your
sins and do as you did then – turn from your sins, I beseech you, turn from your
sins! For if you do not turn from your sins I will come and I will find you and I
will leap upon you like a thief in the night! Listen to me, Andrew! Listen to me if

you have ears! Listen to me if you have ears! Listen to me if you have ears!

OGILVIE *collapses once again and this time,* SANDY *and* ANDREW *are so horror-struck by him that they do not even try to catch him. He lies on the floor gabbling for a moment before passing out again.*

SANDY *(breathlessly)*   He's gane badgy!
ANDREW *(glancing dazedly at* SANDY)   Guid God! Guid God!

SPOTTISWOODE *enters briskly, followed by a* DOCTOR, *a severe-looking young man.*

SPOTTISWOODE   What's happening here? What's the trouble? Andrew?

The DOCTOR *goes to* OGILVIE *and starts examining him.* ANDREW *takes a step back and looks at* SPOTTISWOODE, *shaking his head.*

SANDY   Gin ye want my opinion, m'lord, I'd say that he's gey near it. I mean to say, sir, echt days and nine nichts, I mean tae say…
SPOTTISWOODE *(completely ignoring him)*   Andro. What d'ye think?
ANDREW *(hesitates before he answers)*   I dinnae ken, m'lord. Shair as daith, I dinnae ken. I thocht that… weill, I didnae think he had it in him, I didnae think he had the smeddum tae see it through this far. And nou – nou I hae the idea, I'm jist as shair that he'll see it through till daith. Daith and worse nor daith. I think he's past tholin ony mair o it.
DOCTOR   M'lord, gin this man is no let to sleep within the hour, he'll no survive.
SPOTTISWOODE   Ye're siccar o that?
DOCTOR   Aye, m'lord.

SPOTTISWOODE *paces the floor, hands behind back, deep in thought.*

SPOTTISWOODE   Very well. Andro. Sandy. Bring him a bed.

Exit ANDREW *and* SANDY *hurriedly, followed by the* DOCTOR.

SPOTTISWOODE   Damn ye, John Ogilvie. Damn ye!

Exit SPOTTISWOODE.

Act Two

Scene 1

About a month later. Ogilvie's quarters in Spottiswoode's Castle in Glasgow. As the scene opens, OGILVIE *is discovered sitting on the bed reading a book. He looks up from his reading, closing his eyes, committing a passage to memory. The high-spirited laughter of a woman is heard off.* OGILVIE *lays the book aside, frowning, rises to his feet. Enter* ANDREW, *and, sweeping in behind him,* LADY RACHEL SPOTTISWOODE. *A tall, handsome woman, she is dressed in a floor-length cloak and is slightly tipsy, she keeps her arms under the cloak folded across her chest, and glances about the room with a rather exaggerated inquisitiveness.*

ANDREW *(grumpily)*   Faither, ye hae a visitor. The Leddy Rachel Spottiswoode.

Looking rather uncertain, OGILVIE *steps forward, inclining his head in the merest suggestion of a bow.*

OGILVIE *(guardedly)*   Madam, this is an unlooked-for pleasure.

RACHEL *gives a slight nod and moves past* OGILVIE, *downstage and across, speaking as she does so.*

RACHEL   Weill, Faither, this is hardly what I'd been led to expect. *(She stops one step away from the end of the bed and turns to address* OGILVIE *direct.)* Ye seem to be byordnar comfortable here. They maun be treating ye better nou nor they did when ye were in Embro!

OGILVIE *(pleasantly)*   Madam, it is still...

RACHEL   Is that richt, Andro? Ye'll hae been tellt to treat the Faither a wee thing kinder here in Glesca nor ye did in Embro?

ANDREW   That's no for me to say, m'leddy.

RACHEL *(giggles)*   Andro's no very pleased wi me, Faither. Are ye, Andro?

ANDREW   No my place to be pleased or displeased, m'leddy.

RACHEL   Och, wad ye listen to him, Faither? It's my husband, ye see. He's feart the Airchbishop'll get to ken that I've come to see ye!

ANDREW   He's shair tae, m'leddy. And *he'll* no be pleased.

OGILVIE *is looking distinctly unhappy by this time.*

OGILVIE   In that case, madam, perhaps it would be better...

RACHEL   Och, Faither Ogilvie, dinna you start! There's nae need to fash about John. I ken weill enough hou to handle *him*. I'll tell him myself – in my ain guid time. Andro, as I was just this minute passing the servants' quarters, I've a notion I heard the sound of merriment and conviviality. *(Flatly.)* I suggest that ye go and get yourself a drink.

ANDREW *(hardly able to contain his outrage)*   I am on duty, m'leddy.

RACHEL *(irritably)*   Aw, Andro, dinna you be sic an auld fash! *(Smiles with mischief.)* Faither Ogilvie's a braw-looking cheil richt enough – but he's a man o the cloth and a perfect gentleman, I'm shair. I don't suppose that there's the slightest chance that my honour will be in any danger whatsoever!

ANDREW *(growling)*   Madam…

RACHEL   Andro, that's enough! Dinna argue. Dae what I tell ye. Away ye go! Shoo!

Reluctantly, glowering at them both, ANDREW *takes his leave.* OGILVIE *watches him leave somewhat helplessly.*

OGILVIE   Well, madam – would you care to take a seat?

OGILVIE *goes to take the chair from the desk.* RACHEL *steps over to the bed and sits herself down on it.*

RACHEL   That's very kind of ye, Faither.

Perplexed, OGILVIE *sits down on the chair himself.*

OGILVIE   Well! *(Pauses.)* I'm afraid that I'm unable to offer you any kind of refreshment.

RACHEL *laughs and rises. She throws back her cloak to reveal that she has been holding a bottle and two goblets, hiding them presumably from Andrew.*

RACHEL   No need for apologies, Faither! I brocht my ain!

She places the bottle and the goblets on the table, and, slipping off her cloak, throws it on to the bed. OGILVIE *rises to his feet.* RACHEL *uncorks the bottle and begins to pour.*

RACHEL   Say when, Faither.

OGILVIE   That will be sufficient, madam.

RACHEL *hands him the goblet and pours out a drink for herself.*

RACHEL *(grins)*   Here, I wonder what Mistress Calder and the ither douce leddies o Glesca toun'd say, gin they could see me nou? On my lane wi a man – a Catholic priest! – sipping wine at this time o the nicht! Tut, tut, tut! *(Confidentially, coming closer to him.)* But then, Faither Ogilvie, Mistress Calder and the ither douce leddies o Glesca toun consider me a harlot and a tippler in any case – so we'll no worry about them, eh?

She moves away from him and takes up her seat on the bed.

OGILVIE   Well, Lady Spottiswoode – your very good health!

RACHEL   *(raising her glass)*   And yours, Faither! *(Takes a sip.)* Tell me – are ye keeping better nou?

OGILVIE   Oh yes! Yes, I've quite recovered from my *(pauses)* my experience in Edinburgh.

RACHEL   That's fine, then.

OGILVIE *nods and pauses for an instant.*

OGILVIE   Tell me, my lady, What can I do for you? *(Smiles guardedly.)* I take it you've not come to interrogate me?

RACHEL *laughs.*

RACHEL   Hits, na, Faither. I ken nocht o sic maitters! I wadnae ken where to start! Just a wee social visit, that's aa! There's been sic a lot o clash about the toun anent the ongoings o Faither John Ogilvie that I thocht – ach, I had a notion to come and see ye, that's aa! *(Pauses.)* Efter the morn's morn, I michtna get the chance.

OGILVIE   *(warily)*   No. No. That's true.

RACHEL   Aye! *(Changing the subject.)* They tell me, Faither, that ye left Scotland when ye were nae mair nor a laddie?

OGILVIE   That's correct. I've spent most of my life on the Continent. I only returned last year.

RACHEL   Shairly... it maun hae been a thocht to come back?

OGILVIE *pauses a minute before answering, moving away from her downstage.*

OGILVIE   I have a vocation to serve, madam. It is not for me to be afraid of the conditions in which I must serve it.

RACHEL   *(smiling)*   Dinna mistake me, Faither. That's no what I meant. I was just thinking that Scotland – the place and the folk – maun seem unco strange til ye after aa this time.

OGILVIE   *(faintly surprised)*   Strange? No. No, not really. I was happy enough in Europe, but Scotland, after all, is my native land – I am no foreigner here!

RACHEL   Mmm. *(Change of subject.)* And did ye manage to see your family?

OGILVIE   My family? *(Suspicious of the question, pauses before replying.)* Yes. Yes. I paid a short visit to Banff shortly after I arrived.

RACHEL   *(pleasantly)*   Oh, they'd be pleased to see ye!

OGILVIE   *(laughs bitterly)*   Pleased? No, madam, they were hardly pleased!

RACHEL   *(rising in concern)*   Were they no? But shairly your faither...

235

OGILVIE My father! *(Laughs again.)* My father – and my step-mother and all the rest of them – are heretics! Surely you don't imagine that they'd kill any fatted calves for me?

RACHEL *sits down on the edge of the desk.*

RACHEL Och, I'm no sae shair! Bluid's thicker nor water when aa's said and done!

OGILVIE Water perhaps, madam! Other elements are made of sterner stuff. *(Sighs and walks towards her.)* Look, my lady. My father was asked to make a choice – years ago – between his title and his land on the one hand and his faith on the other. Well you know the choice he made. And if he were asked to make a similar choice – between his property and his blood – which do you think he'd choose?

RACHEL *drains her goblet.*

RACHEL Puir Johnnie! Puir, puir Johnnie Ogilvie! No had much o a homecoming, have ye, son?

OGILVIE *resumes his seat.*

OGILVIE *(with irony)* It certainly has left a lot to be desired!

RACHEL Still, your faither maunnae hae been sae bad! I mean, ye'd shairly hae been a heretic yourself gin he hadnae sent ye...

OGILVIE *rises angrily from his seat.*

OGILVIE Oh that! That, madam, is the greatest irony of all! It was the dying wish of my mother – my real mother, that is – that I should be given a Catholic education. That desire was never honoured until my father married my step-mother – the Lady Douglas – and she saw the opportunity to rob me of my heritage – to seize the title and the property that should be rightfully mine and give them to her own bastard brats! Well, very soon now, I shall be given a greater title – and believe me, madam, there's none of them will have any part in that!

RACHEL *lays her goblet aside thoughtfully.*

RACHEL Faither, d'ye ken wha ye put me in mind o? Wullie Scott.

OGILVIE *looks puzzled.*

RACHEL Och, it's an auld tale. There was this laddie in the Borders – Wullie Scott was his name. A cattle thief. Naethin byordnar in that, of course – they're aa cattle-thieves in the Borders, ye ken. Anyway. Wullie was reivin the kye o a man cried Murray – and Murray keppit him at it. In the normal wey o things, Murray wad hae hinged Wullie Scott and that wad hae been that. But it seems that Murray had a problem. He had a dochter – an ill-faured bitch bi the name of Meg – muckle-moued Meg they cried her – and he couldna get onybody to mairry her and take her aff his hands. So he tellt Wullie, he said 'See here, Scott. I'll gie ye the choice. Ye can hing – or ye can mairry my dochter. What's it to be?' Wullie took ae look at muckle-moued Meg – and he says 'I'll hing!'

OGILVIE *(huffily)* I fail to see the analogy, madam. I am no criminal.

RACHEL I didnae say ye were, Faither.

Enter ANDREW. *He sees the bottle on the desk and eyes* RACHEL *with suspicion.*

RACHEL Ah, it's yourself, Andrew. Aye, I suppose I'd better awa. *(She picks up her cloak and takes it over to* ANDREW.) We hae sic a feck o visitors the nou – I'd better go and do my hostess. *(She hands the cloak to* ANDREW, *who holds it for her.)* Thank ye kindly for the refreshment. *(She indicates the bottle and winks at* OGILVIE.) It's been grand talking to ye.

OGILVIE Likewise, madam.

RACHEL I trust it'll aa go weill for ye at the trial the morn.

OGILVIE *shrugs.* RACHEL *turns to go, then stops.*

RACHEL Oh, by the way, Faither. I never tellt ye the end o the tale. Wullie Scott didnae hing. Naw. He thocht about it and decided that discretion was the better pairt o valour. I heard tell that Meg was a guid enough wife till him and that, in time, he even learned to love her.

OGILVIE Madam, I could never learn to love heresy.

RACHEL *(smiles)* Faither, I fear ye dinna take my meaning yet! Guid nicht wi ye!

Exit RACHEL *and a relieved* ANDREW. OGILVIE *watches them go, puzzled.*

Scene 2

The courtyard of the Castle later that night. WILL, *on guard duty, walks back and forward thoughtfully, holding his spear over his shoulder. He hears a step and comes to the alert.*

WILL Whoa! Stop richt there, whaever ye are!

The DOCTOR *steps out of the shadows.*

DOCTOR It's aaricht, Wullie. It's just mysel!

WILL *relaxes.*

WILL   Doctor! Ye gied me a wee gluff there! Ye're shairly out of yer bed late the
nicht, are ye no?

They approach each other in a friendly manner.

DOCTOR   Aye! Just canna get to sleep, Wull! I keep thinkin about the trial the morn.
WILL   *(nodding sadly)*   Aye!
DOCTOR   Tell me, Wullie… what d'ye think the outcome'll be?
WILL   O the trial?
DCOTOR   Aye.
WILL   That's no for me to say, Doctor. Tae tell ye the truth, I'll no even be there. I'll
no be on duty.
DOCTOR   Aye, but ye've shairly some idea! Will they hing him, d'ye think?

WILL *pauses, looks at the* DOCTOR *a trifle guardedly, turns away.*

WILL   It looks like it, doctor. Aye. It shairly looks like it!
DOCTOR   Mmm. It strikes me ye wadna be aathegither happy about that, Wullie.

WILL *turns to him suspiciously.*

WILL   What d'ye mean bi that?
DCOTOR   *(innocently)*   Naethin! Just that Faither Ogilvie and yourself seem to get
on sae weill thegither that I'd hae thocht…
WILL   Ogilvie's a prisoner. I'm a gaird. Naethin chynges that!
DOCTOR   Na? That's no what I heard.
WILL   Aye, and whit did ye hear?

The DOCTOR *smiles.*

DOCTOR   I'm no shair if I can say, Wullie. It concerns a patient o mine, ye see. It
michtna be ethical for me to tell *onybody* what I ken. Still, a doctor's no the same
as a priest, is he? Whiles, a doctor micht feel it's his duty to betray a professional
confidence…
WILL   *(shaking his head)*   I'm no wi ye, doctor. I've no got a clue o what ye're
talkin about!
DOCTOR   I'm talkin about a patient o mine – a man cried Mayne. John Mayne. Ken
wha I mean?
WILL   *(shocked rigid)*   Oh!
DOCTOR   Aye. Oh Wullie, ye've been an awfy silly laddie!
WILL   I didna mean ony hairm! It was just a wheen letters for his freins – his faither
and his brithers and that – just tae let them ken hou he was! There was nae

hairm...

DOCTOR *goes to him and lays his hand on his shoulder.*

DOCTOR Of course no! Of course there wasna! Still, gin the bishop was to find
   out... (WILL *looks alarmed.*) Aw dinna fash, Wullie! Dinna fash! I'll no say a
   word. Like I said, it wadna be ethical.
WILL *(relieved)* Thanks a lot, doctor! I'll no...

The DOCTOR *looks about him before drawing a yellow parchment from the inside
of his coat.*

DOCTOR Only there's a wee complication. Ane of Faither Ogilvie's brithers has
   sent him a reply!

WILL *backs away from the* DOCTOR.

WILL Naw! No chance!
DOCTOR What for no, Wullie? I mean, in for a penny...

Enter WAT, *none too sober.*

WAT What the hell's gaun on here?

Both WILL *and the* DOCTOR *are terrified.*

DOCTOR Oh! It's yersel, Wattie! *(Pauses uncertainly for a moment.)* I've just
   brocht this message round for the bishop. Wullie here seems to think it's owre late
   in the day to bother him wi it *(goes to put the paper back in his pocket)* but it
   doesna maitter. It'll keep til the morn.

WAT *steps up to the* DOCTOR *suspiciously and puts his hand out.*

WAT See's it here!
DOCTOR It's aaricht, Wat. I tellt ye...

WAT *snatches the parchment from his hand.*

WAT I'll just tak a wee look at it just the same!

The DOCTOR *turns away, very frightened.* WAT *unfolds the parchment and gazes at
it for a few moments without expression. He looks up at* WILL.

WAT What's the maitter wi this? Eh? Naethin the maitter wi this! See, you take it, gie it tae the bishop the morn. *(Turns to* the DOCTOR.) Save ye a trip back, eh doctor? *(Turns back to* WILL.) See? Simple! Nae bother! *(Burps and claps* WILL *on the shoulder.)* I'm awa tae my bed!

WAT *moves off, then stops suddenly, turns slowly and looks at both of them suspiciously, shrugs as if he couldn't care less, then exits. The* DOCTOR *heaves a huge sigh of relief.*

DOCTOR Right! I think I'd better get awa nou, Wullie…

WILL *strides over to him.*

WILL Just a second, doctor. *(Holds up the document.)* I'll deliver this. I've nae option nou – sae I'll gie it tae the Faither. But I'm thinkin that you want tae be grateful, doctor, that nane o us can read.

Without another word, the DOCTOR *makes a hurried exit.* WILL *puts the parchment inside his tunic.*

Scene 3

Spottiswoode's study in the Castle of the Archbishop of Glasgow. It is a well-furnished, comfortable room, the most dominating features of which are: on the right a writing desk and chair, in the centre a large fireplace with comfortable chairs on either side, on the left a small table with a decanter, water and goblets. It is well past midnight and the fire has died. SPOTTISWOODE *sits on the left of the fireplace, a book in one hand and a goblet of wine in the other. He sighs and, laying the book aside on his lap, takes a sip of the wine. His wife,* LADY RACHEL SPOTTISWOODE, *dressed in a nightgown and carrying a candle, enters from the right.*

RACHEL *(reprovingly)* John! Are ye wyce, man? For heaven's sake, what ails ye? Ye should be in your bed!

SPOTTISWOODE *looks up at her, shakes his head and sighs.*

SPOTTISWOODE *(absently, almost defensively)* I hae been reading the epistles of the apostle Paul.
RACHEL *(sarcastically)* Oh. I see. Are ye to be examined in them then – the morn's morn – that ye maun bide up aa nicht in preparation?
SPOTTISWOODE *(with a faint smile)* Woman, your wit is sour.

RACHEL *comes forward and places her candle on the mantelpiece.*

RACHEL   I ken. It's the time of nicht – and the sair trial of haeing sic a husband as I hae.

She sits down opposite him.

SPOTTISWOODE   *(still smiling, rises and takes his goblet over to the drinks table)*   Hae I been sic a bad husband to ye, lass?

RACHEL   *(turning in the chair to smile at him)*   No, John. No. Ye ken better than to speir that. But there was a time when ye'd tell me aathing – a time when ye'd bring aa your sair bits to me.

SPOTTISWOODE   And do ye think that time has gane?

RACHEL   It looks like it, John. It shairly looks like it. St Paul, it would seem, has mair to offer in the way of comfort than I.

SPOTTISWOODE *laughs loudly.*

SPOTTISWOODE   Rachel, there can be smaa comfort for me in these times we live in. The office I hold in our Kirk is hardly a comfortable ane! Will ye tak a cup of wine with me, m'lady?

RACHEL   Dearie me. *(Sighs.)* Just a small one please, John!

SPOTTISWOODE   *(grinning)*   For the stomach's sake?

RACHEL   Aye.

As SPOTTISWOODE *pours the drinks, the smile leaves* RACHEL'S *face and she becomes apprehensive. She turns away from him.*

RACHEL   John – I went to see John Ogilvie the nicht.

SPOTTISWOODE   *(turning, astounded)*   You – what?

RACHEL   I went to see John Ogilvie the nicht.

SPOTTISWOODE   Certes, woman! Whiles ye go past it! What would Mistress Calder and the leddies o the congregation...

RACHEL   *(with a wave of her hand)*   P-y-e-e-h!

SPOTTISWOODE   P-y-e-e-h yourself! Rachel! What in creation garred ye do a thing like thon! Ogilvie has set this toun on fire! If it is kent – and certes, it will be kent! – that Spottiswoode's wife... *(Hands her the goblet.)* I do not ken where ye got the gumption!

RACHEL   *(taking the goblet)*   Weill – I maun admit to being a wee thing leerie about it myself – so I took a rather large glass of this before I went. So they'll maist likely let on that I was fou at the time!

SPOTTISWOODE *is about to take his seat. He turns on her, fuming and speechless. Looking at her, his temper fades and he smiles and shakes his head hopelessly.*

SPOTTISWOODE   Rachel, oh Rachel! What am I to do with ye?

RACHEL *(seriously)*   What am I to do with you, John? I'm sorry if I've offended or upset ye by going to see Ogilvie – but I'd hae thocht myself a sorrier wife gin I had stayed away! John, d'ye no understand? I had to try to discover what it was about this man that was bothering you.

SPOTTISWOODE *(irritably)*   Bothering me! Huh! It's no Ogilvie that bothers me!

RACHEL   Is it no? I'm no so sure! John, ye've no been yourself this while past – ill-tempered, growling and snarling aa owre the place, biding up gey near aa nicht, tossing and turning when ye do come to your bed... Na, na, my mannie, ye'll na tell me that it's no John Ogilvie that's bothering ye! This aa started on the very day he was arrested! Your bad humour started then. I had a notion to speak with the man that had put ye in sic a humour! So I went to see him.

SPOTTISWOODE   And are ye any the wiser?

RACHEL   I am not! I fail to see what there is to worry ye about this man! I canna help but feel sorry for him, but he's a wrong-headed fool! He micht be a cliver fool, but he's a fool just the same.

SPOTTISWOODE   D'ye tell me that, woman? A clever fool?

RACHEL   Ye needna laugh! Ye ken fine what I mean! The man has faith enough, I daresay! Faith of a kind – but is it the Christian faith? I beg leave to doubt it. I jalouse that even a papist micht beg leave to doubt it! That man cares for nobody but himself – his ain hurts and grievances! And how can he hae any sympathy with the concerns and conditions of ordinary folk? He kens nocht about them. He has charm enough to spare and a braw sharp tongue – he'd make a bonnie courtier no doubt. What does he ken o the sufferings o Scotland? He maybe kens principle and argument. He kens nocht o flesh and blood!

SPOTTISWOODE   Principle is necessary, m'dear, in any undertaking – and so is argument. Flesh and blood survive and flourish on the guid maintenance of baith. *(Gets to his feet thoughtfully and walks about.)* What troubles me in this matter is no Ogilvie's faith – I have never doubted nor grudged him that for an instant. He is a man of great faith, of great courage – and of not inconsiderable intellect. Really, Rachel, John Ogilvie is a maist byordnar man. I wish we had a few like him in our Kirk. Paul tells us – as ye weill ken – that every man should bide the way he was when God called him. I cannot blame Ogilvie for his faith – in his own way, he is as true to his principles as, in his place, I would hope and pray to be to mine.

RACHEL   Aye. Maybe. But ye ken as weill as I do that there is mair to this than John Ogilvie's faith! Since Paul appears to be in favour the nicht, I would commend to you the advice given by Paul to the Romans anent their responsibilities to the authorities of the State!

SPOTTISWOODE *(shaking his head irritably)*   Oh it's no that, Rachel! It's no that, it's no that!

RACHEL   Weill what is it then?

SPOTTISWOODE   Ye ken what men say about me – and what they said about your faither?

RACHEL *(hotly)*   And you ken me weill enough to ken that I do not care a docken for what men say. My faither stood fast against the papes – and against the presbyterians! You have done the same and I'm proud of ye baith! What time of day is this to be bothering about what men say?

SPOTTISWOODE   Rachel, I am a man of the cloth! It is my business to take tent of what men say. And they say that we were bocht – that we served the King no out of conviction but for the stipend.

RACHEL   Och, John. Ye ken that's no true.

SPOTTISWOODE   Aye! Aye! But d'ye no understand? We were taking a gamble – your father and myself and the others – we were taking a gamble with our own guid names, with our reputations. We kent that it would take time but what we were ettling to effect was a reconciliation – we thocht that gif the Catholics could bend a wee bit and the presbyterians could bend a wee bit, we could bring them aa intil ae strang kirk. Ae kirk in Scotland and peace in the land!

RACHEL   Aye. That's what ye've aye wanted.

SPOTTISWOODE   It was the king's plan but it was us who had to carry it out –it was men like your faither and me who had to take the gamble. We kent that it would be a gey hard trauchle. A hard ane and a lang ane – your faither died still trauchling. But we kent anaa that it was the only way. And nou *(sighs)* nou we are going to spoil it aa. The morn's morn John Ogilvie will be tried and condemned and the haill thing – years of work – will aa be up in the air!

RACHEL   But John – it's no siccar yet that Ogilvie's to hing!

SPOTTISWOODE   Is it no! Losh woman, ye ken yourself – ye have seen Ogilvie, ye have spoken to him. Is it no obvious what he's after? He pants after the martyr's croun like a dog at a bitch! And they'll gie it to him, thae men that you tell me no to take tent of!

RACHEL   Och, John!

SPOTTISWOODE   Oh aye, they will. Since we came back from Edinburgh, John Ogilvie's name has been on every lip. Gif – no – *when* he mounts the gallows, the Scottish Catholic community'll take him to their hearts and there will be blood. It'll be war aa owre again! As for Ogilvie, he'll hae got what he socht, what he returned to Scotland for. Glory, Rachel; glory and a place in the bloody history of our country! What does he care if the rivers of Scotland run black with the blood of her people, as long as he gets his glory!

RACHEL   But John, that's no your wyte…

SPOTTISWOODE   Did I say it was? Woman, d'ye no understand yet? I hae given everything – my capabilities, my intellect, my honour and my – *oor* guid name – everything to ae single course of action. And the morn's morn, I maun sit doun in that court yonder and watch aa the work that I hae done – and, what's worse – the work I micht hae done being brocht doun and connached by ane fushionless fanatic!

RACHEL *(going to him)*   John, John, my love, ye're making owre muckle of this! *(Sighs.)* Ye said one true thing anent Ogilvie – he's a byordnar man. There's no mony'd have stood what he's stood – I ken what ye did to him in Embro, John –

and if he wants his martyrdom, he's surely earned it. But it'll be an empty thing, folk'll forget aa about it in no time! Hing him, John, hing him and ye'll never see his like again!

SPOTTISWOODE   Will I no? *(Breaks away from her.)* I'm no sure. Oh gin I just had the power, gin I could just get him to listen! Gin I could persuade him! Persuade him to change his mind...

RACHEL   *(with an empty laugh)*   Recant? Fegs John, he'll never do that!

SPOTTISWOODE   Gin he doesna, I'm feared. Gin he doesna I'm feared that I'll be hinging him again and again and again. Owre and owre and owre and owre! Martyrs are a queer-like breed, Rachel – they hae a way of turning into saints. Saints! Saint John Ogilvie – can ye no imagine it? Oh Rachel, I look intae that young man's een and I see a dream – a dream that is alowe with a bitter hatred. And it is a hatred that he has never learned – it is a hatred that he has only dreamed. Oh God! Rachel, how does a man learn sic hatred – how can a man learn to dream sic dreams?

RACHEL   *(quietly)*   John, I'm sure I dinna ken.

SPOTTISWOODE   No more do I, love, no more do I. *(Savagely.)* But, shair as daith, I'd better learn! I'd better learn gin my work in Scotland is to mean ocht ava! For I hae a dream of my own, Rachel, I hae a dream of my own! Christ's sheep maun aa be brocht thegither in ae fauld! *(Stops and smiles a little at his own emotion.)* Paul again, Rachel. Gin we dinna aa eat thegither at the same table, there will be some wha maun gang hungry – while ithers get fou! I want a Kirk in Scotland that will serve aa men. I want a Kirk in Scotland that will bring Catholic and Protestant thegither in the ae faith, in the ae life; I want peace in the land and britherhood and guidwill amang aa men – as the Guid Lord aye intended it should be! That is *my* dream, Rachel, a dream that is biggit nocht on hatred but – I pray to God! – on love!

RACHEL   Ogilvie can never change that, John.

SPOTTISWOODE   No, but he can stop the dream from coming true! He can set the clock back twenty years! Ogilvie can change reality – and it is reality that is important, no dreams! That is a lesson we maun learn here in Scotland! *(Gives a bitter laugh.)* D'ye ken what is the maist absurd thing in this haill business? My auld teacher, my auld lecturer here in Glasgow – Andro Melville – preached the doctrine of the Twa Kingdoms. The temporal and the spiritual. D'ye mind? D'ye mind when King Jamie was seventeen year auld and auld Maister Andro took a grip of him by the arm and tellt him he was 'nocht but God's silly vassal'? Aye, aye. Maister Andro was aye strang for the Lord and against the King! Nou Andro Melville's in the Tower of London for exactly the same reason that John Ogilvie's doun the stair! Would it no gar ye laugh? Gin it wasna so deathly serious would ye not see the humour? Melville, wha railed against the 'Harlot of Rome' and Ogilvie wha cries 'damn aa heretics' with geynear every second breath, are both facing death for geynear the exact same reason. Catholic and Protestant could aye unite better in death than they could in life! But where's Scotland aa this time – where's the sheep that we were aa tellt to feed? They're aa starving to death!

RACHEL *(thoughtfully)*   John, d'ye mind if I tell ye something?

SPOTTISWOODE   Woman, I'd like fine to see the day when I could stop you!

RACHEL   You're a clever fool anaa! Ye are. Oh I'm no complaining! Ye hae great faith, great learning, great generosity and great compassion. But ye've barely enough imagination to fill this cup!

SPOTTISWOODE   Woman, what time o day is this…

RACHEL   Na, na, na, na, na! Just you haud on and leave me have my say! Ye're sitting there, raxing yourself to daith, biding up aa nicht, pouring owre puir auld Paul looking for some divine answer to your predicament – and aa the time, there's a simple solution to the haill affair staring ye in the face gin ye only had the gumption to take a look at it!

SPOTTISWOODE   There is, is there? And what is that, woman?

RACHEL *goes to the mantelpiece and retrieves her candle.*

RACHEL *(turning to him with the candle in her hand)*   Ye're siccar that he'll be condemned the morn?

SPOTTISWOODE   As siccar as I'm standing here.

RACHEL   And ye'll keep him in thon cell there, with a lock on the door and an armed guard ootbye?

SPOTTISWOODE   Aye.

RACHEL   So. Send the guard awa. Unlock the door. What would ye think of that gin you were Ogilvie?

SPOTTISWOODE   Ye think he'd run?

RACHEL *(going slowly to the door)*   Ogilvie's young – he's time yet to be a martyr. *(Grins.)* And I ken what Andro Melville would do in he's place! *(Sweeping out.)* Come awa to your bed!

SPOTTISWOODE, *bewildered, gazes at her departing presence.*

Scene 4

The following day in the late afternoon. The armoury at Spottiswoode's Castle in Glasgow. It is a roughly furnished but rather cosy room which the soldiers use as a sort of common room in their off-duty periods. There is a rack of spears along the length of the back wall and, in front of this, a long low table with a number of stools all about it. WILL *is seated at one end of the table, polishing his helmet and* ANDREW *is at the other, sharpening his sword with a whetstone.* WILL'S *sword and* ANDREW'S *helmet lie on the table. They talk as they work.*

WILL   Andro?

ANDREW   Aye?

WILL   Were you ever mairrit?

ANDREW   *(laughing)*   Naw, no me!

WILL   Whit for no?

ANDREW   Oh, a lot o reasons! Never kent a lassie I fancied enough – at least, I never fancied a lassie that fancied me! *(Looks at* WILL *thoughtfully.)* Thinkin aboot it yersel like?

WILL   Aye. I'd hae tae get oot o here…

ANDREW   Oh aye! Sodgerin's nae life for a mairrit man!

WILL   …but I'm no worried aboot that. I was thinking o packin it in onywey. Nae offence and aa that, Andro, but I dinnae want tae end up like you and Sandy – or, worse yet, like Wattie.

ANDREW   Well, it's up tae yersel, son.

WILL   Aye. Andro, the Faither says I cannae get mairrit – no really mairrit – gin I dinnae get mairrit in a Catholic kirk.

ANDREW   Haw, ye dinnae want tae listen tae the Faither, Christ! He's said a lot, has he no, and see whaur it's got him.

WILL   Aye but – look Andro, gin the Faither hings, there's likely tae be ructions. There micht even be a war! And if the papes were tae win, whaur would that leave me?

ANDREW   Whaur would that leave ony o us? A lot of things can happen in a war, Wullie. Ye micht never see the end o it for one!

WILL   Aye, but if I did! That would mean that I'd hae to be a pape afore I could get mairrit! If the papes won like?

ANDREW   *(laying down the sword and looking at him)*   Wullie, ye're a chynged laddie, dae ye ken that? Ye're an awfy chynged laddie. Jist a few short months syne ye were aa for burnin every pape in sicht! D'ye mind when we brocht Ogilvie in? D'ye mind whit ye were wantin tae dae tae him then?

WILL   I didnae ken the Faither then; I didnae ken – I had nae idea o hou mony folk in Scotland were still papes at hert. Aw, I'm no one o them, dinnae fash yersel aboot that! But I hae tae look oot for mysel and for –

ANDREW   For yer maw?

WILL   For the lassie that I want tae mairry! There are places in Scotland whaur the ministers hae tae tak swords intil the pulpits wi them! Aye! Gin the papes were tae get back…

ANDREW   Wullie, I'll set yer mind at rest! The papes arenae comin back, son. The papes are never comin back!

WILL   *(sceptically)*   I dinnae ken hou ye can be sae shair…

ANDREW   Dae ye no? Weill, I'll tell ye. The papes arenae comin back because the gentry – Faither Ogilvie's ain kind – 'll never let them. Christ, the reason – I winnae say the only reason – why the papes got kicked oot of the country in the first place was so's thae buggers could get their hauns on the ferms and the big hooses and aa the property and treisour that belanged tae the Roman kirk. Ye'll no tell me that they're gonnae hand aa that back for a daft-like thing like religion?

(Laughs.) Ye'll no tell me that Tam o the Cougait's gonnae gie back Melrose
Abbey so that the papes can stop a laddie like you frae gettin mairrit!

WILL *(nodding, still troubled)*   Mebbe ye're richt, Andro, mebbe ye're richt. Still,
gin the Faither hings...

WILL *is interrupted by the excited entrance of* WAT *and* SANDY.

WAT   That's it, then. The pape's tae hing!

WILL   When?

SANDY   On the tenth. Jesus Andro, ye should have seen this! (WILL *picks up his
sword and helmet and leaves the room.)* Here, whit's the maitter wi the boy?

ANDREW   Never mind him. He's got a lot tae learn, that's aa.

SANDY   Aye, him and the Faither's been gettin gey chief this last wee while. He'll
be upset bi the news.

WAT *(taking the seat that* WILL *has vacated)*   Aye and he's no the only ane either!
Ye want tae have seen the greetin in the coort the day, Andro – eh, Sandy? No aa
weemen either!

SANDY *(coming round and taking his seat beside* ANDREW)   Aye, Ogilvie's taen the
trick wi them richt enough. Wadnae mind bettin there'll be a puckle trouble nou!

WAT   B'Christ there will! You jist watch! See, that's the thing wi papes – they
worm awa intae people, turn them against their ain kind. They should hae hung
that bugger months syne! See whit he's done tae young Wullie. He was a guid
laddie that, at one time. But see nou? I'll tell ye this – if there is trouble, I'll be
awfy careful aboot turnin my back on him. In my opinion...

ANDREW *(angrily)*   That's the trouble wi aa you buggers – ye're aa fu o yersels,
ye've aa got opinions! Weill, I've an opinion anaa! *(Picks up his sword and hits
the table with it.)* That's it there! And if there is trouble, Wattie, and I see you
turnin yer back on *onybody,* I'll soon enough gie ye my opinion, son! You bet I
will!

WAT *glares back hatefully at* ANDREW *but says nothing.*

SANDY   Aye, he will anaa! He will! *(Pause.)* Andro...

ANDREW   Aaricht, Sandy. Aaricht. I can see that I'm gonnae get it aa sooner or later
– I can see ye're fair burstin tae let it aa oot – sae it micht as weill be nou. Whit
happened at the trial?

SANDY *(enthusiastically)*   ...Weill, Andro, seein ye asked, I'll tell ye. It was
somethin. It was somethin tae see aaricht! Nou, I'd hae thocht that – after whit
happened in Embro – that the Faither'd have calmed doun a wee, behaved himself
like? Not a bit of it! My, my, but did he no gie them laldy! I'll say this for him –
he's fit for them aa in a slangin match. Is that no richt, Wat?

WAT   Oh aye.

SANDY   He said he didnae gie a rotten fig for the jury, that the judges were aa like
flies swarmin roun a lump o shite – weill, he didnae say shite, bein aa pan-loaf

and a priest and that, but we aa kent whit he meant – he said he wadnae set doun
holy things afore dugs and – tae cap it aa – he tellt the haill coort that the King
was nae mair tae him nor an auld hat! Christ, ye want tae have seen
Spottiswoode's face! If looks could kill, there'd be nae need for a hingin!

ANDREW   In ither wards, he pit the raip aroun his ain thrapple! I thocht he wad.
*(Stands up and, taking his sword, holds it up to the light and looks along the
edge.)* And it's a bluidy waste, d'ye ken that? A man wi he's smeddum and brains
could dae a haill lot o guid!

WAT *(sneering)*   Ye're shairly gettin auld, Andro. Auld and saft! What guid is there
in a papish priest? There's owre mony o the fuckers in Scotland as it is!

ANDREW *(coldly)*   He had echt days and nine nichts of pure bluidy hell in Embro.
You ken that, torturer, you gave him the maist o it – and he never even looked like
breakin! In spite of yer nails and yer mallet and yer clairty wee mind, he never
came near tae beggin for mercy! And as far as the law's concerned, bein a papish
priest isnae a hingin maitter.

WAT *(smugly)*   But he's no hingin for bein a papish priest! He's hingin for bein a
traitor – he wadnae tak the Aith o Allegiance!

ANDREW   Then he should hae got the jile until he did! Och, it's no for me tae say
that he shouldnae be punished – I'm no even sayin that he shouldnae hing! It jist
seems tae me that it's a gey donnert thing for a man like Ogilvie, wi aa his
smeddum and brains, tae fling his ain life awa like that! Ach, whit gars me grue
the maist is the fact that aa this argy-bargy is aboot sweet fuck-all! *(Holds the
naked sword up before him.)* The haun that hauds this sword has killed mair men
nor I hae years o my life – and whit for? Whit some bluidy jyner said or didnae
say in Palestine hundreds o years syne! Christ, it gies me the boke tae think o it!
(Looks at WAT.*)* You'll mebbe no mind on this, but Sandy will. Back in the year o
'96…

SANDY   Oh aye. I mind aaricht. The seventeenth o September riot. I mind thon
aaricht!

ANDREW   The seventeenth o September. In Embro. There was a mob o thousans
that day – aa bearin wappins and wantin tae kill the King. And at the heid o them
aa was the meenisters. Bruce. Welsh. Black. 'For God and the Kirk' they cried
'For God and the Kirk!' And on the ither side – on the ither side, there was anither
mob. And they were shoutin 'For God and the King!' God and the King! The
bluid and the snot ran through the streets o Embro like a torrent that day!

WAT   Oh, aye. I mind on that that anaa. It was a sair business richt enough – but it
was aa King Jamie's wyte…

ANDREW   Oh was it? Aaricht weill, whaur's King Jamie nou? He's still got his
croun on his heid – at least, it's no the same croun but a bigger ane – and whaur's
Robert Bruce? Whaur's John Welsh? Huh! The King's on his throne and the
meenisters are in their pulpits yet! It's aye the same – the meenisters and the
priests and the high-heid anes'll dae the argyin and the stirrin up – but when it
comes tae the killin and the deein, weill there's nane o them can lift up the deid
they left on the streets o Embro that day. And they're never satisfied. When

Ogilvie hings we'll hae anither riot, this time on the streets o Glesca. And it'll no be the meenisters that'll dae the fechtin or the killin or deein – it'll be you and me and Sandy and young laddies like Wullie!

WAT *(laughing, quite insensitive to what* ANDREW *is saying)* Be fair, Andro! Be fair! It'll be Ogilvie anaa!

ANDREW Aw fine Ogilvie. Ogilvie'll gae til the gallows and hae his craig stretched – fine for him! That's what he wants, that's whit he's efter! They'll mak a martyr oot o'm nae doubt – pent his pictur and hing it up on the Vatican waa! Great for Ogilvie! But whae'll fecht the battles that he'll leave ahint him? No John Ogilvie. He's away! *(Sighs and sheaths his sword.)* And so am I. Better get back tae work, back tae the bluidy job!

ANDREW *picks up his helmet and walks towards the door somewhat wearily.*

WAT *(addressing* SANDY *but really taunting* ANDREW) It's like I was sayin, Sandy. Ye cannae trust thae papes. They get in aawhere – even here.

ANDREW *stops and considers* WAT *amusedly.*

ANDREW What's the maitter, Wattie? Ye're shairly no gonnae tell me that ye're worried aboot turnin yer back on me?

WAT *(rises, walks towards the centre of the room)* Turnin my back? I made up my mind on that score as far as you were concerned a while syne.

SANDY *rises and moves away from the table, behind* WAT *who is facing* ANDREW *from the middle of the room.*

ANDREW *(very quietly)* And what dae ye mean bi that, son?

WAT I mean that you're a pape – I mean that you're a Pope's man. I mean that I wadnae trust ye as far as I can throw ye!

ANDREW *(stiffens, goes very quiet)* I hope you're feelin lucky, son!

WAT Ha! Listen tae the hard man! I dinnae need luck for you, ye tired auld priest's (SANDY *very quickly draws his sword and prods* WAT *in the back with it)* bastard!

SANDY *(laughing)* Ha, ha! Wattie, ye werenae mindin yer p's and q's. I micht be a pape anaa for aa ye ken! Will I disarm him, Andro?

ANDREW Naw! *(Strides forward and gives* WAT *the back of his hand across the face.)* Ye daft cunt! I micht hae killed you! Comin the haurd-case! You stick tae yer buits and yer mallet and yer nails! Because the next time you try onythin like thon, the best you can hope for is tae be flung in a cell withoot a door in it. D'ye understand?

WAT *(wiping his cheek where* ANDREW *struck him)* I micht hae kent that the pair o ye wad hing thegither.

ANDREW We aa hing thegither! We aa hing thegither – or we aa end up deid! That's the rule, Wattie. For Christ's sake, get it intae yer thick heid and forget

aboot papes and protestants and bein feart aboot turnin yer back! We'll forget
aboot this – you jist mak shair it disnae happen again, richt? (WAT *makes no
answer.*) Richt?

WAT *(reluctantly)* Aye.

ANDREW *nods and exits.* SANDY *sheaths his sword.* WAT *returns to where he was
sitting.*

SANDY Christ, Wattie, that was a daft-like thing tae try. What got intae ye?

WAT Ach, I got pissed off wi him! Him and aa that talk aboot the seventeenth o
September! Christ, ye'd think the papes'd never done onything!

SANDY I'll no argy wi ye, Wattie. But ye're a lucky bugger tae be sittin there the
nou. Andro's a haurd man, Wat. He's no lived as lang as he has for naethin. His
sword'd have been through your guts afore ye'd got yer ain clear o the scabbard!
Jist dinnae try that again, son. I'm warnin ye!

WAT Aye? Weill maybe… *(looks towards the door)* but I still say ye cannae trust
thae papish bastards!

Scene 5

*Ogilvie's room in the Castle on the night of 9 March 1615. It is slightly more
comfortable than his quarters in Edinburgh (inasmuch as there is a small fire) but it
is just as barely furnished.* OGILVIE, *dressed completely in white, is seated at a table
writing. He finishes, sands the paper, folds it and goes to the door and knocks.*

OGILVIE Will! (WILL *enters.*) *(Handing* WILL *the paper.)* This is the last. You know
where to take it.

WILL Aye.

WILL *takes the paper from* OGILVIE, *puts it inside his tunic.*

WILL *(with a sigh and a shake of the head)* Oh Faither, this is the last for me anaa!

OGILVIE *gives a speechless, unsteady smile but says nothing. Quickly, somewhat
impulsively,* WILL *doffs his helmet and kneels before* OGILVIE. OGILVIE *is taken
aback for a second, then smiles and places his hand on* WILL'S *head.*

OGILVIE Nomine Patris et Filis… The Lord bless you and keep you. (WILL *gives a
small, choked sob.*) Oh Willie. Willie! Arise, my son, arise! (OGILVIE *takes him by
the shoulders and brings him to his feet, talking to him gently and kindly.*) You
must not grieve for me, Will! Do you not remember when I told you – a long time

ago – that this is my destiny? Tomorrow my destiny will be fulfilled. Tomorrow – they are going to put a crown of precious stones upon my head! *(He looks at* WILL *inquiringly.* WILL *nods.)* So no tears, boy. Go now. Go and give my messages and my story to my brethren that the world shall know what happened here.

WILL nods again and turns. SPOTTISWOODE *enters and stands at the door. Coming face to face with him,* WILL *freezes.*

SPOTTISWOODE   Ye hae secured your prisoner, Wull?
WILL *(shakily)*   Aye aye, m'lord. M'lord...
SPOTTISWOODE   Guid. Ye'd best get awa to your bed nou. Ye'll no be wantit again the nicht. *(When* WILL *hesitates.)* Go, boy! It's aaricht!

WILL goes but stops briefly at the door.

WILL   Guidby, Faither.
OGILVIE *(quietly, with a kind smile)*   Goodbye, Will. Take care!

WILL leaves.

OGILVIE *(rather too eagerly when* WILL *has gone)*   Will has been very good to me. I am most indebted to you for putting him at my disposal. I have given him some letters for my family, he has promised to see that they are delivered safely...

OGILVIE lets his rather guilty words trickle away into silence.

SPOTTISWOODE   Family? The Heretics? Ye make a damned poor liar, John Ogilvie. Did ye ken that?
OGILVIE *(with some heat)*   Spottiswoode, I had hoped never to see you again and do not in the least know what you hope to gain by coming here tonight! But since you are here – and will no doubt state your business in due course – I would thank you to spare me your insults for I am completely beyond them now!

Ignoring him, SPOTTISWOODE *paces the floor a little in thought.*

SPOTTISWOODE   Tell me, Faither. Did ye hae any success with the boy?
OGILVIE   Boy? What boy?
SPOTTISWOODE   The laddie! Wullie! Did ye manage to convince him of the true faith?
OGILVIE   That's for you to find out!
SPOTTISWOODE   Aw, Faither, come on! I'm no going to set up a new trial at this time of day! I was only voicing a professional interest, that's aa! And gin ye dinnae wish to tell me, I'll no press ye! *(Pauses.)* Houever, I would be interested to ken if ye tried. Did ye? Did ye try?

OGILVIE *(taken aback)* As a matter of fact – since you ask – I didn't. *(Laughs.)* I didn't. I never even thought of it. I gave him some instruction… Look, Will is no catholic, believe me when I tell you that! Please do not persecute him on my account!

SPOTTISWOODE No, no, no, no, Faither Ogilvie, ye misunderstand me! I'm no interested in the laddie! I ken him for an honest young man and a loyal and faithful servant! It's you that interests me, Faither Ogilvie, you! Ye didna try, ye tell me? Forgive me, Faither – I'll no doubt ye, never fear! – but I find that a wee thing strange.

OGILVIE Not all that strange. Right from the start – from the very day I was taken into captivity – I realised that I had to be strong, that I had to raise my voice and shout. I knew that if I did otherwise, I was lost! That is to say, my cause was lost – there was never any hope for me personally and I knew it. I knew that I had to be strong, I expected nothing from my jailers but blows and abuse. I certainly never expected charity.

SPOTTISWOODE And yet ye got it from Wullie?

OGILVIE Yes. Yes. I never asked for it, I certainly never begged for it – and yet, without I myself doing anything at all, Will changed – he changed from a rough-tongued, bigoted youth into a warm-hearted and decent fellow man. I do not know how I would have kept my sanity and my courage without him. And I? I gave him nothing! Oh he would occasionally ask me a question about faith or behaviour and I would give him my opinion – but I did not minister to him. I gave him nothing!

SPOTTISWOODE Faither Ogilvie. Will is damned. Will is going straight to the fires of hell!

OGILVIE *(outraged)* That's a terrible thing to say!

SPOTTISWOODE Aye, maybe! But I dinna say it – you do!

OGILVIE I have never said any such thing!

SPOTTISWOODE Have ye no? And what have ye been saying this last half-year? You tellt me – in Embro last January – that even the youngest bairn baptised by a presbyterian minister was damned!

OGILVIE I never said that – I said that he was within the Pope's authority as far as…

SPOTTISWOODE …punishment is concerned. I ken. And what if he bides outwith the Pope's authority? What if he never becomes a Catholic? He's damned! You said that, Faither Ogilvie, you believe that! You had the chance to save Wullie's soul – according to your own beliefs – and you threw it away. Ye didna try!

OGILVIE Do not seek to burden me on the gallows with a lost soul! There are other priests!

SPOTTISWOODE Aye. There *are* other priests – or will be. There are episcopalian and presbyterian ministers as well – wha kens? Willie micht weill win to heaven yet! Houever, let us no get into *that* argument! I didna come here the nicht to burden your heart with a lost soul – I came for quite another purpose. *(Very carefully, he pauses to frame his words.)* Faither Ogilvie, when first we met and I speired at ye what had garred ye return to Scotland, ye tellt me – as I mind – that it was to save souls. To 'unteach heresy' was the phrase, as I mind?

OGILVIE   That is correct. That is why I came.

SPOTTISWOODE   Ye haena had muckle success, hae ye?

OGILVIE   Time alone will tell about that.

SPOTTISWOODE   Time? *(Nods.)* Faither, ye are due to hing the morn's afternoon. Ye'll be aware, no doubt, that the courageous – if perverse – manner in which ye hae conducted yourself in the course of the various hearings has attracted a certain popular element, a mob following. And ye will be aware anaa that there is a certain anti-Catholic element in this city. By the morn's nicht, there could be riots. We are expecting riots. We are expecting blood to flow on the streets of Glasgow.

OGILVIE   *(unhappily)*   That is not a consideration that I am in a position to entertain.

SPOTTISWOODE   No. But ye will appreciate that as a man of God and as spiritual leader of this community, I am anxious to avoid needless bloodshed?

OGILVIE   I, too, am a man of God, Archbishop – but if there are riots because of me tomorrow night, it will not be the first time that men have spilled blood over religion – nor, I fear, will it be the last. I repeat – I am in no position to think about it.

SPOTTISWOODE   Faither Ogilvie, do you esteem your life a success? Do you feel that there is nothing left for you to achieve?

OGILVIE   If I could serve my faith in the clean air of freedom, there would be a great deal. But if I cannot live without compromising my faith? *(Smiles sadly.)* It is another consideration I am in no position to entertain.

SPOTTISWOODE   Your faith? Oh, aye. Nou, there's a question… *(Pauses carefully, regards* OGILVIE *thoughtfully.)* Tell me, Faither Ogilvie, what *is* your faith?

OGILVIE   *(angrily)*   Surely I have made that plain enough by this time!

SPOTTISWOODE   Ye havena – that's just what I'm saying! Oh, ye've speechified and argued and swaggered and bragged your way throughout this whole affair – but you have just this minute admitted to me that you had the chance to save the soul of one young man from eternal damnation – and that you did not even try! So I want tae ken, John Ogilvie. What *is* your faith?

OGILVIE   I thought you said that you would not burden my heart with a lost soul!

SPOTTISWOODE   Nor will I! For Wullie is my responsibility and his soul is *not* lost – nor will it be while I hae ocht to do with it! So forget about Wullie – what about yourself?

OGILVIE   You want me to recant!

SPOTTISWOODE   *(sighs, exasperated)*   Since you seem to be unable to understand what I mean, let me put it another way. Are you a Christian – or are you a Jesuit?

OGILVIE   *(looks at* SPOTTISWOODE *speculatively for a moment, then suddenly laughs)* You do! You want me to recant! You want me to save my life by denying my faith!

SPOTTISWOODE   *(snorts)*   It's no possible for a traitor to recant. Damn the Pope to hell if ye like, it'll do you no good. But is your lealty to the Society of Jesus mair important than your lealty to Our Lord Himself? Would you live for Christ – or die for Ignatius? That's the question that I'm speiring at you!

OGILVIE   Spottiswoode, I have been condemned to die – but in condemning me, you and your like condemn all our ancestors, all the ancient bishops and kings, all the priests – all that was once the glory of Scotland! Do you not understand that to be condemned with all these old lights is a matter of gladness and joy for me. God lives, Spottiswoode, posterity lives and the judgment of posterity will not be so corrupt as yours. You call my religion treason...

SPOTTISWOODE *(snapping)*   But what *is* your religion?

OGILVIE   I am a Catholic man and a priest. In that faith I have lived and in that faith I am content to die...

SPOTTISWOODE   Rhetoric. Sheer, empty-headed, bloody-minded rhetoric. To put Catholicism before Christianity is bad enough – but no man will ever be condemned to death in Scotland for that! But you put your Jesuitism before your Christianity and your Catholicism! That is why you are going to hang! Certes, Ogilvie, you are an ignorant man! Your ignorance appals me. What do you ken of folk – plain ordinary common Scottish folk! What do you ken and what do you care that men will kill and die, women will be widowed and bairns will be orphaned because of you and your ill-bred pride? What do you ken of Scotland – guidsakes man, what garred you return after all these years? Ye canna even speak the language! What do you ken of religion? Oh aye, ye've been well trained and can quote Holy Scripture by the mile – but what is your religion to you? 'Feed my sheep' said the Lord – but you hae a gey funny notion of how to feed sheep! You'd feed sheep by killing kings! And that's what it all comes doun to – your religion, I mean. Christianity is a religion of life – the god you serve is a god of daith!

OGILVIE *(stiffly)*   In your judgment perhaps. Posterity, as I have said, will take a different view.

SPOTTISWOODE   Posterity! Ha! And what will posterity hold for you?

OGILVIE   It is not important what it will hold for me, but some day we may have a Catholic Scotland again and if my action...

SPOTTISWOODE   A Catholic Scotland! There will never be a Catholic Scotland any more than there will be a Presbyterian or Episcopalian Scotland! But that's no important – perhaps some day there'll be a Christian Scotland. And how will posterity judge you then?

OGILVIE *(hotly)*   As a man who stood by his principles against the threats and tortures of pagans and unbelievers!

SPOTTISWOODE   D'ye think so? D'ye really think so? What you call your 'principles' will be long-forgotten political issues in less than twenty years time! And then history will see ye as ye really are – the false shepherd who betrayed his flock in the vain hope of winning a martyr's croun!

OGILVIE   And who are you to accuse me of betrayal, you – you Judas! You who betrayed your own cause to the sinful vanity of a decadent and Godless King!

SPOTTISWOODE   I micht hae kent that sooner or later ye wad hae brocht that ane up – but ye needna hae bothered! That charge has been made afore this with greater eloquence than even you can summon – *and* my conscience is clear. I had guid reasons for what I did!

OGILVIE *(laughing)* Oh, no doubt! Hundreds of reasons for leaving your presbyterian ministry and thousands of reasons for taking on your episcopalian diocese!

SPOTTISWOODE Certes but you're the sharp ane! You're the sharp ane richt enough. With half a dozen wits as sharp as yours I could chynge Scotland, I could chynge the warld!

OGILVIE Then it's as well that I'm going to the gallows because you're going straight to hell!

SPOTTISWOODE, struck dumb with horror, stiffens and balls his fists. OGILVIE immediately regrets his words.

OGILVIE Pardon me, m'lord. That was not well said. Whatever our intentions, it seems that we always end up shouting at each other. I know that you did not change your church for material gain – and I believe that you know, that you must know in your heart that I am no death worshipper! God knows I do not want to die! I am as in love with life as any man! But there is no way out of my situation – no way at all.

SPOTTISWOODE There is one way – that's why I'm here the nicht.

OGILVIE *(hopelessly)* I cannot go back on anything that I've said.

SPOTTISWOODE There's no need to. The locks hae been removed from aa the doors and my men hae their orders. Gin ye should decide to leave the Castle the nicht, there's nane will detain ye.

OGILVIE seems about to make some outraged reply, but something in SPOTTISWOODE'S expression makes him hold his tongue. Instead, he moves to his chair and sits down wearily.

OGILVIE And where do you think I could go? What kind of reception do you think I would receive from my brethren were I to run away at this hour?

SPOTTISWOODE That would be up to yourself. But ye are yet a young man – young for a priest at any rate. In time...

OGILVIE Yes, I suppose I might be able to live it down. I would be able to preach again – might even be able to... some day... to come back to Scotland. *(He glances enquiringly at Spottiswoode.)*

SPOTTISWOODE *(doubtfully)* Weill...

OGILVIE No. No. I would never be able to come back to Scotland.

OGILVIE sits brooding in his chair, his head turned away from SPOTTISWOODE. There is a set of rosary beads lying on the table. Absently, OGILVIE reaches over and picks them up, laying them on his lap. SPOTTISWOODE senses that he is tempted by the offer of freedom.

SPOTTISWOODE *(with passion)* Ogilvie! Save yourself, Ogilvie! Save yourself! In the name of the Lord Jesus Christ, I beseech you...

OGILVIE *turns, looks at* SPOTTISWOODE *wordlessly, then looks away.*

SPOTTISWOODE *(throwing his hands in the air)* Fare ye weel, Faither Ogilvie. One way or the other, fare ye weel!

SPOTTISWOODE *starts to leave.*

OGILVIE *(rising stiffly to his feet)* My Lord Archbishop! (SPOTTISWOODE *turns expectantly towards him.)* There is just one thing before you leave.
SPOTTISWOODE Aye?
OGILVIE *(extending his hand)* I would require your hand.

SPOTTISWOODE *almost responds. He looks at the outstretched hand and then at* OGILVIE.

SPOTTISWOODE No. No. This is no game, Faither. This is no game.

SPOTTISWOODE *turns and goes, leaving* OGILVIE *standing with his hand outstretched. Slowly,* OGILVIE *lets his arm fall to his side.*

Scene 6

The hangman's quarters, within sight of the gallows. OGILVIE *kneels in prayer, with his rosary wound round his fingers and his eyes tightly shut.* THE SOLDIERS *stand by watching him patiently. Their swords are drawn and they carry shields. In the distance, the sound of drums can be heard.*
    SPOTTISWOODE *enters impatiently, followed by* THE HANGMAN. *Both check as they see* OGILVIE *at prayer.* OGILVIE *finishes praying, opens his eyes, and rises unsteadily to his feet. He sees* SPOTTISWOODE *as he turns.*

OGILVIE My Lord.
SPOTTISWOODE *(quietly)* Ye are ready now? (OGILVIE *nods.* SPOTTISWOODE *looks about himself in exasperation and says to no-one in particular.)* Better get on wi't then!

Exit SPOTTISWOODE. THE HANGMAN *approaches* OGILVIE *with bowed head.*
OGILVIE *goes to meet him, taking him lightly by each sleeve.*

OGILVIE Be of good heart, my friend. I have forgiven you already. Will...

WILL *turns as he calls.* OGILVIE *goes to him and embraces him.*

OGILVIE   Take care, my son! My time has come. Take care.

WILL, *choked with emotion, turns away.*

OGILVIE   Sandy! Goodbye to you!

SANDY *pumps* OGILVIE'S *hand.*

SANDY   Here's tae ye, Faither. Here's tae ye!
OGILVIE   Wat!

WAT *turns away and spits.*

OGILVIE   Andrew! Can I just say that…
ANDREW   *(roughly)*   Say naethin, Faither! The time for words is past! *(Prods* THE HANGMAN *with his sword.)* Come on, you! Get on wi't. *(Turns to the other soldiers.)* Right. Sandy and me'll tak it frae here! *(They prepare to move off.)*
WILL   Andro…
ANDREW   Aye?
WILL   Can I no come instead o Sandy?

ANDREW *and* SANDY *exchange wise smiles.*

ANDREW   Been on the gallows afore, have ye?
WILL   Naw, but…
ANDREW   Then I'm no wantin ye! *(Softer.)* Listen, son. Ye ken there's gonnae be trouble – bound tae be. There's no an awfy lot o room up by the scaffold thonder. Mair nor twa o us and we'd just be gettin in ane another's road. Best leave it tae Sandy and me, son – we're auld hands at this gemme.
SANDY   Aye, Andro's richt, son. You listen tae Andro. Him and me, we've…
ANDREW.   *(to* SANDY*)*   You shut up! *(To* THE HANGMAN.*)* Come on! Let's dae the job.

They are about to move off again, when OGILVIE *suddenly stops dead and turns to them all.*

OGILVIE   Wait! *(Looks pointedly at* ANDREW, *who makes a pained expression.)* I have one last word for you all. If there are any hidden Catholics among you, I would welcome your prayers – but the prayers of heretics I will not have!

ANDREW *explodes with anger.*

ANDREW   Get him oot o here!

THE HANGMAN *takes* OGILVIE *by the arm, but* OGILVIE *stands his ground.* ANDREW *comes forward and pushes* OGILVIE *in the chest with his sword hand. Between* THE HANGMAN *and* ANDREW, OGILVIE *is pushed and hauled off the stage, followed by* SANDY.

WILL *watches them leave anxiously. Unconcerned,* WAT *sheathes his sword.*

WAT   He doesnae trust ye, son.

A huge roar is heard from outside.

WILL   *(sheathing his sword)*   What's that?
WAT   The auld fella. Andro. I'm sayin he doesnae trust ye.
WILL   *(absently)*   Aye? Weel, he's richt enough, I suppose.
WAT   Aye, ye see, it doesnae dae tae get owre chief wi a prisoner, Wullie. It doesnae dae, son.
WILL   Does it no? Weel, Andro kens I'll aye dae the job. He kens he can rely on me.
WAT   He does, does he? Huh! That's mair nor I wad dae!
WILL   What for no, eh?
WAT   Aw, come on, son! Ye're jokin! See ye there the nou – ye were near greetin! I'm gaun up tae the gallows tae hing a man – wi a big mob like that ane ootby – and the boy that's meant tae be helpin me's greetin like a wean acause the prisoner's tae be hung? Foo! Forget it, son! No danger!
WILL   Aye, weel, it wisnae you that was gaun tae the gallows in any case!
WAT   So what? What the hell's the odds whae goes up? The thing is, Wullie – ye're no reliable. Ye took up wi that pape and there's nane o us can depend on ye!
WILL   Aye, so ye say – but Andro doesna think that! Neither does Sandy. Ach, you, ye dinnae understand onything, you dinnae! I'll no deny I thocht a lot on Faither Ogilvie – but I'm no ashamed o that! He's a guid man…
WAT   Is he…
WILL   You shut yer mooth! He's worth ten o you ony day o the week!
WAT   Aw, is that right? Weel, listen son, I'll tell ye somethin aboot your precious Faither Ogilvie. He's a crappin bastard! He's got a big yellae streak rinnin aa the wey doun his back!

A huge roar is heard from outside. They pause as they hear it.

WAT   I ken. I ken Ogilvie's kind weel enough. And I'm tellin you, Wullie…
WILL   Aw, you get stuffed!
WAT   Listen, d'ye want me tae prove it tae ye? I'm a torturer, son – and part o my tredd's kennin when a man's feart and when he's no. I kent he's kind the minute I clapped eyes on him.
WILL   Aye, when ye went tae meisure him for the buits!

WAT   Aye, he didnae get the buits though, did he? He got somethin worse, I reckon. And I'm no shair but that *that* didnae brak him. I'm no shair but he didnae cough his load tae the Archbishop.

WILL   Balls! Whit the hell are they hingin him for then?

Another huge roar is heard from outside. Again they pause.

WAT   I dinnae ken. But I ken this; mind when he was in Glesca first, just efter the arrest? What was he like? Eh? Ye ken yersel. Doun in the dungeon amang the rats and aa the shit and filth o the day! A twa-hunner pund wecht chyned til his leg! Aye. And hou's he been this past while? A different story. A wee room o his ain, a table, a chair, a bed, visitors tae see him, buiks tae read, wine tae drink, Lady Spottiswoode... Even you have tae admit there's somethin twisted about that!

WILL   There's just the wan thing that's twisted aboot here...

WAT   Listen, hou d'ye fancy a wee bet? Eh? Hou d'ye fancy a wee wager that they'll hae tae turn him aff.

WILL   Turn him aff? What's that?

WAT   Shove him aff, ye fule! He'll get tae the tap o the scaffold syne put up a fecht! They'll hae tae gie him the heave!

WILL   Naw! Naw! No chance! No him! Never him!

WAT   Aye, we'll see then, eh? Just you wait! We'll see.

Enter SANDY, *running.*

SANDY   *(out of breath)*   Jesus Christ, I never saw anythin like thon in aa my born days!

WAT   What happened, Sandy! Tell us what happened!

SANDY *leans against* WILL *for support. He is out of breath for the duration of his speech.*

SANDY   Aw, wait'll I catch my braith! Lads, I'll tell ye... Oh my God!

WILL   What happened, Sandy? What happened?

SANDY   The Faither – he goes up there quite checko, ye ken? Kisses the scaffold – aye, kisses the bluidy scaffold. Then this laddie manages tae get up on the gallows.

WAT   What then?

SANDY   Aw, Andro sorted him aaricht. Nae messin. Boom, boom. Puir laddie. I hope he wasnae thinkin o gettin mairrit.

WILL   Never mind him! What about the Faither?

SANDY   Ogilvie takes his rosary and he slings it intae the crowd...

WILL   Aye, that'd be him right enough.

SANDY   Aye, weel, we get him aa tied up and the hangman takes him up the scaffold. He had a bit o a job o it, what wi Ogilvie's hands bein ahint his back and that – but onyway, he gets him up. Ogilvie's chantin awa at this Latin prayer aa the time. The hangman gets him up – and he says tae him 'Say it, John. Lord have mercy on me. Lord, receive my soul' and Ogilvie says it 'Lord, have mercy on me. Lord, receive my soul'. And then…

WAT   Aye! Aye! What happened then!

SANDY   Aw, Christ I dinnae ken! There was a struggle… the hangman couldnae manage… Andro had tae sclim the ladder and shove the Faither aff!

WAT   I tellt ye! I tellt ye! The bastard crapped it at the last! I tellt ye he was yella, Wullie! I tellt ye! *(Slaps one palm against the other.)* Put it there, son! Put it there!

WILL *loses his temper completely and goes for* WAT.

WILL   Shut up, you! Shut up, shut up, shut up! I'm seik and tired o listenin tae your sneerie tongue…

SANDY   Hi, Wullie, what's this? Keep the heid, son, eh? Keep the heid!

WAT *(sneering)*   Cannae take it, eh?

WILL *pushes* SANDY *aside.*

WILL   I tellt you tae shut up! Shut up – or you'll take it! Ye'll take it frae me! Aaricht!

WAT   Naw! No aaricht! I've taen about as muckle as I can thole…

SANDY *tries to restrain* WAT.

SANDY   For the love o Christ, Wattie! Wad ye no…

WAT *throws* SANDY *to one side.*

WAT   Oot the road! Nae hauf-airsed wee pape's gonnae tell me…

WAT *draws his sword.* WILL *lets out a yell of anger and draws his sword too. He aims a great two-handed sweep in* WAT'S *direction. At that precise moment,* ANDREW *bursts in, hauling* WAT *out of the way of the blow and throwing him to one side.* WILL *is thrown off balance and the impetus of the blow spins him round.* ANDREW *grabs him by the belt and the scruff of the neck and throws him to the other side of the stage.*

ANDREW   What the fuckin hell dae you pair of stupit bastards think ye're airsin about at? I tellt ye, did I no? I tellt ye baith – but you, ye stupit fuckers, ye wadnae listen! *(Pauses breathless, exasperated with them.)* It's done! It's finished! And that's an end tae it!

The Bevellers

by

Roddy McMillan

First performed at the Royal Lyceum Theatre, Edinburgh,
on 16 February 1973, directed by Bill Bryden

Roddy McMillan

Roddy McMillan (1923–79) was born in Glasgow of Gaelic-speaking parents. His mother was from the Isle of Harris and his father, who worked as a docker, was from Ardnamurchan. He left school at fourteen and worked in a glass factory in Bothwell Street, Glasgow (an experience he drew on in writing *The Bevellers)*. He also worked as a biscuit factory's vanboy, which took him all over South-West and Central Scotland. In 1941, on the way home from a night-class when training to be an aero-engineer, he was persuaded by a former schoolteacher of his, the actor Duncan Macrae, to consider acting. This chance encounter transformed his life. At eighteen he joined Glasgow Unity Theatre as an amateur actor, becoming part of its professional company after the war. Following the demise of Unity, he worked at Glasgow Citizens' Theatre for several seasons. During his period at the Citizens' he wrote his first play, *All in Good Faith*. It was initially rejected but, prompted by a fellow actor, Andrew Keir, McMillan resubmitted the script and it was eventually accepted for production at the Citizens' Theatre in 1954 (revived by the Gateway Theatre in Edinburgh in 1958 and 1963). McMillan played the part of Jadie Bryson in that first production.

It has been suggested that the criticism and controversy provoked by his first play contributed to the twenty-year gap before McMillan wrote his second, *The Bevellers*. Looking back at the reception given *All in Good Faith* in 1954, he wrote in 1979: 'Having recently re-read the largely hostile Press reaction… I am again quite shaken by the vehemence and bitterness of the attack, mainly from outside the review columns of the sheets concerned. There were scathing articles, letters of condemnation, letters in defence and indignant demands that the play and Citizens' Theatre should be toppled from a position of civic indulgence and privilege.' *The Bevellers* was a work-in-progress that he revisited and completed at the request of Bill Bryden when an Associate Director at the Royal Lyceum Theatre, Edinburgh, in the early 1970s. (McMillan was a member of the company of Scottish actors that Bryden drew together there.) *The Bevellers*, directed by Bryden and featuring McMillan in the role of Bob Darnley, was first performed at the Royal Lyceum in 1973. In his preface to the published script, Bill Bryden suggested further reasons for the long gap between McMillan's first and second plays: 'The changes that had hindered the progress of a vital Scottish theatre were perhaps partly to blame as well as the author's pursuit of his career as a fine character actor.'

At the time of his early death in 1979, Roddy McMillan had long been established as one of Scotland's leading actors. He worked widely in theatre, film, radio and television. His work in television made him a household name in Scotland in the 1960s through appearances in programmes such as *Dr Finlay's Casebook, The White Heather Club, The Vital Spark* series (in which he played

Para Handy), and the BBC's Hogmanay show. He achieved wider UK fame in the 1970s when he played the title role of a small-time Glaswegian private detective in the networked television series *The View from Daniel Pike.* His last television role was as a Scottish detective in the Thames Television series *Hazell.*

In addition to his considerable talents as an actor and playwright, Roddy McMillan was a gifted composer of Scottish songs and wrote the lyrics for the celebrated *Campbeltown Loch.* He was made an OBE in 1979.

'Among the Pomas, the Wheels and the Slurry'

(Original Preface by the First Director)

Nothing in the theatre has given me more pleasure than directing the play you are about to read. *The Bevellers* was commissioned by the Royal Lyceum Theatre Company of Edinburgh in 1972, just after Roddy McMillan had given a performance of great simplicity, humour and grace in my own play *Willie Rough*. McMillan's first play *All in Good Faith,* over fifteen years earlier, was still remembered with affection for its passion and immediacy, but it had not been followed up. The changes that had hindered the progress of a vital Scottish theatre were perhaps partly to blame as well as the author's pursuit of his career as a fine character actor. It seemed to me, however, that perhaps the time was right to invite him to write a new play. Luckily, when director Clive Perry expressed the invitation, it seemed possible that the challenge would be met. There might be a play. No more than that. It was to be about bevelling. Frankly, I knew absolutely nothing about the subject, but in discussion, rehearsal, and performance I became something of an expert, as did audiences in Edinburgh, Glasgow, and London when this heartfelt tribute to a remembered craft took the stage.

My memories of this time are of hard work and great creative satisfaction. They come in no particular order, but with an intensity that matches this play. The first visit to a bevelling shop on a winter's day in Glasgow. Here, Billy Wells, who began by inviting us all to call him 'the Bombardier', after the legendary fighter, showed us the range and beauty of his work. None of us who were there had bothered very much about glass until that morning. It had been windows and milk-bottles. Now it was patterns and style. I saw why the play had been written. It was obvious that the author's apprenticeship (however short) in this skill was part of the stuff from which the good plays are made.

Next, the mind jumps to the first time the company, wearing their aprons and Deirdre Clancy's clothes (so realistic and natural that it would be insulting to call them 'costumes'), stepped down the wooden stairs into Geoffrey Scott's meticulous set on the Lyceum stage. The proof of its authenticity was seen the next night on BBC Television in a short excerpt from the play which seemed to be coming to you, not from the stage of a theatre but live from a basement under the streets of a great city. Here we were 'among the pomas and the wheels and the slurry' of Alex Freer in the play. This was the proof that our pursuit of dramatic realism had not been in vain.

Humorous memories, too – actor John Grieve giving up smoking and wondering if he'd be too fat for the role of Peter Laidlaw as a result – Jackie Farrell struggling to be fit enough to lift a ton weight every night – Paul Young's pride at being told by Billy Wells that he should take up the trade full time! But more than the humour of rehearsals I have to pay tribute to the stamina of the company as they lived through the emotional terrors of the play day after day for more than a month. Then there was the delight when they seemed to be bevellers. The characters had come off the page on to the stage to the concentration and applause of an audience. To see this is to know why one is in the theatre. This is what it is for. For a director, this is the pleasure and reward of the job. For this I have to thank Jan Wilson, Billy Armour, Andrew Byatt, John Young, John Grieve, Paul Young, Leonard Maguire, Jackie Farrell, and the author himself.

This is an important play for the Scottish theatre. It was written at a time when there was certainly the potential of a theatre, in this country, of European standard. I hope that you are able to read it at a time when that potential is realised.

Finally, I have a fervent wish: that the author does not take another fifteen years to write his next play. I hope that at this moment Roddy McMillan is staring at the blank piece of paper in that, the loneliest of situations. I have the confidence that he will fill it as full of life and love as are the pages that follow.

Bill Bryden, Edinburgh, October 1973

Characters

JOE CROSBY

PETER LAIDLAW

BOB DARNLEY

DAN MATCHETT, *the* ROUGER

CHARLIE WEIR

NORRIE BEATON

LESLIE SKINNER

ALEX FREER

NANCY BLAIR

The play is set in the basement bevelling shop of a glass firm in Glasgow.

Act One

BOB, PETER, CHARLIE, *and* JOE *are all getting ready for work in the morning, taking off their jackets, and putting on their working aprons. The* ROUGER *carries his bike down the stairs;* LESLIE SKINNER, *the Manager, then brings* NORRIE *downstairs.*

LESLIE   Here's the new boy, Bob. Smart boy he looks. Name's Beaton – that right, lad? Norman Beaton.

NORRIE   That's right, Mr Skinner.

LESLIE   This is Mr Darnley, the foreman.

BOB   Boys call ye Norrie?

NORRIE   Aye.

LESLIE   Well, I suppose that's what they'll call you in here. Show him the job, Bob. I'll ring down for you in a wee while. Couple of items I want to show you. Stick in, boy, you'll do fine. Good effort the day, the rest o' you lads.

LESLIE climbs the stairs and goes off.

BOB   Well seen it's Monday mornin. 'I'll ring doon fur ye, Bob.' Ah'll be up an' doon that bliddy stair like a yo-yo. I can feel it in ma watter. Dae ye know whit bevellin is, young Norrie?

NORRIE   Naw.

BOB   It's a' ower the bliddy place, though no wan in a million wid recognise it. No so much o it nooadays, right enough. Time wis there wisnae a boozer or a half-decent shitehouse in the country withoot a sample o the bevellers' craft screwed tae the wa'. Can ye no guess?

NORRIE   Tae dae wi gless, int it?

BOB   Now there's a boy wi his eyes open. Comes intae a bevellin shop where the stuff's stacked on its edges an' says it's tae dae wi gless. A'right, son, let me show ye this.

ROUGER   Watch him, young-yin. He might show ye the gless version o the golden rivet.

BOB   Haud yur tongue, Rouger. See this mirror here, Norrie. That's what we call a mirror, but it's no done yet. No silvered. Well, that kinna border-bit round the gless is a bevel. If that wis woodwork, they might call it a chamfer. Not tae be confused wi yur champer, of coorse. An' there's a few other kinna jobs that's a' in the trade, like the arrisin, the polishin an' that. But ye'll soon see it a'.

NORRIE   An' is that whit I'll be learnin, the bevellin?

BOB   No right away, naw. Ye start at the feedin-up. Joe'll tell ye aboot that. It's his job ye're gettin. C'm'ere, Joe. This is Norrie Beaton, he's gaun tae the feedin-up. Get him an apron.

JOE   Hullo. Crosbie's the second name.

NORRIE   How ye?

JOE   Better noo ah'm aff the feedin-up.

BOB   Don't gie the boy a bad impression. Feedin-up's no a bad job. It's an easy job, an' wan that ye must learn before ye start bevellin.

JOE   Aye, whitever ye say yursel'.

BOB   Aye, well, show him how tae mix the pomas. No too thick, no too thin. Then show him how tae make the brush.

JOE   Okay. Ower tae the bench here.

ROUGER   Whit d'ye say this boy's name wis?

BOB   Beaton. Norman Beaton. Kinna film star's name that, int it?

ROUGER   Naw. Teuchter name, I wid say. That right, eh? Teuchter name yours, int it?

NORRIE   Whit?

ROUGER   Teuchter, teuchter. Ye no know whit 'teuchter' is?

NORRIE   Naw.

ROUGER   This is a very dim youth. You'll learn something here, I'll tell ye. Hear that, Charlie, he never heard o a teuchter.

CHARLIE   Innocent, eh!

ROUGER   Doe-eyed.

CHARLIE   He'll soon loss it. Clear and press, a hundred an' eighty, hah!

CHARLIE *snatches at an imaginary weight and holds it aloft. The* ROUGER *pretends to tickle his armpit.*

ROUGER   Tickle, tickle.

CHARLIE   *(immediately furious, dropping his arms)*   Whit have I said aboot that before, Rouger? One o these times I'll hoist you by the ballocks an' chip ye ower the mill.

ROUGER   Aw, easy, easy, fur Jesus' sake. Bit o fun.

CHARLIE   Or maybe ye'd like a small tournament, jist you an' me. There's the bar in the corner, hundred and twenty pounds. Ten snatches right up, eh?

ROUGER   Wait a minute. That's your game, the liftin, int it? You're on a cert. Whit dis that prove? Superiority in wan field of exertion. I mean, you come oot the road wi me on the bike sometime, I'll show you a fast wheel an' a flash o ma arse as ah leave you gaspin on the highway.

CHARLIE   Never mind the cycle talk. There's the bar. Ten snatches, whit ye say?

BOB   Aw, snatch yur fuckin drawers! Ye're like a coupla weans. Get yur aprons on an' start graftin. A good effort the day now, as Leslie says. Too much shaggin the dog in here lately.

They all break up and start moving towards their wheels.

PETER   Don't worry aboot the Rouger, son. He might try somethin' on wi ye. Don't be feart. He's full o crap. Jist tell him tae come an' see me at the mill. I'll put a hauf-inch level on his tail. Mind, noo.

NORRIE   Is it always like this?

JOE   Worse sometimes. Bevellers are a' mad, ye know. Peter therr couldnae blow a feather aff his nose withoot havin a rigor.

NORRIE   A whit?

JOE   A fit. Takes fits, ye know.

NORRIE   Straight up?

JOE   Aye, jist noo an' again.

NORRIE   Works wi gless an' takes fits? That must be dangerous.

JOE   Oh whit! Ye see him startin tae jerk a wee bit. Next thing Bob's shoutin, 'Never mind the man, save the bliddy job!'

NORRIE   Whit happens?

JOE   Ach, jist lie him doon for five minutes, he gets up bran' new.

NORRIE   Naw, but I mean, ye wunner they let him carry on.

JOE   Nae choice. Cannae get men like him nooadays.

NORRIE   Is he good?

JOE   The best. Noo, look, ye jist take a haunful o pomas an' stick it in the basin. Then ye take the watter an' mix it slowly tae it's jist right. Too thick it clogs the grooves, too thin it skooshes all over the shop and disnae polish.

NORRIE   How d'ye know when it's right?

JOE   Ye jist learn. That's aboot right noo, feel that. Right, noo fur the brush. This pile o straw here an' some string, it's easy. *(Proceeds to make the brush.)*

NORRIE   That's a funny name that, Rouger, int it?

JOE   That's no his name, his right name's Dan Matchett. We call him Rouger because he works wi the rouge. See a' that red stuff ower at his wheel. That's the rouge.

NORRIE   That's a hell of a mess. Whit's it dae?

JOE   Peter pits the bevel on at the mill. Grinds it on wi the hard wheel, the carborundum. Then he pits it on the sander. That's a slightly softer wheel. Efter that it goes tae the polishin – that's Bob's job. Then it goes tae the rougin – that pits the gloss on it.

NORRIE   Whit are the other wheels?

JOE   Wan's Charlie's an' wan's mine. They're vertical fur daein' edges an'…

Suddenly the noise of glass applied to the various wheels blots out all other sound.

NORRIE   *(putting his hands over his ears)*   That's a hell of a noise.

JOE   Ye get used tae it.

The noise recedes after a short time.

BOB   No ready yet, Joe?

JOE   Coupla shakes.

NORRIE   That a real weight-liftin thing ower therr?

JOE   Aye, it's Charlie's. Brought it in hissel'. Practises wi it at dinnertime sometimes.

NORRIE   I'd like tae see him liftin that.

JOE   He'd lift that an' you alang wi it. Don't needle him – he might dae it.

NORRIE   He pit the breeze up the big-fella anyway, didn't he? Does he lose the head easy, that Charlie fella?

JOE   Not always. Fact, sometimes he's very good-tempered. Disnae like anybody takin him down. Winches this bird that works up next door in the printin-works. Noo ye see how tae make the brush? Ye jist take enough straw and fold it, tie it in two places away fae the middle, and cut the ends wi the chisel.

NORRIE   I fancy I could dae that.

JOE   The secret's ye tie it tight – it's got tae be tight. That's it, Bob! *(He carries the basin and brush over to the polishing wheel.)*

BOB   Right noo, you sit there, son, jist beside the wheel. Take the brush, dip it in the pomas. Feed it up on tap o the wheel when I'm usin the surface, and feed it intae the groove when I'm daein the edges. Try it noo, but easy.

NORRIE *soaks the brush and plunks it on the wheel, as* BOB *touches it with the glass. The pomas squirts up into* BOB'S *face.*

BOB   *(wiping the pomas away with his apron)*   Aw, Jesus Christ, naw, naw! No so hard, an' no so much pomas. I've got tae be able tae see tae dae this job, Norrie. Try it again – a wee bit easier.

NORRIE *tries again. This time the brush flies out of his hand and lands over by the bench.*

NORRIE   Sorry, Mr Darnley.

BOB   Away and pick the bliddy thing up. Gie it a run through in the trough. That's it, jist enough tae take the grit oot o it. It's no needin a haircut an' a shampoo. Noo, wance mair, nice an' easy.

NORRIE   That better, Mr Darnley?

BOB   Aye, that's better. Jist pit some on when ye think it needs it. An' stop callin us Mr Darnley. Bob'll dae. But no Bobbie – I'll no stand for Bobbie.

NORRIE   Aye, right.

BOB   Ye see the idea? Noo that bit o the bevel's still rough, but this bit here that I'm polishin is a bit smoother, see that? *(He wipes the glass and holds it up to the light.)*

NORRIE   That's great.

BOB   Well, it's no exactly great, but it'll be a'right. Merr pomas.

NORRIE   Is that ma job, then? Jist sittin here dabbin the brush?

BOB   Refer tae it as feedin-up fae noo on. Like everything else, ye start at the beginnin. It's amazin how much ye pick up when ye think ye're idlin'. I wis feedin-up when I wis fourteen. Sometimes I think I havenae learnt it a' yet. This is a craft, ye know, not jist a common trade. Wan o the few, an' wan o the auldest. Put your mind tae this, ye'll get a job anywhere. Merr pomas. Ah, ye see, that wis you gaun a wee bit heavy again – but don't worry, the time'll come when ye'll be able tae judge it, an' that'll be somethin' learnt, that right?

NORRIE   Aye.

BOB   Is this yur first job?

NORRIE   Aye.

BOB   Ye'll be able tae bung yur mother a couple o poun' at the end o the week noo, eh?

NORRIE   Naw.

BOB   Ye gaun tae keep it a' tae yersel?

NORRIE   Naw, I didnae mean that. Ma mother's deid. Died when ah wis thirteen. Two years ago.

BOB   That a fact, son? Yur faither's still livin, though?

NORRIE   Oh aye. There's ma da, ma sister, an' me.

BOB   An' yur sister looks efter ye, like?

NORRIE   Aye. She's got a job tae, though.

BOB   Yez'll be quite a well-doing wee family, then?

NORRIE   Aye, no' bad.

BOB   Whit dis yur faither dae?

NORRIE   Docker.

BOB   Good job, good job. Merr pomas. She'll wid have been quite young, your mother? When she died?

NORRIE   Forty-four, I think.

BOB   That's young. Must've been sudden, eh?

NORRIE   Aye, it wis during the school holidays it wis. I wakened up wan mornin, an' there wis this noise in the kitchen. A lot o voices. I went through an' they widnae let me in. I jist saw her lyin in a chair. That wis it.

BOB   Ah didnae mean tae make ye greet noo.

NORRIE   Ah'm no greetin. It's a long time. Two year.

BOB   Aye, a long time fur a boy tae be withoot his old-lady. Hear that, youz fullas. This boy here's been tellin me aboot his oul'-wife dyin, and he's no greetin. No much wrang wi a boy that can dae that, eh?

ROUGER   Eh, whit's that, who's dyin? Who's deid?

BOB   Norrie's oul'-lady. He wis jist at school at the time.

ROUGER   Whit wis wrang wi her? (NORRIE *doesn't answer.*) ...It's a'right, young-yin, we're no tryin tae extract ye. Jist askin whit happened tae her.

NORRIE   Heart-attack.

ROUGER   By Jees, eh. That's tough luck. Hey, Bob, wee bit fire on this side here.

The ROUGER *holds out the glass.* BOB *gives it a wipe and holds it up to the light.*

BOB   Aye, ye're right. Ah'll gie it a touch. Noo, Norrie, jist gie the brush the least wee sensation on the wheel therr... ach, I better dae it masel'.

ROUGER   That the only time yur mother wis ever sick?

NORRIE   Naw. Eh, she wis sick wance before – a couple o year before she died.

ROUGER   Hospital, wis she?

NORRIE   Naw, naw.

ROUGER   Couldnae have been too bad, then, wis she?

NORRIE   Oh, she wis bad. It wis in the middle o the night. She suddenly had these terrible pains. She wis moaning – nearly screaming. I had tae go tae the polis station, fur them tae call a doctor.

BOB   Whit time o night wis that?

NORRIE   Hauf past two – three o'clock.

ROUGER   An' wis she a'right efter that?

NORRIE   Aye, a while efter the doctor came.

ROUGER   Did ye see her?

NORRIE   Naw, ma oul'-man told me tae go back tae bed. She wis a bit better in the mornin.

ROUGER   Nae merr pain, eh?

NORRIE   You're hell of a nosy. Whit ye want tae know fur?

ROUGER   Nothin'. Jist askin.

BOB   Ye must've been only eleven year auld then. No much wrang wi a boy that'll go fur a doctor for his mother at three o'clock in the mornin an' him only eleven year auld. Did yur big sister no go wi ye?

NORRIE   She wis bubblin. She couldnae go.

ROUGER   Got a sister, eh? Tell her ah'll take her out some night.

NORRIE   Aye, likely. That your bike over therr?

ROUGER   Yes! Nice machine, int it?

NORRIE   'S all right.

ROUGER   Like tae get yur leg ower it?

NORRIE   Widnae mind.

ROUGER   Leg ower yur sister?

NORRIE   She widnae pish on you if ye were on fire.

ROUGER   Now... I'll remember that.

BOB   Therr ye are, then. That should be a'right. Jist blend it in easy. That should dae... *(The bell rings and the* ROUGER *goes back to his wheel.)* That's him started. Ye ever see wan o' thae monkeys on a string, Norrie? That's whit he thinks ah am. Got tae take the apron aff every time ye go up the sterr in case there's some conshiterified bloddy eediot in the office. Whit's the time? Clock's stopped, bi-Christ! Hey, Joe, see the time – show Norrie here how tae keek, then gie that clock a dunt an' see if it'll go.

BOB *goes off upstairs.* JOE *goes to the back of the shop, mounts a box, and puts his eye to the roof.*

NORRIE   Whit ye daein? Whit can ye see?

JOE   The pavement up there's wan o' thae glazed gratings. Ther' a hole in the gless, an' if ye judge it right ye can see the Greek clock.

NORRIE   Gaun tae let us swatch it?

JOE   Sure. Jist pit your eye up there.

NORRIE *goes up.*

NORRIE   Aw, Christ, I think I've blint masel'.

JOE   Don't pit your eye hard against the hole, it's full o muck. Try it again and jist squint a wee bit tae the left.

NORRIE   Cannae see anythin'.

JOE   Nae wunner, ye've got your eye shut.

NORRIE   Eh, oh aye. I think I can see somethin' noo.

JOE   Can ye see the coffin-end corner?

NORRIE   I think so – aye!

JOE   Jist move a wee touch tae yur left and look up, ye'll see the Greek steeple wi the clock.

NORRIE   Got it, bang in the sights. That's great, int it?

JOE   Oh, aye, great, but whit the hell's the time?

NORRIE   Twenty past nine. Naebody in here wear watches?

JOE   Naw. Too much stour and damp. Even that oul' clock's got a touch o the cramp. *(He goes up to the clock, which is on the wall just above* BOB'S *wheel.)*

PETER   Hey, Norrie – is that your name? Well, c'm'ere, ah want ye. See this brush? Take it up in your airm, yur right airm, and ower yur shouther. That's right... noo, jist you staun therr fur a wee while, an' if ye feel like it, jist take a wee about-turn noo an' again. Anybody comes, shout, 'Beware the amber bead!'

NORRIE *is holding the brush like a sentry, though he doesn't realise it.* PETER *darts into the lavvy under the stairs.* NORRIE *stands quite still for a bit, until* BOB *appears carrying an old mirror down the stairs.*

BOB   The hell ye daein staunin therr, ya bliddy eediot! Pit that thing doon an' come ower here tae ah show ye somethin'. Somethin' that came oot the Ark. An' as for you, Peter Laidlaw, you should have merr sense. I hope a bliddy crocodile gets ye.

NORRIE   Sorry, Bob.

BOB   Don't be sorry, be sensible. Joe, leave *that* rush job the noo an' start on *this* rush job. I want ye tae show the young fella here how tae dismantle this oul' mirror. Go easy wi it. If anything happens tae it, Leslie'll bastricate ye.

JOE   Is it worth somethin'?

BOB   Tae you an' me it widnae be worth a pump, but tae the oul' cow that brought it in it's the light o the world. I wunner where Leslie digs them up. They come in here wi their broken-doon, oul'-fashioned fol-de-rols an' expect us tae gie them back tae them bran' new. Ye'd think we hidnae enough work o wur ain. I think Leslie must be gettin his mutton oot o it. Dirty oul' midden. Anyway, she wants it touched up an' re-silvered. Noo, watch the surface. If ye lay it on the face, lay it on straw or plenty paper.

JOE   No much tae it, Bob. Jist a hauf dozen wee tacks.

BOB   Go ahead, then. I'll feed-up tae the boy's ready.

JOE   Right, we'll lay it on the slant so's the glass disnae touch the bench. You haud wan side, an' ah'll ease the tacks oot.

NORRIE   Ye think it's very ould?

JOE   Oulder than you an' me pit thegither, I'll tell ye that. Might even be an antique. Nae bother, see. Jist two merr... therr we are. We take the back aff, Bob?

BOB   Aye, go ahead, go ahead.

JOE   *(easing the back off, and separating the glass from the frame)*   That's it.

BOB   Jist haud on tae it, ah'll finish this side.

NORRIE   Hey, Joe! Look at this oul' paper that came oot the back. *Evening Times,* October the fourteenth, 1921! 1921! Ye wer right, it is oulder than you an' me pit thegither. Look at that, whisky three an' fourpence a bottle.

JOE   Bit chipped on the side here, Bob.

BOB   Aye, aye. Hey, Peter, c'm'ere a minute. Rouger, you, tae. Charlie, have a look at the edges.

NORRIE   'Fordyce's Annual Sale – women's stockings, wan an' six a dozen.' Hey, Rouger, look at this oul' paper I foun' oot the mirror. It's ancient history.

ROUGER   Nae five-poun' notes in the back o it? Nae confessions tae rape and murder concealed in a secret groove? See the paper. Yah, that's a lot o pap. 'Ladies' combinations, every size.' That's disgustin, that. Look at ye, you're slaverin like a dog wi the dicky itch. Get away! *(He throws the paper away.)*

NORRIE   Hey, easy, easy. I want tae read that paper. *(He bends down for the paper. The* ROUGER *catches him a soft kick on the arse, and he falls against the bicycle.)*

ROUGER   Watch that bike, teuchter!

NORRIE   Bugger you and yur bike. Ah'm nae teuchter.

ROUGER   Ha-ha, so ye've learnt whit it is suddenly.

NORRIE   Naw, ah havenae.

ROUGER   I'll tell ye sometime. No as bad as ye think.

BOB   That's quite a chip oot the side right enough. D'ye think it wid staun the slightest touch o the grinder, Peter?

PETER   Never. It wid shatter instantly.

BOB   Aye, I wis thinkin that masel'. Mebbie a wee rub wi the blockin-stone, then?

PETER   Aye, that might dae it. Need tae go dead easy, a' the same.

BOB   We'll a' need tae go very careful wi it. Hear that, Rouger? You hear that, Charlie?

CHARLIE *is revealed with the weight-bar over his head. He brings it down and with a great* 'Yah!' *drops it. The whole place trembles.*

BOB   In the name o the lantern Jesus, have ye nae fuckin sense? I'm tellin everybody tae keep the heid wi this auld merchandise here, and you're flingin ton weights a' ower the place. It's blohoorable, so it is. Diabastric and blohoorable!

CHARLIE   Nae herm done.

BOB   I've tellt ye a hunner times, this is a glesswork. Ye've only been here nine year, ye should know by noo that this is the last place for a contraption like that. But ye'll get it oot o here. Ye'll get it oot that back door by the end o the week.

CHARLIE   Will you cairry it oot?

BOB   Aw, shite! You want tae grow up. Classic beveller, you! Strong back – weak heid!

CHARLIE   Must keep the strength up, Bob.

BOB   How much strength dis it take tae lift three feet o quarter-inch plate?

ROUGER   Aw, this strength o' yours – whit ye gaun tae dae wi it?

CHARLIE   Use it when the time comes.

ROUGER   Like hauf-past ten at night when you're lumberin Nancy up the high-road? Don't blush, Charlie, we a' know you're a wee bit short o strength in the right place.

CHARLIE   Not at all, I've got it when the times comes.

ROUGER   Oh, ye've got it a'right, but where are ye hidin it?

BOB   Be quiet an' pey attention. You're a bliddy mixer, Rouger. I think you were born wi a needle up yur arse. I must decide the best wey tae tackle this thing.

PETER   I could settle that fur ye.

BOB   How?

PETER   I'll just drap it.

BOB   Ye wull, like hell! Don't you start, Peter, we've had enough kiddin this mornin'.

ROUGER   He might drap it anyway.

The bell rings from upstairs.

BOB *(tearing off his apron as he goes upstairs)*   Whit dis he want noo?

BOB *goes off.*

PETER   Whit did you mean therr, Rouger?

ROUGER   Mean aboot whit?

PETER   When ye said I might drap it anywey.

ROUGER   So ye might, so could anybody.

PETER   That wisnae it, you meant me special.

ROUGER   Oh, ye know me better than I dae masel', like?

PETER   Ah know ye fur a big-mouthed, dyin gett.

ROUGER   It's you that might have the big mouth shortly.

PETER   Any time ye like. Dinner-time, any time, oot the back door therr. I'm no much, but I'll have a go wi the likes o you any time ye fancy it. Arse-holer!

ROUGER   Better watch it, ye'll be foamin at the mooth soon.

PETER   That's it, int it – that's whit ye meant? I might take a wee turn an' drap it. That's whit ye meant. Couldnae haud yur tongue in front o the boy therr. Ye must let *him* know.

ROUGER   It's you that's lettin him know.

PETER   Whatever he says, son, it's no epilepsy – no epilepsy! Take a wee tightness in the throat sometimes – constriction – looks bad, but it's no malignant. So, if this big, lousy, squeezed-up, pox-eye tells ye anything different, ye'll know him fur a five-star bastart liar.

ROUGER   You might get yur go sooner than ye think.

PETER   Go! You? I've seen merr go in a haun-reared, Abernethy fuckin biscuit. Ya common, schoolboard-faced, sodomistic pig, ye!

The ROUGER *moves towards* PETER. *As he goes,* CHARLIE *grips his arm tightly. It's obviously a grip of steel.*

CHARLIE   Away ye go, Peter.

PETER *goes.*

ROUGER   Let go the grip, Charlie.

CHARLIE   Try and get away.

ROUGER   This is atween him an' me.

CHARLIE   Whit's on ma mind's between me an' you.

ROUGER   The strength kick again, 's 'at it?

CHARLIE   That's it.

ROUGER   Aye, well, while you're at it ye might try shaftin some o it through tae that hot-arsed wee barra up in... oh... Christ, Charlie... you'll break ma fuckin airm!

CHARLIE   A'right... Noo, ah'm tellin ye, you lift her name again in here, an' ah'll split ye – take ye apart!

CHARLIE *lets go. The* ROUGER *and* CHARLIE *move away to their wheels.* NORRIE *goes to his seat with the paper.*

NORRIE   Hey, Joe, Joe, listen tae this – in this paper. 'Parents in the Anderston district of Glasgow are invited and encouraged to view the new school to be opened soon, to accommodate children of school age in the district. Classrooms and other facilities will be open to inspection for two weeks from the fourteenth of November 1921, which is the fortnight preceding the school's opening date, November twenty-eighth. The school, which will cater for infants, juniors, and advanced division scholars, will be known as Finnieston Public School.'
    Joe – that's the school ah went tae – honest – Finnieston School. I cannae believe it. Imagine that, eh, oor school, an' here's this oul' paper tellin ye when it opened. That's great, int it? D'ye think ah can keep this paper? Ah'll show it tae the boys. Might even take it in tae show it tae ma oul' school-teacher. Therr ye are, Joe – want tae see it?

JOE   Away ye go, an' don't bother me. Ah've this set tae finish aff the day.

NORRIE   But – d'ye no want tae look at it?

JOE   Beat it ah'm tellin ye, blow!

NORRIE   A'right, a'right.

BOB *comes down the stair and puts on his apron.*

BOB   A'right then, Norrie, come on, we'll get wired in. An' youz get wired in, tae. Cannae go up the sterr but ye're a' squealin murder. I'm tellin yez – if there wis bevellers tae be got ah'd bag the hale bliddy lot o ye. Me tae! I'd bag me tae fur no baggin yez a' years ago. Now then, as Leslie says, a good effort! Think a strong fart wid dae him some good. Feed up, son. Whit's that in yur haun?

NORRIE   It's this oul' paper that came oot the mirror.

BOB   Whit year?

NORRIE   1921.

BOB   Nae photies in it, ah'll bet ye.

NORRIE   Naw, jist readin. It's got a paragraph aboot the opening o oor school in it, askin the mothers and faithers tae go an' inspect it before it opens.

BOB   Whit school wis that?

NORRIE   Finnie – Finnieston.

BOB   Doon Anderston wey, eh?

NORRIE   Aye, d'ye know it?

BOB   Naw. Cowcaddens wis wherr ah wis brought up. Used tae be a bevellin shop doon your wey. Ye know Elliot Street? Aye, well, doon therr. Quite unusual that. The trade wis maistly centred up roon aboot Cowcaddens. Lot o Irishmen in it, tae. Hard men – hard drinkers, a lot o them. Piece-workers, and no often steady work. Used tae wait in the pub tae a few jobs came in and go intae the shop when the gaffer sent fur them. Merr pomas, son. Of course, sometimes they'd been in the pub that long they wernae able tae go tae their work when they wer sent fur. Strong men they were. Had tae be. Some o these jobs they had in the oul' days wid have ruptured ye. Every man saw the job right through – start tae finish – and they had tae be fast at the game. There wis plenty o men tae step intae their shoes if they wernae. Merr pomas. Ye see, Norrie – noo listen – try and get used tae knowin when the wheel needs a bit merr pomas – no hiv me tellin ye a' the time. When the wheel's dry, ye can smell the burnin, see? Try some again… (NORRIE *uses too much pomas, and it squirts up into* BOB'S *face.)* Holy Jesus! Ye had it right, therr – noo ye're away back again. Enough, but no' too much, see. Doot ye widnae have lasted long in the oul' days, Norrie. But ye never know, ye might jist see a job like wan o the ould yins quite soon. This very day, in fact. There's a big job lyin through therr, an' ah've a feelin Leslie's gaun tae tell us tae drap everything an' get oan wi it this efternoon. That reminds me, ah've got somethin' tae dae. In the meantime, you can cairry these two jobs up tae the silverin.

NORRIE   Up the sterr is that?

BOB   Past the cuttin-table an' through the door.

NORRIE   Okay. *(He grabs the glass awkwardly.)*

BOB   Easy, son, easy for the… noo, listen. Always haunle gless gently. If there's two jobs thegither, make sure there's always a bit o paper in between when ye're

277

carryin' them. Like that, see, at the tap. Lift them up easy – wan haun at the bottom an' wan haun on the edge. Haud them a bit tae the side so that they're no movin' in front o ye. Try that. That's no bad. Careful up the sterr, noo, and if they gie ye somethin' tae bring doon, jist take it slow. That's the stuff. (NORRIE *goes off.)* Now, I'll away and phone my granny. *(He goes to the lavatory, his head round the door, shouting to Peter.)* How's that comin wi the hand-block, Peter?

PETER   It's fragile – very fragile – but it'll be a'right, ah think.

BOB   Well, don't spend too much time oan it. We'll jist fake it the best wey we can an' sen it up.

PETER   Don't know who first bevelled this thing, Bob. Think it must have been ould Alex Freer when he wis on the wine. See that?

BOB   Well, ah cannae see roon corners. Jist a minute. A wee bit aff the true, eh?

PETER   The rocky road tae Port Dundas.

BOB   Ach well, that'll nearly dae it. Christ, ye're right. I think whoever did this job wis either blind or workin in the dark. Ye seen any sign o ould Alex Freer these days?

PETER   Naw, it's a while noo. Last time I saw him he couldnae see me.

BOB   He'll never get aff the juice. Well, as long as he disnae come roon here tappin us we'll be a'right. Last time he came in he looked like a bliddy ghost. He wis the colour o pomas.

PETER   That's the wine, Bob, the dadlum.

BOB   Aye, good tradesman he wis. He might be deid fur a' we know.

PETER   Aye, he wis fadin away. Ye feel he wid jist slide doon a gratin an' disappear.

BOB   Bring that ower tae the polisher when you're ready. Take yur time noo, Norrie, an' jist haud it right! (NORRIE *carries a couple of pieces of glass down the stairs.)* Good. Noo drap it first on tae yur shoe – that's it – an' lean it against the wa' – a wee bit oot at the bottom. That's it. See, that's a wee bit merr ye've learnt.

NORRIE   That gless is sherp. Think ah've cut ma haun.

BOB   See it. Naw, that's nothin'. Jist the skin. See these. A few cuts therr, eh? But that's nothin' either. You ask John the cutter tae show ye his haun's sometime. He's got millions o wee cuts.

NORRIE   I don't think ah'd fancy that. Gettin ma hauns a' cuts, ah mean.

BOB   That's funny. When we were boys we couldnae wait tae get wur hauns lookin like bevellers'. Used tae compare them, and sometimes ye'd gie them a wee roughin-up wi a sherp bit o gless tae hurry them on.

NORRIE   That sounds a bit daft tae me.

BOB   Well, son, maybe you're no cut oot tae be a beveller. Never mind. It's no often ye get a real cut, unless there's a flaw in the job an' it comes away in yur haun. Mind wan time when ah wis feedin-up – the beveller wis workin in the groove and the job cracked. Well, see the wey your brush skited aff the wheel therr, same thing happened tae the job. It planed right across the shop and caught this other fulla on the thigh. It went through aprons, troosers, the lot. Severed his hamstring, an' though they got him tae the hospital in time, he never walked right again. That frighten ye, eh?

NORRIE   It's no hell of a cheery.

BOB   Come on, we'll get intae it again. Ye might no believe this, but ah've seen me wi near a mornin's work done by this time. Feed up. Noo watch it – jist got ma heid away in time therr, didn't ah?

NORRIE   The feeder-up no find this a monotonous job?

BOB   Maybe a wee bit, but no too bad. How, you find it monotonous?

NORRIE   Ah thought when ah wis workin time wid fly. Seems as if ye jist sit here lookin at the clock.

BOB   Well, ye should be lookin at the job instead.

NORRIE   Is it a'right if ah keep this oul' paper?

BOB   Tae hell wi the paper. Pey attention.

NORRIE   Naebody seems tae care aboot it except me. I mean, it's kinna historical. I wis gaun tae try an' show it tae ma oul' school-teacher.

BOB   Listen, son, schooldays are over. Noo forget the fuckin paper, an' jist keep yur mind on the job. That wey, we'll get along fine.

NORRIE   Aye, right, sorry.

BOB   Stop apologisin. Jist dae the job. *(The pomas squirts up again.)*

NORRIE   I'm sorry, Bob, so I am. I'll... I'll...

BOB   It's no a hard job this, Norrie, an' ah think you're quite a sensible lauddie, but you're no concentratin. Noo, ah'll tell ye again *(the bell rings)* ...aw, Jesus Johnnie, therr that bastart bell again. Oan wi the apron – aff wi the apron. Ye'd think, bi-Christ, I wis a hure on a hard day. Rouger, c'm'ere! Finish that other side or this bliddy thing'll never get done.

The ROUGER *takes over.* NORRIE *feeds pomas. It's too much. It squirts into the* ROUGER'S *face.*

ROUGER   Ya bastart, ye tried that.

NORRIE   Naw, honest, ah didnae, ah didnae mean it.

ROUGER   Ye did, ya swine. Don't try anythin' funny wi me.

NORRIE   No kiddin, ah couldnae help it.

ROUGER   See that ye dae help it. Feed up right. Bliddy teuchter, a'right, that's you.

NORRIE   Ah don't even know whit you're talkin about.

ROUGER   Hielan, Hielan, Stupit Hielan. Nae wunner they used tae eat folk like you.

NORRIE   Whit?

ROUGER   Hielanmen, they used tae eat them. But their meat wis tough – tyuch – teuch! That's how they called them teuchters.

NORRIE   Ah'm no' Hielan.

ROUGER   Yur oul'-man, then?

NORRIE   Naw.

ROUGER   Yur oul'-lady? Don't like talkin aboot her, dae ye?

NORRIE   Whit should ah talk aboot her fur?

ROUGER   Cat's fur! Ye ever seen it oan a fuckin dug?

NORRIE   Whit ye gettin' at?

ROUGER   Big innocent game noo, eh. Oot at three o'clock in the mornin gettin a doctor. That wisnae cat's fur, wis it?

NORRIE   She was ill. Anywey, it's nane o your business.

ROUGER   Oh, you're right. It wid have held tight if it had been ma business.

NORRIE   Whit the hell ye talkin aboot?

ROUGER   A miss, wis it, eh?

NORRIE   A whit?

ROUGER   Don't come it. You know. A miss. Couple o snorts o penny-royal, an' bang goes the baby. Miscarriage, wis it?

NORRIE   She was sick in the middle o the night... she... she...

ROUGER   Abortion, wis that it?

NORRIE   You're a stinkin big bastart! Don't you talk aboot ma old-lady like that.

ROUGER   She drapped it, didn't she? (NORRIE *dives at the* ROUGER, *who holds the job in one hand and the boy at arm's length with the other.* CHARLIE *and* JOE *look on, but do nothing.*) Got ye gaun noo, haven't ah? Look at him, feet an' a'. She wis like the man wi the barra – it wis in front o her.

PETER   Whit ye daein tae that boy, ya dirty big sod, ye? Can ye no let nothin' alane? Lea' him go or I'll come ower there an' pit ma boot in yur cobblers.

ROUGER   You couldnae pit yur boot in shite. No time ye had a wee convulsion?

PETER   Ya midden! Ya misbegotten, parish-bred midden! Liberty-taker! Ould men an' wee boys, it's a' you're good fur.

The ROUGER *gives* NORRIE *a shove. He lands on his back and begins to cry.* BOB *comes down the stair.*

BOB   I don't know whit you're daein therr, but get on yur feet. Whit ye greetin fur?

PETER   He's greetin because that... big, long-distance sod therr wis tormentin him.

BOB   Ah'm no askin you, Peter. You seem tae be gettin intae a hell of a lot o trouble, son, fur yur first day.

NORRIE   Ah didnae start any trouble.

BOB   Whit happened?

NORRIE   It wis... it wis... cannae fuckin tell ye.

BOB   Ye don't hiv tae tell me who wis aback o it. Whit wer ye sayin tae the boy, Rouger?

ROUGER   Nothin' much. He no tell ye hissel'?

BOB   Ye've got him greetin anyway. If you'll no say whit's goin on, an' he'll no say whit's goin on, we'll never know, wull we? Honest tae God and Jesus, Rouger, you're a needle o the first bliddy mettle. Ah wis readin aboot folk like you. Psychopaths they call them. Ye hear that? Psychopaths!

ROUGER   Aw aye, that's thon wee special roads fur ridin the bike on, int it?

BOB   Wan o these days you'll run intae it, an' ah hope ah'm therr tae see it.

ROUGER   That's been said before.

BOB   Dry up noo, Norrie, it cannae be as bad as a' that.

NORRIE   You don't know whit it wis. He said somethin' aboot ma mother.

BOB   You Charlie, could ye no have done somethin' fur the boy?

CHARLIE   No ma business.

BOB   Nothin's your business, except your sodie-heided weight-liftin. A'right, Norrie, ah don't know whit he said tae ye, but it's no the worst ye'll hear. In this game or any other. Feed up, noo. Come on, come on, move. Feed up.

NORRIE   Ah'm chuckin it.

BOB   Ah tellt ye. You're no in the school noo. You're wi the big men ootside. Yur faither cannae come divin up tae see the heid-maister an' tell him somebody's been unkind tae his wee boy. That's in the past. Make up yur mind tae it, you'll get a lot o knocks afore you're done, specially fae the likes o the Rouger therr, and if you want tae chuck it on the first day, that's up tae you, but ye havenae made much o a stab at it, hiv ye? So either feed up, or take aff yur apron an' pit yur jaicket on. (NORRIE *lifts the brush and starts feeding-up.*) We'll likely be makin a start on that big job sometime in the efternoon. Then ye'll see somethin'. Ye'll see a bit o the trade as it used tae be. Four-handed we'll be tae this job, inchbevel all round. We'll hiv tae use the trestle-board. There's no much o that kind o stuff goin aboot these days.

NORRIE   Whit's it fur?

BOB   Some daft dancin-school wants a matchin mirror fur wan that got broke. Hey, whit's the time? Joe, pit the watter on fur the tea. Ye forgot aboot it. It's hardly worth while noo before dinner-time.

JOE   That's *his* job noo.

BOB   He'll dae it the-morra. An' a' the rest o yur jobs, tae.

JOE   Hope that means runnin doon tae the bettin-shop fur ye.

BOB   Less o yur lip, Joe… Christ, that reminds me. Ah backed three winners on Friday an' didnae collect the money. Ought tae hiv a few quid comin back. Noo, where'd ah pit the ticket? Aye, in ma jaicket. Norrie, take a run doon tae the bettin-shop an' pick up the money fur us. They should jist be open noo. Oot the back door, up the sterr and a hunner yards doon the street on this side. Ye cannae miss it. Run like hell, an' if anybody sees ye, kid on you're no therr. Think ye can dae that?

NORRIE   Sure, nae bother.

BOB   On ye go, then. It's a lovely day ootside. Ye'll enjoy the run.

NORRIE *goes out the back door. The* BEVELLERS *concentrate, swaying gently at their wheels. A moment of peace settles on the shop, and they start to sing. In contrast to what has gone before, the song is sweet and sentimental.*

ALL   Meet me tonight when the clock strikes nine
Down in the glen where the stars brightly shine
And we will walk, love, over the hill
Meet me tonight by the old water-mill.

Evening will come at the close of the day

And to the glen we will both make our way
Your hand in mine, love, over the hill
Meet me tonight by the old water-mill.

They hum the end of the song again to a close, and break off slowly. JOE *goes for the tea and hands it round.* NORRIE *comes back.*

NORRIE   That's it, Bob. Jist a few pence short o eight quid.

BOB   Champion, champion. Jist aboot whit ah thought masel'. No bad fur dollar roll-up, eh?

ROUGER   You're hunted – enchanted.

BOB   Jist makin up fur a' the cripples ah've backed since the season started.

PETER   By Jees, Bob, you're a dab at the accumulators. Ye always back wan stotter. Makes up for a' the stevers.

BOB   You're right, Peter. Jist aboot this time last year ah had two bob – ten pence – gaun fur me on a four-horse roll-up. Jist over fourteen poun' it got me.

JOE   An' ye didnae forget the boy that ran wi the line.

BOB   Ah'm no forgettin him this time either. Therr half a quid. But there wer two o' yez this time. You went wi the bet, and the boy here picked it up. So, a dollar each.

JOE   Whit! Ah've been daein it for donkeys! He comes in here new, an' the first day he goes, he's on a dollar?

BOB   That's right. Ye wur greetin therr a wee while ago for Norrie tae go tae the bettin shop. That wis before ye knew ah had a treble up. So, a dollar tae you, an' a dollar tae the boy.

JOE   *(giving* NORRIE *the money)*   Therr ye are – Pontius.

NORRIE   Ah didnae ask fur it.

BOB   Never mind him. Get yur tea.

JOE   Don't think there's enough left fur him.

BOB   Well, whit d'ye no pit plenty on fur?

JOE   Ah jist pit the usual on. Ah forgot aboot him.

NORRIE   That's a'right, ah've got ma flask.

ROUGER   Oh, a flask, eh? Whit aboot that, Joe? Ye hear that, Charlie? Lord Fauntleroy's sister's sent him tae his work wi a flask an' sandwiches.

CHARLIE   Ye don't need a flask in here. Plenty gas in the ring.

NORRIE   It's jist tae go wi ma dinner piece.

CHARLIE   Ye eatin yur dinner in here?

NORRIE   Aye. D'yez no a' dae it?

CHARLIE   Ah think merr o ma gut than eatin ma chuck in here.

NORRIE   Dis naebody dae it, then?

JOE   You'll be on yur tod in here the minute the whistle goes.

ROUGER   Only wan other man in here at dinner-time.

NORRIE   Who's that?

ROUGER   The beveller's ghost!

JOE   Aye, him an' the rats.

NORRIE   Jesus Christ!

ROUGER   Ye'll be sittin therr an' ye'll feel this cauld thing creepin up the back o yur neck. Ye look roon, an' therr it is, glowin in the dark, the beveller's ghost.

PETER   Ach, the beveller's arse! Don't believe them, Norrie. Many's the good kip ah've had in here at dinner-time, stretched oot on the bench.

NORRIE   Ah didnae believe them anyway.

ROUGER   No much – it wis hingin fae ye.

NORRIE   'S a lot a junk, that ghost stuff.

PETER   Ah'll no be havin a kip the day a' the same. Ah'll be joinin Bob on a wee toddle down tae the boozer fur a gless o that class lager. Ye settin them up the day, Bob?

BOB   Don't mind. No every day ye get a wee turn at the bookies. Ye're a'invitit.

CHARLIE   No me, Bob. Thanks a' the same. Ye know me.

BOB   Good enough, wan less.

JOE   Ah'm on fur a half pint.

BOB   You've had yur dollar. You, Rouger?

ROUGER   Don't know. Ah want tae go fur a spare inside tube fur the bike. If ah get back.

BOB   Ye might be too late then.

ROUGER   That'll no bother me.

BOB   Suit yursel'.

CHARLIE *lifts the weight-bar above his head and lets it fall with a great gasp. Everyone freezes. Nobody says anything.*

ROUGER   That's how tae spend yur dinner-time, young-yin. Try liftin Charlie's weight.

NORRIE   No me. Many times can you dae that, Charlie?

CHARLIE   Often as ye like, within reason. I'll show ye. Wance merr fur luck, eh?

PETER   Aw, Charlie, we're a' fuckin galvanised wi you drappin that thing.

CHARLIE   I'll put it doon nice an easy this time, like a feather.

CHARLIE *lifts the bar again, holds it there, brings it down with one break, then sets it gently on the floor.*

CHARLIE   That satisfy ye, eh, young fulla?

NORRIE   You must have some strength.

ROUGER   Aw aye, an' some knack, tae – ye learn the knack through practice.

CHARLIE   Ye fancy tryin tae learn it, then?

ROUGER   Ah've got some knack o ma ain. Shovin that thing ower yur heid a couple times might look snazzy, but you try shovin a bike up tae Dalmally an' back in wan day. See who'd hiv the knack then. Knackered merr like you'd be.

CHARLIE   Widnae waste ma time.

ROUGER   We wernae wastin time yesterday, ah'll tell ye. We caught six riders fae the Troy Wheelers just below the Falls o Falloch. Four o us, an' six o them. They knew we were on their tail and tried tae shake us on the climb. Suddenly the road ahead wis clear, an' wan o oor boys shouts, 'Jump!' We wer out the saddles like jockeys. As one man we sprinted up the hill an' left them fuckless. We danced away fae them! Burnt off they were – burnt right off! An' that wisnae knack, that wis pedallin, Mac, shovin an' pedallin.

CHARLIE   Bravo. So, how d'ye fancy makin yur name, Norrie? On the bike, or on the bar here?

NORRIE   Don't think ah fancy either o them.

CHARLIE   Ye can sit straight on a bike though, can't ye?

NORRIE   Who cannae?

CHARLIE   So try gettin that thing two inches aff the flerr.

NORRIE   Don't want tae.

CHARLIE   Jist hiv a wee crack at it.

NORRIE   Nae point, ah'd never dae it.

CHARLIE   Jist tae get the feel o it – get a sense o the resistance.

NORRIE   Ah think you're kiddin me.

CHARLIE   Naw, naw, c'm'ere. Pit baith hauns on the bar – a wee bit further apart – noo bend at the knees and jist get the feel o it. (NORRIE *does so and strains at the bar.*)

NORRIE   If I try any harder I'll go through the flerr.

ALL *the men laugh. There is a move towards resuming work. The* ROUGER *spots the red cloth peering out of* NORRIE'S *pocket. He whips it out.*

ROUGER   Here, wipe the sweat aff yursel'… whit the hell's this?

NORRIE   Give us that, you.

ROUGER   Oh aye, gie's back ma drawers. Whit ye daein' wi these? *(He holds up a pair of red ladies' briefs.)*

NORRIE   Give us them, ah said.

ROUGER   Cairry these aboot in yur pocket a' the time, dae ye?

NORRIE   Naw ah don't.

ROUGER   Doin yur knee-creeper an' blaggin them aff the washin lines, then. Is that it?

NORRIE   They're no mine.

ROUGER   Well ah hope tae Christ they're no. We've had a few queeries in here, but never wan o that kind before.

NORRIE   Ach, work them up yur nose. Ah don't care.

JOE   Wherr d'ye get them?

NORRIE   Ye'll no believe us anyway, so whit the hell's the use o tellin' yez?

BOB   Aye well, Norrie, ye must admit it's a kinna unusual article fur a boy tae hiv aboot him.

NORRIE   Ah don't care, they're no mine.

ROUGER   Yur sister's, 's 'at it? Takes his sister's knickers oot wi him. Some boy, eh?

NORRIE   You keep the sister oot o' it! Some bird up at a windae shouted at me as ah wis comin doon the back sterr and threw these things ower.

ROUGER   Oot the work next door?

NORRIE   Aye.

ROUGER   An' you picked them up an' kept them?

NORRIE   They fell right on ma heid. Ah wis in a hurry. Bob said ah wis tae hurry an' no let anybody see me. Ah jist stuck them in ma pocket. Meant tae throw them away later.

ROUGER   Oh, we'll believe that, oh aye. Nae wunner ye're takin yur dinner in here, eh?

NORRIE   Ach, away you an' peddle yur duff.

ROUGER   Whit ye tellin us? Some young fox up therr hauls aff her drawers an' chucks them oot the windae fur ye?

NORRIE   They wernae fur me.

ROUGER   Oh, fur somebody else, then?

NORRIE   Ah don't know.

ROUGER   Naebody in here knows any o the birds in therr, except Charlie.

NORRIE   Ah don't know, ah'm tellin' yez.

ROUGER   Hidin it, eh? Feart somebody might lift ye ower his heid an' drap ye like a fifty-sixer?

NORRIE   Aw, shut it!

CHARLIE   All right, boy, speak up.

NORRIE   Charlie, ah didnae want tae say anythin'…

CHARLIE   Never mind that. Jist tell whit wis shouted.

NORRIE   Ah cannae mind.

BOB   The boy cannae mind. Come on, back tae work, if that's whit ye call it, sittin on yur jacksies hauf the mornin.

CHARLIE   Listen, Bob, it's no often ah go against ye, but ah'm gaun tae hear the version o' this, wance an' fur a.

NORRIE   Aw, right then, it's no ma fault. There wis two or three o these lassies up therr. The windae wis slung open. Wan o them seemed tae be tryin tae stop the others throwin these things, but they came flyin ower the windae, an' wan o them shouted, 'These are fur Charlie. Tell him Nancy says they're on fire and he's the man wi the hose.' *(The men laugh.)*

CHARLIE   *(deeply humiliated)*   Ya little bastart!

BOB   Naw, naw, Charlie. The boy wis keepin it quiet, but you made him speak. That no right, noo? Peter?

PETER   Aye, fair enough. Boy wantit tae keep his mouth shut. Whit the hell's it matter anywey? Only a bunch o lassies sky-larkin'.

CHARLIE   Suppose you're right. Okay, son, forget it. Joke's on me. But it's over. Jist keep that in mind, everybody.

BOB   Whit's the time therr? God stiff me, ah believe that clock's stopped again. Nae

wunner the tea-break went on so long. Dae ye know how tae squint the time up
therr, Norrie?

NORRIE   Aye, think so… *(He goes to the hole in the glass grating.)* It's jist leavin
hauf-past.

BOB   Whit! Oh buggeration! We've less than hauf-an-oor o the mornin left an'
we've hardly turned a wheel. Ah well, wan o these days. Set that clock, Norrie.

NORRIE *goes up to the clock.*

NORRIE   The hauns are stiff, they'll hardly turn.

BOB   Well, spit on it – right on the spindle. That usually dis it.

NORRIE *spits on it.*

NORRIE   Ah think that's it noo.

BOB   Come on then, get some pomas on, an' mind my eye.

BOB *and* NORRIE *start to work.*

NORRIE   Did you think the mornin went past quick, Bob?

BOB   Past quick? It vanished, disappeared. How d'you no?

NORRIE   It seemed quite long tae me. In school you've got different periods. Time
goes quick.

BOB   Back at school again, are ye? Take ma advice, son. Put it behind ye, unless
you're thinkin o gaun back there, are ye?

NORRIE   Naw, nae chance.

BOB   Got tae make the break sometime. So stick in. You might think this is a rough
trade and rough folk in it. But that's jist because we havenae broke away fae the
oul' days – no a'thegither anyway. Ye cannae wipe oot years o' hard men an' hard
graft jist because the machinery changes a wee bit. No that it's a' that different,
mind you. The wheels are a wee bit different here an' there, like the carborundum
stone. That used tae be the ould mill wi the hopper feeder and a sand-drip. That's
when boys younger than you really grafted. Cairryin pailfuls o saun an' sievin it
in the trough beside the mill. They still use them in wan or two places yet, an' if
somethin' had tae go wrang at Peter's end we might have tae use it yet, but it's no
likely. As ah said, there wis a lot o Irishmen in this game at wan time. Haill
families o them. It wis wan o the few trades open tae them. The Rouger's oul'
man wis a beveller. You think he's twistit. Ye want tae have seen his oul' man.
They worked on piece work, each man seein his job through fae start tae finish,
an' they had tae shift. The Rouger's faither wis a beaster. He'd collect his ain
wages at the end o the week an' take the Rouger's tae. That wis the last they'd see
o him tae the pubs shut on Setturday night. They wer lucky if he had enough left
tae get them pigs' feet fur the rest o the week. So maybe it's no surprisin that he's
a wee bit rough. Course they wurnae a' like that, the oul' yins. Some o them could

cut a design wi a wheel that wis merr like somethin' ye'd see in the Art Galleries. Ah wis never a' that good at figure-work masel'. But some o them raised families an' even put them tae the University. Ah see some lawyers' names aboot the toon an' ah can mind their faithers. Bevellers. Hard men, but good bliddy men, some o them. Aye, aye. Ye find the time long, then?

NORRIE Jist keep glancin up at the clock a lot. Disnae seem tae move much.

BOB Ah well, it's no much o a clock. Whit kinna stuff did they learn ye at school?

NORRIE Usual. Bit o maths, science, techy-drawin, composition an' that.

BOB Whit wer ye good at?

NORRIE English.

BOB English?

NORRIE Aye. Might no talk it very good, but ah wis a'right when it came tae writin it doon.

BOB Wisnae exactly ma best subject. Mebbie you're wan o these fullas wi the itch.

NORRIE Eh?

BOB Ah've noticed. There's roughly three kinds o blokes get loose efter school. Wan's like me. Plods along, learns a trade and disnae see much further than a week's work an' his wages at the end o it. A wee bit o security tae keep the wife happy. Other kind's the wan wi a bit o education. They run businesses, buy a hoose, an' never seem tae be short o a few nicker. They might be dumplins, but that bit o education makes the difference. They're usually solid. Third kind's the wans wi the itch. Ah don't mean scratchin theirsel's or anythin' like that. A kind o internal itch. They'd come in an look at a job like this an' say, 'Bugger that – ah'm off!' They might cast aboot fur a while before anythin' turns up, but it usually happens. They might be the kind that tries tae knock aff a couple o wage-vans an' get seven year fur their bother, but they're no exactly the really itchy wans. Naw, the fullas ah'm talking aboot don't seem tae need whit the rest o us need. They've a kinna instinct, an' it gets them through. Some o them turn intae bookies, some do well at the buyin an' sellin, but occasionally ye get wan an' he really makes a name. Nae real start in life, but he's got the itch. We had a fulla like that in oor class in school. He wis good at composition, tae.

NORRIE Ah don't feel very itchy now.

BOB Ah well, we'll see. You're feedin up better. *(The bell goes.)* Stiff me, that's Leslie again. He's got the itch, but ah widnae like tae tell him where it is.

BOB *goes off upstairs. The* ROUGER *and* JOE *start to talk together, hatching something.*

ROUGER Hey, Norrie! Ye really fancy that bike, eh?

NORRIE How, ye giein it away?

ROUGER Naw, but ye could always have a gander at it.

NORRIE Much'll it cost us?

ROUGER Jist thought ye might be interested tae have a look. See these gears here, many permutations ye think's in the cogs therr?

NORRIE   You tell us.

ROUGER   Twelve. A dozen choices when you're nickin along. Hills, flats, corners, take yur pick.

NORRIE *moves towards the bike and becomes absorbed.* JOE *snatches the old newspaper.*

NORRIE   Whit kinna frame is it?

ROUGER   Continental. Top stylin. The lightest frame on the road.

NORRIE   Much it cost ye?

ROUGER   Best part o fifty quid for the frame itsel'. Wheels, gears, brakes, extra. Worth a hundred nicker as it stands.

NORRIE   That's no a bike, that's a space-ship.

ROUGER   Feel the position.

NORRIE   Position?

ROUGER   The relationship between the saddle, the rider, and the haunle-bars.

NORRIE   Whit's that got tae dae wi it? Ye no jist get on an' shove?

ROUGER   That's gringo talk. You see a rider wi his position right, ye know he's a pedaller. Ye see a bloke wi his arse in the air, ye know he's a plunk, a Joseph. Ye can always spot the pedallers weighin thursel's up in shop windaes as they pass.

NORRIE   Ah widnae mind whit ah looked like if ah had that thing under me.

ROUGER   Ye'd get the knock before ye reached Old Kilpatrick.

NORRIE   Ah've shoved a bike before this.

ROUGER   Ye'd get fire in yur gut. Jist like that fire behind ye.

NORRIE *turns round and sees a small blaze on the floor.*

NORRIE   Whit's that fur?

ROUGER   Ye no feel it cauld?

NORRIE   No me.

JOE   Ould papers make very good burnin.

NORRIE   Ye no feart ye set fire tae that straw?

JOE   No chance.

ROUGER   Don't think ye heard him right. Ould papers make good fires. Nice and dry.

NORRIE *(looking towards his bench)*   'S 'at that paper that came oot the mirror?

ROUGER   You're gettin warm. But no so warm as that crap aboot yur oul' school.

NORRIE *tries to kick out the fire and rescue the paper but it's too late.*

NORRIE   Whit ye want tae dae that fur?

ROUGER   Jist a wee game. New boy – first day. Ye've got tae gee him up a wee bit.

NORRIE   Ah don't mind ye takin the rise, but the paper wis somethin' else. D'ye burn the lot o it?

ROUGER   Mebbie no.

JOE *holds up the rest of the paper.* NORRIE *dives for it. The* ROUGER *collars him, while* JOE *puts the rest on the fire.*

NORRIE   You're a coupla animals. Liberty-takers. Yez knew ah wanted that paper.
ROUGER   Teacher's pet. Gallopin back tae get a pat on the heid fur bein a good boy.
NORRIE   Ah thought you wur gaun tae be ma mate in here, Joe.
JOE   No chance, Mac.
NORRIE   Lousy bastards.

BOB *comes down the stair.*

BOB   Whit's that burnin?
ROUGER   Gaun, tell him. Tell the teacher. The big bad boys set fire tae his paper.
BOB   You get some watter on that at wance, Joe, or I'll land ye a severe kick in the arse. Rouger, ye're a lousebag plain and simple. It wis daein ye nae herm tae let the boy hiv the paper, but ye couldnae leave it, could ye? Ah knew yur oul' man. Ah widnae hiv crossed him, but he wis straight in his ain wey. You! When they bury you, they'll use a twisted coffin.
ROUGER   Ma oul' man wis a pig, an' when he got tae the age when he wis past it, ah let him know it, too.
BOB   Aye, don't tell us. Ah mind o his last days at the job. Ye used tae thump him on the chest an' say, 'Gaun, ya dirty oul' pig, ye.'
ROUGER   Mebbie he'll no be the last oul' man tae feel that.
BOB   If that's me you're talkin aboot, ah'll tell ye somethin'. Ye wernae bred fur it. Ah'd cut ye fae yur heid tae yur arse, or ah'd find them that wid dae it fur me. Joe, don't let me catch you at that caper again.
JOE   Only a bit o kiddin, Bob.
BOB   Ye might've burnt the shop doon. Aw right, Norrie, don't staun therr like a stumor. Mix some merr pomas or somethin', but stir yur ideas – the lot o ye. Peter, Charlie. C'm'ere, ah want yez. We're gettin that big mirror-plate through right now. Leslie says we've tae try an' get it started by two o'clock this efternoon, so gie's your efforts, an' we'll get it through against the sterr therr.
JOE   You want me, Bob?
BOB   When ah want you, ah'll ask ye. Any oul' gloves aboot the place?
CHARLIE   Ah've got a couple ower therr.
BOB   See's wan. The right haun.
CHARLIE   They're baith fur the right haun.
BOB   Like the rest o the stuff in here. Two o everythin' – bugger all o nothin'.
ROUGER   Ah hivnae got wan.
BOB   Good. Mebbie ye'll do wan o yur arteries in.

BOB, PETER, *and* CHARLIE *move through to the side of the shop.*

JOE   You've got me in bad wi the gaffer.

NORRIE   Ah got ye in bad? Ah didnae dae anythin'.

JOE   You and yur manky oul' paper.

NORRIE   Well, ye knew ah wanted tae keep it 'cause it wis ould.

JOE   Ould papers oot o ould mirrors are ten a penny in this job.

NORRIE   Ah didnae know that. Yez didnae need tae burn it anyway.

JOE   Ach, get bottled.

BOB, PETER, *and* CHARLIE *begin to appear carrying the glass plate.* LESLIE *comes down the stair.*

LESLIE   Is that you bringing it through now, Bob?

BOB   We're no exactly takin it oot the back door.

LESLIE   See you don't mark the face.

BOB   We're jist lookin for rough corners tae gie it a dunt against.

LESLIE   Careful with the step down, then.

BOB   Aye. The wan-legged man'll go first.

LESLIE   It's all right kidding, Bob, but that's a valuable job. Watch the step, Peter.

PETER   Thanks for remindin me. Ah'd never noticed it before.

LESLIE   You're all in good humour today, I can see that.

BOB   We're a' jist tryin tae get this thing fae wan side o the shop tae the other.

LESLIE   Where are you putting it down?

BOB   We'll lie it alangside the sterr therr. If you'll get oot the road, that is.

LESLIE   Sorry, sorry. You think that's the safest place for it?

BOB   It's the only place fur it. Unless you know somewhere in this shop that ah havenae seen before.

LESLIE   No need for the sarcasm, Bob. Just seeing things right.

BOB   Jist a minute, Leslie. Ah'll talk tae ye in a minute. Now then, fullas, put it doon easy against the lavvy boards and the haun-rail.

LESLIE   You'll have to be careful when you're going into the doings.

BOB   Ma end doon first. Easy, noo, Charlie, easy, Peter. Your end, Rouger, aboot a foot oot at the bottom. That's it. Well noo, that wisnae so bad, wis it, Leslie?

LESLIE   No, quite good, quite good. You laddies be careful going up the stairs. No jumping. You hear that, sonny?

NORRIE   Yes, Mr Skinner.

LESLIE   I suppose you're right, Bob. That's just about the best place for it.

BOB   It's nice an' near the grinder anywey.

LESLIE   When do you think you'll make a start on it?

BOB   Well, we've a few odds and ends o rush jobs tae clear up first. Mebbie two o'clock or hauf-past.

LESLIE   How's that mirror coming along?

BOB   That's wan o the odds an' ends. Right efter dinner-time ah'll gie it a polishin.

LESLIE   Well, as long as you get the big one started this afternoon.

BOB   Honest, ah don't know whit the panic is. We'd be better giein this a full day.

LESLIE   No. Must get it started sometime today.

BOB   You're the boss.

LESLIE   I'll look down later and see how you're managing. How will you tackle it?

BOB   Same wey we always tackle that size o job. A man tae each corner, an' the trestle-board underneath for support. Peter'll do the bevel.

LESLIE   Your best effort, Peter. Keep the bevel true. Use the measuring-stick. Inch bevel all round.

PETER   Aye, right, Leslie.

LESLIE   I'll be off, then. Remember what I told you, boys. Watch the stairs.

LESLIE *goes off – and stumbles on the stair.*

ROUGER   Inch bevel all round now, Peter. Use the measuring-stick.

PETER   I havenae used a measuring-stick in twenty year. When ah dae a job, it's bang on. Nae merr, nae less.

BOB   That man wid drive ye tae drink, so he wid.

PETER   He disnae hiv tae drive me. You're still settin them up, ah hope, Bob.

BOB   Mebbie you shouldnae go the day, Peter.

PETER   The day wan lager sets me aff ma stroke ah'll chuck it.

BOB   Ah, well, it'll no be long noo. Some bliddy mornin this has been.

ROUGER   Whit aboot this yin here, eh? 'Yes, Mr Skinner.'

BOB   Whit d'ye want him tae say – ye want him tae call the manager by his first name, an' him a new boy?

ROUGER   He calls you Bob.

BOB   Aye, 'cause ah told him tae. Right, back tae the graft for the wee while that remains o the mornin. Try an' clear up some o the small stuff.

ALL *return to their wheels and settle again. The singing takes over, and they begin humming the same tune as before.*
The whistle goes shortly. ALL *rush for their jackets and go off upstairs, the* ROUGER *taking his bike.* NORRIE *remains downstairs. At the foot of the stair* PETER *turns.*

PETER   Ye can leave a couple o the lights on, but don't touch anythin' ye shouldnae.

PETER *goes off.*

NORRIE   Aye, right.

NORRIE *is left all alone. He takes a flask and sandwiches from his piece-bag and settles on the bench beside his wheel. After a moment he goes to his jacket and returns with a comic, in which he soon becomes absorbed – so absorbed that he doesn't notice old* ALEX FREER *coming slowly, like a shadow, down the stair.*
Old ALEX *gets very near to* NORRIE *and stands looking round vacantly. He puts*

out a thin hand and touches NORRIE.

NORRIE *(leaping up on to the bench and backing away)* Jesus Christ! Ya whey-faced oul' bastart, ye come near me, ah'll break every bit o gless in the shop ower ye!

ALEX Eh... Eh... Wait, noo... don't be feart, son.

NORRIE Ye might be a fuckin ghost, but you touch me an' ye'll be sorry ye ever snuffed it!

ALEX Aw, ah'm no' a ghost, son. Sometimes ah wish ah wis, an' sometimes ah feel like wan, but ah'll just hiv tae wait ma time. Sorry if ah gied ye a fright.

NORRIE Whit ye daein in here?

ALEX Ah'm nae stranger here. I wis doon here before ye wur born. Best years o ma life wer spent doon here, among the pomas an' the wheels an' the slurry.

NORRIE The whit?

ALEX The slurry – the grindings o the gless that gethers at the bottom o the wheels. You must be new here. When did ye start?

NORRIE This morning.

ALEX Ye'll no have learnt a' the names fur the different wee bits an' pieces roon aboot the trade yet. The burning, the slurry, the culet. Ye know whit culet is?

NORRIE Naw.

ALEX Well, it's no much, but it sounds like something. The scrap gless in the box below the bench therr. The shards, the spikes, the remains o ould jobs bunged away an' forgot aboot – that's culet.

NORRIE Naebody told me.

ALEX Sometimes ah feel like a bit o ould culet masel'. Sometimes in the mornings I feel as if the culet's inside me. Apexes, corners, an' wee sherp slithers o gless tryin tae bust their wey oot ma inside. It's no gless, of course, it's jist the wey ah am sometimes in the mornings.

NORRIE Wur ye lookin fur somebody?

ALEX Ye could say that, aye. Ah try tae stey away, no bother anybody, but then the time comes when ah miss the smell. Ye've noticed the smell? Aye, ye wid. The burning at the polisher, an' that peculiar smell fae the edgers. It's no like anythin' else ah can think o. A kinna funny, limy smell. Nearly sweet. I noticed it the first time ah ever went intae a bevellin shop, an' ah can smell it noo.

NORRIE Is it Bob you're looking fur?

ALEX Aye, Bob. Maybe Peter, or any o the ould-yins. The young-yins, they're different. Widnae gie ye a smell o their drawers if their arse wis studded wi diamonds. Sit doon, son, hiv yur piece. Ah'll hiv a wee sate, tae. Ye're no sure o me yet, are ye? It's a'right, ah'll sit a wee bit away fae ye. Gaun, don't bother wi me. Ah'm Alex Freer... (NORRIE *sits down cagily, and* ALEX *takes a place down the bench from him.*) Whit's making ye hiv yur piece inside?

NORRIE Jist thought that's how they wid a' dae it.

ALEX They used tae, right enough. Nothin' else fur it at wan time. Different noo. No very often they stey in at dinner-time noo. Peter sometimes if he's needin a wee sleep. If he's been feelin a wee bit dizzy or that. An' a very odd time, Bob.

NORRIE   They're no here the day. Bob backed a few winners, an' Peter an' him are in the pub.

ALEX   Are they? By Christ if ah'd known that, ah widnae be here, ah'll tell ye.

NORRIE   Could ye no run doon? Ye might catch them.

ALEX   Run? Ha-ha, Jesus, that's a good yin. Run, eh? Whit's yur name?

NORRIE   Norrie.

ALEX   Well, Norrie, the thing ah want maist right noo is a big gill o wine, but ah couldnae run if they wer at the bottom o Pitt Street giein it away in barrels.

NORRIE   Ye no feelin well?

ALEX   Aye, ye could pit it that wey. Mebbie ah could manage a wee drap o yur tea, if ye've any tae spare.

NORRIE   Aye, sure. Ye want a bit piece?

ALEX   Naw, nae piece, nae piece.

NORRIE *pours out some tea and hands it over.* ALEX *stretches out his hand, which shakes violently.*

NORRIE   Ye cauld or somethin'?

ALEX   Ah'm cauld, ah'm hot – ah'm sweatin, ah'm shiverin. *(He gets the cup to his mouth. It rattles against his teeth.)* God take care o us! Cannae even... cannae even... aw, never mind, son, it's a wee bit too hot anywey.

NORRIE   Sure ye widnae like a bit o piece?

ALEX   Naw, naw. Oh, Jeez, ah'm exhausted. Whit's on yur piece?

NORRIE   Sausage.

ALEX   Cannae mind the last time I had a sausage. Listen, son...

NORRIE   Whit?

ALEX   Aw, never mind... cannae ask ye that. Ye jist started this mornin, eh?

NORRIE   Aye.

ALEX   Ye gaun tae stick it?

NORRIE   No sure. Hiv tae wait an' see.

ALEX   Don't, Norrie boy, don't. Get away fae it. Ye spend yur days grindin gless, an' at the finish yur life's like slurry at the bottom o the wheel. Yur back's like the bent bit o an oul' tree an' yur hauns are like jaurries aboot the knuckles. Ye never get away fae the sound o watter drippin in yur ears. The damp gets in at the soles o yur feet an' creeps right up tae yur neck. Yur face turns tae the colour o pomas an' ye cannae stop it. That Rouger, he tries tae keep the shine on his face by gallopin like a bliddy eediot oot on that bike o his, an' Charlie thinks he can pit aff the evil day liftin that stupit weight o his ower his heid, but they cannae stop it. Somethin' breks doon in the chest, an' the sound o yur voice gets thin, an' wan day you're an oul' man like me, bent an' brittle. Don't stey at it, Norrie. Get somethin' else – anythin'. Get intae the sun an' the fresh air. Get a job on a motor, a van, anythin', but don't stey at this trade. Fur if ye dae, it'll bend ye.

NORRIE   Aye... well... hivnae made up ma mind aboot it.

ALEX   Take ma word, make it up soon.

NORRIE   Thought ye said ye couldnae stey away fae the smell?

ALEX   That's right, oh, that's right. Efter a while it gets intae ye, an wance it gets under ye, it's very hard tae make the brek. Ah'm no sayin there urnae some lovely things aboot this trade, but it's a' in the end-product, like. A bit o figure-work or a good – a beautiful mirror – well bevelled an' set – will staun against anythin' in any craft. Ah've seen work by some o the oul' fullas that wid bring wee needles intae the corners o yur eyes it wis that lovely, but take ma word – it's no worth it. The price fur a' that work has got tae be peyed.

NORRIE   How long have ye been stopped workin?

ALEX   A few year. Must be five or six anyway. Come in here sometimes an' see the boys. Sometimes they bung us a few bob tae get's a gless o wine. Ah'm a wine-mopper, ye know.

NORRIE   'S 'at how you're shakin?

ALEX   That's how, son, that's how. Ye can imagine me haudin a three-foot plate wi a shake like that on, eh?

NORRIE   Dangerous fur ye.

ALEX   Dangerous fur everybody else. Ah'm no sayin the trade did that tae me. That might have happened anywey. But sometimes, stuck doon here wi the mill gaun, the shaddas an' the watter drippin, on bad days ah used tae think, 'This is how it must be efter the big trumpet blaws', an' ah'd grab ma jaicket an' dive oot the back door fur a glass o the ruby red. Time came when ah couldnae come in at a'. No tae work anywey. How long before the rest o them come back?

NORRIE   Good forty minutes yet anywey.

ALEX   Well, ah cannae stey here. The wee funny things are beginnin tae jig aboot at the side o ma eyes. Must try an' see the boys on the road up.

NORRIE   Whit if ye don't see them?

ALEX   Don't know. When it's like this ye never know. Jist hiv tae suffer, ah suppose, jist hiv tae suffer.

NORRIE   Wid a dollar be any good tae ye?

ALEX   Ye mean ye wid give us a dollar?

NORRIE   Aye.

ALEX   Oh, give us it, Norrie, give us it. Ah wis gaun tae tap ye a wee while ago therr, but you're jist a young boy. (NORRIE *gives him the money.*) …Thanks. A dollar's quite a lot the wey ah'll drink it. At least the tap o ma heid'll no come aff. Thanks. Ah'll away noo. Ye'll never know whit this means… it might no make a' that much difference in the long run… but the day, anywey… I'll be safe fur the day, anywey. Cheerio, Norrie. You're a kind boy.

ALEX *goes.*

   NORRIE *sits for a long moment before picking up his comic and starting to read and eat again.*

Act Two

NORRIE *has finished eating and is now roaming around the shop. He has a crack at* CHARLIE'S *weight, but can't budge it. He swings on a thick rafter that juts out from the wall, then, spotting an old loft high up on the side wall, he climbs up into it to see what's there.*

Just then, the ROUGER *comes down the stair carrying his bike, and puts it down.*

ROUGER Anybody here? Wherr are ye, teuchter? Come oot, come oot, we're sellin fruit!

NORRIE *peeps out from the loft, but doesn't answer. The* ROUGER *looks around the shop and decides he's alone. He, too, goes to* CHARLIE'S *weight and has a go, but can't lift it more than shoulder-high.* NORRIE *watches.*

ROUGER Bastart! Five an' a half feet o fuck-all, an' he pits this thing up like a bag o straw. By Christ, ah ever see him oot the road, ah'll burn him, ah'll burn him down tae the rim o his jacksie.

The ROUGER *tries the weight again, but with no more success. He lets it drop on to the floor, and the noise is followed quickly by a rattle at the back door. The* ROUGER *goes through to answer it.* NORRIE *stays aloft.* NANCY'S *voice is heard, off.*

NANCY Charlie here?
ROUGER No the noo. Come on in.
NANCY No if he's no here.
ROUGER 'S a'right, he'll be in a minute.
NANCY Jist tell him ah wis here, eh?
ROUGER Tellin ye straight, he'll be back in a shake. Come on in. Nothin' tae be feart o.
NANCY A'right, ah'm comin, but you keep yur distance, ye hear?
ROUGER Sure, sure. Jist fixin the bike.

NANCY *appears. She is wary of the* ROUGER, *who is slamming the back door and throwing the bolt.*

NANCY Whit's a' the security fur? Leave that back door open.
ROUGER Ah'm no botherin ye. Ye want tae open the door, naebody stoppin ye.
NANCY You'll no be stoppin me anywey an' chance it.
ROUGER That's whit ah'm sayin', int it?
NANCY Jist mind it.
ROUGER You got somethin' against me? *(He goes to his bike and fiddles about.)*

NANCY   Whit d'ye mean?

ROUGER   Ye're comin on as if ah wis gaun tae dive ye or somethin'. Ye hardly know me.

NANCY   Ah know ye a'right. Ah widnae trust you wi a deid cat.

ROUGER   How dae you know aboot me – Charlie been wisin ye up on the shop gossip?

NANCY   Ah jist know, that's a'.

ROUGER   Oh, ah've heard o them, but ah didnae think we had wan o them in here.

NANCY   Wan o whit?

ROUGER   The kind that run tae their mammies or their birds or their wives. 'See whit a bad boy Rouger is – see whit a good boy, me.'

NANCY   Say that in front o Charlie.

ROUGER   You that implied it, no me.

NANCY   Ah'll tell him – see who's smilin then.

ROUGER   Ah don't know whit you're losin the brow fur. You pit the needle intae me, ah stick it back. Nothin' wrang wi that.

NANCY   Ah'm balin out o here.

ROUGER   Suit yursel'. Go or stey, ah'm no botherin ye.

NANCY   Ye mind opening that door then?

ROUGER   Ah don't mind. Jist gie's a minute, an' ah'll open it.

There is a moment of truce. NANCY *looks around the place. She is keenly aware of the* ROUGER, *and not entirely disenchanted.*

NANCY   How can ye work in a place like this?

ROUGER   It's no that bad.

NANCY   It's a dump. Places like this should be demolished.

ROUGER   Maist o them are, but we're still here.

NANCY   Ah widnae work here if ye gave me a mink Rolls-Royce.

ROUGER   Ye'll be gettin that any day noo. Ah mean, when you an' Charlie walk down the aisle.

NANCY   Oh aye, that'll be the day.

ROUGER   Ye no set the date yet?

NANCY   I think the calendar's stopped.

ROUGER   Whit, ye mean tae say Charlie's no sweatin tae get ye signed up?

NANCY   You ask too many questions.

ROUGER   Nae offence. Jist thought ye wanted tae air yur feelins.

NANCY   Aye, but ah don't want tae broadcast them.

ROUGER   Right. Ah heard nothin. Well, that's that. Wull ah open the door fur ye then?

NANCY   Ye in a hurry tae see me aff noo?

ROUGER   Naw, naw. Ah like talkin tae ye. In fact ah like you.

NANCY   Save it, Santy. How can you like me, ye don't even know me?

ROUGER   Well, the cat can look up the queen's drawers, can't it?

NANCY   That's enough! Excuse me!

ROUGER   It's jist a wey o speakin. Ah've seen ye stacks o times, an' in ma ain wey ah've liked ye. Havenae said much tae ye, but then ah don't know wherr ah stand, dae ah?

NANCY   Ye stand wherr ye've always stood, big-yin, right oot in the rain.

ROUGER   That's no exactly fair, is it? Ah mean, fur a' you know, ah could be wan o the nicest fullas in the city.

NANCY   Ah'll never know anythin' aboot that.

ROUGER   Up tae you. Wer ye supposed tae see Charlie?

NANCY   Aye. Said he'd see me at the front o the work at a quarter past.

ROUGER   He must have left late. He sometimes dis a bit o trainin wi the weight therr. Maybe he forgot.

NANCY   Trainin fur whit? The Possilpark Olympics?

ROUGER   Gettin his strength up. Ah mean, a lovely girl like you.

NANCY   Flattery'll get ye nowhere.

ROUGER   Naw, genuine. Ah think you're a lovely girl.

NANCY   The compliments are bowlin me over.

ROUGER   Ah mean it. Terrific body, smashin face, the lot.

NANCY   Don't let *him* hear ye sayin that.

ROUGER   He'll never hear it unless you tell him.

NANCY   You're dead crafty, aren't ye?

ROUGER   Strike me dead, ah mean it, genuine. If ah wis Charlie, you'd be right up on the old pedastal fur ma money.

NANCY   Ah used tae think you wer a dead-head. Gettin quite romantic in yur ould age.

ROUGER   I'll say it again, you don't know me, Nancy. Sit doon a minute, an' if ye'll no fly off the handle, I'll tell ye whit ah think.

NANCY *sits, takes out a cigarette, and lights it.*

NANCY   Fag?

ROUGER   Don't use them. Savin ma strength fur the big event.

NANCY   D'ye think it'll be worth it when the time comes?

ROUGER   No swankin now. If you were ma bird, ah wid look efter ye in a wey Charlie disnae, I don't think.

NANCY   Didnae know ye told fortunes.

ROUGER   See a fulla day in, day out. Jerkin that bar therr ower his nut a hunner times a session disnae mean tae say he's got confidence in the right places.

NANCY   You're daein the talkin.

ROUGER   Ye can tell me if ah'm wrang, but ah believe the strong-man stuff is strictly fur the onlookers. Whit's he like in the heat o the moment, when the defences are down, or when anythin' else is down, fur that matter? Noo don't get the spur. Has he ever set the brush on fire? In the clinch, ah mean?

NANCY   You'd like tae know, widn't ye?

ROUGER   Naw, but you should know. You should know the difference. Four year ye've been waitin, haven't ye? Waitin fur the man behind the muscle tae give ye a charge. Jist wance.

NANCY   Whit ye gettin at?

ROUGER   It's simple. He blouters hissel' intae a trance, breakin tissue, buildin the frame, an' for what? Another night when he leaves ye like a cauld pie on the doorstep.

NANCY   Mebbie ah'm not that kinda girl.

ROUGER   Ye are, Nancy, ye are. You're just waitin for the moment. It might come in a wey that wid surprise ye.

NANCY   Like when?

ROUGER   Let me pit it tae ye this wey. Charlie's a champ fae the finger-nails up. Ah'm like steel fae the waist doon. Ah've got power therr, Nancy. That machine ower therr, that bike, has built me some-thin' you couldnae imagine in yur wildest fantasy.

NANCY   Ah think it's time ah wis leavin.

ROUGER   Jist hing on for a minute, Nancy. Jist a couple o shakes, an' let me state ma case, and if you fancy it, prove it.

NANCY   The men'll soon be here.

ROUGER   We've jist got time. You said you've nothin' against me. Jist you let me take care o you for a minute, an' ah'll have somethin' lovely against you.

NANCY *is almost mesmerised. The* ROUGER *slips his arms around her and half-presses her on to the bench. She is hooked. His hands engulf her, and she almost succumbs then.*

NANCY   No here! For God's sake, no here!

ROUGER   Ower here, then. The straw – a lovely bed for a lovely deed, hen. Come on, don't draw back now. I'll take care o ye, Nancy, that's it, that's it. Ye'll be a'right wi me.

NANCY *allows herself to be led to the straw. The* ROUGER *is a snake-pit of fumbles. Partially out of sight, they seem to be at the moment of her undoing, when suddenly she looks up, catches sight of* NORRIE, *who has been watching fascinated, and screams, 'Who's that up there?' The pair scramble to their feet,* NANCY *pulling up her drawers, the* ROUGER *buttoning up in a fury of frustration.* NANCY *flies to the back door and disappears. The* ROUGER *spots* NORRIE.

ROUGER   Ya knee-crept, Jesus-crept, swatchin little fucker, ah'll cut the bliddy scrotum aff ye! Ah'll knacker an' gut ye, ah'll eviscerate ye! Ya hure-spun, bastrified, conscrapulated young prick, ah'll do twenty year fur mincin you. Ye hear me? Ah'll rip ye fae the gullet tae the groin, ah'll incinerate ye! Ah had her – right therr – ah had her, spread-eagled, waitin fur the knife – an' you blew it. You blew the chance o pittin wan in her, an' wan on Charlie. He's never had her, but ah wid have had her. Another minute, ah wid have scored where he's never scored, an' you shankered it, ya parish-eyed, perishin bastart. Well, whit she didnae get, you'll get. Come doon here, come doon ah'm tellin ye, ah'll pit a shot in your arse that'll feel like thunder. Come doon, ah tell ye, or are ye gaun tae stey up?

NORRIE   Ah'm feart tae stey up, but ah'm feart tae come doon.

ROUGER   You better, young-yin. Ye see this culet? Ah'll make a bayonet o this an' come up therr an' get ye. Ah'll stow ye in the rubbish, an' the rats'll guzzle whit's left o ye. Ah'm comin up!

NORRIE   Naw, don't, don't, Rouger, ah'm comin doon. Don't touch us, eh, don't touch us. Ah never meant tae watch ye, honest, ah'll no say anythin'. *(He drops to the floor.)*

ROUGER   *(grabbing him)*   By Christ, ye'll no say anythin', or ah'll tell them a' ah blocked ye 'cause ye wanted it. Ah'll dae that anywey. *(He begins hauling NORRIE towards the straw.)*

NORRIE   Lea's alane, ya dirty pig. Ah'll tell Charlie when he comes doon that sterr.

ROUGER   Ye'll whit? Ye'll no live that long! Ah'll hiv you stuffed an' parcelled in a coupla shakes.

LESLIE   *(off)*   Whit the hell's the row down there?

The ROUGER *lets go of* NORRIE *and moves to the bottom of the stair, blocking the way out.*

ROUGER   Nothing, Leslie, nothing. Jist a bit o kiddin.

LESLIE   *(off)*   That's a terrible noise. Sounds like a bad day at Hampden. No more of it, now.

ROUGER   Yes, Leslie. Right ye are.

LESLIE   *(off)*   See to it, then.

ROUGER   *(moving towards NORRIE)*   Whit wis that you said aboot Charlie?

NORRIE   Said ah widnae tell him.

ROUGER   Or any o the others?

NORRIE   Them either.

ROUGER   Right. Ah'll gie ye another chance. You say nothin' tae anybody, specially Charlie, an' ah'll let ye aff this time.

NORRIE   Too true you'll fuckin let me aff, 'cause Charlie widnae let you aff.

ROUGER   Noo, don't needle me. Say nothin', we'll forget the haill thing. But you tell him, an' ah'm no kiddin, ah'll take a cuttin oot the culet box, an' they'll be stitchin you for ever.

NORRIE   Ye don't think ah'll be staunin here waitin fur it, dae ye?

ROUGER   Ye mean ye'll be takin a powder?

NORRIE   Ah'll no' be loiterin.

ROUGER   An' whit wid ye say before ye go?

NORRIE   Ah widnae be wastin time.

ROUGER   Ha-ha, by Jeez, ah pit the wind up ye therr, didn't ah? Ye don't think ah mean a' that, dae ye?

NORRIE   Bliddy sure ye did.

ROUGER   Not at all. Whit ye take me fur? Ye heard me tellin Leslie it wis jist a bit o kiddin. That's a' it wis.

NORRIE   Widnae be kiddin if Charlie got tae hear aboot it.

ROUGER   Ah now, Norrie, ye cannae blame me therr, eh? Every man fur hissel', when it comes tae that. Ah mean, Nancy's quite a doll, isn't she?

NORRIE   Well, you leave me alane, an' ah'll be sayin nothin'. Nane o ma business anywey.

ROUGER   That's you screwin the nut now. We'll jist keep Charlie oot o this, 'cause if you open your mouth… ah'll get tae ye quick, believe it.

NORRIE   Jist keep yur hauns aff me.

ROUGER   Sure, sure. Peace an' love, eh?

NORRIE   Piece an' fuckin jam.

ROUGER   Ha-ha… that's good, that. *(The men's voices are heard returning.* BOB *and* PETER *come down first, followed soon afterwards by* JOE.) Remember, no grass. Ye dae, I'll dig you up. New kipper, you.

PETER   Bob, you can take the drawers aff the bookies every day in the week, an' it'll give me pleasure tae stand alongside ye and drink the proceeds.

BOB   If ah make it wance a year ah'm no complainin. Buy ye another pint next year.

PETER   Where'll we a' be then?

BOB   Wi any luck we'll a' be somewhere. No so sure aboot the shop here. It's on its last legs.

PETER   Aye, like the trade.

BOB   Widnae say that, Peter. Maybe no the same class o work as there used tae be, but ther'll always be room fur a good man.

PETER   Well, right now ah havenae got room fur a' that lager. Ah'll away an' pour the totties. 'Oh dropping, dropping, dropping, dropping, hear the pennies fall…'

PETER *goes to the lavatory.* JOE *arrives. The* ROUGER *keeps squinting at* NORRIE.

BOB   Ye enjoy yur piece, Norrie?

NORRIE   No bad.

BOB   Ye no go oot at a'?

NORRIE   Didnae bother.

JOE   The ghost no get ye?

NORRIE   Aye, he wis here.

BOB   Who wis here?

NORRIE   That oul' man.

BOB   Who wis that, then?

NORRIE   Said his name wis Alex. Alex Freer.

ROUGER   Ye didnae tell me that.

NORRIE   Ye never asked us.

BOB   Wis he right in the shop here?

NORRIE   Aye.

ROUGER   Wis he away before ah came in then?

NORRIE   Aye.

ROUGER   Ye sure aboot that?

NORRIE   Well, ye didnae see him here, did ye?

BOB   Christ, dae ye no know if he wis here?

ROUGER   He might have went oot the back… door.

BOB   Ye'd have seen him then, widn't ye? Whit ye gettin intae an uproar fur?

ROUGER   Jist askin.

BOB   Ye sure you're here the noo?

ROUGER   Naw, ah'm up on the rafters, higher an' higher.

PETER *reappears from the lavatory.*

BOB   Hear that, Peter? Ould Alex Freer wis in here, an' the Rouger's no sure
    whether he saw him or no.

PETER   How, wis he invisible?

ROUGER   A'right, forget it. Jist thought he might have slipped away as ah came in.

BOB   Whit's up wi you?

ROUGER   Nothin'. Nothin's up wi' me.

NORRIE   He left a while before the Rouger got here.

PETER   Whit wis he wantin'?

NORRIE   He wis lookin fur you an' Bob.

PETER   Whit d'ye tell him?

NORRIE   Said yez wer doon in the pub.

PETER   That should have been enough tae sen' him gallopin.

NORRIE   He wis kinna shaky.

BOB   Ye mean he wisnae chasin us up tae the boozer when he left here?

NORRIE   Ah'm no sure.

PETER   Did he no put the tap on ye fur the price o a gill?

NORRIE   Naw, but ah gave him a dollar anywey.

JOE   Ye mean the dollar Bob gave ye, ye bunged that oul' stumor?

NORRIE   Ah suppose it wis.

JOE   That's a good yin, eh. First day here he carries the gaffer's stash, then throws
    away the dollar he gets bunged fur it.

NORRIE   Didnae mean it that wey. Jist felt sorry fur the man.

JOE   Whit ye make o that Rouger?

ROUGER   Very ungrateful boy, that. Devious-like.

NORRIE   Aye, like some other people no a mile away fae here.

BOB   Ach, whit's the odds? His dollar, wisn't it? Alex Freer look bad?

NORRIE   He wis sick.

BOB   He'll no get better. Hey, that whistle hasnae went. Time we were started.

CHARLIE *runs down the stair in a fury.*

PETER   See any sign o ould Alex in yur travels, Charlie?

CHARLIE   Saw naebody – naebody – nutt anybody!

CHARLIE *slings his jacket and goes to the weight. He lifts it straight up six times and then lets it fall with a smash. The men cringe and go to their wheels, starting up one by one.*

BOB   Whit's eatin ye, Charlie?

CHARLIE   Forty-five minutes ah stood on that corner. Not a sign, not a whiff. By Jeez, she'll wait fur me, ah'm tellin ye.

ROUGER *(on hot cinders, watching* NORRIE)   Nancy no show up, or somethin'?

CHARLIE   That's right – or somethin'. I'm staunin therr like a motion-less pump... forty-five... fuckin minutes...

ROUGER   Ye must be angry, Charlie, no often we hear you swearin.

CHARLIE   Yeh. By Christ ah'm angry, ah'll... ah'll... *(He goes to the weight again and snatches it overhead.)*

BOB   Aw naw, Charlie, naw. Ye'll hav us a' in the nut-hoose if ye drap that thing again. (CHARLIE *smashes it down.)* That's the grand bastart finale, Charlie Weir! Noo ah don't give a shite if Nancy's running ye shammy-leggit, you're in here tae work, so leave the bleedin heart ootside an' start graftin, an' get that bliddy earthshaker oot o here fur wance an' fur a'. Nine shell-shocked, pile-drivin bliddy year we've had o it, so finish now, finish! Ye get it oot o' here... ah don't care how ye dae it – ye can stuff it in yur back pocket or ram it up yur nose, but oot it goes... Friday at the latest.

ROUGER   That's short notice you're giving him, Bob.

CHARLIE *is not sure where he is. He blinks and gets to work.*

BOB   You get tae yur work, plaster arse. Noo listen, everybody, we get a' the odds and ends an' rush jobs cleared up before we start on the big job this efternoon. Get stuck intae it, now. Norrie, ye got plenty o pomas therr?

NORRIE   Aye.

BOB   Right, where's that oul' mirror nou?

ALL *work for a short spell during which the grinder screeches its loudest, and then goes quiet as* PETER *approaches* BOB.

PETER   Eh Bob, ah'm sorry tae bother ye. Ah should have noticed it before, but the grinder's pretty faur worn doon. Ah don't know if there's enough left in it tae see the big job through.

BOB   That's a' we need. Ah wish tae hell ye had seen that before, Peter. Nae time tae set a new wheel in noo.

PETER   Naw.

BOB   That's a problem right enough. Any suggestions?

PETER No unless we use the ould mill tae we get a new wheel on. It wid be the day efter the morra before the new yin wid be right fur a job like that.

BOB Nothin' left in that wheel therr at a'?

PETER Oh aye, but it might no be enough. Might be doon tae the metal before we knew it.

BOB We'll have a look at it. Norrie, you run up the sterr an' tell Leslie ah wid like tae see him. Let him come doon here fur a change. (NORRIE *goes off upstairs.* BOB *and* PETER *go to the grinder.*) ...Ah don't think that's too bad, Peter. I think it'll jist last. Whit d'ye say yoursel'?

PETER It could last, mebbie. On the other hand, ye know how it goes. Wan minute ye've got a grinder, the next minute you're through tae the wheel.

BOB Ah wid chance it anywey. But jist in case, we'll get the boys tae sieve some saun fur the oul' mill. Hey, Joe, when Norrie comes doon, start gettin' a wee load o saun ower here an' sieve it. Peter, have a look at the belts and see they're a'right. Well, come on, Joe, get crackin.

JOE Whit, sievin saun?

BOB Aye, sievin saun, whit d'ye think?

JOE It's two year since ah sieved saun – ah don't know if ah can dae it noo.

BOB Oh aye, ye'll have forgot the intricacies. Ye cairry saun tae the mill and run it wet through the sieve. That's a hell of a lot tae forget, right enough.

JOE That's no ma job any mair, Bob. Ah'm bevellin noo.

BOB We're a' bevellin! You've done the job before, so show the boy, an' if it ever needs done again, he'll dae it. Get the pails ready, he'll cairry some fur ye.

JOE Ah hate sievin saun.

BOB Ye'll hate gettin a kick in the arse if ah land ye wan. Whit d'ye make o it? Open bliddy rebellion fae the junior staff. If there wis a war on they wid take ye oot in a Mexican hat an' shoot ye. (NORRIE *returns down the stair.*) Whit kept ye?

NORRIE He wis on the phone. He says you've tae go up.

BOB Whit – ye mean tae say he couldnae even... right! Ah'll go up an' ah'll tell him a few things. Jist wance, ye want a wee conference wi the heid o the hoose an' whit happens? He'll no even come hauf wey tae meet ye. *(He starts to mount the stair.)*

NORRIE Yur apron, Bob.

BOB Ach, bugger the apron. You get wi Joe an' learn how tae sieve saun.

NORRIE Whit's a sieve?

BOB Oh by Jeez, ah've heard everythin' noo. Whit's a sieve? Ah'll away up before ma arteries start tae chuck it.

BOB *goes off upstairs.*

JOE Right you! See if ye can cairry a pailful o saun.

NORRIE Ah'll go pail fur pail wi you anytime an' chance it.

JOE Ye should be daein' it by yursel'. No ma' job noo.

NORRIE Ah'll hiv tae learn it first, win't ah?

JOE   Imagine, never heard o a sieve before.

NORRIE   Ah'm waitin fur you tae tell me.

JOE   Rouger, this yin disnae know whit a sieve is.

ROUGER   Oh, riddle me ree, wan two three, up Mick's arse in the breweree.

NORRIE   Thanks fur wisin us up.

ROUGER   Ah said it, didn't ah? Riddle me ree, riddle, riddle, riddle. Never heard o' a riddle? An' ah don't mean a conundorum. The other kind.

NORRIE   Wan o these roun' things?

ROUGER   That's right – wi the meat safe in the end o it.

JOE   Now ye know – so full up two pails an' carry them ower.

NORRIE *fills the pails. They are heavy, and he doesn't find it easy.* JOE *has taken his load out of sight beyond the grinder.*

PETER   That's the stuff, young fulla. Pit muscles on ye, that.

NORRIE   Aye, a' we need's the ankle-chains.

JOE *returns for more sand.*

JOE   Moanin already. Instant greetin-face. Wan load o saun, an' he's knackered.

NORRIE   You lay affa me. I might be out ma class wi everybody else in here, but ah'll give you a run fur it any time ye fancy it.

JOE   Mebbie ah fancy it right now. (NORRIE *drops the sand,* JOE *is a fraction unsure. Just then,* BOB *comes down.)* ...Ah'll see you later.

PETER   Don't let him rummle ye, son. Him an' that Rouger, they're a coupla poe-naggers.

BOB   Some game this, eh? Ye go up the stair tae ask for a bit o' advice, an' whit dae ye get? 'You're the foreman, Bob, you know the job and what's required, it's your responsibility.' That's the manager fur ye.

PETER   Well, he didnae know hissel', did he?

BOB   You're right. Nearly shat hissel' when ah brought it up. Never mind – hauf-past two or earlier we get on wi the big yin. Ma decision. Much saun ye got through therr?

JOE   Eight pails.

BOB   That'll dae. Start sievin it. Back tae the polisher, Norrie... (*He works for a short spell at the old mirror, then holds it up to the light, and decides it's all right.*) Right, Rouger, ye can take this thing an' gie it a finish. Don't waste too much time on it.

The ROUGER *takes the mirror, and* BOB *lifts another job. Suddenly there's a splintering of glass.*

CHARLIE *turns away from his wheel. He has a bad cut on his left hand.*

CHARLIE   Christ, ah'm wounded! Ah'm goutin like a punctured bliddy pig.

ROUGER *(first to move)* Let us see that. Oh, that's bad, Charlie, very bad. Better get
Leslie tae phone the ambulance.

CHARLIE Naw, nae ambulance, nae hospitals! It's jist across the palm. Ah'll get it
bandaged up in the office.

BOB Right enough, Charlie, it looks gey bad.

CHARLIE It's no too deep, it'll be a'right wi a bandage.

ROUGER Never. That's serious, that. Need's stitchin, ah'm tellin' ye. Good
anaesthetic, ye'll no feel a thing.

CHARLIE Nae hospitals, ah said!

BOB Ah think ye better see a doctor anywey.

CHARLIE Nae doctors! Ah'm seein nae doctors!

ROUGER Ye'll feel nothin', Charlie, honest. They'll clean it oot wi a bit o spirit –
well, that's sore, right enough – an' shove the old needle in, draw it thegither, an'
you're bran' new.

CHARLIE Shurrup, Rouger! Ah'm no gaun anywhere. Ah'm gaun up that sterr an'
get a dressin on it.

BOB Ah'll come wi ye.

CHARLIE Ah'll go masel'. Stey away fae me, everybody.

CHARLIE *goes off upstairs.*

ROUGER Therr goes the hero fur ye. Mister Universe. He wis shitin hissel' sidie-
weys in case he had tae go tae the hospital.

BOB That wis a bad cut.

ROUGER Aye, palm o his hand. Nae merr hair growin therr fur a while, eh?

PETER You're a monster, Matchett. A diabonical, lousy big twat. Your mate cuts
hissel', an' you're crawin. You're an imbecile.

ROUGER Ach, away you an fa' aff the spar.

BOB Peter's right. Everybody's bad luck's your excuse fur laughin.

ROUGER He'll no be slingin that weight o his aboot so handy noo, ah'll wager ye.

BOB That's wherr he's always had ye, isn't it?

ROUGER Had me nothin'. Every man tae his ain exertion. Ah'll be nickin up the
Lochside this weekend at the goin rate fur all good pedallers – somethin' he
knows nothin' about – while he's greetin ower his sore mitt an' soilin his drawers
in case he has tae go tae the doctor. He's knackerless. If he ever gets a hard on,
he'll think it's a fart that's went the wrang wey.

BOB Go an' finish that job.

ROUGER Wan dab, half a jiffy, it's yours.

BOB Whit we gaun tae dae aboot that job if Charlie's oot the game? Widnae like tae
trust Joe as the fourth man.

PETER Charlie might jist manage it.

BOB Very doubtful. Did ye get a look at that cut?

PETER Naw, ah wisnae too keen on a close inspection.

BOB Couldnae tell if it wis really bad or no. Ye know, Peter, it's a while since ah've seen a really bad injury at the job. Ah wis tellin the boy earlier aboot the day a hauf plate came aff the polisher an' caught a man in the back o the leg. He never walked right again.

PETER   That Eddie McCance?

BOB   Aye, did ye know him?

PETER   Heard aboot him up in the Northern Glass.

BOB   Ah believe he finished up therr.

PETER   Nice an' near Lambhill Cemetery.

ROUGER   That's you, no much tae it, as you said. Whit's next?

BOB   Jist use yur eyes. Plenty lyin aboot.

ROUGER   You're the gaffer.

BOB   Come on ower, Norrie. We'll set this back in its frame. Go tae ma inside pocket, an' ye'll find a paper therr – seein these intelligent fullas had the good sense tae set fire tae the ould yin. A'right, noo, hauf a dozen tacks or so, an' it'll be restored tae its former glory. Wee tap wi the hammer and jist bend them over gently. That'll haud it lovely. Jist a wee couple merr an' we'll be home. Therr we go. Mind you, when ye see it in that frame, it's right. Aye, dead right. Ah didnae gie it much o a glance when it came in, but noo ah see it, it's all of a piece. Gless and frame in wan union, quite delicate and nicely balanced. Ah don't know who the oul' fulla wis that set his haun tae the bevellin – an' mebbie he wisnae seein too straight when he did it – but ah can read him – ah can see he wis wan o ma ain kind. As ah said before, he wid take it through a' the stages fae the mill tae the rouger, an' if he earned seven an' tanner fur his day's work, he thought he wis king o the land. When ah look in a gless, Norrie, ah don't jist see masel', ah see the age o the job, the quality, the craftsmanship, and the style. Ah can very near see the face o the man that wis therr before me. Here's Leslie comin wi Charlie.

LESLIE *and* CHARLIE *come down the stairs.* CHARLIE'S *hand is bandaged, and* LESLIE *is carrying a crystal bowl.*

LESLIE   He's not too bad, Bob. Bad enough, you know, but not so bad that he'd have to go to hospital.

BOB   Are ye sayin' that fur Charlie's sake or the sake o the big job therr?

LESLIE   No… eh… the job comes into it, of course, but Charlie says he can manage.

CHARLIE   That's right, ah'll manage.

BOB   Aye, but will ye manage yur corner at the job?

CHARLIE   Ah said ah'll manage. I've still got wan good haun.

BOB   It's no the good haun ah'm worried aboot, it's the other yin.

CHARLIE   This good haun' o mine is better than two o anybody else's in here. An' if anybody didnae hear that, they better flush their ears oot.

BOB   Naebody's questionin yur strength, Charlie, but ye need a coupla hauns for this job.

CHARLIE   Look, wan good haun tae support the board an' the other tae keep ma end steady. Ah'll be fine. Ah'll rest the left yin on tap o the job, an' it'll be dandy.

BOB   A'right, if you say so. It's your haun.

LESLIE   You'll get a start made this afternoon, Bob?

BOB   That's whit ah said, an' that's whit we'll dae. Listen, Leslie, dae us a favour. Tell me whit a' the rush is aboot. I mean, why start the day?

LESLIE   I promised the job for delivery on Thursday. If we don't get on with it today, it'll still be down here on Wednesday. It's got to be up the stair tomorrow afternoon at the latest.

BOB   I wish ye widnae pit us a' on the rack like that, Leslie. Whit's that ye've got wi ye?

LESLIE   Well, actually, Bob, it's a small emergency that just came in.

BOB   Ye don't mean ye want us tae tackle that the noo?

LESLIE   Let me explain, Bob...

BOB   Aw, Jesus Johnnie, Leslie, give us a break.

LESLIE   It's a small crisis, Bob. An old friend brought this in just before Charlie came up the stair.

BOB   Oh aye, upset, wis she?

LESLIE   It wasn't a she, it was a he. And he was upset. Look, see the rim there. There's the tiniest piece out of it. It's a presentation – an office presentation – and by some accident somebody has knocked a small chip out of it.

BOB   They should take it back tae the shop an' say it's a bad yin.

LESLIE   Don't think they haven't tried it. They were chased. Anyway, the presentation's at five o'clock this evening. You know, small office party and a few drinks.

BOB   Oh, that's fine, we'll a' go alang.

LESLIE   Come on, Bob, can you fake this so as the chap will never notice it?

BOB   Let us see it. Where is it? Oh, therr? No much in that. If they cannae get that past him he must have microscopic eyes.

LESLIE   They don't want to take a chance he'd spot it. What do you say, Bob?

BOB   A'right, leave it wi us. Wee touch o the handstone an' the polisher, it'll be bang in front.

LESLIE   Good, good. Then you'll start the big one, eh?

BOB   Ah'd like the boys tae get a drap o tea first.

LESLIE   Sure, sure. But right after that?

BOB   As you say, Leslie, right after that.

LESLIE   Thanks, Bob, I'll leave you to it, then.

LESLIE *goes off upstairs.*

BOB   Ah've said it before, an' ah'll say it again. Skinner by name an' Skinner by nature. Nae wunner ould Alex went on the sauce. Joe, make the tea.

JOE   It's made.

BOB   Thank you, son. Anythin' bad ah've said aboot you the day, Joe, cancel it. You're a good, clever, conscientious boy. Get yur tea, lads, quick as ye can. Peter, a wee touch o the handstone on that crystal. Ah'll smooth it aff on the polisher when you're done.

ALL *get their tea. Distantly a pipe band is heard. It gets nearer, accompanied by the sound of marching feet overhead.*

NORRIE   Whit's that?

PETER   Must be that time o the year again.

ROUGER   Aye, the bastarts.

NORRIE   Is it the army?

ROUGER   No quite, but it could be.

PETER   Happens every year at this time. The Academy boys. The Officers Corps, or whatever they call them. Aff tae the summer camp.

ROUGER   Bunch o ponced-up parasitical twats. Mummies and daddies walking alongside the darling boys to see them off at the station.

NORRIE   Wish ah wis gaun wi them.

ROUGER   You'll never see it. Not if ye had six lifetimes.

The band and procession draw nearer and pass by overhead. ALL *listen quietly until they pass. Then* PETER *hands the bowl over to* BOB, *who touches it very gently on the polisher.*

ROUGER   Naw, naw. You'll never be amongst it, young-yin. They're up there, an' you're doon here, an' even if ye wer grindin yur guts tae get up therr amongst it, next year when they go by you'll still be doon here, like the rest o us.

NORRIE   No me. Ah'll no be here.

ROUGER   No good enough fur ye, 's 'at it?

NORRIE   Didnae say that.

ROUGER   Ye fancy yoursel' up therr wi that mob?

NORRIE   Jist fancy gettin away tae hell oot the road. See a bit o the country.

ROUGER   But ye think ye'd make the grade wi the grandees up therr?

NORRIE   No ma style.

ROUGER   But a' this is no yur style either?

NORRIE   Whit ye talkin aboot? Fae whit ah've heard, you're never done gaun on aboot divin oot the country yursel'.

ROUGER   Aye, but on ma terms. Shovin that bike up the road's a different thing a'thegither fae kiss-my-arse and daddy's bankbook. Whit are *your* terms?

NORRIE   No money anywey. Mebbie a job on a van or somethin'. That oul' man, Alex, wis tellin us tae blow this job and get oot in the fresh air.

ROUGER   Ye listen tae him ye'll end up in Carrick Street Model. Did ye believe him?

NORRIE   Don't know. Made sense the wey he said it.

BOB   Don't think ye fancy this game much, young fulla. *(He gives the bowl a wipe and lays it down.)*

NORRIE   Don't like some o the folk in it.

BOB   It's a hard trade wi crude beginnins. Some o that's bound tae have rubbed aff. We're a wee bit on the rough side. Mebbie as time goes on you'll no notice it so much.

NORRIE   Aye.

BOB   Well come on then, fullas, it's now or never. Yur eye in, Peter?

PETER   Bang on.

BOB   Ye fit, Charlie?

CHARLIE   Yes!

BOB   Right! We'll get stevered intae the big yin therr. Youz young fullas might see another job like that in yur lifetimes again, but it's no' likely. We'll start on the grinder therr, but any sign o the wheel packin in, we transfer tae the ould mill. Right, Peter?

PETER   Right.

BOB   Rouger, you an' Joe bring the big trestle-board through fae the back. We'll lie it up against the job an' jist ease it gently ower tae the horizontal. (JOE *and the* ROUGER *go for the board. It is a large wooden frame of four crossed spars. The men complete the operation of placing the board against the plate and tilting it over to the horizontal.* PETER *goes to the corner which will be nearest the grinder.* BOB *calls instructions to the men.*) Easy, noo, lads. Wan step at a time tae we get used tae it. Jist keep it steady when Peter gets his corner on tae the wheel. The board'll take up the vibration.

Just then, LESLIE *hurries down the stair.*

LESLIE   Hold it, Bob. Hold it, boys.

BOB   Hold it? We've jist got tae hold it. We cannae drap it on the fuckin flerr.

LESLIE   No need to use that language in front of young boys, Bob.

BOB   These young boys have got words we've never even heard o. Whit's the panic?

LESLIE   You didn't forget that bowl, did you?

BOB   Christ, is that a' ye want tae ask? We're staunin here wi this thing in wur hauns, an' you're worryin aboot some stupid article that some half-arsed cowboy'll use for a chanty in the middle o the night.

LESLIE   You don't have to be so crude.

BOB   It's lyin ower therr. Gie it a wipe, an' it'll be champion.

LESLIE   You managed to get the mark out?

BOB   Aye, aye. Noo, will ye kindly take a walk up these sterrs an' leave us in peace?

LESLIE   You might be the foreman here, Bob, but you are talking to the manager.

BOB   The manager that didnae gie me much co-operation when I was askin fur yur ideas a wee while ago. It wis up tae me, ye said. A'right, then, it's up tae me an' ah'll see the job done. Away you an' staun up at the front door an' scratch yur arse. (LESLIE *leaves.*) A'right, noo, mind whit ah said, jist take it easy, an' we'll put a bevel on this thing that ye could hing in a palace. *(The job begins.* NORRIE, *standing by, holds his ears. All seems to be going well when* PETER'S *face begins to tighten, unnoticed by the others. Then he begins to jerk, and the plate flaps wildly.)* Mind the job, fur Christ's sake, mind the job! Joe, grab Peter's end. Norrie, get the haud o Peter an' lie him doon. Ye hear me, Norrie, stir yur arse fur fuck's sake, an' get Peter on tae that low bench. (NORRIE *is rooted and can't move.)* Rouger, leave your end tae Charlie and grab Peter. Don't be rough wi him, noo. That's it, lie him doon. Jist leave him, an' gie's a haun wi this thing. Norrie, ya useless young bugger ye, get oot the road. Right, lads, quick as ye can, get this thing against the wa'. Up she goes, easy, noo. How's Peter? Jist leave him, he'll come oot o it soon. Charlie, ye look as though you're in some bother wi that haun.

CHARLIE   It wis fine tae ah had tae take the full weight o the end.

LESLIE *appears.*

LESLIE   What's going on?

BOB   Ach... Peter took wan o his turns. He's lyin oot on the bench therr.

LESLIE   Is it just the usual or is it worse, do you think?

BOB   How the hell dae ah know, ah'm no a doctor. He looks like he always looks when this comes on him. Have a glance at him yursel'.

LESLIE   No, I'll leave that to you and the men. You've dealt with it before.

BOB   Aye, an' ah suppose we'll deal wi it again the next time it happens.

LESLIE   Is the job all right?

BOB   Oh, that's whit's on yur mind? I knew it couldnae be Peter.

LESLIE   That's unfair, Bob. You know Peter's been kept on here despite his disability.

BOB   An' because ye couldnae get his like anywhere else.

LESLIE   I won't argue with you. I'll be in the office if you need me.

LESLIE *goes.*

BOB   Whit's up wi ye, Norrie? You're staunin therr like a stumor.

NORRIE   He's dead, isn't he?

BOB   Who, Peter? Nat at all.

NORRIE   Ah've only seen wan... I mean... he looks like it.

BOB   Ye'll see him worse than that, mebbie, if you're here long enough.

NORRIE   Ah'll no see him. Ah'm chuckin it.

ROUGER   He's movin a wee bit noo.

CHARLIE   Bob, ye mind if ah go up tae the end o the shop?

BOB   Naw, on ye go, Charlie. Ye'll have tae go tae the hospital wi that thing.

CHARLIE   Aye, we'll see.

ROUGER   Ah don't want tae be around when the likes o that happens again. Ah thought we were a' gaun tae be minced.

BOB   Don't make it any worse than it wis. If it had been an ordinary job it widnae have looked so bad.

ROUGER   Couldnae have been much worse. Leslie's right, he's lucky he's got a job.
BOB   An' this shop's lucky it's got Peter. He's got the best eye o any beveller ah
ever met, tae any fraction you like tae quote. An' he can horse it wi anybody...
he's no feart tae bend his back.
ROUGER   You'll no hear a bad word aboot him, will ye?
BOB   No fae you anywey. You're always tryin tae make oot he's epileptic when
he's no. He's had a' the tests, an' they've told him he's no epileptic, not that it wid
worry me in the least if he wis.
ROUGER   Whit dae you think's up wi him, then?
BOB   Ah don't know. Some kind o tension when he's excited or upset.
ROUGER   Jist as well he's got you fur a china.
BOB   That's right, an' don't you forget it. (PETER *sits up slowly.*) A'right, then,
Peter, how ye feelin?
PETER   Ah? Aye. Whit time is it?
BOB   How ye doin, oul' son? You're gey faur away.
PETER   Ah wis supposed tae meet... this big fulla at the corner... he had a parcel fur
me.
BOB   Sure, sure. Wid ye like a wee drap tea tae clear yur heid? Joe, any merr tea
left?
PETER   Took me a' ma time... ye know... ma fingers were thon funny wey... an'
then...
BOB   Jist slipped away, did it?
PETER   Fell aff the spar. Aw, God love us... that you, Bob?
BOB   Aye.
PETER   Are we late?
BOB   Naw, we're no late, plenty o time.
PETER   We're in the shop?
BOB   That's right.
PETER   That's funny, ah thought...
BOB   Easy, Peter.
PETER   Ah pass out?
BOB   Yes.
PETER   Ah break anythin'?
BOB   Naw, naw. Come on, ah'll take ye tae the back door fur a wee bit air.
PETER   Aye, sure. That big bastart tell me tae fa' aff the spar?
BOB   Ah believe he mentioned it.
PETER   He wis right then, wisn't he? Stuck in ma mind.

BOB *and* PETER *go to the back door.*

JOE   You challenged me a while ago.
NORRIE   Naw, ah didnae.
JOE   Ye said ye fancied yur chances anywey.
NORRIE   Ah wis browned off.

JOE   Ah wisnae needlin ye a' that much.

NORRIE   Naw, but he wis.

ROUGER   Now, mind your mouth, you.

NORRIE   Don't worry, I'm sayin nothin'. A' ah'm waitin fur's the five o'clock whistle an' ah'm jackin it in.

JOE   When, the day?

NORRIE   Aye.

JOE   Less than wan day at the job, an' you're turnin it up already?

NORRIE   Ah'd never be any use at it anyway.

ROUGER   How dae ye know?

NORRIE   Ah jist know.

ROUGER   Like it's a' right fur the common grafters, but no fur the likes o you.

NORRIE   It's nothin' tae dae wi that.

JOE   Ah don't get it. It's a job, int it – it's a trade. Whit'll yur oul'-man say when ye tell him?

NORRIE   He'll say try somethin' else.

ROUGER   Whit wis it finally got ye? Seein Peter, wis it?

NORRIE   Didnae help.

ROUGER   Ah thought that sickened ye. Remind ye o somethin'?

NORRIE   You keep your mouth shut, an' ah'll keep mine.

ROUGER   Ah'm easy.

BOB *comes back with* PETER.

BOB   He's no hissel'. Try a wee drap o that tea, Joe. Take Peter wi ye.

JOE   He said he's leavin the day, Bob.

BOB   Who?

JOE   Him, Norrie.

BOB   'S 'at a fact? Well, ah don't suppose wan boy here or therr'll make any difference tae this trade. *(He goes to the foot of the stair.)* Hey, Leslie, Leslie, ye hear me? Wid ye mind comin tae the heid o the sterr fur a minute, ah want a word wi ye? Take that tea slow, Peter, it'll dae ye good. Ah think ye can pit yur jaicket on, tae. Listen, Leslie, ah think we better a' pack it in fur the day. Charlie's no fit, an' Peter should go hame. Ah'll have tae see him up the road. Nae sense in the rest hingin on. Whit dae ye say?

LESLIE   Hold on, Bob, I was on the phone. I'll have to finish the call and think about it.

BOB   There's nothin' tae think aboot. If me an' Peter are no here, there's nothin' the rest can dae.

LESLIE   I'll finish this call an' blow the whistle. It might take a few minutes.

BOB   Got tae be manager, hisn't he? He'll blaw the whistle, but in his ain time. Can ye manage yur jaicket, Charlie?

CHARLIE   Ah'll be a'right.

BOB *and* CHARLIE *begin preparing to leave.*

NORRIE   Ah'm sorry, Bob. Wisnae you ah meant when a said ah didnae like some o
the folk in here.

BOB   Jist as well ye told me that. Ah widnae have slept the night.

NORRIE   An' ah'm sorry aboot the job. Ah mean leavin.

BOB   Don't apologise tae me. You're no comin tae the trade, so forget it. This time
the morra ah'll have forgotten you. It's nae insult tae me if you don't want tae
work at this job. Ah didnae think ye wid stick it long anyway. That's the wey it
goes. New folk don't want tae come intae the game, an' some o them that are at it
don't give a toss fur it. So save yur apologies. Makes nae odds tae me. How ye
shapin up, Peter?

JOE *and the* ROUGER *have been whispering together and now approach* NORRIE.

ROUGER   Jist wan thing you missed in this job, Mac.

NORRIE   Whit wis that?

ROUGER   Ye didnae get baptised.

The ROUGER *and* JOE *grab* NORRIE *and rush him to the trough, where they shove
his head under the water.* JOE *lets go quite soon; but the* ROUGER, *who has* NORRIE
by the hair, holds him under till he almost passes out. BOB *intervenes.*

BOB   Whit ye daein, Rouger, fur Christ's sake, ye want tae kill the boy?

ROUGER   Jist wettin his heid.

BOB   Ye couldnae let him go, could ye? You had tae get the needle in. Ye might've
droont him, ya bliddy eediot.

ROUGER   Fuck him. He's no wan o us.

BOB   He didnae deserve that, anywey.

The ROUGER *collects his bike and brings it to the foot of the stairs to join the
others.* NORRIE *recovers slowly. The whistle goes.* ALL *begin to leave.*

NORRIE   Hey, Charlie, Nancy wis in here at dinner-time. The Rouger tried tae shag
her.

ALL *stop. There is a long silence.*

BOB   Come on, Peter, ah'll take ye up the road.

BOB *and* PETER *leave.*
   JOE *is merely a bystander.* CHARLIE *considers his hand, but advances slightly
on the* ROUGER.

CHARLIE   Ah'm wan-handed, Rouger, but if whit that boy says is true, ah'll take you, ah'll take you, an' ah'll mash ye intae the slurry.

ROUGER   He's a liar, Charlie. Honest tae God on the old-lady's grave, ah'll give ye ma genuine Bible oath, he's a liar.

CHARLIE   Whit made him say it?

ROUGER   Ah don't know, ah really don't know. He jist couldnae take the kiddin, ah suppose, an' made it up fur badness.

CHARLIE   Ah believe ye. Now, you listen, boy, that's the second time you've raised Nancy's name the day, an' each time ye soiled it.

CHARLIE *punches* NORRIE *in the stomach, and* NORRIE *folds up.* JOE, *the* ROUGER, *and* CHARLIE *go up the stairs.*

NORRIE *lies on the floor gasping in pain. After some time, he gets to his feet and begins weeping deep, hard sobs which come from the pain in his body. He supports himself on the trough, but seems unable to make any kind of decision. At last* LESLIE *comes down the stair.*

LESLIE   What's the matter with you, sonny, have they been giving you a rough time? It sometimes happens with new boys. They haven't really hurt you, have they? That's all right, then. I think you better get up the stair. Where's your jacket? I'll get it for you. This bag belong to you, too? All right, come on then, up you go. Your stomach sore, eh? Ah, you'll be all right. Away home to your mother, and you'll be all right.

Curtain.

The Hardman

by

Tom McGrath

and

Jimmy Boyle

First performed at the Traverse Theatre, Edinburgh,
on 19 May 1977, directed by Peter Lichtenfels

Tom McGrath

Tom McGrath was born in Rutherglen in 1940. He is a playwright, poet and jazz musician. During the 1960s he worked in London, where he was features editor of *Peace News* and a founder editor of *International Times (IT)*. He read his early poetry at the first International Poetry Incarnation at the Albert Hall in 1965 alongside American Beat poets Allen Ginsberg and Gregory Corso. He returned to Scotland in 1969 to study literature and drama at the University of Glasgow. He worked in theatre as a pianist, and from 1974 to 1977 was Director of the Third Eye Arts Centre in Glasgow.

His first play, *Laurel and Hardy,* was staged at the Traverse Theatre in 1976. His second, *The Hardman* (1977), was written in collaboration with Jimmy Boyle, on whose life the play draws. McGrath described the collaborative process, in which he as dramatist shaped the play, in an article in 1977:

> I worked with Jimmy Boyle for several months in the [Special Unit, Barlinnie Prison] to produce *The Hardman.* We discussed his life in detail. Sometimes I would have parts of the developing script to read to him, sometimes he would have scenes for me – pub and cellblock conversations, rich in character and zany underworld language. … Writing the play became a balancing act. Somehow I had to stay close to Jimmy Boyle and let the play express his strong views and his version of the story, yet at the same time I had to cast doubts on all that he has to say. He is a man with a question mark over his head. I had to dramatise that question mark.

Tom McGrath's other plays are *The Android Circuit* (1978), *The Innocent* (1979), *Animal* (1979), *1-2-3* (comprising three plays *Who Are You Anyway, Very Important Business* and *Moondog)* (1981), *Kora* (1986), *Trivial Pursuits* (1988), *The Flitting* (1990), *Buchanan* (1993), *DreamTrain* (1999), and S*afe Delivery* (2000). He adapted Tankred Dorst's two-part *Merlin* (1992 and 1993), and Robert Louis Stevenson's *Kidnapped* (1994), translated *Stones and Ashes* by Daniel Danis (1995), and versionised Sophocles' *Electra* (2000). His youth and community plays are *Sisters* (1978), *The Phone Box* (1984), and *City* (1989). His plays for television include *The Nuclear Family* (1982) and *Blowout* (1983).

For the past ten years he has held the Scottish Arts Council-funded post of Associate Literary Director (Scotland). Based at the Royal Lyceum Theatre in Edinburgh, but having a Scotland-wide remit, his role is to encourage new writing for the stage. In addition to his theatre work, he continues to give poetry readings and to play jazz, most frequently at the Traverse Theatre's Monday Lizard Cabaret.

Jimmy Boyle

Jimmy Boyle was born in Glasgow in 1944. He was sentenced to life imprisonment for murder in 1967 and spent fifteen years in prison. In 1973 he was transferred to the Special Unit, Barlinnie Prison, where he discovered a special talent as a sculptor. He wrote a best-selling autobiography, *A Sense of Freedom* (1977), which was dramatised for television, and *The Pain of Confinement: prison diaries* (1984). Since his release from prison he has combined work for social reform with a successful career as a sculptor. In 1999 he made his debut as a novelist with *Hero of the Underworld*.

Editor's note: The first published edition of the play gave the title in its separated form, *The Hard Man.* Tom McGrath has informed me that the title should be given as one word, *The Hardman,* which is the form used in this edition. He says that the distinction is between the Glasgow expression, 'He thinks he's a real hardman', and the more general, 'a real hard man', where 'hard' can have a different emphasis and meaning.

Characters

BYRNE

SLUGGER
RENFREW

BANDIT
JOHNSTONE

DEADEYE
ARCHIE
KELLY
POLICEMAN
CLERK OF COURT
MOCHAN

BIG DANNY
POLICEMAN
LEWIS THE LAWYER
COMMANDO
PAISLEY

LIZZIE
CAROLE
WOMAN'S VOICE

MAGGIE
MAW
WOMAN *(who's with Archie)*
BARWOMAN
DIDI

PERCUSSIONIST

Act One

Lights come down. Darkness. Fragment of a song:

SONG   Oh the River Clyde's a wonderful sight,
   the name of it thrills me and fills me with pride.
   Oh I'm satisfied whate'er may betide,
   the Sweetest of Songs is the Song of the Clyde.

Lights come up on The Windae-hingers – two women, LIZZIE *and* MAGGIE, *leaning out of their tenement house windows. They have their elbows on the window-ledge and are having a conversation across the street.*

LIZZIE   Hullo, Maggie.

MAGGIE   Hullo there, Lizzie.

LIZZIE   Maggie, where did your man come frae?

MAGGIE   Seymour Street. Ah hear it's getting awfae bad up there. Ah think we just moved oot in time.

LIZZIE   Yir no kiddin. Thir wus a man kilt up thair the other night. The Spaniard. Did you know him?

MAGGIE   Oh aye. McTaggart the Mad Spaniard. Everybody knew him. He wus a right bad loat. Ah might've known he'd come tae a sticky end. Whit happened tae him enyway?

LIZZIE   He wus laying oan the street in Maryhill Road – just ootside the HLI pub fur oors an' oors. We wur oan the buses, oan the night-service, an' we saw him laying there up an' doon fur aboot four journeys. Even from the bus in the dark you could see the blood. They say they put the knife in at the bottom of his stomach and ripped him open.

MAGGIE   Did the polis no dae anythin aboot it?

LIZZIE   Naw. Thae jist let him lie thair. They wur glad tae be rid o him.

MAGGIE   And did they no get anyone fur it?

LIZZIE   They never dae in gang fights, dae they? Oh but see efterwards, when they took the body away, we passed back doon oan the bus an aw you could see wus the chalk marks and the blood. And the Spaniard wusnae thair anymair...

Lights down. Windae-hingers withdraw.

BYRNE, SLUGGER *and* BANDIT *rush on the stage in a state of alarm, looking behind them. They are obviously being pursued.* BYRNE *is alert but not afraid. They have stopped for a moment, breathless, looking back.*

BANDIT   Oh my God! Oh... my... God!

BYRNE   *(annoyed)*   Whit's the matter wae yae?

BANDIT   Whit dae you think?

SLUGGER   Aye. Naebody sed enythin aboot fuckin murder…

BYRNE   Ah didnae touch that mug.

BANDIT   No half yae didnae!

BYRNE   Listen, Bandit. You were in another room when it happened – enjoying the party – you never saw nothing. Same goes fur you, Slugger. You saw nothing neither. That mob will try tae put the finger oan me fur it, but ah didnae touch him. Huv you goat me?

SLUGGER   Goat yae.

BANDIT   *(more reluctantly)*   Goat yae.

BYRNE   *(smiling, extending his open palm)*   Right! Put it there, chinas! We're aw in it thegither! *(They both slap his outstretched palm with their hands and say their line.)*

BANDIT   *(slapping)*   We're aw in it thegither!

SLUGGER   *(slapping)*   We're aw in it thegither!

BYRNE   Okay. Let's scarper. Different directions.

SLUGGER   See you doon the boozer.

BYRNE   Aye, in aboot an oor's time. But go tae the other boozer, no the usual wan. They'll be looking fur us there…

Exit BANDIT *and* SLUGGER. *Light change.* BYRNE *steps forward, looking around the audience.*

My name is Byrne. Johnnie Byrne. I was born in the Gorbals District of Glasgow. You've read about me in the newspapers and heard about me in pubs. I'm a lunatic. A right bad lot. What the Judge always calls, 'A menace to society'. I'm speaking to you tonight from a Scottish prison where I am serving life-sentence for murder. What you are going to see is my life as I remember it. What you are going to hear is my version of the story.

SLUGGER *and* BANDIT *run on shouting.*

SLUGGER   Rats.

BANDIT   Chasin' rats.

SLUGGER   Chasin' rats roon the backs.

BANDIT   Chasin' rats roon the backs wae a wee dug…

SLUGGER   Chasin' rats roon the backs wae a wee dug that wus rerr ut brekkin their necks.

BANDIT   It even goat a mention in the papers that wee dug, because it kilt that many rats.

SLUGGER   Hiya, Johnny.

BYRNE   Hiya, Slugger. Hiya, Bandit. Back tae school again… *(This line by way of explanation to audience.)*

SLUGGER   School! School! Back tae school. Ah hate a Monday.

BANDIT   Ah hate the fuckin' school. School's rubbish!

SLUGGER   Aye, whit's it aw aboot anyway? Who wants to learn aw that shite they teach yae?

BYRNE   You're that stupit, yae couldnae learn anythin anyway, even if yae wahntit tae.

SLUGGER   Listen to who's talkin. The teacher says you're a dead cert fur truble. He's goat you marked doon fur the Borstal already.

BYRNE   Fuck 'im.

BANDIT   Fancy doggin' it?

SLUGGER   Aye. Fancy it? We could go doon the shoaps an' dae some knockin'. Fancy it, Johnny?

BYRNE   Och, I don't know. We did that yesterday – and the day before. Ah think we're just wastin' oor time. Bars a chocolate an' boatles o scoosh. Ah wis aboot sick yesterday wae the amount ah ate.

BANDIT   Well, you were the wan that insistit oan goin' back tae the shoap an daein' it agen.

BYRNE   That wis just because ah wus bored. There's no much fun tae it wance you've done it a few times. An' enyway, it's no bars o choclate we need, it's money!

SLUGGER   Back tae that agen.

BANDIT   You bet your life it's back tae that. Money. Lolly. Cash. It aw comes back tae that sooner or later, doesn't it?

BYRNE   Aye, well you know how we were talkin aboot daein a few shoaps at night?

BOTH   Aye.

BYRNE   An' we were tryin tae figure oot how we wid dae the loaks?

BOTH   Aye.

BYRNE   Well, I've been thinking…

BOTH   Miracles!

BYRNE   During the day, when they close up the shop for a coupla hours tae go hame an' huv a bit tae eat an' a wee snooze, maybe a pint doon ut the boozers… they cannae be bothered pittin aw thae loaks oan… it's no worth it fur the shoart time thair oot… and enyway, they know that thieves only wurk ut night… *(He smiles at them. They think about this.)* …So… if we go during the day…

SLUGGER   Goat ye.

BANDIT   Ya beauty.

BYRNE   So whit ur we waitin fur? Cumoan. *(To audience:)* I can't tell you about my chromosomes or genetic structure and I can't say anything about my Oedipus Complex or my Ego and my Id. Battered babies grow up to be people who batter babies. But I got nothing but affection when I was young – from my mother. My father – sometimes we wouldn't see him for days on end then he'd come home triumphant wae presents for everybody and half-bottle ofwhisky in his back pocket.

One night he came home, lifted me up to the window, and said – 'Look down there, son. What do you see?' I saw a brand new, shining motorcar. 'It's all yours,' he said. 'Tomorrow we'll go fur a hurl in it.' The next day I got up and looked out of the window. But the car was gone. And so was my father. And I never saw him again.

I remember my brothers and I at the funeral. There were four of us and we were sitting round the coffin, giggling. We wouldn't have laughed if we'd known what was coming.

SLUGGER *and* BANDIT *run on, pretending to be kids in the street teasing* BYRNE.

SLUGGER   Poorhoose! Poorhoose!

BANDIT   Look ut the Byrnes wae thir big broon suits an their tackety boots. Poorhoose! Poorhoose!

BYRNE   Him an' his brothers sleep four tae a bed!

BANDIT   Poorhoose! Poorhoose!

SLUGGER   *(he and* BANDIT *are exiting as* MOTHER *enters)*   Their mammy's a skivvy fur the West End toafs.

BOTH   *(exiting)*   Poorhoose! Poorhoose!

BYRNE *and his* MOTHER.

BYRNE   Hey Maw. Gonnae lend me half a knicker?

MAW   How? Where are you goin?

BYRNE   Ah'm goin oot wae the boys.

MAW   Where ti? Ah hope you're no going galavantin aw o'er the place and gettin intae trouble an' hiven the polis up at this door?

BYRNE   Ah'm no goin anywhere. Ah just want the money fur the pictures.

MAW   Ah've no goat that much. Here's a dollar, that'll huv tae dae yi. Be in here sharp the night. Ah've tae get up at five the morn.

BYRNE   You know ah'm always in early, Maw.

MAW   Aye. That'll be right. Aw ah know is yir always bringin the polis tae the door and givin that auld nosey bastard across the road somethin' tae talk about.

BYRNE   Don't worry aboot hur, Maw. She's been gossipping oot hur windae so long she's left hur diddie-marks oan the windae sill.

Exit BYRNE.

MAW   Right you. That's enough. Watch yir tongue. Mind and be in here early and nae fighting nor cerryin oan. *(To audience:)* Och, he wusnae a bad boy really. It wus the company he kept. Ah could never believe aw the bad things people said aboot him, no even after he went tae prison. He wus ma son and he wus never any boather tae me. Ah mean, whit chance did he huv? He went alang tae the youth club an him an his mates were barred the very first night. Troublemakers! They were the very wans that needed some help. When he was younger, he wantit tae be an altar boy. But he wusnae allowed because he didnae huv any sandshoes –

and ah couldnae afford tae buy him any. It wus oanly the toaffs that could afford tae kneel oan God's altar. Of course, toaffs tae us wur the people that lived jist up the street. In those days the television wus a new thing and it wus a great sign of wealth if yae hud a telly. We wur lucky if we hud enough tae keep us in food from day to day, nae wonder the boy turned tae thievin. He used tae come home wae presents fur me – things fur the hoose an' sometimes even a bit of money – and he'd pretend he'd worked fur thaim. Ah knew how he'd come by them and ah didnae like it and sometimes ah wid refuse his gifts. But maist o the time ah accepted – ah hud no option.

SLUGGER *and* BANDIT *run on to the stage.* MAW *exits behind them.*

SLUGGER   Nylons.
BANDIT   Bevvy.
SLUGGER   Trannies.
BANDIT   Dresses. We supplied the loat.
SLUGGER   The people couldnae afford tae buy things frae the shoaps—
BANDIT   It was a social service. *(Pointing to himself.)* To our society at any rate. It aw depends which side o the fence yir oan, doesn't it? Presents fur Christmas, a boatle fur Ne'erday, the orders wur always placed wae us. And Johnny Byrne became a popular young man about the Gorbals – a contact much sought after.
SLUGGER   While we made a foartune. Well, no much o a fortune but enough to keep us going for a while. For, after all, we were growing boys...

Enter DEADEYE *and* BYRNE *from opposite sides of the stage. They walk straight into next scene which includes* BANDIT *and* SLUGGER. DEADEYE *speaks through his nose.*

DEADEYE   Hello there, Johnny. Hiya, boys.
BOYS *(together)*   Hiya, Deadeye!

They do this greeting in style but DEADEYE *is intent on his business with* BYRNE. *He is a small man in his forties. He goes straight to the point.*

DEADEYE   Listen, Johnny, ah blagged some shirts there. Dae yae want tae buy any?
BYRNE   Let me see whit like they ur.
DEADEYE   Look at that. The best o' swag, Johnny, an' thair a real bargain so they urr.
BYRNE   How many huv yae goat?
DEADEYE   A gross. And ah'm puntin thaim cheap at a knicker each.
BYRNE   Och, cumon, Deadeye. Yir no trying tae punt thaim tae me at that price.
DEADEYE   Whit dae yae want? Dae yae want me tae throw thaim away? Ye'll no get shurts like that in the shoaps fur under a fiver.
BYRNE   Ah tell yae what, Deadeye. I'll give you half a knicker each fur thaim an'...

DEADEYE   Naw, naw…

BYRNE   …an' ah'll take the loat.

DEADEYE   The loat? A hale gross. You wid never get rid o them.

BYRNE   Let me worry aboot that. You take care o your end and ah'll take care of mine. Where ur the shurts? Doon ut the hoose? Right, Slugger, you go wae the wee yin an' pick up the rest o thaim. Ah'll settle up wae yae later, Deadeye. *(Exit* DEADEYE *and* SLUGGER. SLUGGER *gently persuading* DEADEYE *on his way,* DEADEYE *a bit bemused by it all.)* You take these doon tae Isaac the tailor and tell him he cun huv a groass o thaim ut Thirty Boab each.

BANDIT   Right-oh, Johnny.

Takes shirts and exits. BYRNE *left alone on stage.*

BYRNE   So we'd progressed. We'd started at the age of five, going round the doors collecting firewood and empty bottles, it was only a tiny step to stealing bars of chocolate, and a tiny step further to breaking locks and squeezing through windows. By this time I'd already done an Approved School stretch – for breaking into bubble gum machines, and I was beginning to get a sense of the way things are stacked. I cried my eyes out the night they took me away, pleaded with them and promised I would never do it again – it had only been a joke and I didn't feel I had done anything wrong but it was too late—

SLUGGER *and* BANDIT *have re-entered.*

SLUGGER   Alright, Byrne, stop dreaming. Strip. Wash. Scrub this in your hair, you little heap of vermin – grab hold of that bucket and SCRUB THAT FLOOR!

BYRNE   But I scrubbed it yesterday and the day before.

SLUGGER   Well, scrub it again.

BANDIT   And don't but me, sonny, you're going to have to learn!

SLUGGER   That floor has been scrubbed a thousand times by boys like you down the years, and it'll be scrubbed a thousand times more, because, you know, it's not the scrubbing that counts, not the sparkle off the floor, no it's the lesson you learn while you're scrubbing.

BANDIT   And do you know what that is, Byrne? Or dae yae want us tae tell yae?

SLUGGER   Respect! Respect fur authority!

BANDIT   That's right. Respect fur authority. Authority. *(Brandishes cane.)* Authority.

They are circling him, threateningly. BANDIT *has a cane. He becomes increasingly aroused.*

SLUGGER   Authority and Private Property. *(Irish accent. Mimics priest. Makes blessing in the air.)* Blessed be Private Property Now and Forever Amen.

BANDIT   *(Almost diabolic. Thrashing with the cane in rhythm to the words.)*

Whack Whack Whack
On Your Bare Backside.
Just to make sure
You Don't Try it Again.

Gives a final whack and stands back. Breathless. Wipes his brow. SLUGGER *takes on a mock air of schoolteacher. Produces a tawse from within his jacket and flexes it.* BYRNE *remains cowering back, his hands up to protect himself.* SLUGGER *speaks straight to the audience.*

SLUGGER   Personally I prefer the tawse to the cane – flesh against flesh, it seems more humane.

BYRNE *stands up slowly, with the bucket in his hand, carefully considering* SLUGGER *who is giving the audience a demonstration of how to use the tawse.* BYRNE *lifts the bucket and empties it over* SLUGGER'S *head. Slow blackout on* SLUGGER *dancing in rage with bucket on his head –* BYRNE *and* BANDIT *doubled up, laughing.*
   Lights come back up on the Windae-hingers, MAGGIE *and* LIZZIE.

MAGGIE   Howurr things, Lizzie?
LIZZIE   No bad. They could be better. Ma back's killin me an that doctoar doon the street's nae use at aw.
MAGGIE   Aye. Ah've changed away frae him. No so much because o him but o that bitch that cleans his office. Just because she writes oot his prescriptions fur him, she thinks she's a nurse.
LIZZIE   Aye, she bloody annoys me so she does, the way she struts aboot that surgery like the Queen o Sheba an' hur wae hur hoose like a midden an thae weans o hurs in a terrible state. She ought tae be ashamed o hursel.
MAGGIE   She hud the cheek tae tap a shilling aff o me fur the meter an ah huvnae seen her since. Ah'll be needin it back by Friday tae – ah need every penny!
LIZZIE   Ah'm in the same boat. Ah've goat the man comin in tae empty the meter this afternoon because ah need the rebate. Ah've nae money tae get the tea in fur him comin hame fae work.
MAGGIE   Ah'm expecting that H.P. man. Ah canna pay him this week an ah owe him six weeks awready.
LIZZIE   If ah see him comin ah'll send wan o the weans up tae shout through the letter box.
MAGGIE   Aye and let me know when he goes away cos the old bastard always stauns wae his ear ti the door listenin fur me…

They both withdraw. Enter BYRNE, SLUGGER *and* BANDIT. *Rock beat from percussionist.*

BANDIT   Johnny, the lads up in Shamrock Street wahnt us tae go o'er thair an' gie
    them haunders. There's a team comin doon frae the Calton tae dae them over.
BYRNE   We're a thievin gang. We're no a fightin gang like thaim.
BANDIT   But they're just the next street, Johnny.
SLUGGER   Aye, and if we don't dae it, they'll say we crapped it.

BYRNE *thinks it over.*

BYRNE   Is there weapons?
BANDIT   That Calton team will huv bayonets and chains, boatles – the lot.
BYRNE   We better arm oorsels tae then.
BANDIT   Ah've goat a blade stashed away in the hoose.
SLUGGER   Wait till yae see the chib ah've goat. You'll never believe it.

SLUGGER *and* BANDIT *stage a mock fight behind* BYRNE *as he speaks to audience.*
They have weapons and they stalk one another, leap on one another pretending to
stab and hit.

BYRNE   Blades. Hammers. A splinter of glass. Anything did – just so long as it
    made a mark. A new dimension had entered my life. A new reality had opened up
    for me. Violence. It was inevitable. Sometimes violence has a reason on the streets
    – it's political, or religious, or a junkie killing for drugs – either a reason or an
    excuse. But in the world that I come from, violence is its own reason. Violence is
    an art form practised in and for itself. And you soon get to know your audience
    and what it is impresses them. You cut a man's face and somebody asks you,
    'How many stitches?' 'Twenty' you say, and they look at you – 'Twenty? Only
    twenty? Christ, you hardly marked him.' The next time you cut a face you make a
    bit more certain it will be news.

He turns aside and doubles up holding his head. Rock beat. BANDIT *and* SLUGGER
attend to him.

BYRNE   Ma heid! Ma heid! Ma fucking heid! The bastard kept hitting it wae a
    hammer.
BANDIT   Never mind, Johnny. You made a mess o him.
BYRNE   Ah wus so angry ah didnae know whit ah wus daein. He's no deid, is he?
BANDIT   He's no deid, but you just aboot gouged his eye oot wae that screwdriver
    you were carryin.
SLUGGER   They're aw saying yir crazy. They're sayin yir a lunatic. They're aw
    scairt tae fuck o yae.

BYRNE *straightens up and thinks this over. Smiles.*

BYRNE   That's whit thair sayin is it? That ah'm a lunatic? That's awright then, isn't

it? Ah ahm a lunatic. Ah'll dae anythin! You'se hud aw better watch it! *(They are afraid of him for a moment. He stretches out his palm as at beginning of play.)* It's just as well, eh? *(Smiling.)*
BANDIT *(smiling)* Aye!

They slap hands. BANDIT *and* JOHNNY, SLUGGER *and* JOHNNY.

SLUGGER *(slapping)* We're aw in it thegither.

They are laughing. BANDIT *suddenly on the alert.*

BANDIT Hey, look. Here's Big Danny coming. Somebody said he hud a joab fur you, Johnny, doon at his shebeen.
SLUGGER Yir going places, Johnny.
LIZZIE *(looking out of her window)* Johnny, you're a mug!

BYRNE *looks at her questioningly. Rock beat. Enter* BIG DANNY.

BANDIT *(with a flourish)* Big Danny!
SLUGGER Look at the suit! Get the material!

DANNY *is in his late forties. A flashy suit and tie, well-pleased with himself. Smoking a cigar.*

DANNY *(to audience)* They call me Big Danny and ah run a shebeen. Dae yae's all know what a shebeen is? Well, it's like Prohibition but it's no as big. In Glasgow, when these boys were still boys – before thae goat too big fur their boots – the pubs closed up at nine o'clock. Nine o'clock! Can you imagine it? So thir wur a loat o people wae drooths oan thaim aboot the town and it wus a simple matter, if yae wantit tae make some easy money, tae open up a wee place fur drinkin *efter* nine o'clock. And that's exactly whit ah did. Up a close in the Gorbals. A two room and kitchen. The place stacked wae bevvy. A shebeen! Ah wus in business – fur masell.
—Hullo there, boys. Howzit goin?
BYRNE No bad, Danny. How's things wae you?
DANNY Business is good, boys, but it could be better.
BANDIT Whit dyae mean, Danny?
DANNY *(examining the tip of his cigar)* Can ah ask youse boys a question?
BYRNE Fire away.
DANNY How much ur youse makin in a week frae yir thievin?
BYRNE How much? I don't know, Danny. We don't really keep count.
DANNY Well, that's where youse ur makin a mistake because yae's should keep count. Let's face it, boys, none o youse ur ever gonnae work, ur yi?
BANDIT Dead right we're no.

DANNY   Anyway, youse couldnae get a joab even if ye's wantit wan.

SLUGGER   Which we don't!

BYRNE   Ah hud a joab wance but it wus a waste o time, cooped up aw day wae somebody watching yir every move when yae could be oot oan the streets enjoyin yirsel...

DANNY   Aye. So whit else can ye dae but turn tae thievin. Yir hands are forced.

BANDIT   Nae option.

DANNY   A man's goat tae dae something tae keep himsel alive.

SLUGGER   An occupy his time...

DANNY   But wance ye've done that, yae've goat tae gie it some thoat. Wance a thief – always a thief. There's nae wae oot oh it. And yir maybe young now but youse'll soon be older.

BYRNE   Ah, come off it, Danny. Whit's aw this aboot?

SLUGGER   Aye, whit ur yae leading up tae, Danny?

DANNY   Oh, you'se ur clever boys alright. I can see that – except fur you, Byrne, everybudy knows you're a fuckin Hun. *(They all find this funny.)* So ah'll gie it tae ye's straight – how would youse boys like tae wurk fur me?

BANDIT   Wid we no just.

SLUGGER   Right an aw.

BYRNE   You two shut up and leave this to me. That wid depend, Danny.

DANNY   Whit wid it depend oan?

BYRNE   A loat o things.

DANNY   Like what?

BYRNE   Like what wid we be daein and whit wid you be payin us fur a start?

DANNY   Fur a start? Dae yae mean yae've goat mair conditions? Whit age ur you, Byrne?

BYRNE   Fourteen.

DANNY   Sweet Jesus, only fourteen and look ut him. Wahntin tae figure oot aw the angles before he's properly begun. Look, aw ahm lookin fur is somebody tae hang aboot in the streets at night ootside the shebeen tae bring the customers tae ma door. If youse boys urnae interested, ah can aye try somebody else.

BYRNE   Naebody else wurks in the streets in this part of town, and you know it.

BANDIT   Naebudy else wid dare.

BYRNE   Awright, so whit wid ye be payin us?

DANNY   Ah'm no sayin right now – but ah'll say this, frae the look o you bunch an' the rags yir wearin, it'll be mair than yir making noo. (JOHNNY *is annoyed by this. It looks for a moment as if there might be trouble.)* An' there's no point in lookin ut me like that, Byrne. Ah'm gieing yae a chance. Ah'm gieing yae a chance tae better yirsel. Because ah can see ye've goat – talent. What's your answer?

BYRNE   We'll need tae discuss it.

DANNY   Awright, discuss it then. Is it gonnae take long?

BYRNE   Naw. Just gie us a few minutes... *(Takes the others aside.)* Listen... don't let him see you're too keen. We've goat tae get as much oot oh this as... *(Conversation gets quieter as* DANNY *steps forward to talk to audience.)*

DANNY   Lamentable, isn't it? There ah was – wan big fool leading three young nitwits further intae the hole that he's in. You know what finally happened tae me? Ah didnae dae any big prison stretches, though ah wus in an oot the Bar-L same as the rest o them, but ah wus too weak tae be really crooked an ah took tae the boattle. If yae saw me nooadays it wid be oan a street coarner, wae stubble oan ma chin an ma clothes gone shabby – a hasbeen and a wino, gone beyond all hope. Ah didnae last long as bigshot… *(Returns to the boys.)* …So. Hus the great cooncil come to its decision. Whit a huddle. Youse ur wurse than the City fuckin Chambers.

BYRNE   We'll dae it – if the money's right.

DANNY   The money'll be right. Don't you worry about that. Comoan an ah'll get yies some chips tae celebrate.

SLUGGER   Tony the Tally wullnae let us in his chippy.

DANNY   He wull if ah tell him tae.

BANDIT   Good oan yae, Danny. Ah'll huv a fish supper.

SLUGGER   Ah wahnt a black puddin. Wae a pickled onion.

BYRNE   Could you get us in the pub, Danny?

DANNY   Johnny Byrne, now you're wae me, Big Danny, a loat o doors that previously were closed will suddenly magically be open tae yae.

BYRNE   Aye? That sounds fine.

Enter DANNY. *He has a glass of whisky.*

DANNY   Johnny, you an the boys huv been daein a loat o good wurk fur me.

BYRNE   Yae can say that again, Danny. When you took me oan ah didnae know ah'd be brekkin jaws fur yae.

DANNY   Well, in this game, Johnny, sometimes yae've goat tae be firm.

BYRNE   Aye, or get somebody else tae be firm fur ye.

DANNY   Whit ur you complainin aboot? Yir gettin paid well enough, urn't yae?

BYRNE   Aye. Fur the time being anyway.

DANNY   Naw. No just fur the time being. There's a bit mair action comin your way, Johnny. Ah wahnt tae make you ma right-hand man.

BYRNE   That's wise o you, Danny.

DANNY   Is that aw you've goat tae say. God, you're a close wee bugger. Two years yae've been workin fur me and you've always been so silent. But when you speak ah can feel the evil weighing down on your every word. Can ah trust yae, Johnny?

BYRNE   Whit's that yae've goat in yir hand, Danny?

DANNY   Bevvy. Whit does it look like?

BYRNE   Can yae trust the bevvy, Danny?

DANNY   You must be jokin. Ah see too much of it.

BYRNE   Well, if ye cannae trust yirsel wae the bevvy, yae cannae trust yirsel wae me. Because it's no me or the bevvy you should be worryin aboot, it's yirsel…

DANNY   Aw, don't you worry about me. Ah'll see masell alright alright. Listen, did yae see that yin that owes me the hunner?

BYRNE   Aye, ah saw him.

DANNY   Whit did he huv tae say fur himsel?

BYRNE   He says his wife's pregnant and he's nae money. He says it'll take him another month or two.

DANNY   Whit did you say?

BYRNE   Ah said ah'd be back tae see him in a day or two.

DANNY   Did he get the message?

BYRNE   Whit dae you think?

DANNY   Aye. That's because he knows ah don't mess around. If he disnae come up wae the lolly... You get down and fix that fucker fur me.

BYRNE   Don't worry, Danny. Ah'll gie him a face like the map o Glasca.

Percussion. Rock rhythm. ARCHIE *is rolling a cigarette.* WOMAN *is offstage.*

WOMAN   Archie, are you no comin tae bed?

ARCHIE   Aye, ah'll be through in a minit, Jean. Just you go tae sleep.

WOMAN   Naw. Yae sat up aw last night, noo yir at it agen. An yae canny stay away fae that windae. Whit's the matter wae yae? Ur ye in some kind of trouble? Is there somebody efter yae?

ARCHIE   Naw, naw. Nuthin like that. Ah just cannae sleep these nights. Ah don't know whit it is. It must be wae the baby coming. Maybe I'm worrying.

WOMAN   I'd 've thought you'd be used to it by this time.

ARCHIE *(to audience)*   When somebody's after you, you cannae sleep – unless you sleep wae one eye open. Every noise you hear from the street, could be the noise of him coming. Footsteps on the pavement. A car draws up. The wind shakes and rattles at the window. Sometimes you wish he could come, just tae get it over with, just to put an end to this waiting.

WOMAN   Archie, are you coming tae bed or ur yae no?

Rock rhythms. DANNY *and* BYRNE.

DANNY   Noo that you've been upgraded, whit wid yae like?

BYRNE *(to audience)*   So there I was standing with the sole of my shoe flapping, the buttons off my shirt and big holes all over my vest, and he's asking me what wid ah like. A right good suit with right good material, a brand spanking new white shirt and a tie to match. A pair of handmade shoes that were sparkling with polish. I always wanted to look like he does... *(To* DANNY.*)* I want a suit!

DANNY   A suit? Haw. Haw. I asked him what did he want and he said a suit! Awright, Johnny boy. First thing the morn's morn, down tae Isaac the Tailor...

They break and BYRNE *stands to attention. Enter* BANDIT *and* SLUGGER *carrying suit.*

WOMAN *(she stands screaming at him)*   Monster! Sadistic bloody monster! You cut ma husband's face to shreds!

Drums. BYRNE *is kitted out in suit. Eventually he stands resplendent.*

LIZZIE   Yae never seen that fight last night, did yae?

MAGGIE   Naw. Ah didnae. But big Mary Boyce wus tellin me about it at the steamie this mornin.

LIZZIE   That Johnny Byrne half killed wan o those boys he wus fightin wae. Ah don't know how the poor soul managed tae pick hissel aff the ground the state he wis in.

MAGGIE   That's the thurd fight this week. It's time that Johnny Byrne grew up so it is.

LIZZIE   It's his maw ah feel sorry fur. She works aw day fur those boys so she does. She must be heartbroken.

MAGGIE   He's gonnae end up in Barlinnie the way he's goin. It's time he goat himsel a lassie an thoat aboot settlin doon.

LIZZIE   Aye. Aw him an his pals dae is sit in that pub aw day long drinkin an swearin, an that gaffer o the pub's just as bad because he gies thaim drink fur nuthin.

MAGGIE   He's just goan fae bad tae worse since he got in tow wae that Big Danny.

LIZZIE   That wee niaff!

MAGGIE   Ah think yir right, Lizzie. A lassie wid be the makins o that boy. Sometimes ah think it's the only hope he's goat left.

Enter SLUGGER *and* BANDIT. BANDIT *looking around him.*

BANDIT   Is Johnny no here yet? It's no like him tae be late.

SLUGGER   He'll be wae the burd.

BANDIT   Aye, probably. *(Slightly derisive. Looks around him, taking in the audience.)* Thair they go, Slugger, the honest workin people. Whit a bunch o mugs! They get up in the mornin and go oot tae wurk and get their miserable wages ut the end o the week tae help them pay fur their miserable wee hooses an' their miserable wee lives. Wance a year they're released fur two weeks. The Glesca Fair! An' thae aw go daft! Eejits! Two weeks later it's back tae the grindstone again fur another year.

SLUGGER   Either that or they cannae get a joab an' they go aboot in fuckin poverty.

BANDIT   Well thank Christ that's no fur us. When we want something – we take it. And it doesnae matter who it belangs tae.

SLUGGER   When we take it, it belangs tae us.

BANDIT   Aye and aw the toffs and intellectuals hate oor guts. Because we're the wans that kick in thir doors an climb in thir windaes and run oaf wae aw their nice new presies an their family hierlooms. An they know we don't give a fuck. Efter we've done a place an left it in a mess, ah'll bet they can still feel us in the air roon aboot thaim an they wonder who we are. What we're like. Because it's obvious we don't give a fuck...

SLUGGER   Smash their shoap windaes in. Dynamite their safes. Chib thaim in the street ut night an' run aff wae their money! Naw. They don't like us. They don't like us at aw.

BANDIT   An thae cun stuff their fuckin probation officers up thur fuckin arses. *(Pause.)* Here's Johnny coming. Aw naw, he's goat hur wae him.

Enter JOHNNY *and* CAROLE. *Talking and laughing.* BANDIT *interrupts them.*

BANDIT   Hey, Johnny, fancy goin doon the Railway Club the night fur a bevvy?

CAROLE   I thought we were going out tonight.

BYRNE   Well, you can come alang wae us.

CAROLE   I thought we were going out by ourselves withoot thae two eejits.

Hits her.

BYRNE   Watchit, Carole. Ah've warned you before aboot cheekin me in front o the boys.

CAROLE   That's aw you worry aboot, isn't it? Yir reputation! Aw ahm good fur is cerryin yir chib an cop-watching fur yae.

BYRNE   Naw. That's no aw yir good fur.

CAROLE   Och, shut up you. You make me sick. Wan minit your aw affection, the next yir like a bluddy animal. You shouldnae tell me we're going oot if we're no.

SLUGGER   Oh, wid yae listen tae that. She'll be wahntin tae merry him next.

BYRNE   Right. Hurry up you if you're comin.

CAROLE   Aw, piss off!

BYRNE   Cumoan, lads.

BANDIT   Aye, furget her, Johnny. Ah don't know whit yae see in hur.

BYRNE   Ah'm no asking you tae um ah?

BANDIT   Hey, fancy we'll go doon the Barrowland instead an pick up some burds.

SLUGGER   Nooky!

BYRNE   Aye, ah fancy that. Haud oan. Hey, Carole, gie's ma chib.

CAROLE   Whit dae yae wahnt yir chib fur if yir just goin doon the Railway Club?

BYRNE   Never you mind. Just give us it an less o the questions. *(She gives it to him.)* Right. Ah'll see you later. Right, lads. Doon the Barraland. If any o that Calton mob jump us, we'll be ready for them.

SLUGGER   An ah thoat we wur going doon fur some nooky...

BANDIT   *(triumphant)*   See yae later, Carole...

Exit BANDIT *and* SLUGGER. *But* BYRNE *sits down behind* CAROLE *with his back to her.* CAROLE *speaks to audience.*

CAROLE   Later. Later. That's aw ah ever hear. Aw ahm good fur is keeping his chib an cop-watching fur him. Everybody says ah need ma heid looked going aboot wae him. He's a dead cert road tae trouble, wan way or another. Ah'd like tae say that he was different when he wis wae me – quiet and gentle and affectionate like. But he's no. Ah suppóse he must feel something for me – but if he does, he doesnae show it. Aw he's interestit in is his nookie then it's doon tae the pub wae the boys.

BRYNE   Carole! Carole!

CAROLE   What's the matter?

BYRNE   Scratch ma back, ah've goat a helluva itch.

CAROLE   Goad, yae never know the minit, dae yae? Whereaboots?

BYRNE   Just aboot there. That's it. Naw, a wee bit higher. Naw, lower. That's it. Oh, that's lovely... Rerr...

CAROLE   Here, leave me alane ya durty pig...

BYRNE   Stop it I like it...

CAROLE   Naw, really. Ah've goat soup oan an ah doant want it tae overheat. It loses aw the flavour.

BYRNE   Oh well, you go right ahead wae yir soup, hen. Don't let me stoap yae. Yae'll make somebody a good wife wan o these days.

CAROLE   Aye well maybe one day yae'll huv tae marry me!

BYRNE   Och don't talk stupid!

CAROLE   Ah'm no talking stupid. Did naebday ever tell you the facts o life?

BYRNE   Ah mean whut dae yae wahnt tae be married tae a character like me fur? Ma road's mapped oot fur me. Ah keep a chib over the door an a blade in ma bedroom. That's when ah'm no oan the run or oot causin damage. Ah'm for the Bar-L. It's inevitable.

CAROLE   It doesnae need tae be inevitable, Johnny. Yae can change things, you know.

BYRNE   Aw, gie us a brekk, wullyae? What can ah change? Fuck all.

CAROLE   Well, maybe if yae were married an hud a family...

BYRNE   Ah'd huv tae feed thaem. Or you'd huv tae feed them's mair likely. Just like my ma hud four o us tae feed efter ma father died.

CAROLE   But Johnny, even if yae did dae a stretch, you could rely oan me. Ah widnae mess yae aboot.

BYRNE   That's whit yae say now, but it's a different story when it happens. Look ut Big Jean – her husband's daein four years. She managed tae keep hursel fur him fur a year and that wus that. She started shacking up wae somebody else. Wait till he gets oot.

CAROLE   Ur you comparin me tae that Big Jean?

BYRNE   Naw ah'm no comparin yae tae...

CAROLE   It sounds very much tae me as if yae ur...

BYRNE   Aw in the name o... You know something, Carole?

CAROLE   What?

BYRNE   Ah'd love a plate o soup.

Rock rhythms. Enter SLUGGER, *speaks straight to audience.*

SLUGGER   Ah wus up in Duke Street buying masel a coupla flash shurts an there wus a gemme oan ut Parkheid. The Old Firm. Jesus Christ, whit a bunch o eejits – grown men throwin screwtaps at each uther frae wan side o the road tae the uther, an aw in the name o religion. Ah don't know whit that's supposed tae be aboot at aw. They wurk aw week then oan a Saturday thae go daft an split each other's heids open, then oan a Sunday thair oot tae twelve o'clock Mass un oan their knees. Sheer hypocrisy. *(Enter* BANDIT.*)*

BANDIT   Just so long as thair no taking money oot o oor pockets!

SLUGGER   Right an aw!

BYRNE   *(approaching them)*   Aye, but you'll let Danny take money oot o your pockets.

BANDIT   Whit dae yae mean? It's Danny thut pays us, in' it?

BYRNE   Is it? So far as ah can see, we pay oorsels – underpay oorsels. Danny might hand over the notes tae us ut the end o the week, but that's aw he does. You think aboot it, when we startet wae Danny, we wur just boys. That wus two years ago. An Danny wis just runnin the Shebeen. It wus easy wurk. Noo he's intae everythin – every racket that's going, he's goat his finger in the pie. An' it's us he's using tae dae it. He's goat us breakin jaws fur him an' taking aw the risks, but we're no seein enough return fur it personally.

BANDIT   So whit yae sayin? We'll chin him fur mair money?

BYRNE   Aye. Something like that.

BANDIT   Supposing he says no.

BYRNE   Whether Big Danny says yes or no makes no difference anymore.

BANDIT   I'm beginning tae see whit yae mean.

Enter DANNY.

DANNY   Hello there, boys, howzit goin? Still enjoyin the good life?

BYRNE   Hello, Danny.

BANDIT   Hello.

SLUGGER   Hello.

DANNY   Hey, whit's this? Aw the hellos. Ur you boys claimin me?

BANDIT   Yir gettin awfa sensitive in yir old age, Danny.

DANNY   Less o the old…

BYRNE   It's just that me an' the boys huv been discussin money.

DANNY   Ah should ah guessed. Well, ah suppose youse ur entitled tae a rise wae the way things ur expandin…

BYRNE   We don't want a rise, Danny.

DANNY   Whit dae yae want then?

BYRNE   We're intae yae fur the loat. *(Slashes him.)* We Rule, ya fool.

DANNY   Okay…

Percussion. Pub lights up. DEADEYE *singing. Rock beat.* DEADEYE'S *voice is heard in the darkness. Lights come up on the domestic area.* SLUGGER, BANDIT *and* JOHNNY *are seated, sharing a bottle of cheap wine with* DEADEYE. *Some of his swag is lying on the table.* DEADEYE *sings with his eyes closed, his arms outstretched. It is the Nat King Cole song 'Too Young'.*

DEADEYE *(singing)*   And yet we're not too young to know…
this love may last, though years may go…
and then some day they may recall…
we were not… too young… at all.

The boys laugh and cheer.

DEADEYE *(encouraged)*   I know a millionaire, who's burdened down with care.
BYRNE *(hastily interrupting him)*   Yir a good wee cunt, Deadeye, so yae urr.
DEADEYE   We're aw happy, int wi'? Ah mean we've aw earned a bit an' that's whit matters intit?
BYRNE   Mind, any other swag yae get gie us a chance eh it first.
DEADEYE   Don't worry aboot that, Johnny. Ah know that if ah'm involved wae you an the mob, nae cunt's gonnae bump me fur ma money.
BANDIT   That's right, kiddo. An' you know none o us will bump yae.
DEADEYE   See that big bastard Sid doon ut the Bookies, he tried tae knock ma price doon ti fifteen bob by sayin' the material on the shirts wis shite. The big bastard's worth a fortune as well.
BYRNE   Aye, he's a tight big bastard. Gie him nothin. He likes tae try and take liberties, an there's a loat o talk aboot him bein a grass.
BANDIT   Aye, that's right. He's supposed tae huv told the busies aboot wee Sniffer when he knocked him back fur some jewellery that he blagged.
BYRNE   Ah'll tell yae whit ah'll dae, Deadeye. Frae now on, don't bother dealing wae anybody else. Fae now on, any swag yi get gie me the chance o it and yae can put the word roon aw the young yins that urr blaggin swag an tell thaim that ah'll get thaim a good price fur it.
DEADEYE   Nae bother. Ah'll dae that. There's been too many cunts oot tae bump me recently.
SLUGGER *(at a sign from* BYRNE *he is again bundling* DEADEYE *out)*   Just get the swag sent doon here an' we'll attend tae it.
DEADEYE   Right… Aye… *(Confused.)* Goodbye, Johnny.
BYRNE   Goodbye, Deadeye.
BANDIT   That's the right way, Johnny. Sew the whole district up. We can earn a right few quid if we get these guys in hand. They blag some ace gear.

SLUGGER *re-enters.*

SLUGGER   Auld cunt. Ah thoat he'd never stoap talkin. He wus wahntin tae sing me another song oan the doorstep. Ah telt him tae wander.
BYRNE   Right, Slugger, sit doon. Ah wahnt tae talk tae yaes seriously fur a change.

SLUGGER   It's aboot money. People only talk serious when they're talking aboot money.

BYRNE   Cut it oot, Slugger. Right. Now look. Since we took over frae Big Danny we've taken over his contacts. We're intae everythin. The Docks. The Brasses. Protection. We've goat the loat. An' that's aw right as far as it goes, but ah think we cun take it further.

BANDIT   Never satisfied!

BYRNE   Sure ahm no satisfied. Because ah've come to realise somethin more and more strongly these days. We're no ut the thievin any more, we're runnin a business.

SLUGGER   You don't say. We'll need tae turn the shebeen intae an office then an pit oor names up on the door – J. Slugger, Company Secretary. Knock Three Times – Heavily.

BANDIT   Yeah an' we could get ourselves a nice little secretary with nice little tits and a waggly bum…

BYRNE   *(laughing)*   Awright! Awright! Ya pair o eejits! Anyway, aw ahm leadin up tae the noo is tae say that ah wahnt us tae open a bank account.

SLUGGER   A bank account! Not on your Nellie! You'll huv us paying income tax next.

BYRNE   Naw. There's ways roon that. False credentials. You open an account in an assumed name.

SLUGGER   Frank Costello.

BANDIT   Luciano!

SLUGGER   Jesse James!

BANDIT   Billy the Kid!

BYRNE   *(laughing)*   Fucking Genghis Khan! Ya pair o eejits. Right, listen…

BANDIT   Naw. Wait a minute, Johnny. Ah think we get the point. That'll be aw fine and dandy tae huv a bank account and talk aboot the businees an aw that but…

BYRNE *(annoyed and suspicious)*   But whit?

BANDIT   Well… do you no think you're going a wee bit far these days?

BYRNE   What are you talking about?

BANDIT   You know what ah'm talking aboot. Them two yae done over the other night wae a steakie, that's whit ahm fucking talking aboot an you know it. Wan o these days you're gonnae end up killin somebody.

BYRNE   What are you talking about? Whit's aw this aboot killin people? Huv you been drinkin?

BANDIT   You know fine well ah huvnae been drinking.

SLUGGER   An aw ah know is ah could be daein way wan right now. Cumoan tae fuck. You two wid ergue the hindlegs aff a donkey.

BYRNE   Awright. Cumoan then. You'll need tae watch that drooth o yours, Slugger. You'll be gettin a beer belly.

SLUGGER   It's better than a cut face, Johnny.

BYRNE   So's a loat o things. *(Turns back to* BANDIT.*)* Listen, Bandit, you must be mistaken. Ah never done over those two eejits the other night – ah don't use a steakie – did you furget that?

BANDIT *(resigned)*   Anything you say, Johnny.

BYRNE   Right, cumoan then, pal. Doon tae the boozers.

Percussion. They cross stage to pub area.

BYRNE   Hiya, Carole.

CAROLE   Ah've been here a whole half hoor waiting fur you.

BYRNE   That's tough kid. Whit are yae drinkin?

SLUGGER   Ah'm gettin thaim, Johnny.

BYRNE   That cunt Kelly wus supposed tae be here the night. Ah wunder if he's gonnae show his face.

BANDIT   He's a month overdue us it is.

BYRNE   Ah think he'll come across wae the money awright but – ta, Slugger (SLUGGER *hands in drinks*) – ah think we'll need tae gie him a nice receipt fur it when he does. Just a wee reminder that yae've got tae pay up promptly.

BANDIT   A receipt. Ha, ha. That's it. We'll give him a receipt!

CAROLE   Christ, an ah thoat we wur comin here tae relax.

SLUGGER   We are relaxing, hen.

BANDIT   Oh, oh! Here he comes!

BYRNE   Oh. There he is. The very man ah wantit tae see. Ah wis hopin we might run intae ye.

KELLY   Aye, ah knew you'd be here. Ah heard yae wur lookin fur me. Ah've goat it here. Ah'm sorry it's been so long in coming. But you know how it is.

BYRNE   Naw. Ah don't know how it is, Kelly. Tell me. You were supposed tae pay back a month ago.

KELLY   Ah loast it oan the betting, Johnny. Ah just didnae huv it tae gie ye, otherwise ah'd ah gied yae it wouldn't ah?

CAROLE   Fur fuck sake wid yae listen tae that?

BYRNE   You just keep yir mouth shut. *(To* KELLY.*)* Right. Gie us it then.

KELLY *(handing over envelope)*   There you are.

BYRNE   Count it, Bandit.

BANDIT *(a deft hand at running through the banknotes)*   Aye. It's aw here.

BYRNE   Right. Here's yir fucking receipt!

Sticks knife in KELLY'S *face.*

The Windae-hingers.

LIZZIE   Hullo, Maggie. That wis an awfae cerry-oan last night, did yae see it?

MAGGIE   Naw, ah wus oot ut the Bingo. Whit wis it?

LIZZIE   There wis dozens o' squad cars an' polis raided houses an' shoaps aw o'er the district and there wis blue murder.

MAGGIE   In the name o Goad whit wus goin oan?

LIZZIE   Cun yae no guess? They liftit aw that Byrne crowd in a wunner – including
that whore Carole.

MAGGIE   Whit ur thae daein thaim fur?

LIZZIE   Well, that big beat polis – no that ah can stand him either – but he was
telling Jack in the Dairy that thir arrestin' thaim furr everythin under the sun.

MAGGIE   Ah thoat they wir payin' the polis aff and that wis how they never went
near thaim at aw.

LIZZIE   Aye. And so did everybody else. But they've done the loat o thaim.

MAGGIE   Well, hell mend thaim. That's aw ah cin say. Hell mend thaim!

Windae-hingers withdraw. Enter BANDIT, SLUGGER *and* BYRNE. *They head for the
pub.*

BANDIT   *(laughing)*   That really sickened thae bastards, didn't it?

SLUGGER   Aye. They'll no dig us up in a hurry again.

BYRNE   Ah don't know aboot that. We'll huv tae watch thaim.

BANDIT   The heid busy said he was chargin' me wae everythin under the book, but
ah told him ahm sayin fuck all tae ah see ma lawyer.

SLUGGER   Aye. But ah wis worried. Ah thoat they wur gonnae dae a bit o' gardenin
an start plantin some gear oan us.

BANDIT   Aye. They're better at that gemme than Percy Thrower.

BYRNE   It's just as well wee Rollo the lawyer goat there in time tae stoap them
otherwise we'd be lyin in Bar by noo.

BANDIT   They really hate wee Rollo as he's the flyest mouthpiece in the business
and is wide furr aw their gemms.

SLUGGER   Did yae see their faces when they hud tae let us go? It wus fuckin magic.

BYRNE   Aye but they meant business. And ah think they still mean business –
specially wae me. They three I.D. parades they gave us hid me worried. Ah
thoaght they were gonnae stick some snide witnesses oanti' them tae dig us oot.

BANDIT   Aye. And imagine thaim puttin Big Kelly oan it. As if he wid dig us oot.

SLUGGER   They're fuckin idiots so they urr. Ah mean Kelly knows he deserved it.
Ah cannae understand they busies.

They have entered the pub.

BANDIT   How's aboot a wee bit o service then?

BARMAN   Hullo thair, boys. Ah heard the cops dug yaes up.

BYRNE   Aye. You can say that again. Bastards! But lissen, seein' as things are a bit
hoat furr us ah want yae tae keep these o'er the bar fur us.

Three of them start to unload weapons.

BARMAN   Aye, sure, son. Just gie thaim tae me. Ah'll look efter thaim fur ye.

SLUGGER *(hauling out a meat cleaver)*   Noo ah don't wahnt you cuttin the heids affae pints, big yin!

BANDIT   Right noo ah've been lyin in a rotten cell aw weekend so ah want ah good bath, a burd and a right bevvy!

SLUGGER   Aye. An' we'll huv a right bevvy in here the night! *(He mimics Elvis Presley.)* Let's have a party... oh... oh... oh... let's have a party... ooh... ooh... ooh...

BANDIT   *(taking him up on it and dancing in front of him)*   Dancing to the Jailhouse Rock... Bap!

He throws out his arms and sticks out his leg on the 'bap'. At exactly the same moment two policemen appear. SLUGGER and BANDIT freeze on the spot. JOHNNY is drinking with his back to them. SLUGGER makes ineffectual attempts at speech – pointing at the police and opening and closing his mouth but saying nothing. BANDIT puts a hand on JOHNNY'S shoulder. JOHNNY looks round and takes in the policemen. He stands up slowly. Rock rhythms begin. He faces the policemen, hands loose at his side. He walks towards them. They stand on either side of him. They walk out of pub. BANDIT and SLUGGER exit after them looking furtive and trying to hide. They exit in different directions as quickly as they can.

The POLICE leave BYRNE centre stage. He is handcuffed. He is standing to attention and expressionless. If possible, the next sequence should convey by lighting and flashes that BYRNE is having his photograph taken for police files. He is taken face on. Right profile. Left profile. BANDIT and SLUGGER look in on things furtively from either side of the stage. There is no joy in their chant.

SLUGGER   Rats!

BANDIT   Rats aroon the backs!

SLUGGER   Rats aroon the backs an a wee dug!

BANDIT   It wus a rerr wee dug that.

SLUGGER   It kilt that many rats it goat a medal fur it.

BANDIT   It even goat a menshun in the paper.

Enter CAROLE.

CAROLE   Aye, boys. We're aw in it thegither. *(Sarcastic.)*

BANDIT   You shut up, ya cow. We'll keep things goin fur him while he's inside, an we'll stull be here waitin when he comes oot. Whit aboot you?

All three exit.

BYRNE   *(to audience)*   There is so much that none of you can understand about me and the world I come from and there doesn't seem to be any way of telling it that will finally get you to see the bitterness and indifference I inherited from whatever the system was the series of historical priorities that created the world into which I was born.

I didn't think. I didn't think much about it. I didn't say – there's a system – and analyse it – I was never taught to do that. But I felt. I felt strongly.

There were the haves and the have-nots. I was one of the have-nots. There were the have-nots that worked and the have-nots that thieved, then there were the rest of you – living away out there somewhere in your posh districts in aw your ease and refinement – what a situation!

It made me laugh to see you teaching your religions and holding your democratic elections – and it made me sick with disgust. That was why I enjoyed the sight of blood because, without knowing it, it was your blood I was after.

My first prison sentence was like going to university. I made a lot of new friends and useful contacts and we talked and planned together for the future. It was a top-level conference fur the world I moved in, and fur me it lasted all of two years. Maybe you'd hoped it would teach me a lesson and ah wid 'mend ma ways' so to speak. Well, it did teach me a lesson o sorts. When ah goat oot o that prison ah was ready fur somethin new – something ah had learned tae call 'crime'. Organised crime.

POLICE *re-enter and march* BYRNE *off. Action moves to next scene –* BANDIT *and* SLUGGER *in the pub. Drinking pints.*

SLUGGER   It'll no be long tae Johnny gets oot o' Bar-L noo.

BANDIT   Aye. Ah'll be glad tae see him hame again. Mind'ye he wis lucky only gettin two years fur bladin two guys.

SLUGGER   Ur you kiddin? It wis a fuckin liberty. He hud nae form.

BANDIT   Whit dyae mean? He's done his remand home, approved school and his Borstal.

SLUGGER   Aye but he's never been in Bar before.

BANDIT   Bit it wus a wee sentence fur the High Court.

SLUGGER   The last time ah saw him he wus daein his nut aboot Carole. Somebody hud telt him she wis oot at the dancin and he's no pleased aboot it.

BANDIT   Ah wunder who could ah telt him that.

SLUGGER   Ah wunder. It's no as if he's goat a loat o visitors.

BANDIT   Ach, Carole. She's a cow. She's never away fae the Barrowland an' aw that mob in the Calton urr ridin' hurr.

SLUGGER   You better no let him hear that when he gets hame.

BANDIT   Ah'm gonnae tell him. Ah'm gonnae tell him she's a midden. She deserves aw that's comin tae her.

SLUGGER   It's no Carole ah'm thinking aboot, it's Johnny. It'll break his heart.

BANDIT   That yin doesnae huv a heart. He's an animal.

CAROLE *in domestic area, putting on her eye shadow. Enter* JOHNNY. *He stands staring at her. Silent.* CAROLE *is using a small mirror. She sees him in it.*

CAROLE   Johnny! *(Flings down eyeshadow brush.)* Naebody telt me yae were gettin oot!

BYRNE   Did thae no?

CAROLE   Oh, Johnny. It's great tae see you again.

She runs to him and puts her arms round him. JOHNNY *pulls them away again.*

CAROLE   Whit's wrang, Johnny. Lissen, don't believe whit that Bandit says. He's just jealous. Ah've been faithful tae yae. Ah huvnae been up tae enythin…

BYRNE   *(looks her up and down, taking in her clothes and her make up)*   Aye. It looks like it.

He moves towards her raising his clenched fist. He is wearing a knuckle duster.

CAROLE   Naw, Johnny. No ma face!

Enter SLUGGER *and* BANDIT *dressed in trilbies. Long, dark double-breasted coats.*

BANDIT   *(to audience)*   Mr Byrne is going places!

SLUGGER   He's in wae the Firm, the Big Boys noo. *(Arms out imitating an aeroplane.)* They fly him doon tae London. Thae meet him wae a limousine. The biggest villains in Britain.

BANDIT   And everything is very cordial. Everything is very English.

SLUGGER   Everything is layed oan – booze, gamblin, women – the loat! Nooadays oor Johnny wahnts fur nuthin!

BANDIT   An whit does he dae fur it aw in return? Just a wee bit o business.

SLUGGER   Technical business!

Enter BYRNE *behind them with gun. He aims it around the audience, arm outstretched. Then smiles, twirls it in his hand and puts it in his pocket. Goes to* BANDIT *and* SLUGGER.

SLUGGER   You know your trouble. Yae never hud enough toys tae play wae when yae wur a wean.

BYRNE   Where's the fancy-dress party then?

BANDIT   Aye, dyae like the toags. We goat them aff wee Isaac the Tailor fur a laugh tae see yae aff at the airport.

BYRNE   Ah think the man ahm gonnae meet wid like thaim. Gie's a shoat. *(Snatches hat from* SLUGGER'S *head.)*

BYRNE *is moving his head from side to side jokily with the hat on. But the other two have caught his last remark.*

BANDIT   Who ur yae gonnae meet?

BYRNE *(straightening out, hat on his head, gun in his hand to punctuate the words)* George Raft!

SLUGGER   Naw, cumoan, Johnny. Tell us. Who ur you gonnae meet?

BYRNE *(taking hat off and replacing gun in pocket)*   George Raft. Ah'm tellin yae. The Mafia.

BANDIT   Ur you serious?

BYRNE   Did yae ever know me tae tell a lie? The Mafia wahnt tae move in oan the gamblin club scene in this country an' Glasgow's wan o the target areas. They wahnt tae talk tae me because they wahnt tae keep the local boys happy wherever they go.

BANDIT *(suspicious)*   That's awfae big o them, is it no?

BYRNE   It's because they know if they don't cut us in they'll never get a minute's peace!

SLUGGER   Too fuckin true they widnae. Scotland fur the Scoats. Heeuch!

BANDIT *has detached himself from the conversation. He is looking away from the other two.*

BANDIT   Aye, well that'll be aw fine an hunky-dory then wulln't it – if it aw comes aff. But the business in Glesca will huv tae go oan notwithstanding. Jist as it hud tae when you were in prison. An tonight – oan the eve o your departure fur the Big Smoke – there's wan ur two small local matters outstanding thut only Mr Byrne cun attend tae in his own inimitable style.

SLUGGER   Hear aw the big wurds?

BYRNE   What ur you tawkin about?

BANDIT   Ah'm tawkin about those two eejits up in the Cowcaddens. They've been goin aroon extortin ut the pitch an toss pools fur months – oor pitch an toss pools – an you're lettin thaim get away wae it because they've been making a name fur themself o'er where they cum fae as a coupla real hard tickets!

BANDIT *looks at* BYRNE *challengingly.*

BYRNE   Ur you wahntin yir face smashed in, Bandit?

BANDIT   Aye. Yae cun smash ma face in if yae wahnt tae, Johnny, ah'm no disputin that – but it'll no get yae anywhere. Because you're slippin. You've goat that fond o yir shooter an yir fancy new pals in London thut people ur sayin yir losin yir touch. Like you say, we're aw init thegither and ah'm just thinkin aboot yir reputation because there's a helluva loat depends oan it.

BYRNE *(Serious. Silent. Considers it all for a moment. Speaks at first as if chastened.)*   Aye, well maybe there's something in what you say – *(Pause. Suddenly has* BANDIT *by the collar and is snarling in his face.)* But ah don't like yir way o fuckin sayin it!

Holds BANDIT *by the throat for a moment then lets his hand fall and smiles, suddenly relaxed again.*

BYRNE *(smiling)* Right. Where ur these eejits. Take me to thaim.

Twitchy rock thing from the drums. Billy Cobham. They produce different weapons and begin to lark about, stabbing and flailing at one another. SLUGGER *grabs* BANDIT'S *head under his arm and pretends to punch it with big elaborate gestures.*

SLUGGER *(twisting* BANDIT'S *head about and smiling to audience)* He wouldn't give me his lollipop so I broke his left arm! He still wouldn't give me his lollipop so I broke his right arm! And when he continued with his obstinate refusal I broke his legs, his neck, his nose, his heid, smashed in his teeth, an made his mooth tae bleed an ah goat the fuckin lollipop so there!

BYRNE *is standing away from this smiling as if inspired. He has a knife in his hand. He says his words as if inspired by the knife and the general presence of violence like electricity in the air (but not too inspired).*

BYRNE So there! So there!

BANDIT *suddenly frees himself, jumps up with a karate chop, howling all the way like in a Kung Fu film. From this* BANDIT *and* SLUGGER *go into a karate routine.* BYRNE *starts singing vehemently.*

BYRNE When somebody loves you It's no good unless he loves you *(lunging with knife)* All… the… Way…

Suddenly they have all frozen. The drums have stopped. BYRNE *has dropped his knife. They are looking over their shoulders as if being pursued and in fact we are back at the beginning of the play when we first met the Boys. They have stopped for a moment, breathless, looking back.*

BANDIT Oh my God! Oh… my… God!
BYRNE *(annoyed)* Whit's the matter wae yae?
BANDIT Whit dae yae think?
SLUGGER Aye. Naebody sed enythin aboot fuckin murder!

Domestic interior. JOHNNY *and the Big Brass.*

DIDI *sits with her legs up on the table, flexing one to help her fix the ladder in it with a brush of nail-polish.*

DIDI Whit ah night ah've hid. Doon the Squerr. Wan efter another. Each wan mair pissed than the wan before. An it freezin. Ah hud oan this wee short skirt an ma arse wus like ice. Wan o ma regulars says tae me 'Christ, Didi, yir tits ur blue!' *(Thinks.)* He's no a bad soul that yin. He aye hus a wee drink fur yae. Ah'll say that fur him. Even if it does take him hoors sometimes just tae get it up. Aw it's a hard life. Ah'm another social service. Creative leisure's ma department fur aw the poor bastards thur urnae gettin it elsewhere in the natural wey o things – an ah earn every penny that ah make, you take it from me. A hard life and a dangerous wan. Ma mate Big Elsie she ust tae go aboot in Glesca the same as me wae hur big boots an hur whip under hur belt fur aw the kinky wans. But she wus a junkie – that's the kind o thing this joab makes yae dae – if yir no a junkie yir an alcoholic or yir aff yir heid ur somethin – an she ust tae dae a bit o special business doon in London frae time tae time just tae relieve the monotony, aye, well she endit up in a bedsit in Notting Hill strangled wae hur ain nylons...

JOHNNY *shouts in to her.*

BYRNE   Didi! Didi!

DIDI   Who's that ut this time?

BYRNE   It's me. Johnny Byrne. Let me in quick.

DIDI   *(opening up)*   Oh Goad, yae nivir know the minit, dae yae? (BYRNE *comes in.)* Ur yae awright?

BYRNE   Aye ahm fine. Close the door.

DIDI   What's happened?

BYRNE *relaxes. Recovers composure. Smiles.*

BYRNE   Nothin's happened. Ah've just come roon tae see yae. Huvn't ah aye telt yae yir ma favrit Big Brass?

DIDI   Oh yae've telt me awright often enough but ah don't ever see yae unless yir in trouble. Sit doon. Wid yae like a drap o wine?

BYRNE   Aye. That wid be rerr, Didi.

DIDI   *(extracting a bottle of Eldorado from her handbag and pouring it into cups)* Where's Carole the night then?

BYRNE   Hingin tae mae lip!

DIDI   Aye ah widnae be surprised if she'd followed you here.

BYRNE   Ah very much doubt it.

DIDI   Johnny, whit's wrang wae yir hand? Yir bleedin. Christ, whit's been happenin, yir soaked in blood! Oh my fuck un ah huvnae a bandage nor an elastoplast in the whole place. Here, wait an ah'll get a towel!

BYRNE   It's awright, Didi.

DIDI   *(she has towel)* It's no awright at aw!

BYRNE   It's no ma blood... *(She withdraws from him. He smiles.)* Ah huvnae goat a mark on me.

Straight into next scene, pub interior. BYRNE *rapping to* SLUGGER *and* BANDIT.

BYRNE Okay. Right. So while ah'm away ah'm relyin oan you two tae keep things goin. There'll be a loat o money-lendin an protection tae collect ut the end o the month, and you've goat tae make sure it's paid up promptly. Ah wahnt you tae cover the docks, Slugger, and Bandit, you dae aw the far away places wae strange-soundin names. Oh aye an wan o yae tell Big Wilson o'er in Partick tae screw the nut. He's still feudin wae the Anderson mob. Tell him there's supposed tae be an Amnesty. The Law ur bamboozled becos we're no aw fightin wan another eny mair.

BANDIT We can hardly tell him that now!

BYRNE You know sometimes you really get on my nerves, Bandit.

BANDIT Forget it, then. Sorry ah spoke. You an yir fuckin blood lust. It makes yae say wan thing an do another. Whit aboot Grangemouth?

BYRNE Whit aboot Grangemouth?

BANDIT They sed thair wid be a consignment of whisky comin in if we wur interestit we could huv it cheap.

BYRNE Cheap enough tae make it worth oor while? How many boatles?

BANDIT Mair than enough.

BYRNE You'd better take a van.

SLUGGER Aye. Yae cun hire wan frae Hertz.

BANDIT Fuck Hertz. Ah'll nick wan doon the street.

Enter CAROLE *slowly. Her face is marked.*

SLUGGER Look who it is!

BYRNE *and* BANDIT *turn and see her.*

CAROLE Johnny, can ah speak tae yae oan yir ain?

BYRNE Ah thoat ah telt yae tae fuck off. Ah'm no wahntin tae waste ma time talkin tae you, ya whore.

CAROLE But it's important, Johnny. It's urgent.

BYRNE Right then. If it's aw that urgent tell me it right here and now. Then get tae fuck.

CAROLE The Law ur lookin fur yae. Tae pick yae up.

BANDIT Och, don't give us yir worries, Carole. We've goat the Law paid aff fur miles aroon.

SLUGGER It'll be Constable McWhirter lookin fur mair bribes.

CAROLE It wusnae the usual polis, Johnny. They wur roon ut the hoose askin questions.

BANDIT *(mimics her)* It wusnae the usual polis, Johnny.

BYRNE *(to* BANDIT*)* You shut yir mouth. *(To* CAROLE.*)* Whit did thae wahnt?

CAROLE Thae wahntit tae know if ah'd been ut that party in Cowcaddens where the man was murdered.

BYRNE   Oh aye. And how did ma name get involved?

CAROLE   They thoat ah wus thair wae you.

BYRNE   An what did you say?

CAROLE   Ah sed ah hudnae seen yae and ah didnae know nothin about it.

BYRNE   Then whit did yae dae?

CAROLE   Ah came straight doon here tae warn you.

BANDIT   *(derisive)*   Fur fuck's sake. Did yae leave a trail o breadcrumbs behind yae as yae came?

CAROLE   Johnny, they said they wur gonnae get you on this wan. They're determined.

BANDIT   Ah think you'd better catch that plane, Johnny.

BYRNE   *(on his feet)*   Right. Get in touch wae Rollo the Lawyer an' tell him he might be needit.

SLUGGER   *(exits)*   Ah'll go an get the car.

CAROLE   Johnny, you wur up in Cowcaddens that night, wurn't yae?

BYRNE   Naw. Ah wusnae near the place, wus ah, Bandit?

BANDIT   Naw!

BYRNE   They're just tryin tae hustle me because thae don't like the money-lendin.

CAROLE   Johnny, ah'm worrit aboot yae.

BANDIT   Yir a bit late in the day fur that, ur yae no?

BYRNE   You wait outside, Bandit.

BANDIT   Awright, but hurry up. Remember they might be roon here enytime.

> BANDIT *exits.*
> BYRNE *takes* CAROLE'S *face in his hand.*

BYRNE   That's an awfu bad mark you've goat thair. Did somebody hit yae?

> *He kisses her.*

BANDIT   Ur you two comin or ur yae's gonnae staun thair snoggin aw night?

> BYRNE *alone on stage.*

BYRNE   Alright. You can look down your nose at my money-lending. But the fact was I was providing a social service. When the police finally got me they took away my address book with over three thousand addresses in it. They interviewed every person on that list but not one of them would give evidence against me. Not one of them. Because I'd been prepared to do business with them when you hadn't. While you were sitting back pretending not to notice, I had been there to care for their needs. Alright, my methods with defaulters were quick and to the point, but they weren't any different from your precious world – just a bit less hypocritical and undisguised.

Let's face it. The whole human world is a money-lending racket and if it takes a man's whole lifetime to kill him with his debts. that doesn't make it any the less an act of murder!

Explosion. SLUGGER *and* BANDIT *run across stage behind* BYRNE.

WOMAN'S VOICE   Leave us in peace! Hus there no been enough trouble already?

SLUGGER   You tell that man o yours tae keep his fuckin mouth shut or we'll be back.

Exit SLUGGER *and* BANDIT. *Enter* CLERK OF COURT. *Police come on and handcuff* BYRNE. *He stands, on trial.*

CLERK   *(to audience)*   My occupation is Clerk of Court. Three times I saw that man Byrne on trial for murder and twice I saw him get away with it. Witnesses disappeared. Testimony was withdrawn. Anyone who might speak against him was terrorised into silence and justice was thwarted.

On the third occasion, however, he was found Guilty: him and his cronies and his lawyer with him. It was third-time-lucky. When the Judge pronounced the sentence of life imprisonment for murder, I turned to the press benches, and the police, and even for a moment to the public gallery – and raised my thumb in triumph.

He has his thumb up and he presses it out victoriously on three sides of him.

The windows open and LIZZIE *and* MAGGIE *appear.* SLUGGER *and* BANDIT *come on the stage, putting on prison officer's uniform.*

LIZZIE   So Byrne's goat life imprisonment right enough.

MAGGIE   Aye and it's good riddance tae bad rubbish. That's aw ah can say.

LIZZIE   Aye. There must huv been en evil streak in him somewhere. It's the likes o him get the Gorbals a bad name.

MAGGIE   Aye. *(Pause.)* Whit dyae think o that? The price o meat goin up agane?

LIZZIE   Oh aye. Is it no awful? Ma man says ah should make omelettes. Ah says tae him, cun yae show me how? An he did. He made the tea last night. Omelette an chips. He said he learnt it when he wus daein his national service.

MAGGIE   Aye. It's a pity that yin, Byrne, nivir hud any national service tae dae. That wid huv knocked the nonsense oot his heid.

SLUGGER *and* BANDIT *are now dressed in full prison officer uniform. They stand officially on either side of* BYRNE. *They have become the prison wardens.*

BYRNE   *(to audience)*   I did not do the crime I was convicted for.

Drums. SLUGGER *and* BANDIT *march off the stage with* BYRNE. *The* CLERK OF COURT *follows behind – a little man, by the way – smiling to the audience. The Windae-hingers withdraw.*

SONG   The Sweetest of Songs is the Song of the Clyde.

Act Two

BYRNE *on bunk. Prison cell.* MOCHAN *in next cell listening.* BYRNE *direct to audience.*

BYRNE   When a man goes into prison, he's suddenly cut off. His old friends disappear, and his wife, his family – how can he possibly keep in touch wae them when he's locked away.

He hears that his son's getting into trouble, following in his father's footsteps, but he can do nothing about it. The walls prevent him. The thick walls of justice. Your justice.

Enter JOHNSTONE, *prison officer. Furtive.*

JOHNSTONE   Byrne! Byrne! You're a faither. Your burd's just hud a baby.
BYRNE   When?
JOHNSTONE   Last night. It's a girl.
BYRNE   A girl? Ur they awright?
JOHNSTONE   Aye, they're fine. There's somebody coming, I'll need to go. *(Exits.)*
BYRNE   Naw. Don't go. Come back. Listen! Listen! *(To audience:)* So yir daein time. That's a good phrase for it. Daein time. Because that's whit yir daein awright. Time! Time with no distractions. Plenty of time tae consider the matter. Time tae burn. Time tae waste. Time tae kill.

One year. Two year. Three year. Four.

And if yir lucky you've goat a window you can see through, and if you're even luckier through that window you can see a tree, and you think about the day when you'll see the other side of that tree.

Beans. Sweat. Urine. Insomnia. *(Tries to catch a fly.)*

Poor me. Poor fly. Sharing a cell.

Five year. Six year. Seven year. More.

Thick. Thick. Walls of justice.

Thick. Thick. Heads of justice.

Thick. Thick. Assholes of justice.

Thick. Thick. Whores of justice.

—who do you think you are locking me up in here and telling me it's for life? Telling me I deserve it? My life. Fullstop. Thank you very much. I'm so grateful to you for giving me what I deserve. It must be nice to be in the right because it's shitty to be in the wrong.
JOHNSTONE   Your lawyer's here for you, Byrne.

BYRNE *turns as* LEWIS, *lawyer, enters.*

LEWIS   Sorry I couldnae get here sooner, Johnny. How are you?
BYRNE   In a wee bit o a hurry tae get oot o here.

349

LEWIS   They've put you in solitary.

BYRNE   Aye well there's a fly up in the corner up there. He an me huv been huving a wee bit o a blether. How's Carole?

LEWIS   She's fine, Johnny. She's at home with her mother.

BYRNE   That old bag. Tell hur no tae be giein the wean any o her cheap biddy.

LEWIS   Does she drink?

BYRNE   The old woman? Christ, she'd drink the Clyde dry if it wis full o whisky.

LEWIS   You don't need to worry about the baby. Carole will look after her alright. You can trust her.

BYRNE   Trust her nothing. Lewis, ah wahnt out o here and fast. Ah lay doon oan ma bunk last night and a thoat, fifteen years. Fifteen fuckin years. That old swine ae a judge an' the police lieing their mooths aff. How long wull it take fur the appeal tae come through?

LEWIS   Johnny, I wouldnae pin any hopes on an appeal. They were out tae get you. One way or another. The walls of that court would have had to fall down before you'd have walked out of there a free man. (JOHNNY *is silent.*) I don't suppose you'll have seen your press. *(Hands* JOHNNY *newspapers.)*

BYRNE   *(reading)*   'I was a victim of The Gentle Terror!' Whit's aw this about?

LEWIS   Did you no know? That's the name you go under in the Glasgow underworld. Read further down.

BYRNE   'Father of four William Brown told of the night he was threatened by … John Byrne, better known as The Gentle Terror, who said that if he didn't pay his debt, he would cut off his ears!' Jesus Christ! These people have got wonderful imaginations!

LEWIS   You're good copy, Johnny. There's no a good word to say about yae.

BYRNE   And will that affect the appeal?

LEWIS   Well, it shoudnae but it gives you an indication. They're gloating, Johnny. And now they've got you, they're no gonnae let you go without a struggle. The best you can hope for is a bit of remission and parole from time to time – if you keep your nose clean. And your hands to yourself. I know it won't be easy but I would be misleading you if I told you otherwise.

BYRNE *silent, thinking.*

BYRNE   Why did they put me in solitary, Lewis?

LEWIS   Because of your reputation, Johnny. You're a dangerous man.

Pause. BYRNE *thinks again before he speaks.*

BYRNE   Aye. Well, ah'm no gonnae stop being dangerous, just because ah'm in here. If thae think ah'm gonnae crawl fur a bit o parole, they've goat another thing comin.

LEWIS   A few years ago they would have hanged you.

BYRNE   They're gonnae wish they hud.

Enter MOCHAN, *sweeping the stage.*

MOCHAN   Hello there. Ma name's Michael Mochan. Ah've goat a story too. But youse'll no be wantin tae be bothert wae that. Ah mean, ah'm just an old lag, who wahnts tae know whit ah think? Ah dae keep ma nose clean *(wipes it)* so ah get wee joabs tae dae an ah get aboot mair than the rest o thaim. An that way ah get tae hear a loat an see a loat, an usually ah keep my mooth shut aboot it, but wae the things that happened tae that man, Byrne, well, the time came when ah knew ah couldnae just sit back and watch any loanger, ah wis gonnae huv tae say whit ah hud seen, whatever it cost me… No that it made much difference.

(Pause. Thinks.) Ach, but that aw comes later when ah goat tae know him. So ah'll talk tae yaes later oan – if that's awright. Ah jist thoat ah'd say hello an introduce masel.

Exits.

BYRNE *and* CAROLE *and* JOHNSTONE.

BYRNE   Where's the wean?
CAROLE   Ah left hur wae ma muther.
BYRNE   Yae whit? Ur ye aff yir heid?
CAROLE   Ah knew yae'd wahnt tae see hur but ah wus feart she'd catch the cauld.

BYRNE *is exasperated. He looks at* JOHNSTONE *who is standing by.*

BYRNE   Can you no wait ootside fur a while?
JOHNSTONE   Sorry Johnny. Ah've goat ma orders.
BYRNE   Aye, awright. Yir no a bad cunt, Johnstone. Ah wish there were mair like you in this shithoose. *(To* CAROLE.) It wus him telt me aboot the wean. Otherwise ah'd never huv known. That's the way they treat you in this fuckin place. Huv yae seen Danny?
CAROLE   He's lying low.
BYRNE   Ah'll bet he is, the old bastard. The rest o us inside an' he goes Scotfree. Typical. Ah'll bet he's drinking himsel paralytic. Old swine.
CAROLE   Thae wur aw tawkin aboot you in the hoaspital.
BYRNE   Wur they?
CAROLE   Aye. Aw the women. Lying thair feeding thair weans an you wur the main topic o conversation. You should ah heard the things thae wur sayin.
BYRNE   Ah've seen the papers.
CAROLE   It wus worse than the papers. Wan wife sed yae impaled somebody on the spike o a railin, another wan said yae tortured a man by nailing his feet tae the floor. An thir wus this big fat bitch thair, it was hur eighth, and she sed you wur a hired gun doon in London.
BYRNE   An whit did you say?

CAROLE   Ah never said anythin. Ah kept ma mooth shut.

BYRNE   Ur yae ashamed o me then?

CAROLE   Well, whit dae yae expect me tae dae, haud the wean up an tell them you loat just watch whit yir sayin Byrne's this wean's father.

BYRNE   Well you might've stoaped them tellin lies aboot me at least.

CAROLE   How dae ah know if it's lies. Ah don't know how many people you've kilt, dae ah?

BYRNE   Well ah'll tell yae. Ah've never kilt anybody in ma fuckin life – and don't you furget it.

CAROLE   *(Looking away. Then to* JOHNSTONE.)   Can ah gie him a cigarette? (JOHNSTONE *nods assent. She produces cigarettes from her bra.)*

BYRNE   Whit ur yae daein?

CAROLE   Thae take everythin aff yae doon thair. *(Lights cigarette for him. One for herself.)* That yin Halliday's cerryin oan like a big shoat noo that you're inside.

BYRNE   Whit's he daein?

CAROLE   He wus in the pub last night an he smashed the gantry.

BYRNE   Eeejit!

CAROLE   Tommy the barman says thair aw fighting like cats an doags because you're no thair tae keep the peace.

BYRNE   Aye well you tell Tommy ah'll see tae thaim soon enough.

CAROLE   How come?

BYRNE   Because ah'm getting out o here, that's how come.

CAROLE   Naebday telt me aboot it. When ur yae getting out?

BYRNE   Ah'll no bother, if that's how you feel aboot it. Ah'll just stay here.

CAROLE   Och don't talk stupit!

BYRNE   Whit's the matter wae you? Huv yae goat yirsel a new man awready?

CAROLE   Look ah huvnae goat time tae look fur fellas, ah'm too busy lookin efter your fuckin wean.

BYRNE *raises his arm.* JOHNSTONE *moves to restrain him.*

BYRNE   Aw, don't worry, Johnstone, old boy. She's no worth it. Ur yae married yirself?

JOHNSTONE   Aye.

BYRNE   Any family?

JOHNSTONE   A boy and a girl.

BYRNE   Good fur you!

CAROLE   Wull you stoap talking tae that swine an tell me whit this is aw aboot?

BYRNE   Whit? Oh, ur you still here? Awright, ah'll tell yae. Now listen carefully fur wance in yir life. This is important. It's aboot ma Appeal.

CAROLE   Oh, is that aw.

BYRNE   Whit dae yae mean 'is that aw'?

CAROLE   Well, Lewis hus telt me aw aboot it.

BYRNE   Lewis doesnae huv enything tae dae wae it anymore.

CAROLE   Huv yae changed yir lawyer?

BYRNE   Aye.

CAROLE   Who huv yae goat? Franchetti?

BYRNE   That balloon. You must be jokin.

CAROLE   Who then?

BYRNE   Maself.

CAROLE   You? Since when did you become a lawyer?

BYRNE   *(sits back and regards her with disgust)*   Look ut yae, ya stupit wee whore. Of course ah'm no a lawyer, fur fuck sake. Ah'm no pretendin tae be a lawyer, but can you no understand anything? Do you no understand anything at all? No even aboot me? This is ma life ah'm fighting fur. You've hud a wean tae me an ah wahnt tae see it. No in here. Ah'm glad you didnae bring it in here. Because ah don't wahnt it tae see its faither in a place like this.

CAROLE   It happens to be a she.

BYRNE   Ah thoat a telt you tae listen.

CAROLE   Awright, ah'm listening.

BYRNE   Okay. This is ma life ah'm fightin fur and nobody can fight fur ma life except me maself. But ah'm gonnae need new witnesses and ah wahnt you tae talk tae a few people fur me. Do you understand that?

CAROLE   Which people?

BYRNE   *(Hesitates. Speaks to* JOHNSTONE.*)*   Could you stoap up yir ears fur a minit, Johnstone?

JOHNSTONE   Ah'm afraid the time's up, Johnny.

BYRNE   Aye but we've goat drinkin up time. *(Returns to* CAROLE.*)* Go doon tae the pub and talk tae the Big Yin.

CAROLE   Wullie?

BYRNE   Aye! An' tell him tae talk tae that mob in Shamrock Street an tell thaim ah'll be wahntin tae see thaim up here.

CAROLE   Who do you mean in Shamrock Street?

BYRNE   Never mind that. Just tell him. He'll know whit ahm talking aboot.

JOHNSTONE   Awright, that's the time.

CAROLE   *(annoyed at* JOHNSTONE*)*   Och, awright. Ah'm just goin.

BYRNE   Come here. *(She goes to him.)* Dae's a favour Johnstone an close yir eyes a wee minit. *(They kiss.)* Noo don't you furget that. And next time bring the wean in so that ah can see it.

Enter MOCHAN.

MOCHAN   The course of young love never runs smooth. Aye, well he's making a big mistake handling that Appeal himsel. They'll no like that. There was only one man ah ever knew that managed to really speak the truth in a Court of Law and that wus an old wino ah knew. A right old down-and-outer, reeling aboot in the streets wae a three-week stubble oan his chin an stoapin people fur the price of a cup o tea. Ah niver even goat tae know his name. But ah saw his grand finale in

the Sheriff Court in Glasgow wan day, when he goat tae his feet swayed fae side
tae side straightened himsel up took a deep breath an made a speech oan his own
behalf. This wus him:

Today ah wish tae apologise. Ah wish tae apologise tae ma wife fur the terrible
life ah gied hur tae ma children – who no longer want to speak to me – fur aw
they hud tae go without because of their father – tae aw the people – doctors and
police social workers and ministers of religion – who tried tae give me help only
tae huv the help thrown back in their face and most of all – most of all, he said,
and he swayed a wee bit – most of all ah want tae apologise tae this Court in its
Mercy fur the many times ah spurned its Clemency. Ah apologise!

The whole Court was stunned intae silence. And the Sheriff leaned forward and
said, 'Is there anything you would like to add?' And the old fella looked up and he
smiled and he opened out his arms and he closed his eyes tilted back his head, and
this is whit he said: *(sings)*

I left my heart

In San Francisco…

BYRNE   Your Worship, Ladies and Gentlemen of the Jury, and all the rest of you
wankers out there, here ah ahm, the animal, wae a great big lawbook in ma hand
an thinking.

The animal is thinking. He's beginning tae figure it out. Whit yir legal racket's
aw about, he's sussed it.

So ah thoat ah wus a fly-boy. Ah thoat ah wus hard. But you loat take the
biscuit. Yae beat the band. You've goat the biggest racket of aw and you're the
coolest customers because you're legal – and ahm no?

Ah huvnae done any more than the rest o you ur daein every livin day o your
free lifes, you're just a bit mair lang-distance aboot it, yae've goat a wee bit
finesse – but everything you've goat depends oan thievin and killin o one kind or
another – the only difference is that you make the Laws!

But remember this, the animal is thinking.

MOCHAN *has been standing, leaning on his brush and watching* BYRNE *throughout
the speech.*

MOCHAN   Oh, my Goad, son, yir like a wild stallion wae a man oan its back. Why
don't yae just give up an' gie yirsel peace? Yir an awfae hard man.

(To audience:) But he was never hard enough because he couldnae keep
control o himself. He suffered frae frustration. He hud aw this energy bilin up
inside him an he couldnae get it oot. So there would always come a moment when
he wid snap an it wid come oot o him like a torrent. An that wus his undoin. Fur
aw that he wus thinkin, he felt too much, an' he let his feelins run away wae him.

It wus because o that he never actually goat tae make his appeal as you'll see in
a minit. The famous story ah'm sure you've never heard aboot – 'Johnny Byrne
Meets the Commando' better unknown as brawn beats its brains oot agen—

Exits with brush.

Attention returns to BYRNE.
Enter Second Prison Officer, RENFREW, *closely followed by* THE COMMANDO *who is Assistant Governor of the prison.*

RENFREW   Okay, Byrne. Oan yir feet. The Assistant Governor's here tae see yae.
BYRNE   The Assistant Governor. What's he wanting?
RENFREW   Don't be impudent. Get on your feet.
BYRNE   Just a minute. Who do you think you're talking to?
COMMANDO   Okay, Renfrew, outside. I'll deal with this alone.
RENFREW   Are you sure, sir? I'll be right outside, sir.
BYRNE   Yes, sir. No, sir. Three bags full, sir.
COMMANDO   You wanted to see me, Byrne.
BYRNE   Ah don't, what gives you that impression. I could think o nicer sights.
COMMANDO   Don't smart-talk me, Byrne. You've been demanding to see someone for the last ten days.
BYRNE   Aye, that's right. Ah think it wis ten days. Might huv been eleven. Ah'm no sure. You lose track of time in this place. You know whit ah mean? Aye but ah think you're right, now that you come to mention it ah huv been asking tae see someone, but ah widnae huv said ah wus *demanding* anything, and ah don't think the person ah wus asking tae see is you. Ah wanted tae see the guvnor, no his assistant. And by the way, ah'll smart-talk you anytime ah like.
COMMANDO   How dare you, Byrne. I won't have talk like this in my prison.
BYRNE   Oh, it's your prison, is it? Ah wus beginnin tae wunder who owned it. Ah knew it certainly didnae belang tae me. Ah wid huv arranged the furniture different.
COMMANDO   You can make things worse for yourself, you know.
BYRNE   No much worse, surely.
COMMANDO   Yes, but you can make things easy for yourself or you can make them hard, depending on how you behave.
BYRNE   Ha! Ha! That's funny. That's… that's 'rich', as they say, me behave maself; ah'm no capable of behavin maself can you people no understand that? Oh, you're a joke so yae ur, comin intae me daein a lifer and telling me tae behave maself. You behave yourself. Awright, so if you've been sent doon tae talk tae the animal yae might as well talk tae the animal. The animal is hoping you have to discuss the witnesses fur its Appeal.
COMMANDO   No, I haven't come here to discuss. I've come here to tell you something. There's nothing to discuss.
BYRNE   Oh? And what is there to tell me?
COMMANDO   You're not going to be allowed to interview the witnesses. Not in this prison. If you want to have witnesses interviewed, you'll have to get a lawyer to do it for you.
BYRNE   But I'm handling my Appeal myself. I'm entitled to interview witnesses to

prepare my case.

COMMANDO   Not if I think there might be a security risk involved.

BYRNE   What?

COMMANDO   I think you heard what I said.

BYRNE   Aye. Ah heard you awright. Ah just couldnae believe what ah wus hearing. Ah don't think you know this, china, but ah know you. You're the wan thae call the Commando. That's the wurd you like tae put aboot this place – that yir wan o the real dirty squad that fought against old Adolf. The Commando. Aye, yir reputation's preceded yae.

COMMANDO   And I've dealt with harder men than you, Byrne.

BYRNE   Maybe you have. Maybe yae huvnae.

COMMANDO   But thae never had so much to say for themselves as you seem to have.

BYRNE   You'll have to excuse me. You know, it must've been that life imprisonment sentence the judge passed oan me, it must have give me a shock or something but a strange thing has happened since ah came in here – ah've started thinking. And now that ah've started, ah just cannae seem tae stop. And wan o the things ah've been thinking, it's a funny thing this, but I don't really think you think there's a security risk involved at all. You don't seriously think ah wid try tae escape, dae yae? Naw. You're just withholding ma witnesses frae me because… *(grabs hold of him)* you're so… fucking… vindictive!

COMMANDO   You let go of me, Byrne.

BYRNE   Naw. Ah'm no letting go o you until you tell me ah'm getting your signature on that piece of paper that ah need!

He is holding THE COMMANDO *with one hand and forming up the other into a clenched fist under his face.* THE COMMANDO *speaks nervously over his shoulder.*

COMMANDO   Renfrew?

BYRNE *finally loses patience and smashes him in the face, snarling with disgust.*

COMMANDO   Officer! Officer! Come quickly!

BYRNE *has let go of him and is laughing happily at the sight of* THE COMMANDO *lying on the floor.* RENFREW *and* JOHNSTONE *run in. They grab* BYRNE *from behind, one on either arm,* BYRNE *is still laughing happily.* THE COMMANDO *gets up and straightens himself out.*

COMMANDO   You'll hear more of this, Byrne.

BYRNE *is still laughing. This next bit is fast. He breaks in mid-laugh and suddenly he is serious, concentrated. Then he swings up, using the grip of the screws as a lever, taking both feet off the ground and kicking him hard in the groin.* THE

COMMANDO *keels over. Grunting with the pain.* RENFREW *leaves go of his grip on* BYRNE *and goes to* COMMANDO'S *assistance.* BYRNE *has relaxed.* JOHNSTONE *keeps a grip on his arm but perhaps it is not so intense as it was a moment before. As* RENFREW *speaks to* JOHNSTONE, *he is bundling* THE COMMANDO *out of the cell.*

RENFREW   Ah think you'd better lock him up. Ah seem tae remember he's a pal o yours.

JOHNSTONE *locks cell door.* BYRNE *shouts through it, laughing, his hands up at his mouth – cupped.*

BYRNE *(shouting)*   SOME FUCKIN COMMANDO!

His laughter dies away and he is sobbing and gasping. He is desperate and sad. He escapes down the door with his hands, the side of his face pressed against it. He lies on the floor silent, his face resting forehead-down on his arm.

Percussion.

MOCHAN   That wus just before ah met up wae him. That wus the beginning o the end wac Byrne and prison. Or maybe you should say the beginning of the ending because it husnae ended yet. Anyway, a strange thing happened in a Glasgow Court following the events just sccn. The charge was read out that the accused, John Byrne, had, on such-and-such a day, assaulted a senior prison officer. That wus awright. Nothin unexpected aboot that. Whit wis strange wus the next bit. His lawyer gets up and says:

LEWIS *has walked on during these last words. He delivers his speech formally out to the audience. Immediately after making his speech, he exits. No personal contact is made with audience.*
    In behind MOCHAN *and* LEWIS' *speeches,* BYRNE *is set upon by* RENFREW *and* JOHNSTONE *who force him, struggling, into a strait-jacket. Both men are hitting him with batons. Eventually they have him in strait-jacket.* RENFREW *continues hitting him long after might be considered necessary.* JOHNSTONE *restrains him.* BYRNE *is left lying on the stage. The strait-jacket is saturated in blood.*

LEWIS   I am unable to defend my client on this charge because I have not been able to find him. When I went to the prison to prepare his defence, I was told he had been taken away but no-one would tell me where…

Exit LEWIS.

MOCHAN   Ah knew where he wus and ah saw the state hc came in. He wus in Peterheid and he wus in the solitary block where ah used tae dae some o ma sweeping. And that wus where the real troubles started. Because, among other things, that's where he met a big screw called Paisley. Ah'll tell yae mair aboot him later an ye'll see a wee bit fur yirsel.

BYRNE *is on stage in strait-jacket. He struggles to get out of it. At first there is percussion. Then there is only his voice as a stab against the silence.*

BYRNE   Fuck! Fuck! Fuck! Fuck You!
Fuck You, You Bastards.
Fuck You Fuck You Fuck You.

The percussion answers the rhythm. Builds to a crescendo when he bursts the strait-jacket. Then he is on his knees facing the audience. He opens out his arms and roars. He falls slowly backwards, arching himself in a yoga asana. The back of his head (nape of neck) and his heels (soles) touch the floor, but his back is arched between them. What do his arms do? Please see, I. S. Iyengar's 'Light on Yoga' for further details. Gradually this can be relaxed. MOCHAN *approaches and looks in at him.* BYRNE *is flat on his back.*

MOCHAN   Johnny Byrne!
BYRNE   Who's there?
MOCHAN   It's Michael Mochan.
BYRNE   Hello there, Michael. Nice tae meet yae. Ah've heard a loat aboot yae. How ur yae daein old-timer?
MOCHAN   Ah'm daein fine. An' what aboot yirsel? An' less o the old-timer.
BYRNE   Ah'm awright. At least ah'm here. Ah've arrived. But it wus a rough journey getting here. Ah think ah'm suffering fae screw-lag. Wid yae mind just telling me where ah ahm?
MOCHAN   Christ, dae yae no even know that? Did they no even tell ye where they were taking yae? You're in Peterheid. Solitary detention wing. Yir no allowed any visitors ur nuthin, so ye'll huv tae make the best o me. Ah'm the only conversation yir gonnae get in here that isnae a crack in the heid. Ah hear yae burst yir strait-jacket.
BYRNE   Ach, it wus weakened. It wus ma ain blood that weakened it. It wus saturated.
MOCHAN   They must huv gied yae some goins over. Wus that done before yae goat here or wus some o it done after?
BYRNE   Some ae it wus here. There's a big bastard aroon here an he wus knockin fuck oot o me. Ah hud tae crack him oan the jaw.
MOCHAN   Did he huv a moustache?
BYRNE   He might huv hud. Ah wusnae really hoping ah'd ever huv tae identify the bastard agen. Aye, but ah think he did.
MOCHAN   That sounds like him.
BYRNE   Who in particular?

MOCHAN   Paisley. Some o us caw him the Reverend because he hates aw Catholics. Wae a name like yours, you're a gonner. He's a sadistic big bastard. And there's been several cases of brutalisation in this prison because o him in the last two months.

BYRNE   Aye. Well ah'm gonnae get tae the governor aboot him.

MOCHAN   He's been had up two or three times but he always gets away wae it. The last time it was fur buggering two of the young prisoners. Everybody knew he'd done it, including his own lawyer, and when he got him off wae it, he wus sick. The lawyer was sick. So there you are, even his own lawyer.

BYRNE   Aye, well let him come for me. I'll be ready for him.

MOCHAN   Did you say you'd cracked his jaw?

BYRNE   That's right.

MOCHAN   Well, don't you worry. He'll be coming for you alright.

Drums. A march. Enter PAISLEY, JOHNSTONE *and* RENFREW. *They face straight on to the audience.* PAISLEY *is one step in front of the other two who form the tips of a triangle behind him. He speaks direct to the audience.*

PAISLEY   I'm Paisley. I'm the one. The bad screw. The one who brings disrepute on all his hard-working colleagues who are making the best of a very tough job. I'm the sadist. The one that's got too much of a taste for the sight of blood. That's what they say. I know it only too well. The prisoners don't like me because they know I don't mess about. I believe in discipline and I believe in using hard methods to tame hard men. And the other... *(pause)* screws don't like me because they know I'm the one that does the dirty work for them.

They know what this prison would be like if we didn't get tough from time to time. They don't want to walk in fear of their life from day to day when they're going about their job, any more than you would. So they tolerate me. I'm *their* hard man. And they feel a wee bit guilty about me because I'm an aspect of themselves they don't like to admit to. Just like you should be feeling guilty about us because we're the garbage disposal squad for the social sewage system. You people out there, that's the way it works for you – you've got a crime problem so you just flush it away one thug after another in behind bars and safely locked away. The cistern's clanked and you can think you can leave it floating away from you to the depths of the sea. Well, ah've goat news fur you – it's pollution. Yir gonnae huv tae look ut it. Because if yae don't, wun day it's gonnae destroy yae. But in the meantime, dirties like me, well, let's just say we're a necessary evil. Very necessary.

BYRNE and MOCHAN   *(together)*   Screws! Screws!

On the chant of 'Screws, Screws' the drums start their march again. The three SCREWS *march over to* BYRNE'S *cell. Drums stop when they are ranged around* BYRNE. *Important that* MOCHAN *observes all that is happening.*

PAISLEY   Okay, Byrne. On your feet. You're going for a wee walk.

BYRNE   Where are you taking me?

PAISLEY   For a wash. You stink.

BYRNE   It doesnae take three of you to take me for a wash.

JOHNSTONE   Come on, Johnny, it's okay.

BYRNE   Johnstone! Ur you followin me or somethin?

RENFREW   Come on. Get these on. *(Puts on handcuffs.)* We'll decide on staffing in this prison, no you.

BYRNE   *(to Paisley)*   Could ah no be handcuffed tae somebody else? This guy's breath stinks. Ah'm sure you'd be much nicer.

PAISLEY   Cumon, Byrne, get going and keep the mouth shut. You're going to have plenty of chance tae talk. We've goat one or two questions to ask you.

BYRNE   Wait a minute. What's all this about? I might've known you lot wouldnae give a fuck supposin ah never washed fae wan year tae the next.

PAISLEY   *(pushing him)*   Cumon, get moving.

BYRNE   Watch it! Paisley. On second thoughts, you stink more than he does.

PAISLEY *threatens him.*

BYRNE   That's right, ya coward. Ah know all about you. You used tae be a hitman fur the moneylender doon the docks. Did yir 'colleagues' know that?

PAISLEY *hits him.* BYRNE *spits at* PAISLEY. PAISLEY *enraged.* JOHNSTONE *restrains him.*

JOHNSTONE   Take it easy.

PAISLEY   Cumon, move him.

Drums. They move BYRNE *out of cell towards a sink which represents the washroom. As they cross stage to it,* BYRNE *is tugging and pulling at the handcuff which attaches him to* RENFREW. *The effect should be comic.* MOCHAN *follows them across and watches from a concealed position.*

PAISLEY   Okay, Byrne. Get in there.

BYRNE   Ah'm no going in there. No wae the three o you and no witnesses.

MOCHAN *makes a thumbs-up sign to the audience to let them know he is keeping an eye on things.*

PAISLEY   *(pushing him roughly)*   Get in!

RENFREW   *(who has been pulled off balance by* PAISLEY'S *pushing)*   Hey, go easy!

BYRNE   *(now in wash area)*   Aye, you heard whit the man said.

PAISLEY   Okay, Byrne. We're taking the handcuffs off, but no funny business. There's a sinkful of water for you tae wash yourself.

The handcuffs are removed. BYRNE *looks at them all as if he might start some trouble but then he turns away laughing scornfully, as if he has decided they are not worth the effort. He sits down at the sink and enjoys the water.*

BYRNE   Oh, this is rerr. Ah suppose you thoat animals like me wouldnae like water. Did yae bring the DDT powder too?
PAISLEY   Give him the towel.

JOHNSTONE *gives him a towel which* BYRNE *takes reluctantly.*

BYRNE   Is that aw the wash ah'm gonnae get? Fur fuck's sake, ah never even goat time tae dae behind ma ears. Whit aboot a shave. Surely youse can run as far as a shave. Or is shaving forbidden too?
PAISLEY   You're damn right it's forbidden. We know what you do wae a razor, Byrne. Dry yourself off. Ah've goat some questions tae ask yae.
BYRNE   Oh ho! This is when we find out what it's all about, eh? *(Dries his face.)* Okay, fire away. Paisley. I'm intrigued. *(Aside to* RENFREW, *quickly.)* You didnae think ah'd know a word like that, did yae, Renfrew?
PAISLEY   Stoap playing the innocent, Byrne. What's aw this aboot a prisoner's charter?
BYRNE   What? A prisoner's charter. Don't ask me, Ian, ah don't know anything aboot anything as intelligent as that. Ah'm an animal.
PAISLEY   We've found a copy of it in the main block and we know you're behind it. There's been nothing but trouble since you were brought here.
BYRNE   What does it say?
PAISLEY   You know fucking well what it says. A more humane system and investigations… investigations of brutality in this prison…
BYRNE   That sounds like interesting reading. Ah wouldnae mind a copy o that if yae can spare wan.
PAISLEY *(threatening)*   Don't mess with me, Byrne. What's going oan? You'd better tell us or it's more than your life's worth.
BYRNE *(thinks about it)*   Ah'm tellin you nothing.
PAISLEY   Awright! Give him a duckin.

They force BYRNE'S *head under water. He struggles throughout.*

JOHNSTONE   Will we bring him up?
PAISLEY   Naw. Keep him down a minute longer. We'll make him talk. Don't you worry.
JOHNSTONE   We'd better be careful.
PAISLEY   Listen, son. Don't you try tae tell me. How long huv you been in the prison service?
JOHNSTONE   Two years.
PAISLEY   Aye, well ah'm comin up fur ten years. So you just keep yir mouth shut.

(Pause.) Okay. Let him up…

BYRNE *is released from the water. He shakes his head about and starts shouting as he does so, struggling with* RENFREW *and* JOHNSTONE.

BYRNE   Fuck you, you homosexual bastard, Paisley, and fuck King Billy!
PAISLEY   Okay. Give him another ducking. *(They hesitate.)* Go on, do it. *(They do.)* Fur fuck sake, do you see whit he's like. Kindness'll get you nowhere wae that yin. Okay. Bring him up again.
BYRNE   Fuck!
PAISLEY   Awright, Byrne. You'd better start talking or you'll go under a third time and this time you won't come back up.

BYRNE *looks up at him slowly, thinking things over.*

BYRNE   Awright. So what is it you want to know?
PAISLEY   There's something being planned. Some kind of unrest among the men.
BYRNE   That's right.
PAISLEY   What is it?
BYRNE   They're gonnae cut your balls off. (PAISLEY *hits him.)* They're gonnae cut your balls off an' then they're gonnae serve thaim up tae the governor oan toast.
PAISLEY   Okay. Put him under again. And this time… *(They have his head under water.)* This time… don't bother… tae bring him up!

In darkness, noise of prison riot begins. Men's voices shouting. Various sounds emerge clearly from it. 'Up on the Roof'. Perhaps the Prisoner's Charter is read out at this point. Last sound to emerge across the crowd noise is a voice through a public address hailer:

'If you come down peacefully, with no trouble, there will be no recriminations… I repeat that… no recriminations if you come down peacefully…'

BYRNE *is lying on his bunk.* MOCHAN *speaks through to him excitedly.*

MOCHAN   Johnny, waken up. Quick. There's a riot. The men ur up oan the roof an the press and television's here an everything…
BYRNE   *(groggy)* What?
MOCHAN   They're demanding an investigation into prison brutality… Oh, ur you awright. Christ, ah thoat they wur gonnae go the whole way wae yae that time, Johnny. If Paisley hud hud his way, they wid have, but Johnstone chickened oot o it.
BYRNE   Ah must ah blacked out.
MOCHAN   You're lucky yir lungs didnae burst.

Sound of loudhailer in distance.

BYRNE   What's that?

MOCHAN   They're bringing them down. They've been telt that if they come doon peacefully there'll be no recriminations against the ringleaders.

BYRNE   Thank Christ fur that. They think ah'm the masterplanner. Masturbator's more fucking like it. Shower o wankers!

MOCHAN   Sssh! Listen!

Man howling in the distance.

MOCHAN   It sounds as if they're bringing thaim up here to the solitary wing.

BYRNE   Aye, and that doesnae sound much like 'no recriminations'. *(Man's voice shouting louder.)* 'They're kicking me, boys. Leave me alane. Ah hud nothin tae dae wae it'.

BYRNE   So much fur reason. So much fur the peaceful approach. Bastards!

MOCHAN and BYRNE   *(together, banging and making as much noise as possible)* Bastards! Bastards! Bastards! Bastards!

Percussion. The March again. Screws enter to BYRNE. BYRNE *immediately on the ready for a fight.*

PAISLEY   You've been creating a bit of a din doon here, Byrne. Did yae think we wouldnae hear you?

BYRNE   Ah wahntit yae tae hear me because ah could hear whit you were up tae ya dirty swine. You're a pig. A disgusting Protestant pig.

RENFREW   Look at him, the animal, ready fur anuther fight.

BYRNE   That's right, crabcrutch, ah'm ready fur you enytime.

They pull their batons.

BYRNE   Oh, it's the big sticks, is it? Gie me wan and ah'll ram it up yir arse.

JOHNSTONE   Don't make things worse fur yourself, Johnny.

BYRNE   Aw, cumon, less o the old pals act wae that thing in yir haun. Whit's the matter wae you loat enyway? Wull your old ladies no let yae get it in anymore? Is this how yae ease yir frustrations?

PAISLEY   *(to others)* Haud him. *(They grab hold of* BYRNE. PAISLEY *speaks to him with the baton held back, viciously ready for action.)* I'm going to enjoy this, Byrne. Aye, you're right. It is frustration. There's been a loat o faces ah've wahntit tae punch and couldnae an' a loat of skulls ah've wahntit tae crack – and couldnae. But wae you ah've got a perfect excuse tae let it aw come out...

BYRNE *kicks him and at the same time jumps on* RENFREW. *He jabs his fingers repeatedly in* RENFREW'S *eye, finally getting a hold on the eye, straining as if to gouge it out. He is pulled off by* JOHNSTONE *and* PAISLEY *beats him about the head with his baton.* RENFREW *lies howling on the floor, his hand over his injured eye.*

RENFREW   Ma eye! Ma eye! What's he done tae ma eye!

PAISLEY   Aw shut up. You'll survive. *(Kicks* BYRNE *who is unconscious.)* And so will he. Worst luck. Ah think he'll need tae go tae a special place. A very special place.

JOHNSTONE *(he is helping* RENFREW)   Listen, Paisley, there's bound to be an inquiry about this. Renfrew's injured.

PAISLEY   Yes. You're quite right, Johnstone. There probably will be an inquiry. But that's no gonnae bother us, is it? No unless you start getting loose wae yir tongue.

JOHNSTONE   But they'll see the marks on his head.

PAISLEY   That's because he fell on the floor, whilst attacking a prison officer, isn't it? You saw it with your own eyes. You did see it, didn't you?

JOHNSTONE   …Fell on the floor… They'll never accept that.

PAISLEY   They've accepted it before. Plenty o times. Come on. We'd better get this yin tae a doctor. *(To audience.)* Listen, if you excuse him *(indicates* BYRNE) on the grounds that he's a product of this shit-heap system, then you'd better excuse me on the same grounds.

Drums. They exit.

BYRNE *stands up slowly, composes himself and walks out of cell towards audience. Before he speaks he smiles. He begins his speech by mimicking the upper-class tones of a Judge.*

BYRNE   Ladies and Gentlemen of the Jury. In this trial, as in all criminal trials, the Judge and the Jury have different tasks. Your task is, at the end of the day, to bring in a verdict on the Charge on the Indictment before you. *(Own voice.)* The trial wus a farce. Old Mochan got up and did his bit, right enough. He stuck his neck right out and told them the whole story – detail by detail, as he had seen it wae his own eyes. It wus obvious he was telling the truth but that didnae make much difference. *(Smiles again. Judge's voice.)* You must make up your minds on the credibility and reliability of the evidence you have heard. The matter of the verdict, credibility and reliability, which facts are proved, and which not, are matters for you alone…

BYRNE *smiles. Next part is done with off-stage voices.*

VOICES   What is your verdict?
    The verdict is Guilty.
    Is that verdict unanimous or by a majority?
    It is by a majority.

BYRNE   My lawyer passed me a note. It said 'You didn't stand a chance. It was either you or three married men. They didn't dare do otherwise.' After that I went on yet another journey.

Enter three SCREWS. *They lay hands on* BYRNE, *handcuffing him. They push him into centre stage and begin to construct the cage around him.* PAISLEY *punctuates the making of the cage with the speech of the prosecuting advocate, which he delivers with great relish.*

PAISLEY   My Lord, I move for sentence. The Accused is 24 years of age and I produce a Schedule of previous convictions, and your Lordship will see that there have been *fifteen* previous convictions dating from when the accused was a juvenile. The initial convictions are of offences of dishonesty. In particular, in 1963, he was sentenced to two years imprisonment for assault to severe injury and assault by stabbing... February 1963, sentenced to imprisonment for assaulting the police and attempting to resist arrest. Two years imprisonment in 1965 for assault and again in October 1965. 1967 sentenced to life imprisonment for murder. 1968 another 18 months for assaulting the assistant governor of one of Her Majesty's prisons, and now, here's a wee bit more for you. Tell him, Renfrew!

RENFREW   *(also taking off judge)*   John Byrne. You have a deplorable record and you are now serving a sentence of life imprisonment for murder. *(Loud send-up 'tut tuts' from* PAISLEY *and* RENFREW.*)* I cannot emphasise too much that if you are to serve your sentence of imprisonment in such a way as to obtain some remission, you must behave yourself. (PAISLEY *and* RENFREW *nod sagely at this.)*

PAISLEY   Did you hear that, Johnny? Behave yourself.

RENFREW   The sentence I am about to pronounce will have some effect – *(laughing in his own voice)* you bet your fucking life it'll have some effect – *(Judge's voice again)* some effect in that it will be taken into consideration if and when you are released, when the time comes for consideration *(own voice)* but only consideration – of your release. I now sentence you to ha ha ha four years' imprisonment.

PAISLEY   Hear that, Johnny? Another four years on top of what you've already got. If you ever get out of here, it will be in your coffin. See you later!

Exit SCREWS.

MOCHAN   John Byrne, you've gone beyond the physical wae these people. It's no your body they're trying tae break – it's yir proud spirit, because that's what they really fear.

Exit MOCHAN.

Percussion, very quiet and twitchy, behind next sequence. Fluorescent light comes on. It hurts BYRNE'S *eyes, his head. He tries to stretch up towards it. Fails. Each time he fails another light comes on. He tries to climb up the bars. Fails. Another light. He crouches, concentrates, prepares to spring. Leaps up, hands stretched out towards light. Falls back on to floor. Another light goes on. Sits with his hands over his eyes. Enter* RENFREW.

RENFREW   What's this animal? Going to sleep? Sleeping's not allowed, especially not during the day. Yes, it's during the day, animal. I'll bet that surprised you. Never mind. It's nice and bright in here anyway. Isn't it? Look, ah've brought a bit of food for you.

BYRNE *takes his hands from his eyes and looks at food.*

RENFREW   Hungry, are we, animal? Well, there you are.

Puts plate down outside of bars. BYRNE *tries to reach it with his arm but it is too far away from him.*

RENFREW   Oh, sorry. Can you not reach that? Wait and I'll move it a wee bit closer for you.

Picks up plate and spits in food. Puts it down within BYRNE'S *reach.* BYRNE *looks at* RENFREW, *looks back to food. Stretches his arm out slowly through the bars, staring at* RENFREW *who moves back a little. Still staring at him he begins to eat the food – very deliberately – with his fingers.*

BYRNE   You think you're going to break me, don't you?
RENFREW *(indicating patch on his eye)*   Well, you're not exactly my favourite person, Byrne, you could say that.
BYRNE   Well, I've got news for you. I've got something in me that can't be broken, not by you nor by anybody else – no matter what you do to me.
RENFREW   Is that a challenge?
BYRNE   You don't need any challenging. You're going to try it anyway. And your food tastes like fucking sawdust. *(He throws it out through the bars.)*

RENFREW *stands up.*

RENFREW   Right, Byrne. That's just what I was waiting for. Paisley! Johnstone! *(They enter.)*
PAISLEY   What is it?
RENFREW   Look at the mess this animal's made. He's getting aggressive again.
PAISLEY   Oh well. We'll need to do something about that, won't we? Haud yir noses, boys, we're going into his smelly cage…

SCREWS *enter cage. While* PAISLEY *is talking,* JOHNSTONE *searches with his hands along top edge of cage.* RENFREW *holds his nose and looks under chamber pot.*

PAISLEY   So how do you like your new quarters, Byrne? This is the Cage and you're in Inverness. Lovely part of the world, Inverness. Too bad yae cannae get tae see any of it. Aye, yir nice and secure, Byrne. There's these bars, then there's the four walls round the bars – solid concrete. Then there's us… Awright, get your clothes off.

BYRNE   What is this?

PAISLEY   Get them off or we'll tear them off you.

BYRNE   Come on and try.

JOHNSTONE   We need to search you, Byrne. Official procedure.

BYRNE   Official procedure, my arse. *(Pointing at Paisley.)* It was that bastard's idea.

Starts taking his clothes off angrily. When he has stripped BYRNE *places his hands as a shield for his genitals.*

PAISLEY   Okay, search them too. *(Referring to clothes.)* Right, Byrne. Stand against the wall. Oh, look at him. Frightened somebody's gonnae manhandle you, ur yae? Don't worry, we don't want tae know about your disgusting body. Stand against the wall. Okay Renfrew. Search him. Spread your legs, Byrne.

RENFREW *searches him, looking under his armpits, between his toes, finally probing his rectum.* BYRNE *reacts violently to this.* RENFREW *gets away from him fast.*

PAISLEY   Oh, look. He's sensitive.

BYRNE *is looking aggressive.*

PAISLEY   *(as they leave the cage)*   Ah see you've goat that dangerous look again, Byrne. Well you can save it fur later. We're no quite ready fur that yet. But we'll be back. Oh aye and ah think we'd better take your clothes. You never know what mischief he might get tae wae them, do you lads?

Takes clothes. BYRNE *rushes at them but the cage is locked.*

PAISLEY   Too late, Byrne. It's too late for you for anything. Your time's up. You've become one of the living dead.

BYRNE   No. So long as I'm fighting, I know that I'm alive.

PAISLEY   Aye, well ah've telt yae – we'll be back. And we're gonnae knock the fighting out of your system once and for all.

Drums. Exit SCREWS. PAISLEY *pauses.*

PAISLEY   Cover yourself, you disgusting bastard.

BYRNE *makes V signs at* PAISLEY *who laughs. Drums continue. Scotland the Brave.* SCREWS *exit. Starts to pace the interior of the cage. Jogs on the spot. Jogs round the cage. Stops, overcome with weariness for a moment, resting his head against his arm.*
    Begins again, doing press-ups and other exercises. Sits down and adopts Yoga half-lotus posture. He feels the floor with the flat of his hand, then runs his hands over the bare skin of his body.

Enter CAROLE. *She stands looking into the cage.*

CAROLE   Hello, Johnny.
BYRNE *(Putting his hand over his eyes. Turning his head away.)*   No! No!
CAROLE   Speak to me, Johnny.
BYRNE *(fist clenched against his brow)*   I've got to sleep. Got to sleep.
CAROLE   You can change things, you know, Johnny.
BYRNE   Shut up! Shut up you bloody ghost.

Exit CAROLE. *Enter* KELLY.

KELLY   Hiya, Johnny. Dae yae like ma scar? You gave me it, Johnny. Remember?

Enter DIDI.

DIDI   Aye. Remember, Johnny? Yir Big Brass knew how tae treat yae well. But ah think you've hud yir oats just wance too often.

Enter LEWIS.

LEWIS   There might be a loophole, Johnny, a legal loophole.
CAROLE   Five year six year seven year more.
DIDI   Eight Nine Ten Eleven Twelve Thirteen… Whit age ur you?
KELLY   They're knockin down the Gorbals. The old place will be gone by the time you get out. If you ever get out.
DIDI   If he ever gets out of here it'll be in his coffin.

Enter PAISLEY.

PAISLEY   Aye. And we'll make sure the lid is well screwed down. *(All other characters freeze.)* We've come fur yae animal. We've come tae break yae.

BYRNE *stands up.*

BYRNE   Come on then.

Enter JOHNSTONE *and* RENFREW.

BYRNE   Ah promise yae ah'll make it as unpleasant as possible. If yir gonnae break me, yir gonnae break yersels tae. *(Laughs.)* Ah hud a dream under these bright lights, you know, that wis forty winks youse didnae know ah'd hud...

PAISLEY   *(to others)*   He's roon the twist. When ah came in he wus talking tae himself and staring like a lunatic.

BYRNE   Ah dreamt ah hud company. A wee fly, buzzing about the place. It came down and landed on ma arm and flew away again. So ah chased after it and ah caught it. Ah watched it buzzing in ma hand for a minit, then a dropt it intae that chanty there. Right intae aw the piss and shit that's all ah've goat left tae show fur ma life. And ah watched it struggle and swim about. Then ah spat oan it. It wus in real trouble then, flailing about. Ah said, Hello there, wee brother. Ah know exactly how you feel. And ah watched it struggle towards a large lump of shit and crawl up on it for refuge. A moment later ah wus wakened by more of your banging and thumping. And ah could smell your stinking bodies and your smelly feet all the way through those concrete walls. Ah could hear you talking. Ah ran ma hands over ma body and it felt sharp and strong. Ah felt ma own skin and it amazed me. Ah touched the floor. It was so alive, so *there*. Ah could feel every speck of dust. And when ah looked down, the dust was like jewels, when ah breathed, the air was like nectar. It was strange. Ah felt happy. Ah felt happier than I'd ever felt in my life before. Happy. And grateful. Grateful just to be standing here, breathing in the stinking air. Alive. And ah thought. If that shit could help the fly, it can help me too. *(He cakes his body in shit from the chamberpot.)* So come on. Come on and get me. *(Smears over his face.)* How much of it can you accept?

During this speech the SCREWS *have drawn out their batons. At the end of the speech they have their batons held up menacingly and* BYRNE *stands facing them. At the ready. The lights go down slowly. As they go down, the various characters exit slowly taking off their costumes. The words are delivered wearily and sadly as they exit.*

RENFREW   Rats.

JOHNSTONE   Rats aroon the back.

CAROLE   Rats aroon the back an a wee dug.

PAISLEY   Rats aroon the back an a wee dug that wus rerr ut breakin their necks.

RENFREW   It kilt that many rats it goat a mention in the papers.

CAROLE   It broke that many necks, it goat a medal fur it.

BYRNE   *(lights are almost out)*   My name is Byrne, Johnny Byrne. This is my version of my story.

Select Bibliography

1. Plays

Bryden, Bill, *Willie Rough* (Edinburgh: Southside, 1972)

Bryden, Bill, *Benny Lynch: Scenes from a Short Life* (Edinburgh: Southside, 1975)

Bryden, Bill, with Susanna Graham-Jones, translation of *Il Campiello: A Venetian Comedy,* by Carlo Goldoni (London: Heinemann, 1976)

Bryden, Bill, *Old Movies* (London: Heinemann, National Theatre Play, 1977)

Bryden, Bill, *The Big Picnic,* in *Theatre Scotland,* 3:10 (Summer 1994), 27–43

Campbell, Donald, *The Jesuit* (Edinburgh: Paul Harris, 1976)

Campbell, Donald, *Somerville the Soldier* (Edinburgh: Paul Harris, 1978)

Campbell, Donald, *The Widows of Clyth* (Edinburgh: Paul Harris, 1979)

Campbell, Donald, *The Cutting-off Piece,* in *A Writers Ceilidh for Neil Gunn,* ed. Aonghas MacNeacail (Nairn: Balnain Books, 1991), 159–92

Campbell, Donald, *The Heid-Nipper,* in *Scotland's Languages* (Glasgow: Jordanhill College/A.L.T.E.R., 1993), 10–13

Campbell, Donald, *Nancy Sleekit,* in *Theatre Scotland,* 3:12 (Winter 1995), 31–6 [Adapted from a Victorian monologue by James Smith]

Conn, Stewart, *Fancy Seeing You, Then,* in *Playbill Two* (London: Hutchinson, 1969)

Conn, Stewart, *The King,* in *New English Dramatists: 14* (London: Penguin Books, 1970)

Conn, Stewart, *In Transit* (New York: Breakthrough Press, 1972)

Conn, Stewart, *The Burning* (London: Calder & Boyars, 1973)

Conn, Stewart, *The Aquarium, The Man in the Green Muffler & I Didn't Always Live Here* (London: John Calder, 1976)

Conn, Stewart, *Thistlewood* (Todmorden: Woodhouse Books, 1979)

Conn, Stewart, *Play Donkey,* in *A Decade's Drama: Six Scottish Plays* (Todmorden: Woodhouse Books, 1980)

McGrath, Tom, and Jimmy Boyle, *The Hard Man* (Edinburgh: Canongate, 1977)

McGrath, Tom, *Laurel & Hardy* (Glasgow: Midnight Press, 1988)

McGrath, Tom, adaptation from the translation by Ella Wildridge of *Merlin* by Tankred Dorst and Ursula Ehler, in *Theatre Scotland,* 1:1 (Spring/Summer 1992), 19–37

McGrath, Tom, *Buchanan,* in *Theatre Scotland,* 2:5 (Spring 1993), 39–56

MacMillan, Hector, *The Sash* (Glasgow: Molendinar Press, 1974)

MacMillan, Hector, *The Rising,* in *A Decade's Drama: Six Scottish Plays* (Todmorden: Woodhouse Books, 1980)

McMillan, Roddy, *The Bevellers* (Edinburgh: Southside, 1974)

McMillan, Roddy, *All in Good Faith* (Glasgow: Scottish Society of Playwrights, 1979) [Act 2, Scene 2 was published in *Saltire Review,* 1:2 (August 1954), 38–45]

2. Interviews and Autobiography

Bryden, Bill, 'Bricks on our Shoulders', in *Theatre 74,* ed. Sheridan Morley (London: Hutchinson, 1974), 126–32 [Gives an account of his time at the Royal Lyceum Theatre and his promotion there of new Scottish drama]

Bryden, Bill, ''Member 'At?', in *Jock Tamson's Bairns: Essays on a Scots Childhood,* ed. Trevor Royle (London: Hamish Hamilton, 1977), 78–87

Brown, Ian, 'Cultural Centrality and Dominance: The Creative Writer's View – Conversations between Scottish Poet/Playwrights and Ian Brown', *Interface,* 3 (Summer 1984), 17–67 [Includes interviews with Stewart Conn and Tom McGrath]

Campbell, Donald, 'Four Figures in a Personal Landscape', in *Jock Tamson's Bairns: Essays on a Scots Childhood,* ed. Trevor Royle (London: Hamish Hamilton, 1977), 99–111

Campbell, Donald, 'Till All the Words Run Dry', *Theatre Scotland,* 4:13 (Spring 1995), 23–8 [Interviewed by John Clifford]

McGrath, Tom, 'Scots Folk Irish Folk', in *Across the Water: Irishness in Modern Scottish Writing,* ed. Jim McGonigal, Donny O'Rourke and Hamish Whyte (Glendaruel: Argyll Publishing, 2000), 120–24

Selerie, Gavin, ed., *The Riverside Interviews 6: Tom McGrath* (London: Binnacle Press, 1983)

Wright, Allen, 'A Writer Demands to Work' [Interview with Stewart Conn], *The Scotsman,* 29 July 1992

3. Critical/contextual texts

Bain, Audrey, 'Striking It Rich?', *Theatre Scotland,* 3:11 (Autumn 1994), 16–24 [Records the first 21 years of the Scottish Society of Playwrights, founded 1973]

Bold, Alan, *Modern Scottish Literature* (London: Longman, 1983), Part 3: Drama

Campbell, Donald, *A Brighter Sunshine: A Hundred Years of the Edinburgh Royal Lyceum Theatre* (Edinburgh: Polygon, 1983), Chapter 10

Campbell, Donald, 'The Fraying Rope: Part 1, The Audience', *Cencrastus,* 42 (Spring 1992), 3–8; 'Part 2, The Artists', *Cencrastus,* 43 (Autumn 1992), 32–6; 'Part 3, The Authors', *Cencrastus,* 44 (New Year 1993), 6–10

Combres, C., 'Le Théâtre de Stewart Conn, Poète et Dramaturge Ecossais', *Caliban,* 17 (1981)

Corbett, John, *Language and Scottish Literature* (Edinburgh: Edinburgh University Press, 1997), 100–3

Findlay, Bill, ed., *A History of Scottish Theatre* (Edinburgh: Polygon, 1998), 269–80

Hutchison, David, *The Modern Scottish Theatre* (Glasgow: Molendinar Press, 1977), Chapter 11

Hutchison, David, 'Roddy McMillan and the Scottish Theatre', *Cencrastus,* 2 (Spring 1980), 5–8

Lenz, Katja, 'Modern Scottish Drama: Snakes in Iceland – Drama in Scotland?', *Zeitschrift für Anglistik und Amerikanistik,* 44:4 (1996), 301–16

McDonald, Jan, 'Scottish Women Dramatists Since 1945', in *A History of Scottish Women's Writing,* ed. Douglas Gifford and Dorothy McMillan (Edinburgh: Edinburgh University Press, 1997), 494–513

MacMillan, Hector, 'Scots Theatre – or Theatre in Scotland', in *Catalyst,* 3:3 (Summer 1970), 14–15

MacMillan, Hector, 'The Future of Political Theatre in Scotland', *New Edinburgh Review,* 30 (August 1975), 32–3

McMillan, Joyce, *The Traverse Theatre Story* (London: Methuen, 1988), Chapter 7

Morgan, Edwin, 'Glasgow Speech in Recent Scottish Literature', in *Scotland and the Lowland Tongue,* ed. J. Derrick McClure (Aberdeen: Aberdeen University Press, 1983), 195–208 [Includes discussion of language in some 1970s plays]

Paterson, Lindsay, 'Donald Campbell: Playwright in Search of a Method', *Cencrastus, 6* (Autumn 1981), 6–8

Scullion, Adrienne, 'Feminine Pleasures and Masculine Indignities: Gender and Community in Scottish Drama', in *Gendering the Nation: Studies in Modern Scottish Literature,* ed. Christopher Whyte (Edinburgh: Edinburgh University Press, 1995), 169–204

Stevenson, Randall, 'Scottish Theatre, 1950–1980', in *The History of Scottish Literature: Vol. 4, Twentieth Century,* ed. Cairns Craig (Aberdeen: Aberdeen University Press, 1987), 349–67

Stevenson, Randall, 'Looking for a Theatre, Looking for a Nation: Recent Scottish Drama', *Graph* (Winter 1988), 21–4 [Traces developments over the previous twenty years]

Stevenson, Randall and Gavin Wallace, *Scottish Theatre Since the Seventies* (Edinburgh: Edinburgh University Press, 1996)

Unwin, Stephen, Alan Pollock and Jenny Killick, eds., *The Traverse Theatre 1963–1988* (Edinburgh: Traverse Theatre, 1988)

Walker, Marshall, *Scottish Literature Since 1707* (London: Longman, 1996), 263–75

Wells, Patricia, *Scottish Drama Comes of Age* (Ann Arbor, Michigan University Microfilms International, 1987) [Includes detailed analysis of Donald Campbell's *The Jesuit,* Tom McGrath's *Animal,* and Robert David Macdonald's *Chinchilla*]

[Note: For a more extensive bibliography of criticism, and of plays by other 1970s writers, see Alison Lumsden's 'The Scottish Theatre since 1970: A Bibliography', in *Scottish Theatre Since the Seventies,* ed. Randall Stevenson and Gavin Wallace (Edinburgh: Edinburgh University Press, 1996), 215–24.]